Moodle®

FOR

DUMMIES®

by Radana Dvorak

WILEY

Wiley Publishing, Inc.

Moodle® For Dummies®

Published by
Wiley Publishing, Inc.
111 River Street
Hoboken, NJ 07030-5774
www.wiley.com

WILEY

About the Author

Radana Dvorak holds a PhD in computer science from the Queen Mary, University of London, a master's degree in knowledge-based systems (AI) from the University of Sussex, and a BA from the University of Michigan. Radana has been involved in eLearning since 1989, when her research in human computer interaction focused on computer-based training (CBT). She has been a researcher and a university instructor who taught in the United Kingdom, Cayman Islands, and the United States. She has also spent some time in the software industry. Currently, she is an adjunct professor at Portland State University and owner of eLT Solutions LLC. Her focus is to help organizations with the development of learning courses using learning content management systems and integrating Web 2.0 technology to meet the changing needs of educators, trainers, and learners.

Dedication

To my children, James and Anna, and my parents for their ongoing encouragement and support.

Author's Acknowledgments

I want to go back a number of years and thank three professors: Professor Mike Sharples who supervised my master's degree at the University of Sussex and was instrumental in introducing me to the area of eLearning (dubbed CBT in 1989). His vision and dedication inspired and excited me about the possibilities in education. Mike Sharples is currently Professor of Learning Sciences and Director of the Learning Sciences Research Institute at the University of Nottingham. I want to thank Professor Peter Johnson for accepting me to the computer science PhD program at Queen Mary, University of London, and Professor Stephen Summerville, who was instrumental in my research interests and supervised my Ph.D. His vision, enthusiasm, and dedication to his students are admirable. Our discussions about AI, communicative structures transferring to online communication, the future of online books and education, all pre-Web, were vital in my research and love for the field.

I want to thank my Portland State University graduate students; it has been an absolute pleasure and privilege to teach them. They are the most dedicated and hardworking bunch of students I have ever taught. Martin Dougiamas, the original developer of Moodle, believes that in a true collaborative online teaching environment, everyone is both a teacher and a learner — this has proved to be true with my students.

That brings me to thank Martin Dougiamas for developing Moodle and the wonderful Moodle community around the world. The developers, the dedicated forum helpers, and the teachers, many of whom wear all three hats, are integral to Moodle's success.

This book owes a great deal to the fabulous Indianapolis Dummies Tech group at Wiley Publishing. Thank you, Kyle Looper, for believing in Moodle and giving me the opportunity to write this book; Leah Cameron for initial feedback and editing instructions; and Nicole Sholly, the project editor, who spent hours ensuring this book is crafted in the *For Dummies* style. This group of people is professional, nice, and a sheer joy to work with.

Finally, I am grateful for my wonderful children, Anna and James, and indebted to them for putting up with my nocturnal working existence, blurry eyes, and disconnected nature while trying to meet deadlines.

Publisher's Acknowledgments

We're proud of this book; please send us your comments at http://dummies.custhelp.com. For other comments, please contact our Customer Care Department within the U.S. at 877-762-2974, outside the U.S. at 317-572-3993, or fax 317-572-4002.

Some of the people who helped bring this book to market include the following:

Acquisitions, Editorial, and Media Development

Project Editor: Nicole Sholly

Acquisitions Editor: Kyle Looper

Copy Editor: Virginia Sanders

Technical Editor: Bill Bateman, Humboldt State University and owner of Web2oh.com consulting

Editorial Manager: Kevin Kirschner

Media Development Project Manager: Laura Moss-Hollister

Media Development Assistant Project Manager: Jenny Swisher

Media Development Associate Producers: Josh Frank, Marilyn Hummel, Douglas Kuhn, Shawn Patrick

Editorial Assistant: Amanda Graham

Sr. Editorial Assistant: Cherie Case

Cartoons: Rich Tennant (www.the5thwave.com)

Composition Services

Project Coordinator: Katherine Crocker

Layout and Graphics: Carrie A. Cesavice, Samantha Cherolis, Lavonne Roberts, Corrie Socolovitch

Proofreaders: Toni Settle

Indexer: BIM Indexing & Proofreading Services

Special Help: Heidi Unger, Jennifer Riggs

Publishing and Editorial for Technology Dummies

    Richard Swadley, Vice President and Executive Group Publisher

    Andy Cummings, Vice President and Publisher

    Mary Bednarek, Executive Acquisitions Director

    Mary C. Corder, Editorial Director

Publishing for Consumer Dummies

    Diane Graves Steele, Vice President and Publisher

Composition Services

    Debbie Stailey, Director of Composition Services

Contents at a Glance

Table of Contents

Introduction

*I*f you've been thinking about putting your class online, this book takes you from thinking to doing. *Moodle* (Modular Object-Oriented Dynamic Learning Environment) is an open source eLearning software platform that was originally developed by Martin Dougiamas. Moodle enables educators to create online courses supporting rich interactions between educators and their learners. Moodle enables instructors to add content and combine activities into sequences that guide learners through structured learning paths.

Moodle also has also another meaning besides Modular Object-Oriented Dynamic Learning Environment. The second meaning is more interesting: It means a slow-paced process of enjoyable tinkering, fiddling, and experimenting that can lead to insight, creativity, and innovation.

Moodle continues to evolve and improve because the developers, instructors, and learners find creative and novel ways to use it. Moodle is freely distributed under the terms of the GPL. You can redistribute it and/or modify it under the terms of the GNU General Public License as published by the Free Software Foundation. See `http://docs.moodle.org/en/License`. Join the 39.5 million Moodle users; you'll have fun.

About Moodle For Dummies

This book is useful for instructors and trainers working in educational organizations or the business world who want to put their teaching content online. I provide step-by-step processes starting with the most useful tools and activities in Moodle. I use screen shots to illustrate steps, including creative and helpful hints how various activities have been used in the eLearning environment. By the end of this book, you'll have gained the skills and confidence to design complete interactive courses to deliver completely online or to supplement your face-to-face classes.

Here are just some of the things that you — as an instructor or trainer — can do with this book:

✔ Find out what eLearning is all about and how to design and develop great Moodle courses.

✔ Discover all the things Moodle allows you to do, such as linking and embedding Web pages as well as uploading your files in most industry-standard formats. (You can upload the create class notes, for instance.)

✔ Add collaborative tools, such as wikis, forums, glossaries, RSS feeds, chat sessions, lessons, and multimedia content to create a rich learning environment.

✔ Quickly create assignments and quizzes to evaluate learners' progress and use the powerful Quiz module to take grading off your hands and push results to the grade book.

✔ Discover online grading and the grade book to simplify your classroom life.

✔ Discover the Moodle community to share ideas, tools, and expertise to help you succeed — all for free!

IT staff and troubleshooters will also find this book useful because it can

✔ Help you set up Moodle training sessions (in plain English) for personnel.

✔ Help you understand what teachers are up against. If you're a system administrator, knowing what teachers need can help you better serve those needs.

✔ Assist you with the installation and administrative tasks to get Moodle going.

Students of all education levels use Moodle, and because this book covers tools and features that students use in Moodle — such as blogs, profiles, wikis, glossaries, databases, and forums — this book is also helpful to them.

Foolish Assumptions

For starters, I assume you've heard how online education, or *eLearning,* is changing education. You've heard about Web academies, credit recovery, and completing college and university courses to gain diplomas, certificates, and degrees online. You may have possibly taken a class online. Right now, you may be thinking, "Yes, this must be something important, and I better get involved." Here are some other assumptions I make:

✔ **You're somehow involved in education and/or training but don't have any previous experience with Moodle or other similar software.**

✔ **You have an inquisitive nature and aren't afraid of trying new technologies.** You have an appetite to learn and share your knowledge.

✔ **You have a computer and an Internet connection and possess the basic skills to use them.** These skills include (but are not limited to)

- Sending/receiving e-mail messages and attaching documents to and downloading them from e-mail messages

- Manipulating word processing documents, such as Word, PDF, and Open Docs files.

- Navigating your computer hard drive or USB drive to find files

- Organizing files and folders, creating new files, and saving files in correct places on your computer

✔ **You have access to Moodle or can download it.** Moodle is free, but you may need a Moodle partner or Internet service provider (ISP) to host your Moodle site.

✔ **You (or your system administrator) are willing to read parts of this book to get your Moodle course up and running.** Doing so doesn't really take too long, and you don't need much experience with learning content management systems to work with Moodle.

Conventions Used in This Book

To help you navigate this book efficiently, I use a few style conventions:

✔ Terms or words that I want to emphasize or define are *italicized.*

✔ Web site addresses, or URLs, are shown in a special monofont typeface, `like this.`

✔ When I refer to a Moodle *site,* I mean the LCMS that contains all the courses. A site can have many courses, and a site is managed by the system administrator, or in Moodle terms, the person in the Administrator role.

When I refer to a *course* that means one course, or class, contained on the Moodle site.

✔ When I refer to *learners,* I mean students and trainees. Although we are all students when we're learning, often this concept is misinterpreted to refer to students in an educational organization only. Training programs in businesses prefer to use different terms. Trainee, test/exam taker, and team participant are examples of a few terms frequently used.

Moodle user accounts have a Student role, and I use this term when I explain a process or procedure involving the Student user account.

✔ Numbered steps that you need to follow and characters you need to type are set in **bold.**

What You Don't Have to Read

The rule of thumb for this book is that you don't need to read what isn't relevant to your task at hand. Whether you have experience with Moodle or are absolutely clueless, it doesn't matter. Browse this book, and you'll find just the right starting point. Isn't that what the *For Dummies* books are all about? This book is structured modularly, so you don't have to read the Technical Stuff icons. If you work for an organization that has a system administrator looking after Moodle, you don't need to worry about the technical stuff or anything that says Administrating Moodle. If you're an IT guru, you can avoid the sections on how to develop the eLearning course and how to structure great online courses.

How This Book Is Organized

Moodle For Dummies is split into five parts and has a companion Web site. You don't have to read the book sequentially, and you don't even have to read all the sections in any particular chapter. You can use the Table of Contents and the index to find the information you need and quickly get your answer. In this section, I briefly describe what you find in each part.

Part I: Getting Started with Moodle

This part is a great place to find out everything there is to know about Moodle. Here you get a bird's-eye view that helps you understand the Moodle world and explain what's what to get started. You find many things you can do with Moodle, understand what it takes to design a great online course, and get clued in on terms like *Digital Native, Generation X*, and *Generation Z*. This part also gets you ready to begin building your very first Moodle front page, the first step in creating your online course. When you're through with this section, you can impress your friends and colleagues with your eLearning skills and Moodle knowledge.

The first and most important part of creating your online class is to not get carried away. Don't let the cool modules (such as RSS, embedded videos, and links to outside resources) compromise your teaching methods by trying to impress learners and colleagues. Identify your objectives and use Moodle to enhance your teaching methods, not alter or worse, hinder them.

Part II: Creating and Managing Course Content

I know you want to start putting your content, your know-how, and your expertise online ASAP. This part shows you how. You'll have something up in no time. You find out how to add resources, such as uploading your files to your course, creating Web pages, and linking to resources on the Internet. I also shed light on adding video and sound files to create a multi-media-rich teaching environment, and show you how to embed YouTube or TeacherTube videos in your Moodle Web pages. You also figure out how to use the grade book and assessment tools to evaluate your learners' progress and knowledge.

Part III: Adding Activities to Your Moodle Course

Here's where the fun begins. You read how to use forums, chats, messages, and blogs to engage your learners in communicating and expressing them-selves in Moodle. Moodlers believe that in a true collaborative environment, everyone is a learner and teacher. This is where you can set up activities and let your learners create projects, share them, and learn from each other. Wikis, glossaries, and database tools are ideal for creating and sharing knowledge. I also introduce you to the powerful Quiz module, which enables instructors to create any type of quiz, worksheet, or test using multiple choice, true/false, matching, short answer, and essay questions. You can add comments, and then Moodle automatically grades the questions and adds the score to the grade book. You also find out how to create assignments that learners can upload to Moodle for you to grade and record.

This section also shows you how to set up news feeds to push Web content to your Moodle class. For example, you can bring up top stories on any topic from the BBC or CNN, or you can push any journal or e-zine publications right to your course front page, wiki, glossary, or database. Only your imagi-nation can stop the possibilities.

Part IV: Moodle Management

This part is all about managing your content, optimizing your files for smooth running, and backing up your data. The chapters show you how to replicate your course, rename it, and use it again. Put in the work once and replicate from then on. I know how important it is to collect user reports to keep on top of your learners or show impressive statistics to your department head, so I reveal all this knowledge. This part also covers all the techie administrative aspects of Moodle and how to keep it running smoothly. Not for the faint hearted, but with fabulous hand-holding explanations and direct references to Moodle online documentation and links to wealth of information in Moodle forums, you find your way even if you don't have a technical background.

Part V: The Part of Tens

People love *For Dummies* books for all the extra tips, hints, and advice the authors share. This part gives you things to think about before you jump into building your first Moodle course, and it gives you useful, creative ways to keep your learners involved in your Moodle course.

The companion Web site

Although I get very excited about the companion Web site (located at www. dummies.com/go/moodlefd), you aren't required to visit it to be able to create a Moodle course — everything you need is contained in this lovely book. On the site, however, I include a few extras that you may find useful. So, if you're feeling adventurous, you can browse for templates, an online course checklist, good practice and Moodle chat, forum, and blog etiquette tips, and more.

I encourage you to visit the companion site and to contact me (radana@ eltsolutions.com) if I need to add anything else to make your life just a bit easier. Of course, if you think it is absolutely brilliant just as it is, let me know that, too. I will pass on credit where it's due.

The Moodle For Dummies Cheat Sheet

The *For Dummies* Cheat Sheets live online at Dummies.com. To find this book's Cheat Sheet, go to www.dummies.com/cheatsheet/moodle.

The Cheat Sheet takes you on a tour of the Moodle interface, explaining modules and tools along the way. You also find a list of resources (with links) that can help get you started Moodling, provide you with support and community, and deliver news to you about all things Moodle. Finally, I provide shortcut keys particular to Moodle.

Icons Used in This Book

What's a *For Dummies* book without icons pointing you in the direction of really great information that's sure to help you along your way? In this section, I briefly describe each icon I use in this book.

This icon points out helpful information that's likely to make your job easier.

This icon marks a general interesting and useful fact — something that you may want to remember for later use.

This icon highlights lurking danger. Pay attention to this icon and proceed with caution. But don't worry, you really can't destroy or mess up too much.

When you see this icon, you know that there's techie stuff nearby. If you're not feeling very techie, you can skip this info.

Where to Go from Here

You picked up the book off the shelf or ordered it online, so don't marvel at the attractive black and gold cover, get started! If you've never used Moodle, start with Chapter 1 and then read about creating successful eLearning courses followed by creating your first front page.

If you've used learning content management systems similar to Moodle or have experience with Moodle, browse the contents and then jump in where you feel most comfortable. If you have Moodle available in your organization, get on the phone or e-mail your system administrator and tell him you're ready — get him to set up a Teacher account so that you can name your course and jump right in.

Don't be afraid to make mistakes. There's no such thing as a mistake when you experiment and try something new because no matter what you do, you learn from it. Moodle software is robust and backed up, so you can't really corrupt it. Now jump in and start Moodling.

Part I

Getting Started with Moodle

In this part . . .

This part hopefully inspires and excites you so much that you won't be able to contain yourself and will want to digest the whole book and start creating Moodle courses immediately. The part begins with an overview of Moodle and briefly explains its conventions, terminology, and tools. After that, I discuss methods of online learning, how to develop great Moodle courses, and how to use Moodle to support your teaching goals. The last two chapters of this part contain nuts and bolts information that gets you started building your course front page and creating your first Moodle course.

Chapter 1

Discovering Moodle and What You Can Do

*U*sing new software applications isn't always easy and can even be overwhelming if you focus on the ever-changing Internet and all the new software and gadgets that keep appearing. When you want to use a new software, you must think about the time (and possibly money) you need to invest initially to set it up, and then there's the pressure of learning the new software. If the thought of using a new piece of software — such as Moodle — makes you reflexively reach for a bottle of something, take a deep breath and allow me to ease you into learning a few basics about Moodle. Before you know it, your worries will be left behind.

I begin the chapter with a brief definition of Moodle and show you some numbers of how many people and organizations use Moodle. Next I explain some useful terminology and conventions to get you started and help you navigate Moodle. Finally, I dive in to an explanation of software acronyms to alleviate any confusion about the space Moodle occupies in this eLearning (also referred to as *distance learning*) market.

Meeting Moodle

Moodle is a large, Web-based software package that enables instructors, trainers, and educators to create Internet-based courses. Moodle is an acronym for Modular Object-Oriented Dynamic Learning Environment. Moodle provides a robust system and an organized, easy-to-use interface for learning over the Internet. One of the greatest advantages in sticking with Moodle is that developers have kept the look and feel consistent over the years, and they promise to continue to keep it consistent so that each upgrade doesn't feel like it's a piece of new software.

Moodle enables educators and trainers to create online courses. Moodle's home page (Moodle also calls it the course front page) displays, in its basic form a link to a list of participants (including the teacher and students), a calendar with a course schedule and list of assignments, resources, activities, updates, and news. This book explains all of Moodle features, including online quizzes, forums, glossaries of terms, wikis, access to documents, and links to other Web resources, and more.

Moodle is referred to as a course management system (CMS), learning management system (LMS), virtual learning environment (VLE), or more recently a learning content management system (LCMS). Near the end of this chapter, I explain the differences among these terms and why I refer to Moodle as an LCMS.

So why would your organization use Moodle, or why should you learn to use Moodle? I can give you a number of reasons. Moodle is

- ✔ **Widely used, domestically and globally:** As of January 2011, more than 39 million registered users are using Moodle. This list shows you a few other stats (the numbers are from `http://moodle.org/stats`):

  - *Registered courses:* 4,303,011

  - *Users:* 40, 590, 582,899,203

  - *Teachers:* 1,190,743

  - *Enrollments:* 18,794,573

  - *Largest site:* 59,920 courses with 225,546 users

  - *Site with most registered users:* Open University 714,310 (Moodle. org has 1,030,779)

  - *Countries using Moodle:* 213

  - *Languages:* 83

- ✔ **The largest community of users around the globe for a distance learning software:** Moodle has an incredibly large and active community spanning the globe. It has been vital to the success of Moodle, and I can guarantee that if you post a question to the help forums, someone will be awake, somewhere around the globe, and you will have a reply. It's like a 24/7 tech support group. See `http://moodle.org/forums`.

- ✔ **Based on a sound educational philosophy:** Moodle is based on sound pedagogical principals and educational philosophy, making it one of the few LCMS that's learning-centered instead of tool- and gadget-centered.

✔ **Free:** There's no initial cost to purchase the software and no license fees! Moodle is open source software, meaning it's free and governed by GNU Public License (www.gnu.org/copyleft/gpl.html). You may think that nothing is free. Moodle *is* in that you don't have to pay for the software or the upgrades or license, installation, and training (what the marketing and sales team try to get you to commit to when you purchase large software packages).

But in some respects, you are partially correct in thinking that everything has a cost attached. If you add development time to build your course, time to learn the software, and Web-hosting costs, Moodle is not free.

Understanding Moodle Basics

If you want to explore Moodle and perhaps are excited to start developing your first Moodle course, you need to know a few details about Moodle to navigate it and speak the language. The following sections help get you started.

Creating a Moodle account and logging in to your course

You need just a couple things to get started with Moodle:

✔ **An account with a username and password:** Aren't you glad to learn that Moodle is secure? You need a Teacher, a Course Creator, or an Administrator account in order to have editing privileges and create courses.

You can contact your system administrator to set up an account for you. If you will be responsible for looking after Moodle, refer to the discussion regarding roles and registration in Chapter 3 and also the discussion regarding Moodle system administrators in Chapter 13.

✔ **A URL:** The URL depends on your organization or a third-party company that will host your Moodle site.

If you have an account and a URL, open your Web browser (Moodle works best with Internet Explorer and Firefox) and go to the URL. If this is your first time accessing your Moodle site, you come to a page similar to Figure 1-1.

Next time you return to the course, either you see just the login box as shown in Figure 1-2 (or Figure 1-1) or you go straight to a list of courses on your Moodle site with a login link in the top-right corner. You have a number of options to log in, all quite straightforward and simple.

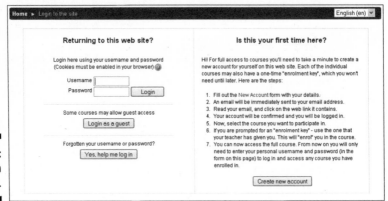

Figure 1-1:
The Login
page.

Figure 1-2:
Returning to
the Moodle
Login page

The Safari, Google Chrome, and Opera browsers do not show all capabilities
of the built-in HTML editor in Moodle, and there are a few issues with the Chat
module using Safari. To be safe, I recommend using Firefox or Internet Explorer.

Navigating the Moodle interface

Finding your way around the Moodle course front page is not difficult when
you understand some of the basic terminology and where things are located.
Before I begin to help you familiarize yourself with the Moodle interface, you
need to understand some terms that I continue to use throughout the book,
and the explanation in this chapter will make more sense. These terms are specific to Moodle, so it's a good idea to use them as your reference starting point.

✔ **Moodle site/Moodle site front page:** Refers to the Moodle software platform that contains all of your organization's courses and blocks with
utilities for managing the site. Figure 1-3 shows an example of a Moodle
site front page, which includes all the courses available on the site.
There is a login link in the top-right corner, a site calendar, site news,
and the Site Administration block. When a reference is made to a *site,*

it's available to all courses and all users in the site. Organizations usually run only one Moodle site.

A Teacher or Student account would not be able to see the Site Administration block located on the left in Figure 1-3. See Chapter 4 for more information on user roles.

✓ **Moodle course:** A Moodle course is much like a real-world course, but online: It's a collection of lessons, assignments, quizzes, documents, projects, grade book, and class discussions. An instructor constructs a syllabus, which is posted on the course front page, and students can download instructions, upload completed assignments, and collaborate through wikis, chats, and online forums.

✓ **Course front page:** Refers to the course home page — it's your work space and where your learners come when they log in to your Moodle course. On your course front page, you have more tools available to you than your learners do. These additional tools enable you to build and edit your course.

Click to toggle editing on/off

Log in/out status

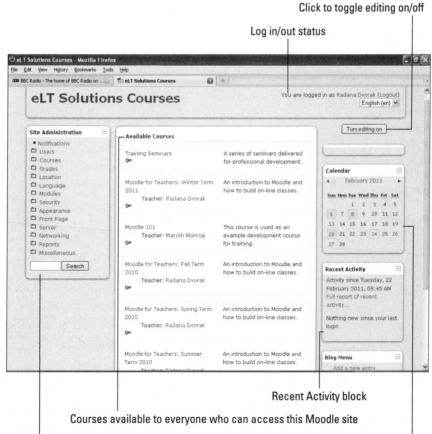

Figure 1-3:
The Moodle
site front
page.

Recent Activity block

Site Administration block

Courses available to everyone who can access this Moodle site

Calendar block

A number of settings offer the instructor controls and tools to add content (called *resources*) and modules such as Wikis, Forums, and Quizzes (called *activities*). The course front page is broken into course sections by week or topic (there are other settings that enable you to set up the course to meet your teaching requirements), and you can add resources and activities to each section.

Chapter 3 goes into detail about each editing tool, icon, block, and menu. Figure 1-4 shows what a teacher view of the course front page looks like without the editing features enabled. Figure 1-5 demonstrates the same page with the editing features enabled and number of activities and resources listed under the different sections (topics or units).

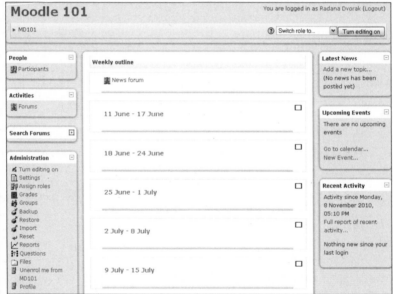

Figure 1-4:
The Teacher
view of the
course front
page.

The course front page includes *blocks* on the left and right sides with the center column reserved for the course content. Blocks are tools — kind of like containers for you and your learners. For example, you have blocks for a calendar, search box, lists of activities and resources, participants, newsfeeds, and so on. Many blocks can have links to various activities. By default, each course front page has specific blocks, such as Participants, Latest News, Upcoming Events, and Recent Activity. You can get more information on blocks later in this chapter and in Chapter 3.

When you first access your course, familiarize yourself with the course front page. Find the Turn Editing On button, located in the top-right corner, and click it. You see your course front page come to life, displaying colorful editing icons, including the Activity and Resource drop-down lists appearing in each section. A new Block drop-down list also shows up on the right side. Explore and familiarize yourself with what you have available.

Figure 1-5:
The editing
tools are
available.

If you don't yet have access to your own Moodle course and want to explore and try editing, go to the Moodle.org demo site at `http://demo.moodle.net`. You can sign in as a teacher, a student, or an administrator, and you can access courses and demos in many different languages. Don't worry about making any changes; the server is refreshed back to the original every 20 minutes.

Understanding Moodle terms and conventions

Moodle uses a number of terms and specific conventions particular to the software. In the following list, I mention and explain some of these terms and conventions to help you ease into the book:

- ✓ **User:** A specific participant who is allowed to enter a Moodle site. Each user account has a specific role, which carries a set of permissions.

- ✓ **Roles:** Roles are user accounts identifying the participants in the site and course. Each role has a set of permissions with capabilities to interact with Moodle. When Moodle is installed, it automatically creates a set of default roles — Administrator, Teacher, Non-Editing Teacher, Course Creator, Student, and Guest — which I define in Chapter 4.

✔ **Capability:** Capabilities are Moodle features. Each activity has specific capabilities and certain roles have the capabilities assigned to interact in different capacities with the activities. For example, a Teacher role can post discussions to the News forum, but a Student role can only read a news forum and not post to or reply to it. Capabilities are further discussed in Chapters 4 and 13.

✔ **Permission:** Permissions are specific settings for capabilities. You have four options: Not Set/Inherit, Allow, Prevent, or Prohibit. See Chapter 13 for more details.

✔ **Activities:** You can add separate, interactive learning activity modules to your course. They are robust, and each one can be set up to work with individual students, groups, or everyone in the course. The Add an Activity functionality is enabled when you click the Turn Editing On button. (See Figure 1-5.) The drop-down list appears in each section/week of your course. Many of the activities can be graded and push information to a course grade book. The activities available are shown in Figure 1-6.

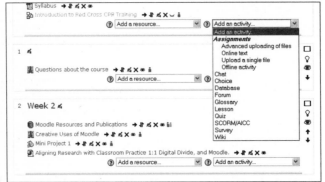

Figure 1-6:
The Add
an Activity
drop-down
list.

✔ **Resources:** Moodle resources are types of tools that enable you to include almost any kind of file, including multimedia files and links to resources on the Internet. Resources include simple text pages, Web pages including a WYSIWYG editor, IMS packages, and more. Like activities, you add resources by using a drop-down list when editing is turned on. Figure 1-7 shows the drop-down list of various resources.

Chapter 3 goes into detail about the various modules and how to use each one.

✔ **Blocks:** Blocks are container-like tools that provide specific information or functionality. There are more than 16 types of blocks, many of which are flexible so that you can use them for a variety of functions. For instance, the HTML block can display a short video on the course front page. The Blocks block appears bottom of the right column when you turn on editing. (See Figure 1-8.)

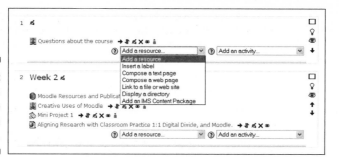

Figure 1-7:
The Add a
Resource
drop-down
list.

Figure 1-8:
The Blocks
drop-down
list.

Clarifying Moodle and CMS, LMS, VLE, and LCMS

Moodle continues to be referred to by a number of acronyms that may cause confusion. You've probably heard of few (if not all) of these terms and may be wondering about the differences among them. In the following list, I describe each and highlight the similarities and differences:

✔ **VLE:** A virtual learning environment is a software system designed to support teaching and learning in a form distinct from a managed learning environment (MLE), which focuses on management. A VLE usually uses Internet browsers to deliver instructions and assessment tools, such as quizzes. More recent VLEs include wikis, blogs, and RSS.

✔ **LMS:** A learning management system (LMS) is a software system that enables the management and delivery of online and instructor-led training content to learners. Most LMSs are Web-based to facilitate anytime, anyplace, and any pace access to learning content and administration. You will see LMS and VLE used interchangeably.

✔ **CMS:** A content management system (CMS) is a repository for data, where *data* can be defined as any type of file, such as documents, movies, sound, pictures, and so forth. CMSs are frequently used for storing, controlling, revising, collaboratively sharing, and publishing documentation. Usually a CMS serves as a central repository. This is most likely the oldest term used to refer to software like Moodle.

✔ **LCMS:** A learning content management systems (LCMS) combines the powers of CMS and LMS. An LCMS is defined as a system that creates, stores, assembles, and delivers eLearning content that can be personalized. It delivers the content in the form of learning objects. Though an LMS manages and administers all forms of learning within an organization, an LCMS concentrates on online learning content, usually in the form of learning objects.

Because of Moodle's extensibility and its separate modules that can be used with individual learners, saved, and reused (wiki, database, blogs, and so on), I refer to Moodle as a LCMS throughout the book.

An LCMS such as Moodle gives instructors, course authors, and designers the ability to create eLearning content more efficiently. The goal of an LCMS is to create small chunks of content to meet the needs of individual students or groups of learners and to offer capabilities to update and change the content as and when needed with ease. For example, traditionally, an entire course would be developed and then adapted to multiple audiences. With a LCMS, instructional designers are able to create content chunks that are reusable.

The LCMS can also provide certification and tracking for individual learners who need specific knowledge. LCMS can deliver degree courses or training to certify for regulatory needs, professional licensure, or quality control. For instance, a construction company using a new piece of heavy equipment can use an LCMS to ensure that all workers are fully trained on the processes and health and safety. The training includes certification tests employees need to pass in order for a company to receive insurance certification. These tests, set up as separate modules, can be easily updated or changed to support employees' needs (second language, learning disabilities, and so on) and/or changes made by the regulatory organizations. LCMSs are used in high schools, Web academies, colleges, universities, and companies.

Keeping Moodle Versions Straight

I wrote this book using version 1.9.9, and it covers Moodle versions up to version 2.0 (which was recently released). I have confidence that this book will help you set up courses and teach you all you need to know for versions 1.8 through 2.0.

The main changes in the new release are designed to give third-party developers more flexibility and scalability and to integrate Web 2.0 technology. Moodle 2.0 is still viewed as *beta* at the time of writing this book, which means the changes are essentially transparent to you as the end user. (Again, though, the material covered in the book is applicable to get you going if want to upgrade to Moodle 2.0.)

Moodle docs, which are referenced throughout the book, are for versions pre-2.0 with notes where upgrades have taken place. Unless you're a developer or actively want to test the software for bugs and intend to contribute to the development of 2.0+, I strongly recommend that you use the latest version, 1.9 (which to date of publication is 1.9.10), because as the Moodle.org site reports, minor upgrades to Moodle 2.0 are found weekly, and patches will be released regularly. Hence why you see versions 2.0; a month later you see 2.1; and then 2.1.1

Moodle has been consistent with every new release, leaving the front page, navigation, and setup pages for teachers and learners the same. For most instructors and teachers, the main difference they will see is changes in how files are handled in the new versions. As with any new releases, there are bugs and minor issues, and the Moodle forums are quite hot with activities around these issues. No doubt all minor issues will be resolved over time.

Please see the Moodle 2.0 release notes at `http://docs.moodle.org`. Many forum discussions still say there are improvements to be made and changes in the wind. I know I will be sticking with 1.9+ versions for my teaching courses for some time yet, though I'm excited about the future possibilities, especially the potential for integrating third-party modules and mobile apps.

Determining Where to Host Moodle

If your organization doesn't support a Moodle site and you cannot convince your System Administrator to download it for you to the organization's server (even after you've tried bribery), you will have to look at other options. In a crunch, your three options are on your computer, on your server, or through third-party hosting. The following list highlights a few pros and cons to help you to decide the best option for you:

- ✓ **Running Moodle on your computer:** Running Moodle on your home computer is not really a difficult process, setting it up doesn't take too long, however getting your Moodle site online is more cumbersome. If you want learners to access your course, it's a complex process involving a Web server, and you may as well use a third party to host it. However, if all you want to do is learn how to build a course and play, then it's a good way to start. Make sure you read the system requirements before you download it.

To download Moodle on your own computer, go to `http://moodle.org/downloads` and scroll down to Moodle for Windows or Moodle for Macs OS X and follow the instructions.

✔ **Run on your own server:** If you have your own Web server, I assume you have the skills needed to set up Moodle. Go to `http://moodle.org/downloads` and click the Standard Moodle Packages link.

✔ **Third-party hosting:** There are few options for third-party hosting. You may find non-profit organizations that offer free hosting for educational organizations. For example, Key-to-School `http://www.keytoschool.com` or similar organizations such as ORVSD (Oregon Virtual School District), a free resource for online teaching learning, offers free hosting to Oregon educators. Check with your district education office for information on similar government- and grant-funded programs.

Many ISPs support open source software and enable you to download Moodle. You have to make sure you have Linux hosting and the ISP supports MySQL. This is a good option if you have few technical skills. Most ISPs will not provide technical support for third-party software.

If you need technical support with the third-party hosting option, I recommend that you contact a local Moodle.org partner. These partners will host, maintain, and provide a secure environment for your Moodle site. Moodle partners are located in many different countries. Go to `http://moodle.com/hosting` for a list of companies that have partnered with Moodle.org.

Chapter 2

Designing Great Moodle Courses

● ●

In This Chapter

▶ Discovering Moodle's origins and the teaching methods behind it

▶ Understanding diversity of your learners

▶ Choosing your instructional design philosophy and methodology

▶ Becoming an online instructor

● ●

*I*know you're itching to start building your Moodle course. However, before you dive in to the next chapter and start building your course front page, I recommend taking a few minutes to learn about how Moodle originated and the underlying pedagogical theory that brought instructors, teachers, and developers around the world to embrace it and develop Moodle to the point where it is today. With this information, you can impress your friends, family, and colleagues when they ask what Moodle and Moodling are and what exactly it all means.

If you take one thing from this chapter, it should be that no matter what technology you use to create and enhance your course, it should be based on sound instructional design principles. Don't fall into the trap of selecting your media before you identify your course objectives. The medium and media should not compromise your teaching methods to fit the technology; instead, use the technology to enhance your teaching so you can reach and support the learning strategies your learners have developed.

The Philosophy and Evolution of Moodle

Like with anything new you undertake in your profession that may require a new way of working and/or thinking, having knowledge about that new thing can ease your anxiety. To help you understand how to use Moodle successfully, I encourage you to understand its origins and the principles on which it was built. In addition, you can benefit from becoming familiar with the new terminology, eLearning methodologies, and the role in education that Moodle occupies.

eLearning defined

Before shedding a light on the educational philosophy of Moodle, I need to briefly define *eLearning* in case you're new to the concept. eLearning is a vast area in education and training that has gained much attention in the last ten years. eLearning is an umbrella term representing learning and training carried out using computers connected to the Internet, interacting with Web-based software. The basic tenet is to be able to learn anytime and anywhere. In this book, you may find I use the terms eLearning, online learning, and distance learning interchangeably. Other terms you may have heard or be familiar with include

- ✔ Distance learning and distance education
- ✔ eTraining, computer-based training, and technology-based training
- ✔ Online learning and online education
- ✔ Web-based training
- ✔ Technology-enhanced learning

The birth of Moodle

The brain child behind Moodle is Martin Dougiamas. In his past, Martin had to use CMS (content management system) in education, and he found it difficult to use and not at all intuitive or supportive to meet his teaching objectives and students' learning needs. As a result, he decided to complete his graduate degrees in Computer Science and Education and create something better — he must have had a *eureka!* moment somewhere along the way. Combining his degrees in education with his computer science degree, Martin developed an online learning environment that is based on pedagogical principles and is learning-centered rather than tool-centered. Martin's interests in social constructionism, which bases learning on collaboration and social activities to create new knowledge for others to see and use, drive Moodle.

Martin and the current development teams continue to evolve Moodle by adding new technologies and enhancing older tools and modules. One of the strongholds close to all Moodle users' hearts is that when enhancements and changes are made, the look and feel stay the same for users. The simple, familiar, and reliable user interface is transferable from older versions of Moodle, and the familiarity of standard editing tools has made Moodle a favorite LCMS (learning content management system) around the world.

Note: LCMS, LMS (learning management system), and CMS (content management system) are used interchangeably in the distance learning community. I define their differences in Chapter 1.

From Martin's initial work on Moodle, the following principles underpin Moodle's ongoing development:

- Everyone is a potential learner as well as a teacher, and in a true collaborative environment, everyone is both.

- People learn by creating, developing, and expressing something for others to use and see.

- People can learn by just curiously observing the activity of their peers.

- A learner-centered environment needs to be flexible and easily adaptable, capable of quickly responding to the needs of all participants within it.

- From the constructionism theory mentioned earlier, if you can understand the essence of what others are trying to convey, you can teach in a more transformational way.

Choosing an eLearning method

There are a number of ways instructors use eLearning to teach, enhance, and support their course goals. You can use Moodle for any type of eLearning you may be involved in. Generally, current eLearning courses use one of the following three models:

- **Distance learning** is simply defined as "structured learning without the physical presents of the instructor." This definition evolved from the first Annual Conference on Distance Learning in 1989 and is still used today.[1]

- **Blended learning** is learning in a traditional classroom where instructors use eLearning systems to enhance their teaching. It's defined as "combining online delivery of educational content with the best features of classroom interaction and live instruction to personalize learning, allow thoughtful reflection, and differentiate instruction from student-to-student across a diverse group of learners." This definition evloved from the International Association for K-12 Online Learning.[2]

- **Hybrid learning** is a type of learning that's a combination of in-class and online teaching. In-class work is not replicated online. Hybrid learning is often used when practicum, labs, or demonstrations are required. It's almost the best of both worlds and is still one of my favorite ways of teaching.

Discovering How Moodle Can Support Instructional Design Strategies

Learning appears to be most effective when learners are involved in creating something for other learners to see or use. This is one of the strengths of Moodle. Table 2-1 lists a number of eLearning strategies and highlights how you can use Moodle to support them. There are many learning strategies, and by no means is this list exhaustive. Discussion about learning theories and pedagogy for online instruction is not for this book to tackle (unfortunately), and because you've picked up this book, you may have some background understanding and/or experience and expertise in this area. See the companion Web site for resources if you want more information about instructional design.

Table 2-1	eLearning Instructional Strategies		
Instructional Strategy	*Pedagogy*	*Description*	*Moodle Features That Can Support the Strategy*
Lecture, presentation, and instruction	Information transfer	Transfer knowledge to learners through interaction, reinforcement, questioning, discussions, immediate feedback.	Lecture notes, video lectures (upload files), chat, and forum discussions
Drill and practice	Assess learning (remember/evaluate)	The desired learning outcome is accomplished by repeating a task or behavior. Transfer knowledge from working memory to long-term memory.	Quizzes, lessons, assignment, and glossaries
Demonstration	Information to attain performance and/or create an artifact	Transfer skills by descriptive use of procedures for tasks, events, and processes.	Lessons, wikis, forum discussions, databases, and resources

Instructional Strategy	Pedagogy	Description	Moodle Features That Can Support the Strategy
Brainstorming	Goal-oriented communicative and collaborative interactions effective for problem solving; using cognitive strategies such as understanding, analyzing, applying, and evaluating	Individual or group problem-solving where analysis, critical reviewing, and imaginative methods are used to achieve understanding and improvement to an agreed outcome.	Forum discussions, chat, wikis, and databases
Guided discussion	Communication and interaction/active participatory learning	Create a synchronous exchange of information.	Chat or live streaming videos (need to integrate live video conferencing tools)
Illustration	Understanding, analyzing, and evaluating	Portrays examples, can be real-world examples, graphically making use of abstract concepts.	Resources (adding or linking to illustrations), wikis, glossaries, and databases
Case study	Understanding and problem solving	Guide students to understand realistic situations and find viable solutions.	Lessons and resources
Role play	Understanding and applying new knowledge; communication and interaction	Learners take on characters from history or characters from a play/novel and have to engage in conversations as those characters.	Forum discussions, real-time videos, uploaded videos, and linking to other resources
Imagery	Information transfer, understanding, analyzing, evaluating, applying	Visualization of artifacts and events. Learners internalizing visual imagery related to learning — it can recreate artifacts or experiences in the learner's mind.	Resources (linking to or adding), wikis, and forum discussions

Understanding Our Learners and Generational Differences

Learners are unique: They have numerous learning styles and different ways information is viewed and assimilated. Educational theorists have identified many different types of learning styles that reflect how the information may be perceived, organized, and processed.[3] Learners assimilate in different ways (visually, aurally, or kinesthetically), and some forms may work better than others for individual learners. The neat aspect of using Moodle is that you, as an instructor, can learn about your learners and present information to support them using the medium in various modalities — other than kinesthetic, of course, because you would need virtual reality for that. (Perhaps in the near future the brilliant Moodle developers will design virtual Moodle classrooms that will support a kinesthetic preference.)

If you're new to the area of eLearning, keep in mind that your knowledge, content expertise, and experience are the valued commodities, not the software. Do not compromise your teaching methods and let the medium drive the content.

Moodle has provided instructors with tools and flexibility to enhance the teaching and learning experiences, not hinder them. For example, just because you *can* use newsfeeds (RSS; see Chapter 14) with Moodle, don't feel you need to integrate newsfeeds because other instructors are using them or because students think they're cool. Use newsfeeds *only* if they play part in your learning objectives. Moodle is not prescriptive — it's extensive. *You* determine how you will use it with your learners. There are no limits, so put your creativity to work, and you may find new uses for it. Moodle is where it's at today because of educators finding new needs and developers working to provide new features to meet those needs.

Moodle is capable of supporting different learning types. However, instructors can be trapped in designing and compromising eLearning courses by preconceived and misunderstood ideas bandied about in the media (or from software vendors) about generational diversity and technology uses. The media is saturated with terms such as "generations X, Y, Z," "digital natives," and "digital immigrants" (or "migrants"). Although it's important to understand how the different groups may use technology and the type of strategies they use to interact with the medium, it's more important for you to understand that you don't compromise your teaching methods and choose media based on these generalized views.

When you're developing a Moodle course, remember that just because a learner may be familiar with technology and can scan, read, or send back text at what seems like the speed of light, it doesn't mean that the learner will have sophisticated learning skills in a system such as Moodle.

Throughout the rest of this section, I define digital natives and digital immigrates and outline some of the general patterns the diverse groups demonstrate when it comes to using and interacting with technology. *Note:* I include references at the end of this chapter that can claim some of the original research and publication in this area. This list is by all means *not* exhaustive, but the list is enough to get you going if you want to research the space. The Internet is saturated with information, including blogs, ezines, and tweets.

Digital natives

The term *digital natives* usually refers to learners born after 1985 to date because they have grown up connected to some media. Although the generalized characteristics appear somewhat accurate across the board, the group covers far too many years when you think about the way technology has evolved and is being used. Researchers have subdivided this group, further demonstrating technological diversity among the generations. Here are the main distinctions to keep in mind when designing your Moodle course:

- **Generation Y (born 1977–1994):** This group is technologically sophisticated and has learned to rely on technology, though you need to watch these group members and not assume that they have capabilities when it comes to Web 2.0 and eLearning.

- **Generation Z (born 1995–2012):** This generation still holds a lot of unknown factors, and technology companies are having a difficult time keeping up with its demands. This generation has also been referred to as the *i, net, quiet,* and *palm* generation — members of this generation are less verbal because most of their communication is through electronic devices. The learners of this generation are impatient, seem to expect immediate results, and multitask with tech devices at exceptional speeds. They don't like to read instructions — most jump in and get on with it. Their expectations of technology are demanding.

  This generation will take to eLearning and will push boundaries. Generation Z doesn't seem to understand the concept of plagiarism — if you don't believe this, ask any secondary school teacher about this issue!

The following list gives a summary of the distinguishing characteristics for digital natives (born 1985 to date):

- Look at graphics first, access text-based media last

- Are play-oriented

- Are always connected

- Multi-task connected to at least one e-vice (electronic device)

✔ Process things at *twitch speed*

Twitch speed thinking (coined by Mark Prensky) is the speed of thinking/processing that is required during video games, action films, and music videos, where viewers are exposed to "more than 100 images a minute."

✔ Expect immediate results

✔ Expect information to come to them or accessible at one click

✔ Do not read instructions, especially step-by-step outlines, but jump straight in

✔ Do not process as linearly as previous generations

✔ Are impatient if technology is not quick enough — find something else to do

✔ Do not stay with tasks as long

✔ Trust the medium

✔ Do not expect things to go wrong

Digital immigrants

The term *digital immigrants* describes learners and instructors born before 1985. This group has also been more affected with wars, recessions, and changes in the workplace than digital natives. The following list briefly summarizes the subgroups and the impact technology had on them:

✔ **Post-war cohorts (born 1930–1945):** This group uses and likes "traditional" forms of reading and learning and tends not to like social media. These learners require and read procedural instructions. They like information written down on paper so they can make sense of it. This is a group that needs encouragement, help, patience, and time. As much as many of these learners resent the new eLearning medium, many can absorb it when challenged to do so.

✔ **Baby Boomers I (born 1946–1954):** Born in good economic conditions, this group embraces technology by spending money on new IT consumer products. The learning methods of this group are traditional as for post-war cohorts, and the group is often resentful toward having to change its teaching/learning methods later in life.

✔ **Baby Boomers II (born 1955–1965):** This group has taken to technology quicker than expected. Members of this group generally love technology and have surprised the consumer market by taking to social networking much more readily than expected. They blog, read e-zines, and use social networks; however, when asked, they still much prefer to work in paper. Their learning methods are traditional, as with Baby Boomers I, but they see the benefits and needs of eLearning. They aren't as resentful to the changes. This group makes up many teachers, instructors, and academics in the work force today. They've been the driving force behind the development and use of information technology and spend more money on technology than any other group.

✔ **Generation X (born 1966–1976):** Seen by researchers as probably the best-educated group, it's also the most skeptical group. Members of this group are pragmatic and practical, embrace social networks, and take to technology quicker than the preceding generations in this category. This group's members are not resentful to change, but instead, expect constant change — this is what they have witnessed and experienced. They've seen most change in the gaming and PC markets. Don't assume that learners in this group have sophisticated eLearning skill — they don't. They have good IT skills, and most likely have some knowledge of eLearning.

In this list, I provide a summary of distinguishing characteristics for digital immigrants (born before 1985):

✔ Process information in a linear fashion

✔ Work at conventional speeds

✔ Like step-by-step instructions

✔ Read text first and like procedural instructions

✔ Are work oriented and don't multitask with electronic devices

✔ Are use to (and like) standalone problems and concepts

✔ Generally do not take to technology as quickly as digital natives

✔ Do not expect information to be brought to them but like looking for information

✔ Do not trust online environments as much and question information more than the digital natives do

✔ Expect things to go wrong

✔ Expect constant change

✔ In the case of the older portion of the group, do not embrace social media

✔ Also regarding the older portion of the group, need more hand-holding and encouragement

Course-Building Checklist

I spent some time in the first part of this chapter discussing how important it is to not compromise your learning strategies, expertise, and experience to fit into the new medium of Moodle. A better approach is to use the Moodle modules to enhance your teaching. Moodle is built on pedagogical principles, and the freedom it gives you should not hinder in any way what you and your learners are trying to achieve — it should help support your goals. I outline a number of techniques and strategies for you to consider when you start building your Moodle course.

Some of the methods and strategies in this checklist are very basic and no doubt are part of your syllabus. Your syllabus is a good starting point — use it to think about how you can add to the units/weeks by using the various modules (such as forum discussions, wikis, quizzes, linking to resources, and so on) to enhance and support what you're trying to achieve.

One cool thing about Moodle is that you can quickly make changes and alterations based on your learners' needs. If you have a group that is more advanced, or has come to your course with skills you were not aware of, you can quickly alter your strategy to make your course more challenging. If the group needs more hand-holding and explanations, you can link to supplementary exercises, upload extra work, and rework the online syllabus in few short steps.

Here are a number of techniques and strategies to consider before you start building your course:

Course Starting Point — The Introduction

✔ Has an e-mail been prepared/sent to your learners informing them about how to gain access your course?

✔ How will learners contact you? Instruct them to use e-mail and/or use messaging in Moodle.

✔ If this is a large Moodle site that's part of your organization, is there technical support? Provide learners with technical support contact — you'll save time if someone else can troubleshoot.

✔ If learners need to use a different language for the browser, how will you get the information to them?

✔ Will you be using the news forum from day one? How will you inform your learners to begin? READ FIRST PLEASE documents are useful, though the younger generations may skip them altogether if they have login info and can jump straight in.

Course Organization and Design

✔ Are font styles, content layout, and organization consistent throughout the course? Do you need to follow departmental or organization protocol and design?

✔ Will you be using an introduction session with a syllabus and course schedule to teach learners how to navigate your course?

✔ Will you give any type of training and/or introduction on how to use Moodle?

✔ Are course goals and objectives identified in your syllabus and in your introduction unit?

 Make sure that the goals and objectives in your syllabus also appear in your introduction unit. Even the slightest omission or rewording can cause confusion. I tend to copy pages or upload the whole syllabus just to make sure!

✔ Are activities and resources organized in a logical and consistent manner as you progress through the duration of the training session or course?

✔ Do you use your organization's academic calendar if you're teaching by term/semester? Doing so avoids a great deal of confusion. If you use topic/unit organization, you can use the calendar tool and cross reference it.

✔ Have you posted dates and times for assignments to be submitted and due dates for forum discussions?

✔ Are objectives measureable and linked to assessments? How will you inform your learners about how you intend to assess them? Setting up a rubric can be useful.

✔ Does each unit/week include materials as outlined in your syllabus? What method will you be using? Will the method be the same for each module, or will it change from unit/week to unit/week? Either way is fine as long as you inform learners when you divert from your syllabus.

✔ Do learners know what they need to do to access the first activity and complete it? Have you included this as part of the training discussed earlier?

✔ Are all assignments and quiz instructions clear? Where can learners access instructions and guidance? Are instructions available per activity in the intro or somewhere else? Be consistent.

✔ Do learners know how the Assignment module works so that they can submit assignments online?

✔ Do learners know how to access the forum and chat? Can they learn how to access them as part of training or instructions given when the activity is introduced?

✔ Is the content interactive?

✔ If students are asked to respond to other students' discussion forum postings, are deadlines set to enable this? For example, they need to post responses by a certain time and date in order to allow time for comments by you and other students before the discussion forum closes.

✔ Are learners involved in creating real-world artifacts and/or involved in real-world experiences in the online course?

✔ What is the mixture of instructional strategies you're providing? Do they support learning goals?

✔ Are you using multimedia (such as videos, audios, and podcasts)?

✔ Are students reflecting on course readings, from textbooks, journal articles, and so on?

Involving your learners in collaborative activities

✔ How will you engage your learners in the course? How will they collaborate with other learners?

✔ How will learners interact with the content in the course to meet learning objectives? Do your learners have all the software they need? (For example, if you upload PowerPoint files to Moodle, how will you make sure they all have PowerPoint?) Plan for alternatives.

✔ How will learners be encouraged to be identified and heard in the course? Encourage the use of profiles to build their Moodle persona and communicate with other Moodlers.

✔ Which activity will require for your learners to collaborate or interact with their peers? How will this be achieved?

✔ Will learners be meeting online only? Or will they meet both online and offline?

Course Communication

✔ How will learners be introduced to you and each other?

✔ Will you make available an area where learners can interact with each other? Will it be an open, free-form area? Creating a general learner forum is one option.

✔ How will you set up group work or group projects to support communication? Consider using forums, chat, FAQs, and messaging.

✔ Will learners be given the opportunity to give feedback on the course? How?

Assessment and Evaluation

✔ Are your instructional and assessment strategies aligned with your objectives?

✔ Are you using a variety of assessment strategies in the course?

✔ Will you give learners access to their grades? Will you use the grade book? Will learners be able to compare their assessment to the course average?

Instructor Feedback

✔ Are students provided with feedback for each activity?

✔ When will you give feedback? How will the learners be informed that you have given them feedback throughout the duration of the course?

Miscellaneous

✔ Did you check about copyrights? Your course should not contain anything that is under copyright protection. You need written permission to use content by the author or publisher (including scanned articles and book chapters). You can directly link to Web resources and databases to which you have access. For more information on copyrights, visit these sites:

- The Digital Millennium Copyrights Act (DMCA) at `www.copy right.gov/legislation/dmca.pdf`

- Regarding international copyright, a copyright act that covers all countries does not exist. Refer to `www.whatiscopyright.org`, which provides information for educational purposes.

✔ Will anyone other than you have access to your course? Do you need to grand access to assistants, student teachers, guests, mentors, or parents? How will you protect learner information?

Busting Moodle Myths

If you've undertaken the task of searching the Internet for information on learning content management systems and software to develop online learning, you probably found fantastic reviews on many products (promoted by vendors) or a lot of negative rhetoric about the whole area of distance learning, the software, and so on. Many people, mostly those from the digital migrant groups, have had to deal with adapting to continual changes in the workplace due to technological changes. I believe that teaching and training continue to be affected, more so than any other industry, and I sympathize with the ambivalence and often the cynical stands that instructors take.

The following set of myths has been compiled thanks to help from the millions of users spanning the globe. (More than 200 countries use Moodle.) No doubt you're familiar with some of these statements and have thought about some (if not all) of the issues presented here. You can find more myth busting at the Moodle.org site: `http://docs.moodle.org/en/Top_10_ Moodle_Myths`.

Myth 1: I have to be terribly tech savvy to use Moodle.

If you know how to attach a document to your e-mail, set up a Facebook or LinkedIn account, and open a variety of files, you can start using Moodle. Start slow, use resources to upload documents for your students to access, and create links to Web sites. When you and your learners are comfortable with Moodle, you can start exploring the cool tools such as discussion forums, wikis, chat, glossary, quizzes, grade book, RSS, and so on.

Myth 2: Using Moodle effectively means being on the computer 24/7.

Not at all!! When you start using new software that's very different from what you are use to, and if it has many different tools, it takes a bit of time to learn. Moodle is an online learning management system that you can learn in stages. You don't have to understand everything about it before you begin using it. Start slowly and build as you become more comfortable. If you've used other content management systems, the skills you developed are transferable, and Moodle will be easy to use!

Realistically, you and your students need to spend time in front of a computer because the more you use Moodle, the less time it will take to add an activity or a resource. Thanks to the consistent interface, adding content will become second nature after you've set up a course and used the modules regularly. Your Moodle comfort level just depends on what you use it for and how much you want to develop a course that will ease up your time in the long run. (For example, developing quizzes takes time, but once completed, Moodle marks them and places results into a student grade book.)

Myth 3: Moodle is not designed for my group of learners or customers.

Moodle is being used successfully in primary, secondary, and tertiary education, including in a variety of subject areas such as languages, science, mathematics, drama, art humanities, and ESL (English as second language). It has also demonstrated success in a wide variety of educational training programs as well as corporate and government training settings.

Myth 4: Students will love Moodle because it is online.

It is important not to make this assumption. Just because you put your courses online doesn't mean that your students will find it more interesting, love it more, and spend more time with the content to get better grades. As with traditional classroom settings, you need to find ways to get students interested in the learning activity and get them to ask good questions; when you do so, they will become more interested in the online content. Moodle and other LCMSs enable you to select tools to enhance your teaching methods and your learning goals. Even digital natives, those who are so independent when it comes to technology, will still look to you and enjoy your involvement and feedback, benefitting from your knowledge, experiences, expertise, and guidance. All students desire and value feedback. Making learning a valuable experience is what drives Moodle, not trying to make it fun.

No matter how technically comfortable you are using a new LCMS like Moodle, nothing can replace good teaching methods. You must always design courses based on sound pedagogical principles, strive to build relationships with your learners, and encourage your learners to build relationships with each other. These factors remain the essence to successful uses of Moodle.

Myth 5: Moodle is just one more thing in our busy schedules that we have to learn.

This myth is often coupled with the thought that, once your organization gets a new head of IT (again), that person will convince the powers-that-be to switch to some other, new Web-based educational software in a year or two. So you're thinking, why should I bother learning about it now?

This is a realistic concern that all instructors and supporting staff have when any new software is introduced. However, there is a number of strong arguments why Moodle is a smart educational and business decision for organizations. Keep reading: This info may put your mind at ease.

- Moodle has been around for many years and is used in more than 200 countries. The United States, the United Kingdom, and Australia are in the top ten. (The United States has the most users, and other top countries include Spain, Brazil, Germany Mexico, Portugal, Colombia, Italy, and China.)

- Moodle is open source software, which means it's free to all profit and non-profit organizations. Managers don't have to worry about license fees, and they face no requirements to employ someone from a company to do the upgrading, fixing, training, and so on. Difficult economic conditions have forced many companies to terminate license products, but that has not been a problem for open source software. Well-rooted open source software is a good business decision. Once used, there's no reason to switch.

✔ Moodle has many features in common with other LCMS/LMSs, and students will be using LCMSs in tertiary education; skills are transferable. By offering good-quality courses and instructing learners how to use Moodle, you are preparing them for college and helping them develop skills if they're already in college.

Moodle tools are so diverse that by learning how to use them effectively in an LMS environment, you will develop skills that you can take to your next employer. These skills will be useful if you continue in education or need to take continuing education credits. You can continue to develop Web 2.0 skills by experimenting and making use of the tools Moodle makes available for instructors. (Just think how impressed your learners will be if instead of asking them to link to specific Web sites for articles or latest news, you set up newsfeeds so that the information will come to them!)

References

1. Alexander, J.B., Andrews, A.E., harmer, N.D., Keller, J.W., Trainer, M.S. (1989). *Distance Learning Conference Proceedings*. Los Almos, NM: Los Alamos National Laboratory.

2. Watson, J. "Blended Learning: The Convergence of Online and Face-To-Face Education, iNACOL Promising Practices in Online Learning," 2008. Retrieved from `www.inacol.org/research/promisingpractices/NACOL_ PP-BlendedLearning-1r.pdf`

3. "Learning Styles and Pedagogy In Post-16 Learning." Learning and Skills Research Centre, Department of Education and Skills UK (2000). Retrieved from `www.hull.ac.uk/php/edskas/learning%20styles.pdf`

Additional References

✔ "Developing Minds with Digital Media: Habits of Mind in the YouTube Era," by M. Weigel and K. Heinkkenne (2007). You can read the article at `www.goodworkproject.org/wp-content/uploads/2010/10/ No-51-Developing-Minds-with-Digital-Media.pdf`.

✔ "Digital Natives A Field Study: Twitch Speed Thinking," by Susan Redmond (2005). You can find this article at `www.slais.ubc.ca/ courses/libr500/05-06-wt1/www/S_Redmond/index.htm`.

✔ "Digital Natives, Digital Immigrants," by Mark Prensky (2001). You can read this article at `www.marcprensky.com/writing/prensky%20- %20digital%20natives,%20digital%20immigrants%20-%20 part1.pdf`.

- ✔ "Digital Natives, Digital Immigrants: Some Thoughts from the Generation Gap," by Timothy VanSlyke. This article is part of The Technology Source Archives (May/June 2003). Check it out at `http://technologysource.org/article/digital_natives_digital_immigrants`.

- ✔ "Generations X,Y, Z and the Others," by William J. Schroer. You can read it at `www.socialmarketing.org/newsletter/features/generation1.htm`.

- ✔ "The Net Generation Goes to College," by Scott Carlson. This article appeared in *The Chronicle of Higher Education,* October 7, 2005. You can read this article at `http://chronicle.com/article/The-Net-Generation-Goes-to/12307`.

- ✔ "Reaching Younger Workers Who Think Differently," by, Marc Prensky. This article was the cover story of the January 1998 issue of *The Conference Board's magazine, Across the Board.* To read the article, go to `www.marcprensky.com/writing/Prensky%20-%20Twitch%20Speed.html`.

- ✔ "Speech by Rupert Murdoch to the American Society of Newspaper Editors," Washington, D.C. April 13, 2005. You can read the transcribed speech at `www.newscorp.com/news/news_247.html`.

- ✔ "What Babyboomers Want from Technology," by Ray Williams B. (2010). This article is from *Psychology Today,* February 7, 2010. You can find this article at `www.psychologytoday.com/blog/wired-success/201002/what-baby-boomers-want-technology`.

Chapter 3

Building Your Course Front Page

*F*amiliarizing yourself with the Moodle course front page is the first step. The second step is becoming as comfortable with it as when you stand up in front of your learners in a traditional classroom setting and use slide presentations, a white board, overhead projectors, and (if you're truly old school) a chalkboard and chalk. (I can just see the glazed look of a youngster reading this.) This chapter gives you the knowledge and skills required to start adding and editing content in your Moodle course.

I start by going over each functionality of your course front page and then define and explain standard features used throughout Moodle. After that, I shed some light on quirky conventions and how to reuse what you develop. "Do it once and never do it again" is my Moodle motto, so in keeping with that, after you learn how you will design and develop your Moodle course, you can jump to Chapter 14 and find out how to clone it.

This book's Cheat Sheet at Dummies.com lists all the functions summarized in the tables that appear later in this chapter. (For more about accessing the Cheat Sheet, see the inside front cover.) You will benefit from printing the Cheat Sheet and keeping it handy when you start playing with Moodle. This is the only thing I ask you to print, I promise. I, too, am aiming to live a green lifestyle.

Understanding Front Page Basics

This chapter assumes you have a Moodle site and a teacher, a course builder, or an administrator account. When you or your IT administrator first set up your Moodle course, it appears on the site front page. Chapter 4 explains the basic course setup, course setting, and Moodle site basics. I know that this seems out of order, but you really can start building your front page before you do those other tasks. It's only when you want to start getting learners in your course that you need the deeper understanding outlined in Chapter 4. In this chapter, I explain tool functionality and how to put tools to use in detail. This section is here to help you get comfortable with Moodle so you can start building your course with confidence.

Depending on how your administrator set up the site front page and your course(s), when you access it using a standard Web address (the URL), you see a page similar to Figure 3-1. The site has a Calendar block and a News block on the right and a list of courses in the center. If you're logged in as I am in the figure, you can see your username in the top-right corner as well as a Logout link.

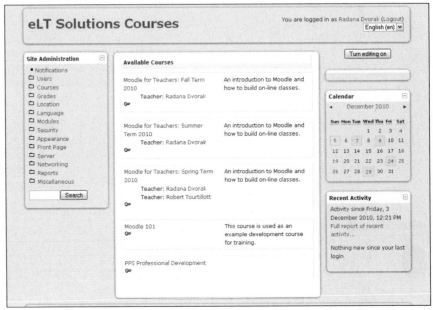

Figure 3-1: A site front page.

If you aren't logged in, the top-right corner displays the same link, but the link states You Are Not Logged In (Login). Click the Login link and then enter the username and password given to you by your Moodle administrator in the new login window, as shown in Figure 3-2. If you're running Moodle on your server or using an ISP to host your Moodle site, see Chapter 13 for an explanation on how to set up your site, course, and user accounts.

Returning to this web site?

Login here using your username and password
(Cookies must be enabled in your browser) ?

Username radana
Password   [   ]   Login

Some courses may allow guest access
[Login as a guest]

Forgotten your username or password?
[Yes, help me log in]

If this is your first visit to your organization's Moodle site, you will soon realize the site front page layout is different from your course front page. The site front page provides general information that's useful to all instructors and courses, and it may contain blocks displaying specific news items, updates, and so on. The main area is used for listing the courses available on the site. You may see a key icon under a course title, which means that the course is locked and anyone wishing to access it needs the password. The courses may also include short descriptions and the name of instructor. You can make these changes by using the course Administration block in the Settings subsection, explained later in this chapter, in the section "Default blocks."

To access your course, you can either click its title or click the Login link as discussed in the previous paragraph. Either one of these actions takes you to the login screen shown in Figure 3-2. Entering your username and password takes you to your course front page.

When your course is first set up and you log in, the first page that you come to is the *front page,* and the basic layout looks similar to what's shown in Figure 3-3 although the design (the *theme* in Moodle-speak) may look different. Themes are fun but not the most important aspect of your course. (Chapter 13 covers themes.) It's up to you how you lay out and use the front page for your learners.

Figure 3-3:
What you
see when
you first log
in to your
Moodle
course.

In Figure 3-1, in the upper-right corner (under the course title) are a few items that will become your best friends:

✔ **Moodle help icon:** Clicking the question mark in the yellow circle takes you to help files. This icon appears throughout all the Moodle screens, and I discuss it further later in the chapter.

✔ **Switch Role To drop-down list:** This drop-down list enables you to select a different role to view your course as you're developing it. Different roles come with different functionality, as explained in Chapter 1. As a teacher, your options are Teacher, Non-Editing Teacher, and Student.

I highly recommend that when you make any additions and changes to your course, you view it as a student and test it by opening files, linking to resources, and so on to make sure your learners see what you want them to see and access. Use the same drop-down list to return to your role as Teacher.

✔ **Turn Editing On button:** Clicking this button instructs Moodle to display all editing icons so that you can make changes to your blocks and layout and so that you can add activities and resources to your course. Figure 3-4 shows the same front page with editing on. To turn off editing, click the same button.

Figure 3-4:
When
editing is
turned on,
your front
page looks
similar to
this image.

Editing Fundamentals

Moodle gives you resources to set up, edit, and maneuver almost every aspect of your course. The editing tool icons are structured into four groups: general, middle column (the main course section), blocks, and activities/resources. I describe each group here and show you what the icons look like.

General icons

  Two general icons — the help icon and the main editing icon (both shown here) — are used across all Moodle tools. Some of the icons will also be available to your learners in activities they have permission to develop and edit, such as wikis, glossaries, and databases.

Middle column

The middle column is the main course section. After you've chosen a format for your course (weeks or topics are most frequently used), Moodle provides you with specific tools to add, alter, and customize the main section used by your learners. You can add a summary to the sections by selecting the stand-alone edit icon. You move sections, resources, and activities up or down to change the order in which the course is displayed. You can hide whole sections from learners or make them visible. If you set up your course by topics, you have an extra icon allowing you to set it as the current topic. You can also compress and display only the current topic (kind of an accordion functionality). Table 3-1 lists the icons used in the middle column.

Table 3-1	Editing in the Front Page's Middle Column	
Icon	**Icon Name**	**What It Does**
	Help	Moodle opens a help window with a brief explanation.
	Edit item	The edit icon, located in the upper left of each section, is specific to adding a summary to the particular section.
	Close/hide item	Item is visible to students. If you click this icon, the item will not be visible, and the eye will close.
	Open/show item	Item not visible to students. If you click this icon, the item will be visible, and the eye will open.
	Make current	You see this lightbulb icon only if the course is set in topic format. This icon allows you to make the particular unit the most current one.
	Move (up)	Click the up arrow icon to move your resource/activities up within the section (if you have number of listings) or to new sections.
	Move (down)	Similar to the preceding icon, this icon moves objects down.
	See one week/ topic	These icons are available at all times, no need to turn on editing. By clicking one square, Moodle collapses all sections, leaving only the top one and the one you selected to view. This is a useful functionality if you have many weeks or units because it saves you from scrolling. This is available for students also.
	See all week/ topic	Clicking the stacked rectangle expands all the sections. (You can think of this rectangle as an accordion.)

 In the main course section, when you turn on editing, the standalone edit icon for the summary is displayed at the top of each section, located above the News forum and below the date or unit titles. (Refer to Figure 3-4.) The editing icon for the summary allows you to place content right at the top of each section. Instructors use this space for titles with images, short instructions, summaries of weekly or unit events, or highlights about any other learning goal–related activity to draw learners' attention.

When you click the edit icon for the summary, Moodle opens a summary page with a Web-based editing text box, enabling you to use the space creatively. Don't forget to click the Save changes button when you finish adding content to the summary. See Figure 3-5 for a neat example of how the summary is used with a history course.

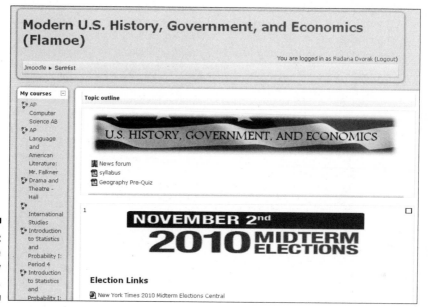

Figure 3-5: Using the summary creatively.

Blocks

Blocks are tools that add information or functionality. Blocks are loaded to the left or right of the middle area of the course's front page (refer to Figure 3-3); some appear by default, and others you must add. Each block has its own functionality and is related to the course or a specific learning objective. People, Activities, Search Forums, Administration, Latest News, Upcoming Events, and Recent Activity are just some examples of blocks you can use in your course. I discuss individual block functionality in detail in the "Course Blocks" section, later in this chapter. Editing features allow you to relocate, hide, or remove blocks. A block's editing icons, shown in Table 3-2, appear on each block and are particular to only that block.

Table 3-2		Icons Used with Blocks
Icon	**Icon Name**	**What It Does**
	Assign roles	In specific blocks, you can add permission to user roles.
	Hide	Block is seen by your learners. Click the icon to hide the block from your learners.
	Show	Block is not seen by your learners. Click the icon to make the block visible to your learners.
✖	Delete/remove	When you click this icon, the block is removed from the course. You can activate it again by adding it by using the general Blocks utility that's available when editing is turned on. See the "Course Blocks" section later in this chapter.
↑	Move up	Moves a block up.
↓	Move down	Moves a block down.
➡	Move right	If located on the left side of the main viewing area, moves the whole block right.
⬅	Move left	If located on the right side of the main viewing area, moves the whole block left.

Activities and resources

Resources allow you to add content to the course, and *activities* are collaborative and/or interactive modules you add to the course. Both make up the bulk of your online learning environment. You can add these modules from drop-down lists when editing is turned on. Editing icons appear next to every activity and resource (refer to Figure 3-4), which allows you to make changes by selecting the appropriate icon. Table 3-3 shows the editing icons for activities and resources.

Table 3-3	Icons Used with Resources and Activities	
Icon	*Icon Name*	*What It Does*
	Update	Clicking this icon takes you to the settings or update page for the activity or resource, allowing you to alter any aspects of it.
	Hide	The resource or activity is visible to learners. Clicking the icon hides it.
	Show	The resource or activity is hidden from learners. Clicking the icon reveals it.
	Move right	Clicking this icon indents the resource or activity. Right/left arrows appear on an indented resource or activity so it can be moved back. (Refer to Figure 3-5.)
	Move up/down	Enables you to reposition your resource or activity within the section or to another section. After you select the arrows, open rectangles appear throughout the page showing where you can move the resource/activity. Click where you want to position it.
	Move [resource/ activity] to this location	Appears when you click the move up/down arrows. Find the place where you want to move the particular item and then click this icon — Moodle moves the item.
	Delete	Clicking this icon deletes the resource or activity. Moodle prompts you, asking whether you're sure you want to delete it (as a safety net for folks who have speedy fingers).

Viewing and Updating Participants' Profiles

Profiles are powerful and useful tools for you and your learners. Personal profiles give everyone in the course a real identity, and when everyone is engaged in collaborative activities, it makes the course more personal. If you use Moodle as part of a traditional course or as blended learning initiative, learners and instructors get to know each other. If you use Moodle for complete online teaching and/or training, it's much harder to develop rapport with your learners, and it's harder for learners to get to know each other and build working and collaborative relationships.

You can access profiles by clicking the Participants link in the People block. By default, Moodle places the People block in the top-left corner of your front page. (Refer to Figure 3-3.) The top part of Figure 3-6 shows an empty profile with the learner's name; country; city; e-mail; user status (in this case, student); and if assigned to a group, the group. This info is all set up when the learner is registered for the course. The bottom part of the figure shows the same profile completed with a picture, a descriptive paragraph, and the learner's interests. The great thing about profiles is that they make everyone involved in the course more real. Completing a profile is one of the first activities I teach my students when they come to one of my courses.

Figure 3-6:
An incomplete profile on the left, with completed one on the right.

Notice the tabs that appear above the information about the virtual student. The Profile tab in Figure 3-6 shows the completed information about a particular learner. The second tab from left — the Edit profile tab — is where you go to edit the profile. The user profile, with basic information (including country, city/town, name, e-mail address, courses, and roles), is set by Moodle when the learner is enrolled in a course. The remaining tabs provide other functionality that you can use to enrich your course and help you meet some of your course learning objectives. Read on for an explanation of these tabs.

Learners don't see all the tabs shown in Figure 3-6 and described in the following sections. A student account only has three tabs: Profile, Edit Profile, and Blog.

Edit Profile tab

All user accounts can edit their profiles, including changing their usernames and passwords. The following list shows you how you can edit and update your profile. I suggest you give your learners some basic instructions so they can personalize their profiles.

Select the participant by clicking the Participants link in the People block.

You can access a profile from anywhere that a learner's or teacher's profile link appears. Moodle takes you to the Participants page, as shown in Figure 3-7. For example, when learners add to a forum discussion, their photo, name, and time of the submission are included in the forum. The name of the learner is a direct link to his or her profile.

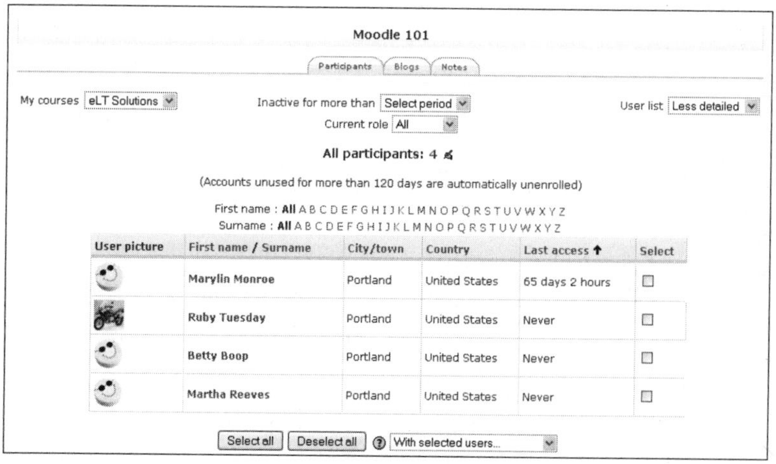

Figure 3-7:
The Moodle
Participants
page.

Click the name of the participant you want to view, and Moodle takes you to the student's basic profile. When you first access your or a learner's profile, the basic information added to register the learner for your course is visible, with the standard Moodle smiley instead of a picture.

✔ **General Information:** Click the Edit Profile tab, and Moodle takes you to a page where you and your learners can edit the General Information provided when the learner enrolled in the course. (See Figure 3-8.) Note the Description field; this is where you should add something about yourself. Encourage your learners to use this space to tell everyone in the course about themselves and upload a picture to replace the default, Moodle Smiley. The profile page, earlier in Figure 3-6, shows how the profile appears when saved.

Your students can change their passwords from the General section on the profile page.

✔ **Description:** In the Description text box (shown in Figure 3-8), every user account can add anything about themselves. You can add several paragraphs, and Moodle adds a scroll bar if a learner writes a complete and unabridged biography. If you encourage your learners to add information about themselves, make sure you set a good example by completing your own profile.

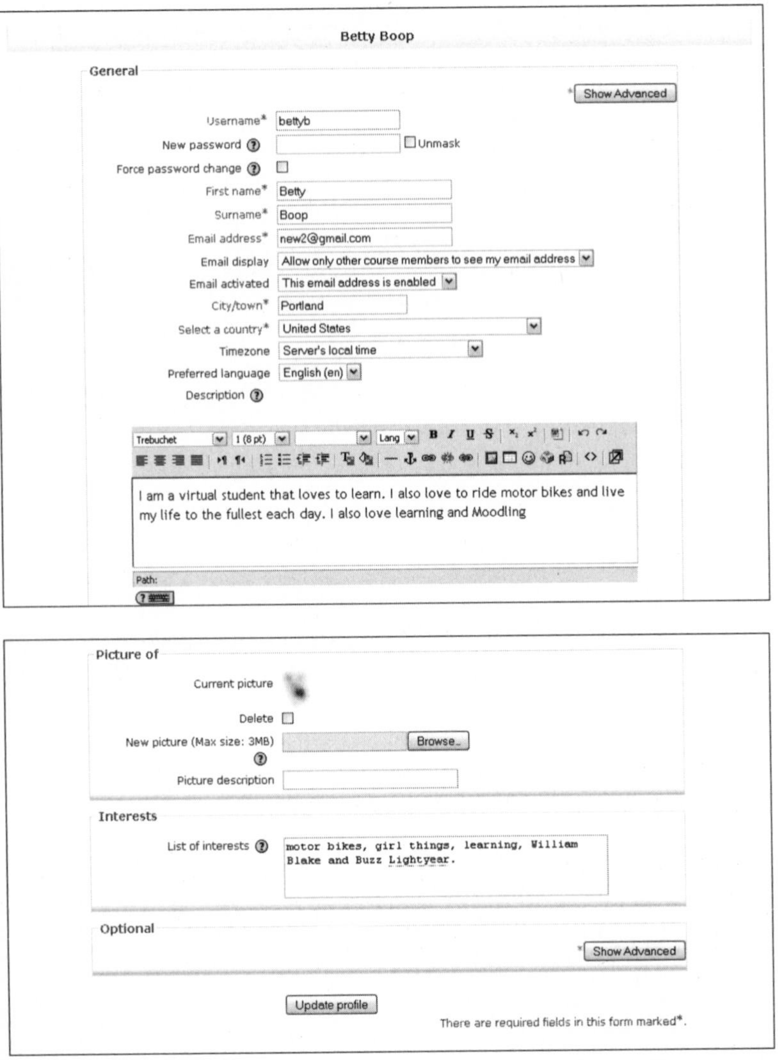

Betty Boop

General

		Show Advanced
Username*	bettyb	
New password ⑦		☐ Unmask
Force password change ⑦	☐	
First name*	Betty	
Surname*	Boop	
Email address*	new2@gmail.com	
Email display	Allow only other course members to see my email address ▾	
Email activated	This email address is enabled ▾	
City/town*	Portland	
Select a country*	United States ▾	
Timezone	Server's local time ▾	
Preferred language	English (en) ▾	
Description ⑦		

Trebuchet ▾ 1 (8 pt) ▾ ▾ Lang ▾ **B** *I* U S | ×₂ ײ | ▦ | ⟲ ⟳
▤ ▥ ▦ ▧ | ¶ ¶ | ⋮≡ ⋮≡ ⋵ ⋵ 🅣 🄰 | — ⚓ ∞ ⚛ ⚛ | 🖽 ⬜ ☺ 😊 🎦 | ‹› | ▨

I am a virtual student that loves to learn. I also love to ride motor bikes and live my life to the fullest each day. I also love learning and Moodling

Path:

Picture of

Current picture		
Delete	☐	
New picture (Max size: 3MB) ⑦		Browse...
Picture description		

Interests

List of interests ⑦	motor bikes, girl things, learning, William Blake and Buzz Lightyear.

Optional

Show Advanced

Update profile

There are required fields in this form marked*.

Figure 3-8:
Filling out
a student
profile.

- ✔ **User Picture:** Add a picture by using the browse button. Using the picture description field, learners can add a caption. Often some learners do not like to display a photo of themselves, but they will upload clip art or an image somehow related to them with a caption. Encouraging them to use pictures and captions helps learners get to know each other.

- ✔ **Interests:** Personalizes you and your learners. In the field, add several words or a sentence describing your interests and hobbies. For example, you can enter **reading, music, tennis, and camping with my family**.

- ✔ **Update Profile button:** Don't forget to save changes by clicking the Update profile button. When selected, Moodle returns you to the Participants page.

Forum posts tab

When you click this tab from the profile, Moodle shows you a list of all the discussion topics created by the particular learner and any replies to forum posts. It's an excellent overview for you to check whether a particular learner has been active in the forums because it summarizes that person's forum activity.

Forums, blogs, and notes are communication tools, which I discuss in Chapter 8.

Blog tab

In Moodle, blogs are accessible only through learners' profiles — that's where they're created by the learner and can be read by all the people enrolled in your course (if permission is set to be read by other course members). Blogs can also be accessible via blog tags. For information on blogs, see Chapter 8.

Notes tab

This tab allows you to add notes related to the particular learner. These notes are not available for learners to read; they are for you and other instructors (if you make them available to other instructors).

Activity Reports tab

The Activity Reports tab (shown in Figure 3-9) provides you with information on all activities of any particular learner in your course. When you click the tab, you're taken to the Outline Report (which is the leftmost link under the tabs).

Figure 3-9:
Find information about your learner's activities on the Activity Reports tab.

The Activity Reports tab includes the following links to reports:

- ✔ **Outline Report:** A general summary of the different areas of the course the learner has viewed.

- ✔ **Complete Report:** Lists every part of the course a learner has visited and whether she has contributed to the activity, such as a forum discussion.

- ✔ **Today's Logs:** A report of all activity for the last 24 hours. This report includes a graphical representation and detailed listing of time of accessing activity, IP address, and so on.

- ✔ **All Logs:** Similar to Today's Logs, a bar graph and a listing show you all the activity of a particular learner from the day the course started.

- ✔ **Statistics:** A graphical representation and a table listing monthly activities of resources and activities viewed and posted. It's a useful, quick overview.

- ✔ **Grade:** A summary of all the learner's graded activities for all courses in a Moodle site. Visit Chapter 7 for details on grades and the grade book within Moodle.

Roles tab

Moodle enables you to view a summary of the roles the participant has within a course. You can override and/or add permissions for the particular learner. Find more about Moodle roles in Chapter 1.

Course Blocks

Blocks provide extra tools and features to your course. Moodle enables a number of blocks by default (refer to Figure 3-2) when the course is created, and these blocks appear in the left and right columns of the Moodle interface. Moodle enables you to add more functionality to your front page from the main blocks drop-down menu, which only appears when editing is turned on. (Refer to Figure 3-5.) You can relocate blocks or close them so that they aren't accessible. Read on for explanations of the blocks and how your learners can benefit from them.

Default blocks

The following blocks, by default, appear on the left:

- ✔ **Activities:** Lists all activities and resources you set up for your students. As soon as you set an activity, Moodle lists it in this block, and it becomes an active link to a table displaying quick access to these activities. The links include the generic titles such as quizzes, forums, chats, lessons, wikis, and resources. This block is a handy overview and a quick way to get to an activity. See the section "Resources and Activities," later in the chapter, for even more details.

- ✔ **Search Forums:** A search text field enabling you and your learners to search all the course forums for a word or phrase. This block supports simple searching, such as typing words with spaces. For exact matching, use a plus sign (+). For an exact phrase, use quotation marks around the phrase *"like this"*. Click the Advanced Search link if you want to use a more sophisticated search. This block is useful if you have many forums and many learners using them. I tend to position the Search Forum block below the Administration block on the left.

- ✔ **Administration:** Soon to become your Moodle best friend! This block is where you can find tools for managing your learners, enrollment, your course setting, access your files, and more. The majority of the tools are visible only to you, and your learners get to see just two tools: Grades and Profile. Table 3-4 lists all the tools and icons and gives a short explanation for each.

Table 3-4	The Administration Block Tools	
Icon	**Tool**	**Functionality**
	Turn Editing On	Functions the same as the button at the top-right corner of the front page. Moodle adds it here for easy access to minimize scrolling.
	Settings	Enables you to set up your course to make it appear just as you want for your learners.
	Assign Roles	Roles are assigned in two contexts: site and course. The strength for course roles is being able to add or take away permissions for activities. See Chapter 4 for a detailed explanation.
	Grades	All your learners have access to their grades. This link takes you to the grader report and takes your learners to their grades. There are two parts to this: grades and grade book. Grades are the marking you set for your activities. The grade book is a container, an archive where all the grades and feedback are stored. See Chapter 7 for details.
	Groups	Enables you to create groups of students within your course. You can do this globally or per activity. See Chapter 4 for more information.
	Backup	Enables you to back up your course or part of the course. See Chapter 14 for more info.
	Restore	Restores your backup. You can rename it and copy it to another course in Moodle. Chapter 14 provides a thorough explanation.
	Import	A tool for importing activities, reports, logs, and statistics from other courses.
	Reset	Enables you to remove all user data from a course while retaining your activities and resources. See Chapter 14 for details.
	Reports	Gives you access to all user data, reports, logs, and the activities learners accessed. See Chapter 14 for more information.
	Questions	Takes you to your question pool, where you can create quiz questions or add them to your existing quizzes. Chapter 11 has more details.

Icon	Tool	Functionality
	Files	Takes you to your files folder, where you can move, upload, delete, and modify files.
	Unenroll Me	An option to unenroll students from a course. Depending on how enrollment and permission are set up, by default, students don't have the option to unenroll.
	Profile	One of the two tools accessible to student accounts. See the earlier "Viewing and Updating Participants' Profiles" section for more details.

✔ **Course Categories (or Courses):** The Courses block lists the categories and/or courses in the Moodle site. This block enables you to move among the courses. It's useful to your learners if they are enrolled in more than one Moodle course because they can quickly navigate among the courses.

The following blocks, by default, appear on the right:

✔ **Latest News:** Posts made to the News Forum are highlighted in this block, including a link to access the older news postings. Moodle is set up to show three latest news item. You can change this to display more or fewer new items: In the course Administration block on the left, click the Settings link and then click the News Items to view the latest news posted to the news forum.

✔ **Upcoming Events:** When you post an event to the calendar (available as an additional block; see the following section) and when you set dates in activities such as assignments, the events are listed in the Upcoming Events block. The listing is a link to the event as well as a useful reminder for your learners. Moodle provides so many different modules listing deadlines, your learners won't be able to find an excuse.

✔ **Recent Activities:** This block lists the activities you post as well as the updates you make to the resources or assignments.

Additional blocks

When you turn on editing (by clicking the Turn Editing On button at the top-right corner), the Blocks drop-down list appears with several utilities you can add (many of them very useful and which I use regularly). I describe each in this list:

✔ **Blog Tags and Blog Menu:** See Chapter 8 for details on how the Blog Tags and Blog Menu blocks are displayed.

✔ **Calendar:** I always enable the Calendar block as soon as I set up a course and move it up left or right side, so learners can easily see it. As soon as you set up an activity or a resource, it gets listed in the calendar. An administrator can create calendars to be listed on the site front page informing all users about events related to all courses. For example, if the site administrator will be running maintenance on the server and there will be a certain period of time when users won't be able to log in, the date(s) and time(s) can be listed in the site calendar. Instructors (those with the Teacher role) can also enable one or more calendars for their courses. Events can be exported into other calendars or software programs.

After enabling the calendar, the following tricks can help enter listings:

- *Color coding:* Notice the color-coded key used for events listed for everyone in a course, for groups, and for users only.

- *Adding entries:* To add an entry to a day (remember: due dates on activities are automatically pushed to the calendar), click the month. The month is a link that takes you to a full calendar view page.

- *Adding events:* When you click the New Event button, Moodle takes you to a new window. Follow the instructions — the fields are straight forward. Make sure you click the Save Changes button on the last screen.

✔ **Global Search:** The Global Search block provides user with a search input box that searches the complete Moodle course. Advanced search features are available.

✔ **HTML:** Use this block to create your own unique block for the front page. By using the HTML capabilities, you can add media (such as images, video, and sound). You don't have to give the block a name; you can leave it totally blank and just add an image.

✔ **Loan Calculator:** A basic calculator enabling your learners to calculate interest rates.

✔ **Mentees:** This block enables an instructor to set up mentor roles and gives mentors quick access to their own profile pages. Mentors can be anyone who has a relationship to your learner — for example, a parent, industry supervisor, or really anyone working with a learner who may want/need access to the Moodle course. The block becomes activated only when the mentor role is activated. This particular role must be assigned viewing permission and then assigned to the student account he or she will view. See Chapter 4 for more detailed explanation.

✔ **Network Server:** This is an admin functionality you may have permission to enable. It allows learners to access different Moodle sites to enroll in a course.

✔ **Online Users:** This block shows a list of all users logged in to your course. The list is refreshed every 5 minutes. You can enable and delete this block, though if don't have administrative privileges, you can't change the time setting for refreshing the list.

If part of your assessment is looking at how long students are viewing your course material, a good check is to look at log files and reports and view the activities students have accessed. Just looking at whether they're logged in is not a conclusive measure of being an active participant.

✔ **Quiz Results:** This block enables you to choose a quiz (there must be a quiz in the course for this block to be enabled) and show the highest and/or lowest grades on the front page. After you bring up the block, you need to select the Editing icon and configure the block. You can select the quiz (if you have more than one in the course), how many highest/lowest grades to show, whether to show the grades anonymously, and the format of the grades (percentages, fractions, or absolute numbers). Figure 3-10 shows the editing screen (on the left) and how the block is displayed when configured.

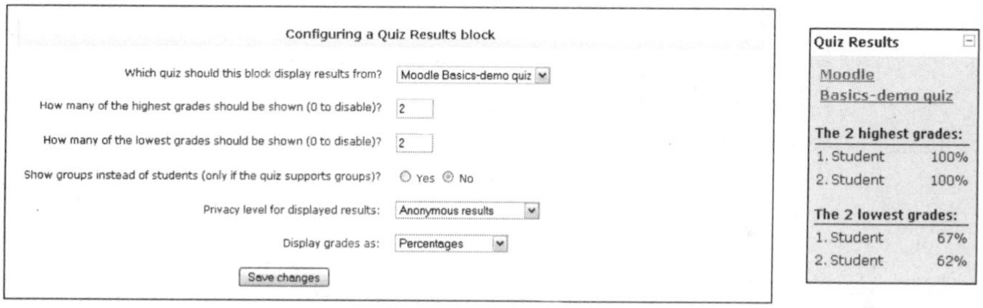

Figure 3-10:
Including a
Quiz Results
block in
your course.

Configuring a Quiz Results block

Which quiz should this block display results from?	Moodle Basics-demo quiz
How many of the highest grades should be shown (0 to disable)?	2
How many of the lowest grades should be shown (0 to disable)?	2
Show groups instead of students (only if the quiz supports groups)?	○ Yes ◉ No
Privacy level for displayed results:	Anonymous results
Display grades as:	Percentages

Save changes

Quiz Results   □

Moodle
Basics-demo quiz

The 2 highest grades:
1. Student   100%
2. Student   100%

The 2 lowest grades:
1. Student   67%
2. Student   62%

✔ **Random Glossary Entry:** You can use this block with your glossary to randomly show various entries. You can also use this block editing text box for other goals such as an image or a quote of the day. The block entry changes every time the front page is refreshed. For more information about the glossary, see Chapter 9. Note that you need to configure the tool by using the edit icon and completing a number of fields.

✔ **Remote RSS Feeds:** This tool enables you to add newsfeeds from external resources, such as Web sites, to show up in your Moodle course front page (or site). You can add news headlines, journal article releases, recently added documents, and so on. When you enable this block, you're given a link telling you to configure it. Follow the Moodle instructions.

✔ **Section Links:** This block enables you and your learners to quickly access week or unit sections in your course. Whether you set up the course by weeks or topics, the numbers that appear in this block act as links to the particular sections. This block is useful if you have many topics. I tend to use it over 10 weeks of units. If you make use of this block, it works best to move it up, so it's clearly visible. I tend to position it right under the People block.

✔ **Tags:** Anything tagged in your course glossary or blog appears in this block. It can be overwhelming and messy, and I recommend that if you use tags, use them for blocks or glossary entries only.

Moodle has few other useful blocks you can download by visiting the `http://moodle.org` modules and plugins database. Some of the blocks that have been added include: YouTube, Flickr, Side Bar, Progress Bar, Unanswered Discussions, and Simple Clock.

Resources and Activities

Resources and Activities are two unique utilities, each providing you with a different set of tools to help add content and interactive modules to your course.

The Activities block, located on the left side of the course front page, lists all the activities and resources you set in your course. When you add a new activity or resource to your course, Moodle adds it to the list in the block. The activity or resource is listed with the icon representing and name representing the module. The name of the module is a direct link to the activity or resource. When you first begin setting up your course, you see only the news forum listed; as you add Resources and Activities, the list will grow.

When you want to add resource or activities to your course, turn on editing, either from the Turn Editing On button at the top-right corner of your front page or from your Administration block, Moodle enables all editing features and opens the Resources and Activities drop-down lists — both shown in Figure 3-11 — in each section/week of your course.

✔ **Resources:** When people in the Moodle community make a reference to Moodle resources, they mean content that you can create within Moodle, link to on the Internet, or upload files (such as PDFs, Word documents, spreadsheets, PowerPoint files, video, and sound). Chapter 5 discusses how to add resources to your course. All resources are depicted by the icon shown in the margin and are listed in the Activities block. Figure 3-11 shows the resources you can add to your course through the Resources drop-down list.

Figure 3-11: The Resources and Activities drop-down lists, and the Activities block.

✔ **Activities:** The drop-down list includes all the interactive and collaborative modules that you can add to your course. When you first set up your course, all you see are the default blocks and the News Forum. The drop-down list lets you explore and add collaborative functionality that makes your course stand out to the learners as more than just static content. Making good use of these modules engages your learners and enables you to meet your instruction goals using various modes of interactivity. Activities are covered in depth in Part III.

Unlike the resources, which are all grouped and listed in the Activities block under one icon, clicking the icon for an activity in the block (see Figure 3-11) leads you to a list of the particular activity. The icons are also used in the week or unit sections within your course. Familiarizing yourself with them helps you maneuver through your course with ease.

Understanding and Implementing Moodle Conventions

Moodle uses specific conventions, icons, and fill-in fields throughout all its tools and features. The most common and oft-used of these conventions — the Moodle Help system and the settings for resources and activities — are ones that you may want to continue to reference, so I discuss those here. When you become a regular Moodler, these will become second nature. Developers of Moodle have kept to the same layouts for every version, which makes you quickly fall in love with it, knowing that after you learn a way of doing things, it won't be changed — thank you, development team!

Moodle Help system

Wherever you see the help icon, you can click it to open a small help window defining or briefly explaining the term or functionality.

Resources and activities settings

Each of the setup pages for all activities and resources has several groups, each containing any number of steps, always ordered in the same sequence. The following sections summarize the settings and explain some of the conventions. You see these setup pages when you set up a resource, such as linking to a file, or an activity like a forum discussion or a quiz.

General settings

The General settings are shown in Figure 3-12. Each setup page requires you to enter a name in the field, a summary (which I recommend because the summary is listed in a table when learners access the activity or resource from the activity block), and then content. Specific activities have other settings particular to the activity, such as setting dates (for instance, for a chat or forum discussion) or linking to a Web site or file.

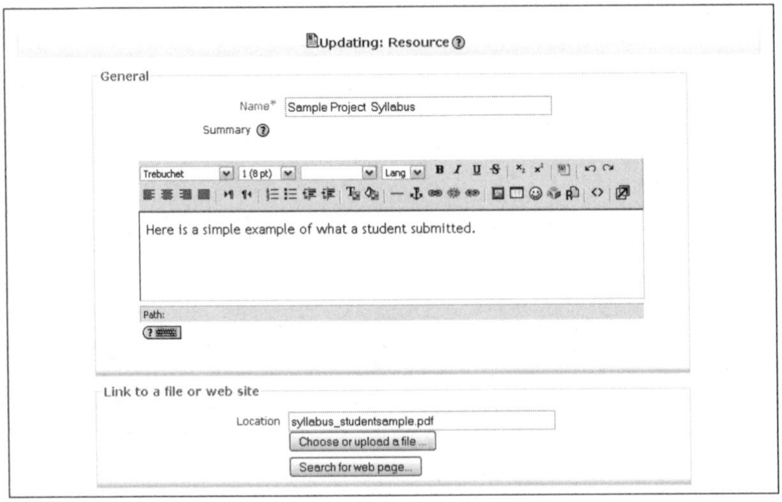

Figure 3-12: The standard Moodle general settings for resources and activities.

Window settings

The Window settings, shown in Figure 3-13, enable you to set up your new activity or resource in a new window or the same window. If the activity or resource opens in the same window, select the check box to show course blocks enabling learners to navigate back. Often when learners have finished with the activity or resource, they close it by clicking the red X in the top-right corner. In Moodle, this action closes the Moodle session, and learners have to log back in.

Unless pop-up windows are blocked by your system administrators, I recommend opening the resource or activity in a new window. When you select New Window from the drop-down list, Moodle lets you select a number of different options. If you aren't sure what to pick, leave the default settings; they work well!

If your system administrator has blocked pop-up windows, try anything, including bribery, to get him to enable them for your Moodle site. Take up the issue with him. The pop-up windows will help you structure the course and help your learners to use and navigate the course with ease. You have a number of choices when you enable a new window and you can make your selections depending on your needs.

Parameters

The Parameters section, shown in Figure 3-14, contains advanced features that you most likely won't use. The parameters are useful when you want to send data about your learners and course to another site. For example, you may want to send information about your learners from your Moodle site to another schools server, which will give learners access.

If the parameters aren't displayed, click the Show Advanced button on the right. Next select the options you require. Depending what the server is requiring, you can choose it from the drop-down list. For example, you just may need the learner's e-mail address, or you may need a combination of e-mail address and learner ID. Moodle provides you with every exception possibly required, and you can use up to five. There are 30 parameter type entries that you can use. (Table 5-1 lists the most widely used parameters. You can see the remainder by opening the Choose Parameter drop-down list.)

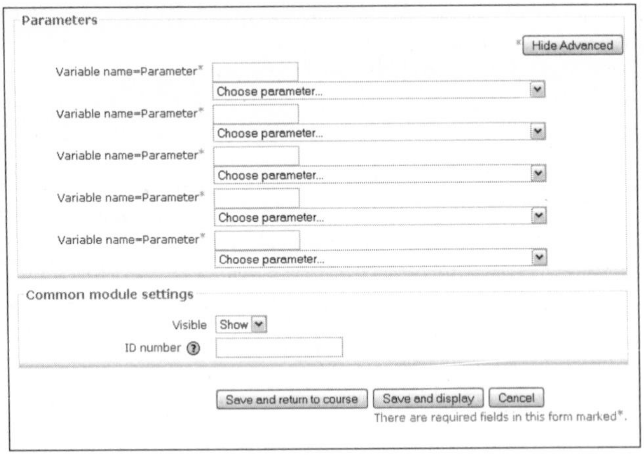

Figure 3-14:
The
standard
Moodle
Window
settings
for param-
eters and
Common
Module
Settings.

Common Module Settings

Most resources and activities include these items (refer to Figure 3-13):

- **Group Mode:** If groups are set up at the course level, this option is available. Moodle by default enables activities by group setting if forced is turned on and set to Yes. If set to No, group selection can be set to one of three levels:

  - *No Groups:* Every setting is same for all groups (for example, assignments are submitted in one area).

  - *Separate Groups:* Students carry out task or activities in separate, designated groups.

  - *Visible Groups:* Students can choose to associate with a group or see other group activities.

- **Visible drop-down list:** Enables you to hide or show (eye closed/opened) and activity or resource. For example, you can set up many activities and resources but choose not to make them visible to learners until you're ready for the information or activity to be presented — planning ahead!

- **ID Number:** ID setting is useful if you have many activities and resources. It is easier to track in log files, grade book, or exporting them to spreadsheet. If you decide to use ID numbers or combination of numbers and characters, either use a standard system used within your organization, or make up a logical system that's easy to understand and identify. If you're using grade calculations, you'll be required to set up an ID. You can leave this field blank.

Common Module Settings are also used in resources and activities, but they don't include all the options for both. For instance, group settings are not used in resources, and parameters are not used with activities.

Password settings

Moodle developers understand that you have to deal with far too many passwords, so wherever you may want to use a password, you see a check box. When you select this check box, Moodle reveals the password you set. This must be one of my most-loved setup functions because I have no need to keep a spreadsheet of passwords ever again when working with Moodle.

Chapter 4

Creating Your Course

• •

In This Chapter

▶ Setting up your course on a Moodle site

▶ Mastering registration

▶ Adding learners to your course and keeping them there

▶ Understanding everything about Moodle user roles

▶ Creating groups

▶ Letting everyone know your course is ready

▶ Setting up PayPal so you can charge for your course

• •

*W*hen you've created your Moodle course and you have the beginnings of it ready to go, you can start announcing it to the world (or your organization) and get learners into your course. Teacher and Course Creator user accounts have permissions enabling you to structure and make changes to the Moodle default course settings. This chapter helps you enroll learners, set permissions, and get the word out. I also explain a few basic settings that can help you organize and deliver a fabulous course.

For this chapter, I assume that you

✔ Have a Moodle site running on a hosted server, or you have access to it through your organization or educational establishment.

✔ Your course has been set up.

✔ You're ready to structure your course to meet the needs of your learners and achieve your teaching goals.

If you don't have a site and/or course set up, please go to Chapter 3 and Chapter 13, where I tell you how to get your own Moodle site and walk you through adding your first course. This chapter guides you through only some of the site settings.

Exploring the Front Page Settings and Enrollment Options

To access the course front page settings, click the Settings link in the Administration block (located on the left side, as shown in Figure 4-1). Moodle takes you to Edit Course Settings page. These settings enable you to decide how you want things to appear to your learners and structure the course layout to meet your learning objectives. In the following sections, I describe these settings (in groups, as they're divided on the Edit Course Settings page) so that you can make changes if you don't want to keep the Moodle default settings.

Figure 4-1: The basic layout of course front page, with the Administration block on the left.

As you look over these settings and make changes, remember two things:

✔ When you're done, click the Save Changes button at the bottom of the Edit Course Settings page.

✔ Any field marked with an asterisk is a required field, and you must fill it in.

General

This is the largest group on the Edit Course Settings page. The following list describes each setting (as shown in Figure 4-2):

- ✔ **Category:** Categories are set up by the site administrator. They can help instructors and learners quickly find their courses if the site is large. The Moodle default category is Miscellaneous, and your site admin may have a list to help structure and organize the site. For example, a university Moodle site may be organized by schools (for instance, medical school, business school, dental school, and so on) or departments (such as math, science, engineering, humanities, and the like). If you have a Teacher or Course Creator user account, you will not be able to create new categories or change the names unless you have Administrative capabilities.

  If you want to change category names and create new categories, go to the site Administration block and click Courses. As mentioned previously, you need to have an Administrator user account or privileges added to your Teacher or Course Creator account.

- ✔ **Full Name:** Enter the full name of your course as it may appear in a course catalogue, such as **Moodle 101** in Figure 4-2. This is a required field.

- ✔ **Short Name:** Enter the short name as used by your organization, such as **MD101**. This field is also required.

  If you don't have a specific short name, make one up! Moodle won't let you set up the course without a short name. The short name will appear in the navigation bar.

- ✔ **Course ID Number:** Enter the unique course alphanumeric ID.

  This field has a variety of uses, and it can be left blank. It's mainly set up in case an organization has a unique identifier for each course and needs to synchronize the IDs with backend data systems used for courses and enrollments. Students don't see ID, but if they need to see it because it's listed in a catalogue, you can use it as part of the course short name.

- ✔ **Summary:** The summary appears on the course listing page for your learners to see. Enter a sentence or short paragraph depicting the nature of your course.

- ✔ **Format:** Moodle allows you to set a course format to support your teaching requirements. The drop-down list gives you a number of options:
  - *Weekly Format:* This is one of the most popular formats, which allows you to specify start and end dates and any number of weeks you want the course to run.

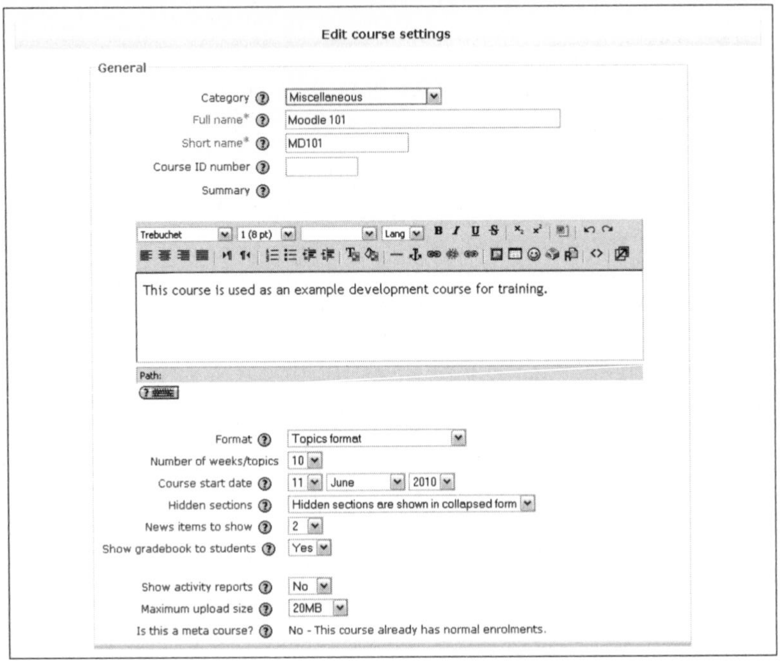

Figure 4-2:
The Edit
Course
Settings
page.

The course dates will be listed based on the course start date you enter, with the current week highlighted. This format is useful if you structure your course by your organization's academic calendar and your learners move at a similar pace. Figure 4-3 shows an example of this format (on left).

- *Topics Format:* With this format, the course is organized by topics or units, and you choose how many topics you want to structure the course. The right side of Figure 4-3 shows an example topic outline.

  This is a useful format if time is not a constraint and some topics have more activities or take longer and/or build on knowledge from previous topics. Moodle adds numbers for topics, which you can change using the front page editing tools described in Chapters 3 and 5.

- *Social Format:* The main focus of the social format takes on the structure of one main forum discussion. This format isn't often used for courses, but it's used to create departmental or organizational discussions around issues. For example, one school district used a social format to involve teachers in a discussion on training needs and training courses. Check out Moodle Lounge, an open forum to chat with other Moodle users at `http://moodle.org/course/view.php?id=55`, `http://moodle.org` to see how this format is being used.

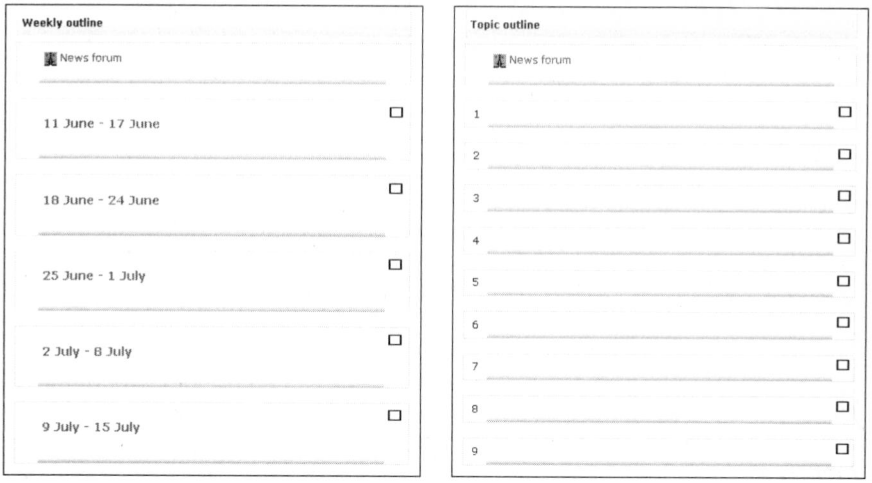

Weekly outline

News forum

11 June - 17 June ☐

18 June - 24 June ☐

25 June - 1 July ☐

2 July - 8 July ☐

9 July - 15 July ☐

Topic outline

News forum

1 ☐

2 ☐

3 ☐

4 ☐

5 ☐

6 ☐

7 ☐

8 ☐

9 ☐

Figure 4-3:
Course front page showing a weekly format.

- *LAMS Format:* LAMS stands for Learning Activity Management System. This is an open source format that has been used for a few years by instructors. The system uses a Flash-based authoring environment. Moodle developers integrated the LAMS format so that instructors can incorporate LAMS-based activities into a Moodle course, benefiting from Moodle tools. LAMS is not widely used because it is a bit dated. Instructors and organizations are adopting Moodle or other similar open source content management systems or Web 2.0 tools.

- *SCORM Format:* SCORM stands for Sharable Content Reference Model. SCORM and AICC are standard content packages that are used by a variety of applications that support the format. Moodle enables you to use this package either as a complete course format or within individual activities. For example, if you set up a complete course with Adobe's Articulate, you can use the SCORM format and make it available on your Moodle site. For more information, go to `http://docs.moodle.org/en`.

If you use the entire course in a SCORM format, your learners can't interact with the Moodle tools. It makes more sense to create SCORM activities.

- *Weekly Format, CSS/No Tables:* This format is very similar to the weekly format without the table layout. You get more flexibility for displaying variety of activities. Older browsers may not be able to display this format.

✔ **Number of Weeks/Topics:** Choose the number of sections from the drop-down list.

You use this drop-down list only with topic and weekly formats. Ten is the default, and you can choose up to 52. You can add sections as you find the need. Moodle adds any new section to the bottom of the list.

✔ **Course Start Date:** Specify the course start date. If you're using a weekly format, the start date appears in the first week. Choose your date to coincide with the date that you want logs to start and your course to be visible to students. If you set the date after you want the learners to see sections, they will be unable to view them.

✔ **Hidden Sections:** This function enables you to display a collapsed section to your learners, showing them the unit title.

I suggest you leave the default setting (Hidden Sections Are Shown in Collapsed Form) unless you want to hide the topic completely because each activity and resource can be hidden.

✔ **News Items to Show:** From the drop-down list, select how many news items you want to show in the News block that appears on the front page (right side column).

✔ **Show Gradebook to Students:** Use this drop-down list to determine whether your learners have access to their grade book.

By default, Moodle enters a grade for every graded activity that is displayed to the learners from the Grades link on the course front page. Unless you have a particular reason for not wanting learners to see their grades and class average, I suggest you allow learners to view their grade books.

✔ **Show Activity Reports:** Displays all Moodle activities to learners.

Similar to the reports available to teachers from the Administration block, if you enable the activity report for students, they can view all of their own activities. Unless you have a particular learning objective for the learners to view their Moodle participation (for example, you can get them to chart, graph, use spreadsheet from the data obtained), I don't suggest enabling this feature. These log reports can place an extra load on the server if you have a large number of learners enrolled in your course. You may even find yourself battling your system administrator on this one.

✔ **Maximum Upload Size:** This option limits the size of files your learners can upload.

You should know how much space your course has and then set this option appropriately. Making this option much smaller than system allocation is wise. Beware; students will use up space quickly when they realize they can do exciting things with their projects and upload video files and sound files.

✔ **Is This a Meta Course?** This is purely an enrollment functionality, meaning a meta course automatically gets students enrolled from one or
more courses. A *meta course* in Moodle is a course that is linked to any
number of other courses to ease registration. See Chapter 13 for more
information.

Enrollments

The Enrollments settings (shown in Figure 4-4) enable you to make decisions
about the people who enroll and what they can see and do.

✔ **Enrollment Plugins:** Moodle has various plugins, including internal
enrollment and PayPal to manage the course enrollment.

This concern may be taken off your hands if the system administrator
controls the enrollment; in that case, just leave the default. You can find
more details on enrollments later in this chapter and in Chapter 13.

✔ **Default Role:** Allows you to set a default login roll for everyone that's
enrolled. Moodle sets this to Student, and I strongly recommend that
you leave the default if you and your administrator want any control
over your course.

✔ **Course Enrollable:** You have three options: No, Yes, and Date Range.
If you select Yes to allow self enrollment, the grayed out Start and End
Dates become active, and you can set the range as required.

This setting has no effect if users are enrolled using an external
database.

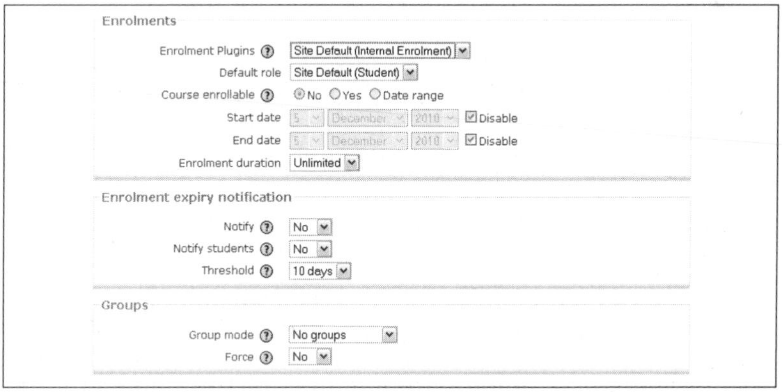

Figure 4-4:
Course
Administra-
tion Block:
enrollments,
groups, and
availability
options.

✔ **Enrollment Duration:** This function sets how long a student can be enrolled in the course, *not* how long self enrollment is available (as many instructors believe). Another way some people use this setting is to automatically unenroll students from a course instead of deleting them manually.

Be careful about how you set this; for example, if you set it for 28 days, all students will be locked out of your course after the duration. If you aren't sure what to select, leave the default setting.

Enrollment Expiry Notification

Use the Enrollment Expiry Notification settings (refer to Figure 4-4) if you want users notified when their enrollment is about to expire. You have just a few things to adjust here:

✔ **Notify:** Select Yes from the drop-down list if you want all other registered users, other than student accounts, notified.

✔ **Notify Students:** Select Yes from the drop-down list if you want students notified.

✔ **Threshold:** From the drop-down list, select how many days prior to the course expiration date the enrolled accounts should be notified.

Groups

Moodle enables you to set up groups for your course or any activity and assign any number of learners or teachers (or other user accounts) to the groups. For example, if you teach three different sections of the same course, you can set up three different groups, or you can assign groups to participate in different forum discussions. I explain groups in more detail later in this chapter in the "Managing Activities and Projects with Groups" section, but you see the following two settings here. (Refer to Figure 4-4.)

✔ **Group Mode:** You have these three choices:

• *No Groups:* You have one course with no groups for activities.

• *Separate Groups:* Groups see and participate in only their own group. Other groups are invisible.

• *Visible Groups:* Each group member participates and works in his own group but can also see other groups' work. For instance in Forums, everyone can see groups' postings, but can post discussions and replies in only their own group.

✔ **Force:** If you force groups, you don't have to set up groups in specific activities, and you can assign learners to specific groups. See the section "Managing Activities and Projects with Groups," later in the chapter, for details on creating groups.

Availability

The Availability settings (shown in Figure 4-5) determine the availability for registered users and guests.

✔ **Availability:** Enables you to hide your course or make it available to students. If you're making it available, I recommend that you set an enrollment key.

✔ **Enrollment Key:** Select any alphanumeric key. Anyone who wants to view your course needs this key to be able to access it. One nice Moodle feature is that if you forget the key, you can select the check box, and the key will be displayed.

✔ **Guest Access:** Determine whether guests can access the course. Using the drop-down list, you have a choice of letting them in needing a key, not needing a key, or not letting guests in at all. Guests can only read content; they can't interact or add to any activity.

✔ **Cost:** If a payment gateway has been added as an enrollment plugin, you can set the cost in the field, and students have to make a payment before they can enroll in the course.

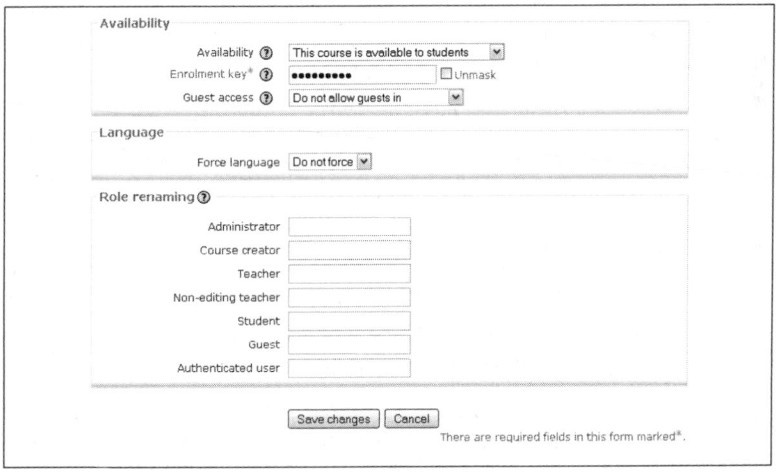

Figure 4-5:
Control
course
availability.

Language

Select an option from the Language drop-down list if you want to force a language. If you force the language of the site, the Moodle interface is presented in that language, and students can't change languages within personal profiles. I recommend you accept the default setting (Do Not Force) shown in the preceding Figure 4-5.

Role Renaming

Moodle enables you to rename roles in your course. For instance, instead of Teacher role, you may want to change it to Instructor, Tutor, or Facilitator. The Student role can be named Participant, and Non-Editing Teacher can become Mentor or Substitute. Moodle allows you to change role permissions for most of the roles in the course. See the later section, "Implementing Moodle Roles and Course Permissions." Note that the default role names, as they appear in Figure 4-5, may have been changed at the site level by your Moodle administrator. Even if they've been changed already, you can still change the names for your course.

Adding Learners to Your Course

The methods to enroll learners in your course fall into two categories: manual registration and self registration. The Manual method is part of the Administrator role, a responsibility that falls to the Moodle administrator. If, however, you're wearing both hats, instructor and administrator, you can review enrollment in Chapter 13.

Enrolling learners through self registration

In this section, I take you through the process of self registration, which Moodle refers to as *internal enrollment;* it's the default setting in Moodle. Using this method is the most efficient and effective way to get learners into your course.

What URL that you use for Moodle depends on how your organization or Internet service provider has it set up, and it can take any number of forms. For example, it can look like http://*nameoforganization*.com/moodle or http://*moodle.nameoforganization.org.*

TIP

Testing your course

When you're in the middle of creating a fabulous course for your learners, you need to have learners in your course. At this point, you may be asking yourself,

- Will learners be able to navigate my course?

- Will learners read the right information to start?

- Are my instructions for assignments and quizzes easy to understand?

These are all great questions, and the only way you can answer yes to all of them is to get a few students to test your course. Run a minipilot session, observe your students, and get feedback. Your test students can be previous students; students from your current courses; or if you're setting up training sessions, a colleague or two. Rounding up testers who will do a complete run-through of your course and give feedback is a valuable exercise, and it will put your mind at ease. To prevent self-induced panic, just be sure to set all this up with plenty of time for testing before you launch your course.

Give your leaners these instructions to follow to self enroll:

1. Go to the Moodle site URL (Web address) provided by the system administrator or instructor.

A screen appears, asking whether you're returning to this site or it's your first time here. See Figure 4-6.

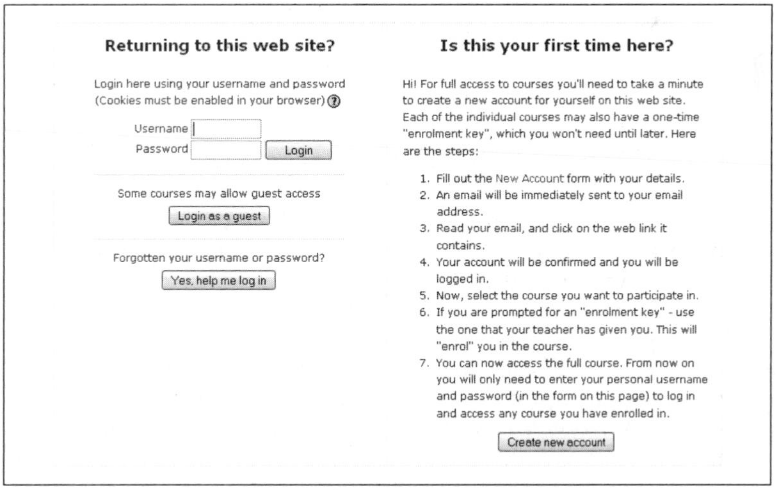

Returning to this web site?

Login here using your username and password (Cookies must be enabled in your browser) ⑦

Username |
Password [   ] [Login]

Some courses may allow guest access
[Login as a guest]

Forgotten your username or password?
[Yes, help me log in]

Is this your first time here?

Hi! For full access to courses you'll need to take a minute to create a new account for yourself on this web site. Each of the individual courses may also have a one-time "enrolment key", which you won't need until later. Here are the steps:

1. Fill out the New Account form with your details.
2. An email will be immediately sent to your email address.
3. Read your email, and click on the web link it contains.
4. Your account will be confirmed and you will be logged in.
5. Now, select the course you want to participate in.
6. If you are prompted for an "enrolment key" - use the one that your teacher has given you. This will "enrol" you in the course.
7. You can now access the full course. From now on you will only need to enter your personal username and password (in the form on this page) to log in and access any course you have enrolled in.

[Create new account]

Figure 4-6:
Moodle
login page.

2. **Click the Create a New Account button on the lower-right side of the screen.**

   The New Account page appears, as shown in Figure 4-7.

3. **Choose your username and password.**

   With Moodle versions 1.9.7 and higher, your password has to be at least eight characters long and include at least one lowercase letter, at least one uppercase letter, at least one digit, and at least one nonalphanumeric letter (such as %, #, *, or !).

4. **Fill in the remainder of the fields, making sure your e-mail address is valid.**

   Note that all these fields are required in order for you to successfully create an account.

5. **Select the Create My New Account button.**

6. **Log in to your e-mail account.**

   You should receive a confirmation within a couple minutes of submitting the Create My New Account form. You must click the link in your e-mail, which confirms your registration and takes you to the Moodle site. You also receive a default Welcome message.

The Welcome message that learners receive is standard, and you need administrative permissions to make changes to or disable it.

When self enrolling, your learners may either enter your course, or enter your organization's site front page. If they enter the organization's front page, a number of courses may be listed. New learners need to select your course from the list. Most often, a pop-up window appears because the learners need a key to enter your course. (I highly recommend requiring a key, or you may never know who is in your course!) The learners can enter the key into the pop-up window. After entering it, they are automatically registered for your course. This is a one-time procedure. Next time they come to the course, they will need to enter only the username and password.

If your course doesn't require a key, the learners will be directed straight to your course. They will be required to enter their username and password every time they revisit the course.

If you set a key for your course, make sure you give the key to students with the URL and registration instructions.

Enrolling learners through manual enrollment

If your learners are manually enrolled in a Moodle site, they need to receive the username and password from you or your Moodle administrator before they can enter the course. If they have the login information and the organization's Moodle Web address, they need to access the Moodle site (by placing the URL into a browser) and then enter their username and password on the left side. (Refer to Figure 4-6.) As discussed previously, if your course has an enrollment key, students are required to enter it. This is a one-time procedure. Next time they come to the course, they will need only the username and password.

If your learners are using Mac computers, advise them that the Firefox browser is much more compatible with Moodle than Safari.

Here's the catch with manually enrolled students: Before they can access your course, you need to add them by assigned role in the course. This process is slightly different than the preceding one. To add learners who are manually enrolled, follow these steps to add them into your course.

You would follow the same process for adding non-editing teachers or guests to your course.

1. **Click the Assign Roles link in the Administration block of your course front page.**

   Moodle takes you to an Assign Roles in Course: *[Course ID]* page, as shown in Figure 4-8.

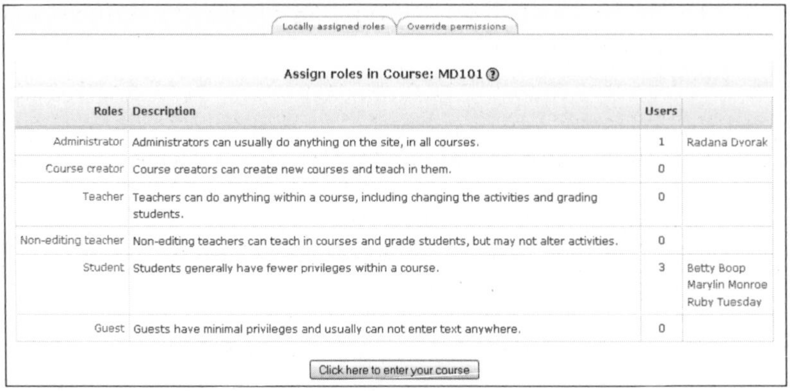

Figure 4-8: Assigning roles in your course for manually registered users.

2. **Click the Student link in the left column in the table.**

   Moodle takes you to the Assign Roles in Course: *[course short name]* page, as shown in Figure 4-9.

Figure 4-9: Adding students (assigning roles) to your course.

3. **Select the learner in the list of students on the right side.**

   You can select multiple learners by holding down the Ctrl or ⌘ key while clicking the names.

4. **Click the Add button between the columns to move the selected learners to the left column.**

   You can remove learners from the course by highlighting names in the left column and clicking the Remove button.

5. **Click the Assign Roles in Course:** *[Course short name]* **button at the bottom when you finish moving the names.**

   Moodle takes you back to Assign Roles page (shown earlier in Figure 4-8). You can return to your course by clicking the Click Here to Enter Your Course button.

To make sure all your learners are in the correct course, go to your course front page and click the Participant link in the People block located, by default, in the top-left column. If all your learners are listed, you are set to start teaching and Moodling — enjoy!

Unenrolling learners from your course

In the unimaginable case that a learner may need to unenroll from your course, you have two options:

✔ You can remove the student from the course on the Assign Roles in Course: *[course short name]* page. (Refer to the preceding steps and Figure 4-9.)

✔ You can allow for *self unenrollment.* Moodle, by default, does not give student accounts permission to unenroll themselves from courses.

To enable students to unenroll themselves from any course, follow the steps in this section. Note that to take these steps you need either administrative privileges or permission status on your Teacher role enabled.

If your IT administrator is new to Moodle and/or wears too many hats and Moodle tasks are a low priority, see whether you can bribe him to set a few extra permissions on your Teacher role so you don't need to keep running to him (or inundating him with threats such as you're going to jump off the building if he doesn't help you). Knowing how to change permissions on rolls will impress him.

1. **In the Site Administration block, (located on the site front page), click the Users link to expand your options. Click the Permissions link and then click the Define Roles link below that.**

   Moodle opens a new Roles page with three tabs on the top. On the Manage Roles tab, roles are listed in the left column, editing options in the right. See Figure 4-10.

Figure 4-10:
Role man-
agement.

2. **Click the editing icon opposite the Student role.**

   Moodle opens the Edit Role page. (See Figure 4-11.)

3. **Scroll down until you see moodle/role:unassignself in the column on the left.**

4. **On the right, select the Allow radio button.**

5. **Click the Save Changes button at the bottom of the page.**

   You have to scroll down quite a bit. The role change is enabled immediately when students log in.

Returning to your course, switch your role to Student view (by using the drop-down list in the top-right corner of your course front page). Notice in the students' Administration block (the third down on the left, as shown in Figure 4-12) that Moodle has enabled an Unenroll Me from *[Course short name]* link.

Moodle default settings allow teachers to unenroll themselves. You may be enrolled in a number of different site courses that you may have shared with your colleagues or just enrolled in to have a look. Often, Moodle administrators change this unenroll permission to prevent teachers from mistakenly unenrolling themselves. If this is the case and you have permissions to access to the site administration settings, follow the preceding steps to change permission status on the student roles; in Step 2, instead of selecting the Student role, select the Teacher role. You can then continue and change the permissions as outlined in Steps 3-5.

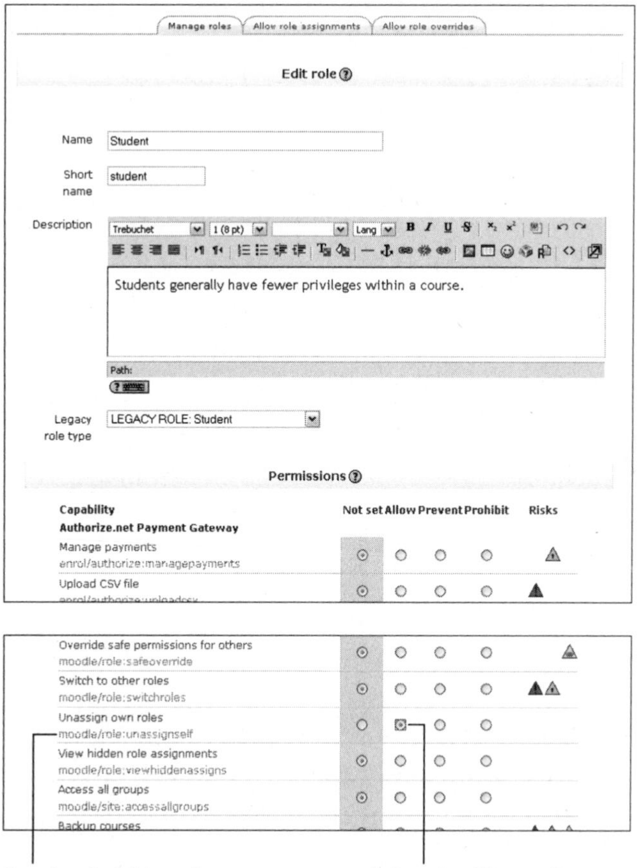

Figure 4-11:
Editing a
student role.

Scroll to find this option.   Select the Allow radio button.

Figure 4-12:
The student
view of the
Administra-
tion block.

Implementing Moodle Roles and Course Permissions

I've touched on Moodle roles in every chapter so far, and it's high time to spend a few minutes defining them, how they affect course capabilities, and what you can do if you want changes made to your course. Even though you may think that you don't really need to worry about roles and permission capabilities, and all this is starting to sound like you may have to put on your techie hat, don't be disheartened. Having a basic understanding of where to find more information if needed will give you skills to manage how your learners and anyone else coming to your course can interact with it. Read on — I promise it's worth your time!

Even if you don't have an Administrator permission status, this information will be useful in persuading and/or helping your IT admin to set specific permissions on your account so you have more control over your course. "The most valuable commodity I know of is information," said Gordon Gekko (played by Michael Douglas in the 1987 film *Wall Street*). This statement is true here as well: The more you know, the more you can help others help you.

Understanding roles and permissions

Moodle has a number of predefined rolls, as shown in Table 4-1. Each role has certain capabilities and permissions assigned to it that specify what a user can do within a Moodle course and/or site, and a user can be assigned multiple roles, such as Administrator and Course Creator.

For example, an Administrator role can restrict chat being used for all courses on a Moodle site. Or permissions can be added to a Student role to have Teacher role privileges for managing course activities such as wikis or glossaries.

Table 4-1	Moodle Roles and Their Capabilities
Roles	*Description*
Administrator	The most powerful role! If offered, take it, but with caution. You will be able to do anything, but that may come at the price of other instructors making demands. (Keep it quiet!)
Course Creator	This role allows you to create new courses and teach in them. Ask for this role also or permission to create new courses on your Teacher role. Course creator is automatically assigned a Teacher role.

Roles	Description
Teacher	Someone with a Teacher role (the most widely assigned role for instructors, trainers, and teachers) can do anything within a course, such as making changes within a course, grading, and grade book and changing activities. Teacher roles can't create a new course. Ask for extra permissions for specific capabilities like creating new courses.
Non-Editing Teacher	This role is great for a substitute teacher. She can teach in the Moodle course and add grades, but she can't set up resources or alter activities. You can rename this role to appear friendlier and not so restrictive.
Student	The student role is the main user of Moodle. It role has few privileges, unless they're given to the users by the teachers, such as being able to edit forums.
Guest	Guests can only read and link to specific resources. They can't participate or add to anything, thank goodness!
Authenticated User	A default role for all users who are logged in to Moodle. This role is set up so that if a user has more than one role, when he is logged in as that role (such as Teacher), it does not conflict with any other role (for instance, the Student role if the Teacher has both).

When it comes to discussing roles and how values function within permissions, you need to understand these three basic terms:

- **User:** A specific participant that is allowed to enter a Moodle site. Each user account has a specific role, which carries a set of permissions.

- **Role:** Identifies any particular user's position, such as Teacher, Student, Guest, and so on.

- **Capability:** Depicts particular Moodle features using a specific syntax. For instance, moodle/glossary:rate changes the capability on a student account giving permission for a student to rate a glossary entry. Moodle has thousands, well, actually, more than 150 capabilities associated with roles.

- **Permission:** Decides whether a specific user can use a capability within Moodle activities. There are four settings that you can manipulate: Not Set/Inherit, Allow, Prevent, and Prohibit. When changing permission status from Moodle defaults, please refer to Table 4-2 (later in this chapter), which describes Moodle warnings assigned to specific capabilities.

To view roles and assign users the roles, click the Assign Roles link in the course Administration block. Moodle takes you to the Assign Roles in Course: *[course short name]* page. Notice the difference between what you see with a

Teacher role (shown on top in Figure 4-13) and what you see if you have an Administrator role or a Teacher role with permissions changed to give you a capability to override roles (shown on the bottom).

	Locally assigned roles		

Assign roles in Course: MD101 ⑦

Roles	Description	Users	
Non-editing teacher	Non-editing teachers can teach in courses and grade students, but may not alter activities.	0	
Student	Students generally have fewer privileges within a course.	4	Betty Boop Marylin Monroe Martha Reeves Ruby Tuesday
Guest	Guests have minimal privileges and usually can not enter text anywhere.	0	

Click here to enter your course

	Locally assigned roles	Override permissions	

Assign roles in Course: MD101 ⑦

Roles	Description	Users	
Administrator	Administrators can usually do anything on the site, in all courses.	1	Radana Dvorak
Course creator	Course creators can create new courses and teach in them.	0	
Teacher	Teachers can do anything within a course, including changing the activities and grading students.	1	Marylin Monroe
Non-editing teacher	Non-editing teachers can teach in courses and grade students, but may not alter activities.	0	
Student	Students generally have fewer privileges within a course.	4	Betty Boop Marylin Monroe Martha Reeves Ruby Tuesday
Guest	Guests have minimal privileges and usually can not enter text anywhere.	0	

Click here to enter your course

Figure 4-13:
Viewing and assigning roles.

Setting up roles

You can create a new role and call it what you want (something intuitive that makes sense to everyone is a good start), and you can assign permissions to fit your course needs. Useful roles that instructors have used are the

✔ **Blogger role,** for specific students to use an activity.

✔ **Parent role,** for providing parents access to view the Moodle course and specific information about their child (for example, projects, grades, blogs).

✔ **VIP role,** assigned to a guest (such as an author, an actor, the President, or other professional) so that the guest can contribute to forums and answer questions.

You need permission for this capability or an Administrator role to set up new roles.

Follow these steps to set up a new role:

1. **Go to the Site Administration block on the site front page.**

2. **Click Permissions to expand the list and then click Define Roles.**

   Moodle takes you to Roles page with three tabs on the top (as shown in Figure 4-14). You can change permission status from this page by selecting the role.

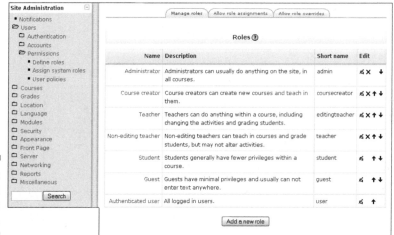

Figure 4-14:
Define roles
on this
page.

3. **Click the Add a New Role button.**

   Moodle takes you to the Add a New Role page, which is shown in Figure 4-15.

4. **In the Name field provided, give the role a name.**

   You can combine two words to name a role, such as Student Teacher, Teacher Instructor, or Teacher Professor.

5. **(Optional) Add a short name, which will be displayed in the profile for all users to see, and a description.**

6. **From the Legacy Role drop-down list, select a legacy role type.**

   Note: Legacy roles are the default roles and useful to select only if you are using an older version of Moodle, or if the new role you are creating is very similar to one of the Moodle default roles. You can leave the default None if you are using Moodle versions 1.9.+.

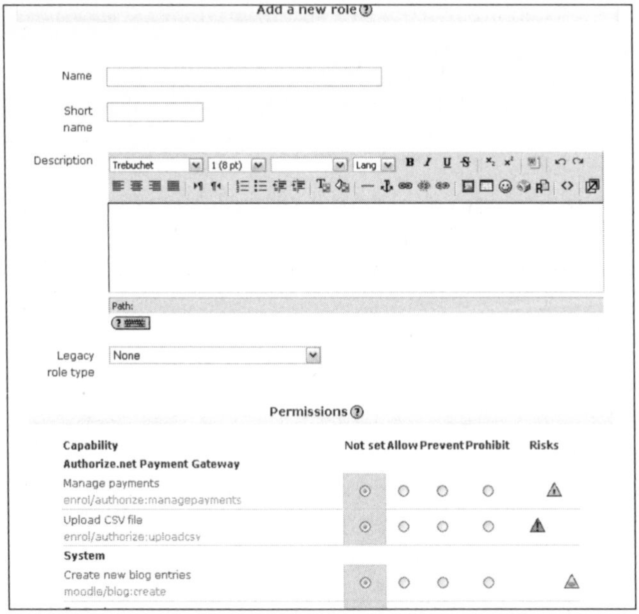

Figure 4-15:
The Add a
New Role
page.

7. **Scroll down the long permissions list to set the permissions for the new role.**

8. **Click the Add a New Role button at the bottom of the page.**

   Moodle returns you to the Role page with the new role added, as shown in Figure 4-16. For this example, I added the Teacher Instructor role.

REMEMBER

A number of the capabilities have warning triangles listed in the Risk column. (Refer to Figure 4-15.) I recommend you pay attention to them when you set permissions to specific capabilities; if you aren't sure what certain risks mean, check by clicking the link Moodle Docs for This Page, at the bottom, or go to `http://docs.moodle.org/en/Risks`. See Table 4-2 for an explanation of the warning triangle symbols.

Table 4-2	Risk Warning Descriptions
Icons	*Description*
Blue triangle	Users can gain access to private information or other users.
Yellow triangle	Users can send spam to site users or others.
Red triangle	Users can add files and text that allow cross-site scripting.
Green triangle	Users can change site configurations and behavior.

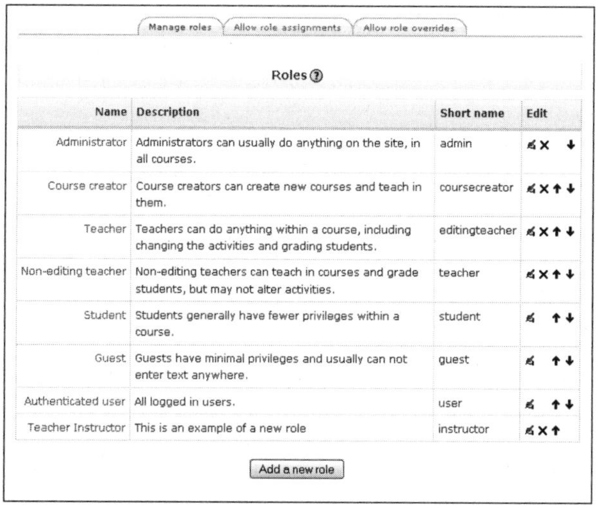

Manage roles | Allow role assignments | Allow role overrides

Roles

Name	Description	Short name	Edit
Administrator	Administrators can usually do anything on the site, in all courses.	admin	
Course creator	Course creators can create new courses and teach in them.	coursecreator	
Teacher	Teachers can do anything within a course, including changing the activities and grading students.	editingteacher	
Non-editing teacher	Non-editing teachers can teach in courses and grade students, but may not alter activities.	teacher	
Student	Students generally have fewer privileges within a course.	student	
Guest	Guests have minimal privileges and usually can not enter text anywhere.	guest	
Authenticated user	All logged in users.	user	
Teacher Instructor	This is an example of a new role	instructor	

Add a new role

Figure 4-16: The Roles page with the newly created example role,Teacher Instructor.

Overriding roles

You can override role capabilities at the course level or for specific activities. Moodle gives you these three options:

- **Override at Course Level:** This override affects all participants in the course. The Administrator can put restrictions on a role, specific to a course.
- **Override for a Particular Activity for All Participants:** You can give participants extra capabilities for a particular activity, such as rating glossary entries or being able to reply to news forums, which by default students cannot do.
- **Override for a Particular Participant (Student):** For example, if you want a student to be the course calendar monitor, you would set the permissions at the particular user account. You can give students various status and responsibility to help you manage the course (for example, approving glossary, wiki, or database entries, and so on).

To make changes to the roles, go to the Administration block on your course front page and click the Assign Roles link. Moodle takes you to a new page with these tabs: Locally Assigned Roles, and Override Permissions (as shown earlier in Figure 4-8). If you don't see these tabs, speak to your system administrator.

Overriding a role in an activity and assigning a role in an activity sound similar, but they aren't; so I detail the process for each in the following sections.

Overriding a role for an activity

If you want to add or restrict capabilities on any course activities, follow these steps:

1. **Choose an activity from your course, such as a Forum, and click the Update This Forum button (top right).**

2. **On the Override Permissions tab, select the role you want to override.**

   In this example, I'm changing the Student role. Moodle takes you to Override Permissions in the particular activity you have chosen; notice it cites the title of the activity at the top of the page. (See Figure 4-17.)

| Settings | Locally assigned roles | Override permissions |

Override permissions in Activity module: Questions about the course ⓘ

Role to override [Student ▾]

Capability	Inherit	Allow	Prevent	Prohibit	Risks
Course					
View hidden activities moodle/course:viewhiddenactivities	⦿	○	○	○	
Access all groups moodle/site:accessallgroups	⦿	○	○	○	
Trust submitted content moodle/site:trustcontent	⦿	○	○	○	⚠
Always see full names of users moodle/site:viewfullnames	⦿	○	○	○	
Forum					
Add news mod/forum:addnews	⦿	○	○	○	⚠
Create attachments mod/forum:createattachment	⦿	○	○	○	⚠
Delete any posts (anytime) mod/forum:deleteanypost	⦿	○	○	○	
Delete own posts (within deadline) mod/forum:deleteownpost	⦿	○	○	○	

Figure 4-17: Overriding a role.

3. **Change the permissions by selecting the radio buttons.**

   The permissions that the Student role already has are denoted by the square boxes around the radio buttons.

4. **Click the Save Changes button at the bottom of the list.**

   Moodle alters the capabilities the next time anyone with the role you just altered logs in to Moodle and accesses this particular activity.

   When altering permissions on the capabilities, make sure you pay attention to the warning triangles. (Refer to Table 4-2.)

Setting a participant's role override for an activity

If you need a student to be a forum moderator to update the calendar settings, grade assignments, and so on, you can set a user role override for a particular participant (such as a student). The steps are similar to assigning a role in your course. To assign extra capabilities to a specific participant's role, follow these steps:

1. **Select an activity or tool, such as a Forum (in this example), and click the Update This Forum button (top right).**

2. **Select the Locally Assigned Roles tab.**

   Moodle takes you to the Assign Roles in Activity Module: *[Module Name]* page.

3. **Select the role you want to assign to a specific participant in your course.**

   In this example, I've chosen Non-Editing Teacher. (See Figure 4-18.)

4. **In the list on the right, select the name of the user to whom you want to give the new role and then click the Add button.**

   The learner is added to the list and has all the capabilities of that role for the particular activity. Notice in Figure 4-18 that I chose Ruby Tuesday and moved her to the left.

5. **Click the Assign the Role in the Activity Module button at the bottom of the page**

   Your learner has the permission capabilities of that particular role for the activity.

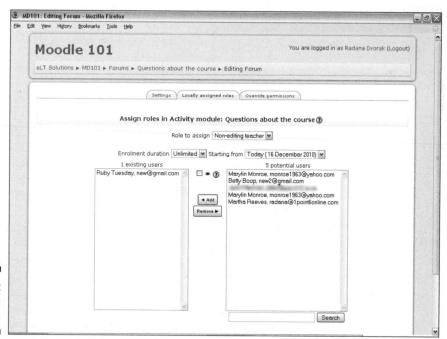

Figure 4-18:
Assigning
a role.

If none of the preset roles are appropriate for what you want to do, you or your Moodle administrator can create a new role, which you can then assign to specific participants in your course and/or particular activity.

Managing Activities and Projects with Groups

Moodle has a very useful tool for manipulating and managing groups of learners and teachers within each course: the Groups functionality. This tool provides an effective way to manage activities, projects, or the complete course. For example, if you, as an instructor, have three periods of the same course, you don't need to set up three different courses; instead, you have just the one course and you organize the different courses into three groups in the course. This functionality is set up at the course level. If, on the other hand, you have one very large course, you can use groups to set up sections.

If you set up groups in the course or at the activity level, you can run the groups completely independent of each other. You can also set them up as partially separate groups, allowing for some interaction, such as each group can see each other groups' activities (for instance, a wiki) but cannot interact or add to the other groups' activities.

To set up groups, they must be enabled in the course settings. Groups are enabled by default. If you don't see the Group icon and link in your course Administration block, contact your Moodle administrator.

There are three group mode options that you will see when you're adding resources and setting up activities:

- ✔ **No groups:** Groups aren't used in the course; every learner participates in all activities.

- ✔ **Separate groups:** When using separate groups, you split up the course, and participants in the groups can add to and see only their own work or participate only in activities for their group, such as a group forum discussion.

- ✔ **Visible groups:** Learners contribute and work in their own groups, but they can view the work of other groups. For example, if you set up groups for wikis and make them visible groups, learners can access the other groups' wikis and read the entries, but they can contribute only to their own wiki.

On your course front page, groups are indicated by the two small figure icons next to the activity if groups are visible groups. If both figures are filled, that indicates visible groups. If only one figure is filled, and one gray, the activity is set up for separate groups.

Before you start using groups, you need to create your groups, set them up, and then add learners (and teachers) to the groups. Moodle makes this process quite easy for you, and it takes just a few steps.

1. **Go to your course (not site) Administration block and click the Groups link.**

   Moodle takes you to your course Groups page.

   Notice two columns in Figure 4-19: Groups (on the left) and Members Of (on the right). The Members Of column lists all possible users you can add to the groups.

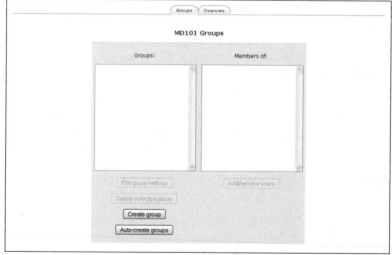

Figure 4-19: The Groups page showing the Create a Group button.

2. **Click the Create Group button under the left column.**

   Moodle takes you to the Create Group page shown in Figure 4-20.

3. **Set options for your group:**

   - *Group Name:* Add the name. This is a required field. The group name will appear in various places in your course.

   - *Group Description:* Add a brief description identifying the group and, if relevant, its purpose. Note that this description will appear above group members on the Participants page.

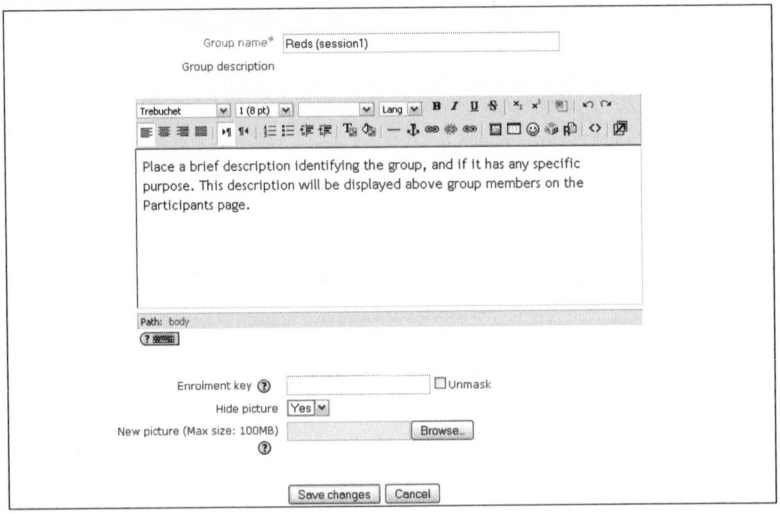

Figure 4-20:
Creating
your group
editing
page.

• *Enrollment Key:* If you set an enrollment key for the course and for the group, anyone who enrolls in the course is also enrolled in a group. Students need to know only the group enrollment key. Set the first letter for each group enrollment key to be the same as the course settings key. If a student forgets the key, a and types in the incorrect characters, Moodle displays a pop-up window and gives the learner a hint using the first character of the key.

• *Hide Picture:* Use the drop-down list to hide learner profile pictures. If you allow for pictures to be shown, they're listed with every activity throughout the course. Showing pictures can use up your allocated space if you have many students.

• *New Picture:* Moodle enables you to upload a picture for the whole group.

4. **Click the Create Group button.**

Moodle returns you to the Groups page with your new group added in the Groups list. (See Figure 4-21.)

Notice the three new group setting buttons under the Groups column.

• *Edit Group Settings:* Enables you to edit groups you have created.

• *Delete Selected Group:* Allows you to delete the group.

• *Auto Create Group:* Enables you to create groups automatically.

Note that unless you have created a group, the first two buttons are grayed out.

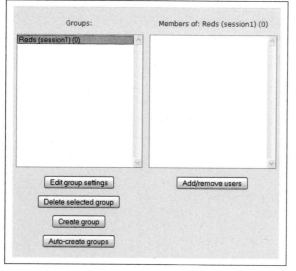

Figure 4-21:
The Groups
page
displaying
the newly
created
group, with
a number
of new
buttons
below the
Groups field.

Under the right column is an Add/Remove Users button.

5. Click the Add/Remove Users button to add learners to your new group.

Moodle takes you to the Add/Remove Users page. (See Figure 4-22.)

6. Select a student from the Potential Members list on the right by clicking a name. Then click the Add button.

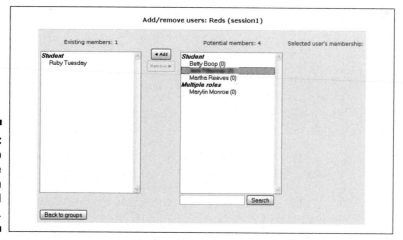

Figure 4-22:
Add users to
or remove
users from
a selected
group.

The user is added to the new group. You can select multiple learners by holding down the Shift key (or ⌘ key on Macs) and clicking the names. A participant with multiple roles can be in different groups. You can also have a student in more than one group. This flexibility is useful if the particular student has extra permissions for particular capabilities.

7. **Repeat the steps to create more groups and add students to the different groups.**

Letting Everyone Know about Your Course

If you're part of an organization such as an educational or training department, you probably don't have to worry too much about attracting students to your course because you have assistance and support. If, however, you need to advertise and market the course yourself, where do you start? The best option is to go through your professional organization. If you managed to get your course certified for professional and/or continuing education credits, you can use the professional body or educational establishment that granted you the certification. Here's a list of other sources you may find useful:

- ✔ Professional organizations, such as ASTD
- ✔ Social network sites, such as LinkedIn, Facebook, Ning, and Twitter
- ✔ Video sites, such as YouTube
- ✔ Blogs, such as Blogger (Google blog) and Google buzz
- ✔ Moodle.org and the Moodle community

Charging for Your Course

From Moodle version 1.8 onward, Moodle has a PayPal enrollment plugin allowing you to charge for your courses and set up a payment system. The PayPal enrollment plugin has to be enabled through the Site Administration block on the site front page. Assuming you have administrative privileges, follow these steps:

1. **If you haven't done so already, go to** `www.paypal.com` **to set up a PayPal merchant account.**

2. **Go to the Site Administration block on the site front page and click Courses to expand the list.**

3. **Click Enrollments.**

   You're taken to the page shown in Figure 4-23.

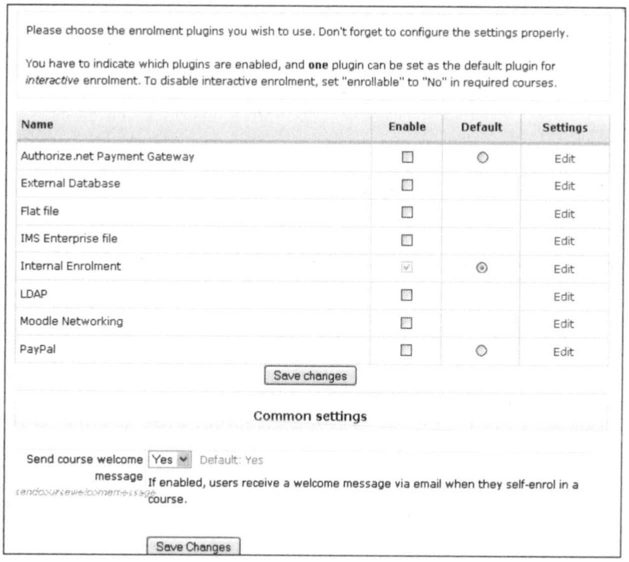

Figure 4-23:
The
Enrollments
page,
enabling
online
payment.

4. **Select the check box in the Enable column for Authorize.net Payment Gateway and click the Save Changes button.**

   Moodle tells you it has saved the changes and provides a button to continue, which takes you back to the previous page.

5. **Click Continue.**

6. **Next to Payment Gateway, click the edit link, and Moodle takes you to the page shown in Figure 4-24, instructing you to turn on the plugin. Follow the instructions on the page.**

7. **At the bottom of the page, select the Turn loginhttps On check box, and Moodle takes you to the HTTP Security page, shown in Figure 4-25.**

8. **Select the Use HTTPS for Logins check box.**

9. **Click the Save Changes button.**

You can have separate costs for each of your courses on your Moodle site. If you set any course to Zero, students are not asked to pay when they log in. If a site default cost is set up, you can override it by setting an individual course cost.

Figure 4-24:
The Moodle
Authoriza-
tion Net
Gateway
Payment
page.

Authorize.net Payment Gateway

The Authorize.net module allows you to
set up paid courses via payment
providers. If the cost for any course is
zero, then students are not asked to pay
for entry. Two ways to set the course
cost (1) a site-wide cost as a default for
the whole site or (2) a course setting that
you can set for each course individually.
The course cost overrides the site cost.

Note: If you enter an enrolment key in
the course settings, then students will
also have the option to enrol using a key.
This is useful if you have a mixture of
paying and non-paying students.

Please ensure that you have "turned loginhttps ON" to use this plugin
in Admin >> Variables >> Security >> HTTP security.

[Save changes]

Figure 4-25:
The HTTP
Security
setting
page.

HTTP security

Use HTTPS for logins ☐ Default: No
loginhttps Turning this on will make Moodle use a secure https connection just for the
login page (providing a secure login), and then afterwards revert back to the
normal http URL for general speed. CAUTION: this setting REQUIRES https to be
specifically enabled on the web server - if it is not then YOU COULD LOCK
YOURSELF OUT OF YOUR SITE.

Secure cookies only ☐ Default: No
cookiesecure If server is accepting only https connections it is recommended to enable
sending of secure cookies. If enabled please make sure that web server is not
accepting http:// or set up permanent redirection to https:// address. When
wwwroot address does not start with https:// this setting is turned off
automatically.

Only http cookies ☐ Default: No
cookiehttponly Enables new PHP 5.2.0 feature - browsers are instructed to send cookie with
real http requests only, cookies should not be accessible by scripting
languages. This is not supported in all browsers and it may not be fully
compatible with current code. It helps to prevent some types of XSS attacks.

Regenerate session id ☐ Default: No
during login Regeneration of the session id during each login request is highly

When students try to enroll for your course, they are presented with a payment page asking them to pay the specify amount before they can enroll. If
you've set an enrollment key in the course settings, the students have an
option to enroll using the key. The enrollment key is useful if you have paying
and nonpaying students in the course.

You are now ready to start taking payment for your course when a learner
enrolls.

Set the cost to be competitive with other courses.

Part II
Creating and Managing Course Content

The 5th Wave   By Rich Tennant

"I know it works on infomercials, but I still wouldn't separate paragraphs in your introduction to your online classmates with 'But wait, that's not all!' and 'Act now, and I'll include this impressive list of hobbies!'"

In this part . . .

The fun really begins here because you're ready to add content to your Moodle course. In these chapters, you find out how to compose Web and text pages, link to other sites, incorporate video and audio files, and make your life easier with the Moodle grade book.

Chapter 5

Adding Content to Your Course: Resources

● ●

In This Chapter

▶ Enriching your Moodle course by adding resources

▶ Adding content and files (including multimedia) to your Moodle course

▶ Using Web-editing tools to compose Web pages

▶ Embedding and editing graphics with the Moodle graphic tool

▶ Creating directories for your content

● ●

*A*fter you become familiar with the layout of Moodle and the flexibility of the front page and blocks (discussed in Part I), you're ready to start building your course. Most likely you have an idea of what you want to teach (after all, you are the content expert), and you have an outline or syllabus of how you structure your information and knowledge for teaching specific subjects. With that knowledge, you can start adding content to support your learning methods and learning goals, which I show you in this chapter. (If you aren't sure where to start, review Chapter 2, which gives you guidance on how to design great Moodle courses.)

You access the Moodle editing tools to change the appearance of and add functionality to your class. I describe the editing tools in Chapter 3, and they're also listed on the book's Cheat Sheet at Dummies.com. (See the inside front cover for more details on the Cheat Sheet.)

Adding Resources to Your Course

In Moodle, all the tools that help you add content are called *resources,* and you find them in the Add Resources drop-down list in each section and week of your course. The tools in the drop-down list aren't ordered according to any specific way of using them.

Inserting a label

A *label* is simply a bit of text and/or graphics that you can add to the top of each course front page in each topic or week. You can use labels to add a unit title, a short introduction or explanation, or brief instructions telling your learners what to do next. To insert a label, follow these steps:

1. **Click the Turn Editing On button in the upper-right corner of your course front page.**

2. **In the section where you want to add a label, open the Add a Resource drop-down list and select Insert a Label.**

   Moodle takes you to an Adding a New Label to Week (or topic) page, shown in Figure 5-1.

3. **Add text for your label in the text box editor.**

   This is a required field, as denoted by the asterisk. Note that you can be creative here: Use it for a heading, use different color text, or create bullet points if you want a short outline.

4. **In the Common Module Settings area, choose whether you want to make the label visible to your learners.**

   (Other resources and activities have a few more Common Module Settings.) Selecting Yes from the Visible drop-down list makes the label visible to your learners. If you select No, it will be hidden until you want to make it available for viewing. This option may be useful if you're planning a few weeks ahead and you want to coordinate topics. You can make it visible by updating the label and changing this option, or from the course front page, open the Eye icon when editing tools are on. See Chapter 3 for more information about editing tools.

5. **Click the Save and Return to Course button, which takes you to the front page of your course, where you can see your new label.**

   The bottom of Figure 5-1 shows the new label I saved. To preview what the page looks like, click the Save and Display button instead of the Save and Return to Course button.

Be creative with positioning. Notice you can indent the label by using the right-pointing arrow when you have the editing features turned on.

Note the *navigation bar* at the top of the course front page under the title in Figure 5-1. On this screen, the following links trace the steps "CI810⇨Labels⇨ Editing Labels."

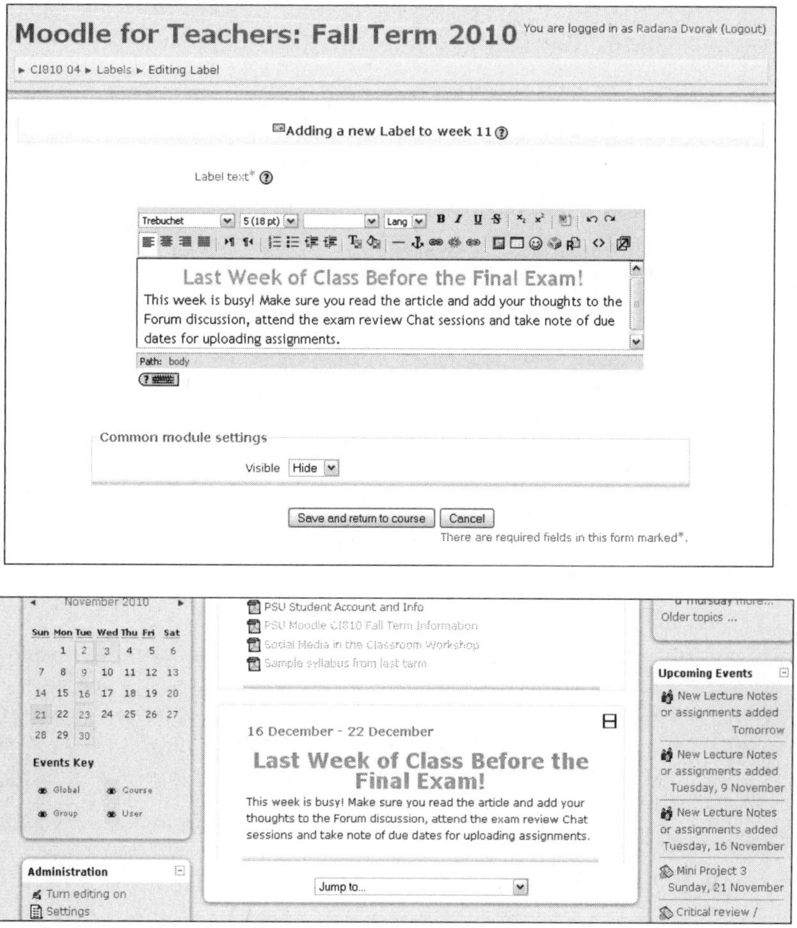

Figure 5-1:
Inserting
a label.

Composing a text page

A *text page* is a simple page you can use for instructions or some basic information. The editing features are quite limited, and the pages you create using plain text can appear dull. Because of the textual limitation, I rarely use text pages. Within the same group of resources, Moodle provides the option of adding a Web page that has more functionality and editing capabilities. See the next section.

After knowing the limitations, if you want simplicity and speed, adding a text page may be a useful resource for you. Follow these steps to create a text page:

1. **Click the Turn Editing On button in the upper-right corner of your course front page.**

2. **In the section where you want to add a text page, open the Add a Resource drop-down list and select Compose a Text Page.**

   Moodle takes you to the Adding a New Resource for Week (or topic) page.

3. **Enter a name (required) for the text page.**

4. **(Optional) Add a summary.**

   The name and summaries appear in the Resources outline and are both accessible to all learners. The Resources outline is a good overview, so it's important you name the resource so it's understood by your learners. Short summaries provide further explanation and identification of how the resource is tied to the learning goals. You and your learners can access the Resources outline from the Activities block on the course front page, located right under the Participants block on the left side.

5. **In the Full Text area, add the content for your text page in the text box.**

6. **From the Format drop-down list, select a different format to display the text.**

   Although you don't have text editor functionality to format the text, Moodle tries to improve the layout and look and feel of the page. Plain text is the default, or you can choose Moodle auto format, HTML format, or Markdown format. Any of the formats will improve the look slightly, though you may as well use the Web page and editor to add information.

   Using a text page is useful if you copy and paste text from a number of Web pages or Word and PDF documents. You don't have to worry about bringing the back-end code with the documents or using a clean code utility. I discuss clean code tools in the "Using the Moodle Web Editor" section.

7. **From the Window drop-down list, select whether you want to open the text page in a new window.**

   The default is to open it in the same window. By asking Moodle to open the page in a new window, you have a number of options to deselect window functionalities and also change the default size. Read these carefully because you need to allow for most of the default settings; otherwise, you may restrict learners from using basic window functionalities. If the Window options are not displayed, click the Show Advanced button on the right. Refer to Chapter 3 for an explanation of the different settings.

   I suggest that, unless your system administrator has blocked all pop-ups, you enable resources to open in a new window. If you don't have a new window opening up and you don't enable the Moodle navigation bar, learners have to close the resources by clicking the red X in the right corner. Consequently, this action also closes the Moodle session, and they have to log in again, which can become frustrating for learners if they have to do this a few times. If you cannot use the New Window option, select the Show Navigation check box so that Moodle adds the navigation bar or instruct learners to add the browser back arrow.

8. **Choose the Common Module Settings as you would when you set up any Moodle activity or resource.**

   I discuss Common Module Settings in Chapter 3.

9. **Click Save and Return to Course button.**

   Moodle returns you to the course front page. You see the link to your new text page with the text page icon in front of it. If you click the name of the text page, you're taken to it, or it will open in a new window (depending how you set it up; Chapter 3 identifies and explains all the standard Moodle icons). As an alternative to clicking the Save and Return to Course button, you can preview what the page looks like by clicking the Save and Display button.

Composing a Web page

You can use a Web page for all the same tasks as the text page discussed in the preceding section, but Web pages include more functionality and options. A Web page has a full editing toolbar and HTML WYSIWYG editing capabilities. (WYSIWYG stands for What You See Is What You Get.) In addition to creative text capabilities, you can add graphics, embed YouTube video clips, embed sound files, and include links to other sites. See the "Using the Moodle Web Editor" section, later in this chapter, where I explain in more detail the Web page editor capabilities and adding graphics.

To set up a Web page, follow these steps:

1. **Click the Turn Editing On button in the top-right corner of your course front page.**

2. **In the section where you want to add a Web page, open the Add a Resource drop-down list and select Compose a Web Page.**

   Moodle takes you to the Adding a New Resource for Week (or topic) page.

3. **Enter a name for the Web page.**

   Anything marked with an asterisk, as shown in Figure 5-2, is a required field.

4. **(Optional) Write a summary.**

   A summary is useful to learners because they see it in the Resources outline page. You and your learners can access the Resources outline from the Activities Block on the course front page, located right under the Participants block on the left side.

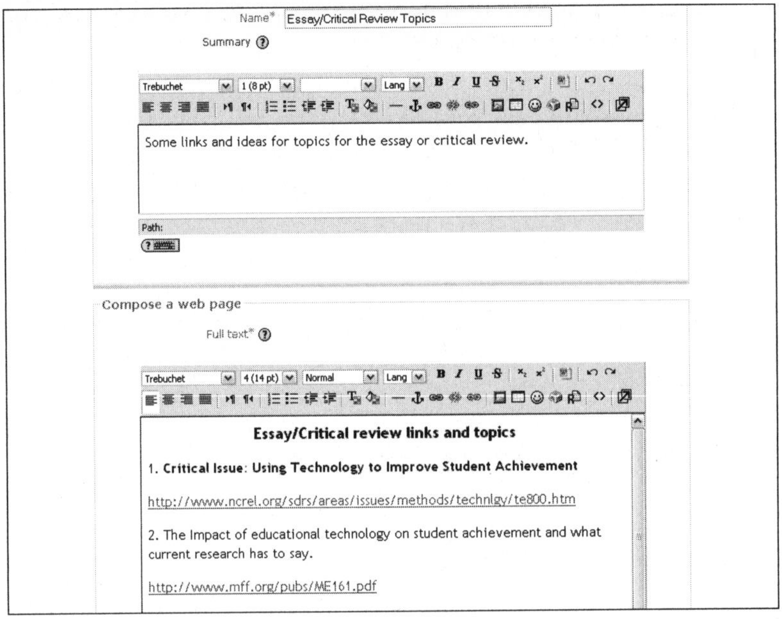

Figure 5-2:
Setting up a
Web page.

5. **Add content for your Web page in the text box provided (as shown in Figure 5-2).**

   You can use various styles and graphics, embed YouTube videos, and/ or link to resources. You can make it as creative as you need. If you copy and paste text from another file, make sure you first paste the text into Notepad or use an application to clean up the HTML code; otherwise, it can look messy. If you're familiar with HTML, you can paste straight from Word or other applications and then tidy it up. (I explain accessing HTML by toggling from text to HTML in the "Using the Moodle Web Editor" section.) However, I find the process much quicker when I just copy the text into Notepad and then copy and paste from Notepad to the text field.

6. **From the Window drop-down list (see Figure 5-3), select New Window so the page opens in a new window.**

   The default is Same Window. If you open the Web page in a new window (I recommend that you do), you have a number of options to deselect window functionalities and also change the default size. If the Window options are not displayed, click the Show Advanced button on the right, and Moodle opens the extra selections. For more information about the new window and menu bar settings, see Chapter 3.

7. **Choose the Common Module Settings as you would when you set up any Moodle resource or activity.**

8. **Click the Save and Return to Course button, and Moodle returns you to the course front page.**

   You see the link to the Web page, with the Web page icon in front of it. Clicking on the title will take you to the Web page. (You can see an example in Figure 5-4.)

   As an alternative to clicking the Save and Return to Course button, you can preview what the page looks like by clicking the Save and Display button.

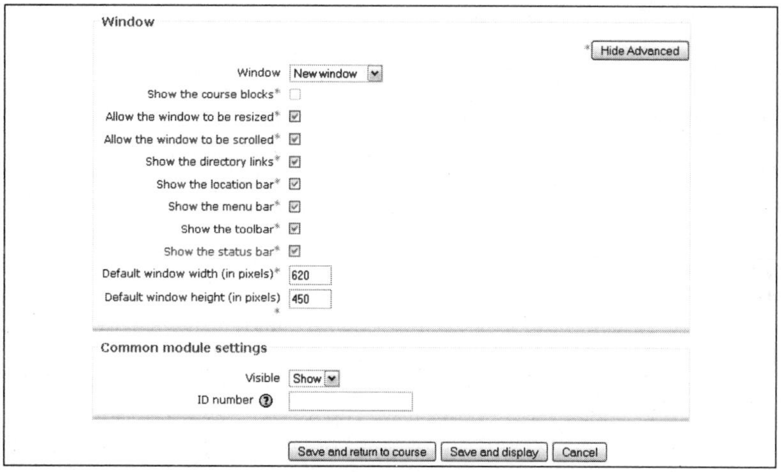

Figure 5-3: Choosing how the window displays.

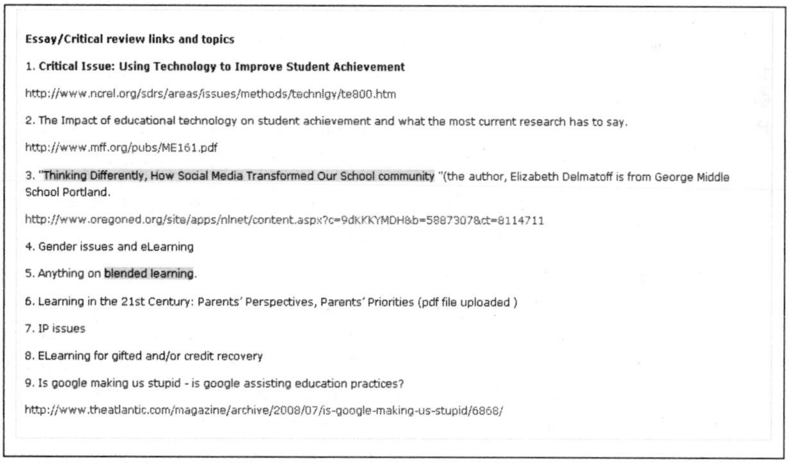
Essay/Critical review links and topics

1. **Critical Issue: Using Technology to Improve Student Achievement**

http://www.ncrel.org/sdrs/areas/issues/methods/technlgy/te800.htm

2. The Impact of educational technology on student achievement and what the most current research has to say.

http://www.mff.org/pubs/ME161.pdf

3. "Thinking Differently, How Social Media Transformed Our School community "(the author, Elizabeth Delmatoff is from George Middle School Portland.

http://www.oregoned.org/site/apps/nlnet/content.aspx?c=9dKKKYMDH&b=5887307&ct=8114711

4. Gender issues and eLearning

5. Anything on blended learning.

6. Learning in the 21st Century: Parents' Perspectives, Parents' Priorities (pdf file uploaded)

7. IP issues

8. ELearning for gifted and/or credit recovery

9. Is google making us stupid - is google assisting education practices?

http://www.theatlantic.com/magazine/archive/2008/07/is-google-making-us-stupid/6868/

Figure 5-4: A completed Web page.

Linking to a file or a Web site

Learning how to compose a Web page in Moodle is relatively easy, and you can quickly add content to your course, as shown in the previous section. Moodle has another useful tool to add content by linking to a Web site or one of your files. No doubt you have many different types of informative files you've used, such as PowerPoint, Excel, and Word files, PDFs, sound files and video files, or any other type of industry-standard files. Moodle enables you to upload and link to these files. You can also link to various resources on the Internet. I first explain how to upload and link to a file you've created, followed by how to link to a Web site.

Uploading and linking to your files

You can easily upload any file you've created for your Moodle class or used in your course on different systems. Remember that your learners need to have the appropriate software on their computers in order to view certain files. For example, if you upload a PowerPoint presentation, your learners need PowerPoint to view it.

If you aren't sure your learners have the software for the type of file you'd like to upload, be creative by saving the file in a second format and uploading both. For example, when I upload a PowerPoint presentation, I also save the presentation as a PDF file with the same name as the presentation; after I upload it, I position it right under the PowerPoint presentation. Most computers come with the Adobe PDF reader installed, or users can download it for free from `http://get.adobe.com/reader`.

To link to a file you created, follow these instructions:

1. **Click the Turn Editing On button in the upper-right corner of your course front page.**

2. **In the section where you want to add a file, open the Add a Resource drop-down list and select Link to a File or a Web Site.**

   Moodle takes you to the Adding a New Resource for Week (or topic) page.

3. **Fill in the Name field (required; shown on the left side of Figure 5-5) for the file as you want it to appear on the front page.**

   It does not have to be the name of the file as stored on your computer.

4. **(Optional) Fill in the Summary field.**

   This field is useful to learners because they can view the summary on the Resources outline page.

5. **Link to the file by clicking the Choose or Upload a File button under Location (shown on the left side of Figure 5-5).**

Moodle takes you to a directory that stores all the files you've uploaded. The first time you upload a file, this directory is empty. Unless a file is already in the Moodle directory, you have to upload the file from your hard drive or thumb drive. Figure 5-6 shows you what the page looks like with files listed.

6. **Add files to the directory:**

   a. *From the directory page, click the Upload a File button.*

   Moodle provides you with the standard Browse button and a field to locate the file you want to upload.

   b. *When you locate the file on your computer, click the Upload button, and your file appears in the directory.*

   c. *Select the check box to the left side of the file you want to upload to Moodle and click the Choose link on its right.*

   Moodle automatically returns to the setup page and puts the path into the Upload a File field. Figure 5-7 shows the file I chose, as it appears in the Location field.

Figure 5-5:
Linking to
a file or
Web site.

Figure 5-6:
The
directory.

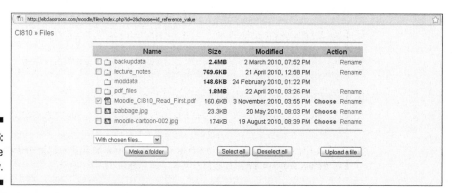

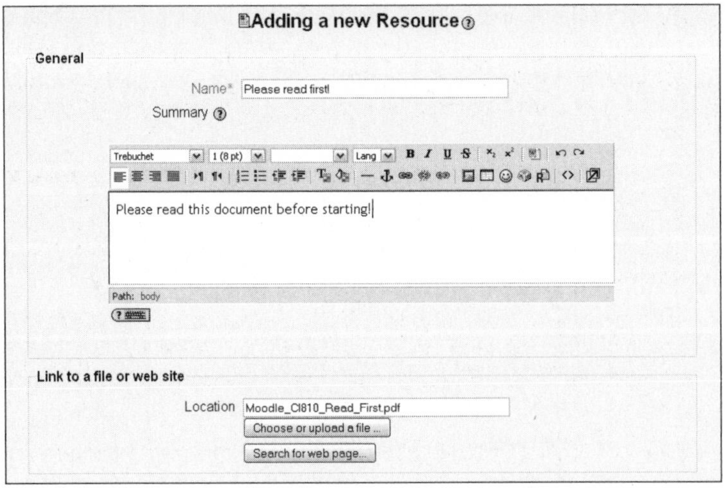

Adding a new Resource ⑦

General

Name* | Please read first!

Summary ⑦

Trebuchet ▾ | 1 (8 pt) ▾ | ▾ | Lang ▾ | **B** *I* U S ×₂ ×² 📷 ▾

▤ ▤ ▤ ▤ | ¶◀ ¶▶ | ⅗ ⅗ ⅗ ⅗ ⅗ ⅗ — ⅗ ⅗ ⅗ ⅗ | 🖼 🖼 😊 ⅗ ⅗ | ◇ 🖉

Please read this document before starting!

Path: body

⑦ 📋

Link to a file or web site

Location | Moodle_CI810_Read_First.pdf

Choose or upload a file...

Search for web page...

Figure 5-7:
Choosing
a file.

It's important that after selecting the file in the directory, you don't click the Upload button. It seems that's what you would want to do, but that button only takes you back to the Browse field in the set up Resources editing page. Clicking Choose uploads the link to the Add a Resources page.

7. (Optional) Select the Force Download check box.

Moodle provides you with an option to force files stored in Moodle to be downloaded, rather than being displayed in the browser window. If you want learners to save specific files on their computers or if they may have browser or multimedia plugin issues, select the Force Download check box. This option may be useful for Word, PowerPoint, PDF, sound, or video files.

8. Select whether you want the file to open in a new window.

See Step 7 in the previous section "Composing a Web page" for an explanation.

For now, ignore the Parameters section, which is used with linking to other servers. See the "Linking to Web sites" section (Step 4) for a detailed explanation.

9. Choose the Common Module Settings as you would when you set up any other resource or activity in Moodle.

10. Click the Save Changes button.

Moodle returns you to the course front page, to the section where you added this resource. You see a link with the title and file type listed under the section where you added it. Moodle doesn't have separate icons for document types; the same Resources icon is displayed related to all linked files, such as PDF, MP3, Word, PowerPoint, and so on.

Linking to Web sites

This procedure is very similar to linking to a file, as described in the preceding section, except that you don't have to store the link in a directory like you do a file. To link to a Web site, follow these steps:

1. **Follow Steps 1–4 in the preceding section, adding a name for the link in the Name field.**

2. **Add the location (the Web address) of the page you want your learners to visit.**

   You can copy and paste the Web address or click the Search for Web Page button. Moodle launches Google in a new Web page. If you paste the link, make sure you don't include http:// two times — notice it's already set in the field.

3. **Select whether you want the Web page to open in a new window.**

   See the Step 7 in the previous section "Composing a Web page" for an explanation.

4. **(Optional) Set parameters.**

   Parameters are advanced features that you most likely will not use. The parameters are useful when you want to send data about your learners and courses to another site. For example, you may want to send information about your learners from your Moodle site to another school's server that will give learners access. If the parameters aren't displayed, click the Show Advanced button on the right. Select the options you require, as shown in Figure 5-8.

5. **Choose the Common Module Settings as you would when you set up any course resources or activities.**

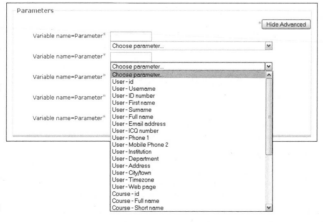

Figure 5-8: The Parameters settings of the Resources page.

6. Click the Save Changes button.

Moodle returns you to the course front page, to the section where you added this resource. You see an icon depicting the Web link and the name you gave to the link.

Depending what the server requires, you can choose a parameter from the drop-down list. For example, you may need the learner's e-mail address, or you may need a combination of e-mail address and learner ID. Moodle provides you with every exception possibly required, and you can use up to five parameters — pretty clever, don't you think? Thirty parameter type entries are available, and I list the most widely used ones in Table 5-1. You can see the remainder by opening the Choose Parameter drop-down list.

Table 5-1	Selected Parameter Options
User	Id
User	Username
User	First name
User	Surname
User	Full name
User	Email address
User	ICQ number
Course	ID
Course	Full name
Course	Teacher

Creating a directory and folders

If you need your learners to access many files that you've uploaded, displaying directory, depicted as a folder, that contains all the files on the course front page is simpler and easier for your learners. You can structure folders by unit, theme, or types of files, such as links to resources or lecture notes. Your learners can open the folders and subfolders and open the files they need from there instead of scrolling through many different files.

To set up a directory, you first need to create the folder that will hold your files. If you put it in the root directory (the default directory created by Moodle), learners will be able to access all files, which you may not want. To create a folder, follow these steps:

1. **From your course front page, click the Files link in the Administration block.**

   Files are denoted by a folder icon and is the third from the bottom. Moodle takes you to your directory page, as shown in Figure 5-9.

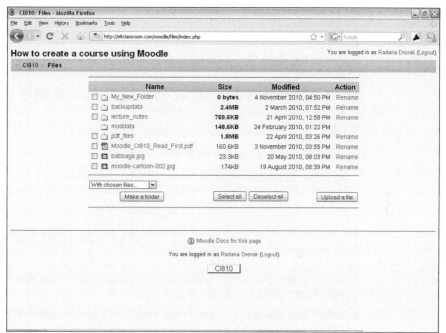

Figure 5-9: A Moodle directory.

2. **Select a folder, choose With Selected Folder from the drop-down list, and click the Make a Folder button.**

   Moodle takes you to a new window where you can name your folder.

3. **Name your folder and then click Create.**

   Moodle takes you back to your folder screen with your new folder. Figure 5-9 shows a number of folders.

4. **Use the navigation bar to return to your course front page.**

Setting up a directory involves first creating the folder and then putting files in it. *Note:* The "directory" that you create on your course front page is the *folder* you created in your files utility. (It's a slight mix of terms in the Moodle language and can be confusing.) Follow these steps to set up a directory on your course front page:

1. **Click the Turn Editing On button in the top-right corner of your course front page.**

2. **In the section where you want to add a directory, open the Add a Resource drop-down list and select Display a Directory.**

   Moodle takes you to the Adding a New Resource for Week (or topic) page.

3. **Fill in the Name field for the new directory, which is required.**

4. **(Optional) Add a summary.**

   The summary is useful to learners because they see it on the Resources outline page.

5. **Select the directory you want to display in your class from the drop-down list.**

6. **Choose the Common Module Settings as you would when you set up any course resources or activities.**

   I discuss Common Module Settings in Chapter 3.

7. **Click the Save Changes button.**

   Moodle returns you to the front page, to the section where you added this resource. You see the folder with the name. (This folder is the directory you will be choosing.)

After you create your directory, you need to fill it with your files; to do so, follow these steps:

1. **Go back to your folder directory by clicking the Files link in the Administration block.**

2. **Select the check box next to the files you want to move to the folder. (Refer to Figure 5-6.)**

3. **Under the With Chosen Folders drop-down list, click the Move to Another Folder button.**

   Moodle refreshes the page, and at the top of the page, you see a statement confirming the number of files you've selected for moving.

4. **Select the folder where you want to move the files by clicking it.**

   The folder will open with the files there.

5. **Click the check box next to the files, and then click the Move Files Here button.**

   Moodle moves the files. You will see them as the page refreshes.

6. **Return to your front page by clicking the class name in the navigation menu.**

Once you have created a number of directories and added files to them, when you choose Add a Directory from the front page Resources menu, you will see a drop-down list of all your folders.

Adding an IMS Content Package

IMS Content Packages are packaged resources that have an agreed specification format (IMS format) enabling them to be re-used in different systems. It's a standard file format you can use without having to convert the material into new formats. If you have purchased or developed online instructional material that can be saved as an IMS Content Package, you can upload it to Moodle. Another way to look at it is like a PowerPoint slide show that you have used for training. If it has navigation, images, small quizzes, video clips, and sound, you can add it as a IMS content resource and use it within your class. You would find that if you uploaded a PowerPoint slide show, you would lose the extra features listed.

1. **Click the Turn Editing On button in the top-right corner of your course front page.**

2. **In the section where you want to add IMS Content, open the Add a Resource drop-down list and select Add an IMS Content Package.**

   Moodle takes you to Adding a New Resource for Week (or topic) page.

3. **Fill in the Name field for the resource.**

   I recommend giving it a name that best identifies the purpose, such as Exam Review or Supplementary Material.

4. **(Optional) Fill in the Summary field.**

   This field is useful to learners because they see the summary in the Resources outline page. You can elaborate here or give brief directions.

5. **Add an IMS Content Package using the file uploading function discussed in the preceding section.**

   Follow Steps 7-9 in the earlier "Uploading and linking to your files" section.

   Your IMS Content Package is most likely zipped. After you select Choose link, Moodle automatically unzips the file.

6. **For the Window option, decide whether you want to display the IMS Content Package in the same window or a new window.**

7. **(Optional) Set the display parameters.**

   Different from the parameters discussed earlier in the chapter, these parameters relate to display and navigational features available in your IMS CP. If you aren't sure what to choose, the safest bet is to accept Moodle defaults.

8. **Choose the Common Module Settings as you would when you set up any course resource or activity.**

   I discuss Common Module Settings in Chapter 3.

9. **Click the Save Changes button.**

Moodle returns you to the course front page, to the section where you added this resource. You see a link with the title and file type listed under the section where you added it.

Using the Moodle Web Editor

Like most software tools that allow you to enter content and format it, Moodle has its own Web-based editor with all the industry-standard functionality and a few Moodle-specific extras. I can reassure you that you will be comfortable with most of the features because you have used them with other programs, such as Word and Outlook. You can find this editor in most resources and activities modules you set up for your learners and anywhere you can create or send content, such as forum discussions, feedback for grades, and so on.

Figure 5-10 shows you the tools on the toolbar. (When the editor is open, place the cursor over the icon to see the name of the tool.) Many of these tools, such as Bold, Italic, and Underline, are familiar tools that appear in many applications. Others, such as Clean Word and Anchor, may be unfamiliar to you if you're new to Moodle. I explain these tools in some detail in the following sections.

Cleaning Word

The Clean Word tool cleans most of the Word formatting from your pasted text. If you use this button, or copy and paste from Notepad, you won't transfer the HTML code and any other setting, meaning it looks better and loads faster. If you've seen text with various characters and tags, that means someone copied and pasted and didn't clean it up.

You can download free HTML filter packs. There are a number of different applications for different operating systems. This book is beyond the scope of assisting you with finding the correct software and installation. I tend to use Notepad. You can paste your content into Notepad, and then copy and paste from Notepad.

Creating anchors

An *anchor* links terms within a document or outside the document within Moodle and also to Web sites. To use the Anchor tool, follow these steps:

1. **Highlight the word that you want to become an anchor and click the Anchor icon.**

   A small window pops up, asking you to name the anchor.

2. **Type a name for the anchor.**

3. **Click the Link icon (described in the next section).**

   Another small window pops up.

4. **From the Anchor drop-down list, choose the word you anchored and from the Target drop-down list, choose Open In New Window.**

   Your link to another resource is created.

5. **Click the Save Changes button at the bottom of the page.**

   Moodle takes you back to the course front page.

6. **Test the text you anchored to make sure it works.**

   Your anchored word(s), once linked to another resource or linked to another place in the same document, will look like any other active link.

You can create a set of anchors as you're preparing the document and later select the anchors when you want to link them to other Moodle resources or activities, or to Web sites.

Anchoring and linking don't work within a wiki module. You need to use a different method to link wiki pages and link to external resources.

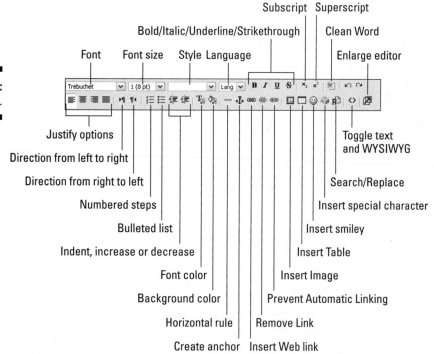

Figure 5-10: The toolbar.

Using the Web link tools

The Moodle HTML editor enables you to link to information external to Moodle, such as Web sites, internal resources, activities, or within the current page. You need to use this tool to link your anchored text. The link tool constructs a way to the external Web page, internal resource, or within the same page using the text you anchor (explained in the preceding section) as the link to the resource.

Inserting Web links

To insert a Web link into your document, follow these steps:

1. **Highlight the text in your document that you want to act as a link and then click the Insert Web Link tool (shown in the margin).**

   For example, if you were to type **For more information, visit www. dummies.com/moodle.**, I recommend highlighting www.dummies.com/moodle and making it a link so that learners can simply click those words to be taken to the Web site.

   A new small window pops up. (See Figure 5-11.)

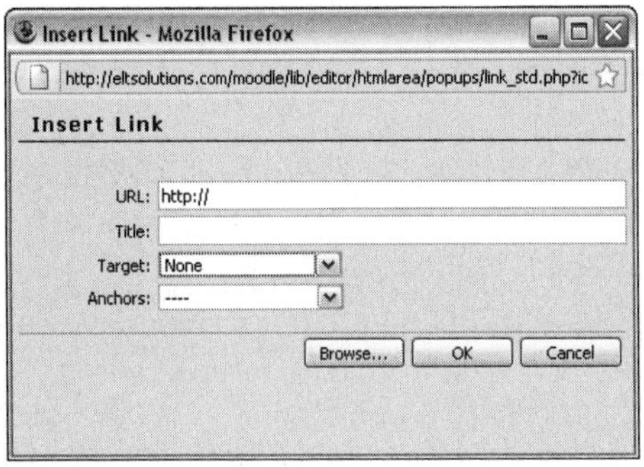

Figure 5-11: Inserting a Web link.

2. **Provide the Web site address in the URL text field.**

   Notice that Moodle already places http:// in the field, so you shouldn't include this when you're adding the address. If you do, the double http:// results in a broken link (the dreaded 404 Error).

   If the link is internal on the Moodle site, click the Browse button to find your file within the Moodle course, saved in a Moodle directory that holds all your files.

3. **Write a title for your link in the Title field, located under the URL field.**

   This is the text that will appear when the mouse rolls over the link. It does not have to be the URL.

4. **From the Target drop-down list, choose where you want to open the new document.**

   I recommend selecting To a New Window. The other options are Same Window, Same Frame, and Other.

5. **From the Anchors drop-down list, select the Anchor you created on the page.**

6. **Click the OK button to save the link.**

 Clicking the Remove Link icon depicted by the broken link to remove the HTML links you've created. Make sure you highlight the text before clicking the Remove Link icon.

Preventing automatic linking

 Clicking the Prevent Automatic Linking tool (depicted by the link with a red X icon) blocks selected text from being linked to other resources and activities. Moodle allows for automatic linking if the filter has been enabled at the site level. For example, if your course uses a glossary, Moodle links the term throughout all activities and resources. Seeing many terms as highlighted links can be distracting in quizzes, assignments, or in forum discussions. This tool enables you to prevent this cross-site automatic linking.

Inserting an image

 Any resource or activity (including the News forum) that has the HTML editor capabilities allows you to upload images to your site folders and embed images into your content. Adding images can support many different learning activities. For example, adding a world map and linking from the map to countries, cities, or demographic and geographical representations can enhance content. Images can also be used for quizzes and assessment activities. There are many different uses for pictures. Use your imagination and a variety of media to enhance your students' learning experience.

To add an image to your content, take these steps:

 1. **Select the Insert Image icon in the editor menu bar.**

   Moodle opens a new window with the image-editing tools that help you add and adjust the picture, as shown in Figure 5-12. In this example, I'm preparing an image to include in a quiz question.

 As with all Web-based tools, you should use the JPG, GIF, or PNG image format.

2. **Click the Browse button to find and select the image you want to use.**

   Moodle places the address of the file's location in the Image URL field.

3. In the Alternate field, add an image title or other text.

You have to fill in the Alternate field, or the image won't be saved into your content. The alternate text appears when a learner moves her mouse over the image.

Notice in the example in Figure 5-12, I didn't add the name of the person in the photo because I'm asking learners in a quiz to identify who it is. (If I added the name, learners would obviously have the answer.)

After completing the preceding steps, you can save the image (proceed to Step 5), and it will appear in your text bar. To adjust the size and layout of your image, go to Step 4.

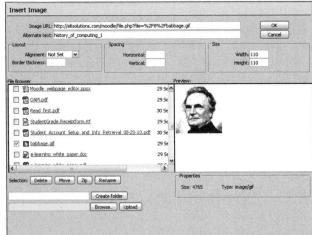

Figure 5-12: Embedding an image.

4. Use these additional options (shown in Figure 5-12) to resize and position the image.

This is not a required field, but something you may need to do to create a size appropriate for the resource or activity.

- *Layout:* You can set the layout of the image in relation to the text. For example, the Alignment drop-down list allows you to choose, left, right, text top, middle, baseline, absbottom (absolute bottom), middle, or top. For the Alignment drop-down list, the default is Not Set. You can also put a border around the image or leave it without. Not entering any digits into the Border Thickness field leaves the image without a border. Thickness is decided by entering the number of pixels.

- *Spacing:* The horizontal and vertical spacing is the space between text and the image, and is also measured in pixels. If you leave the fields blank, the text appears right next to the image. I recommend 5–10 pixels for each field. Of course, if you don't have any text, only the image, there's no reason to add anything to these fields.

- *Size:* In the figure, notice that I added the size, in pixels, of the image. I wanted it small so that it would fit in the matching question type. You can play with the width and height sizing to prepare the image for your requirements. Remember to keep the same proportions as the original so the image doesn't look blurry or distorted.

5. **Click OK (to the right of the Image URL field) to save your changes and return to your editing window.**

Notice the two fields and three buttons in the lower-left corner of the Insert Image dialog box. Use the buttons — Create Folder, Browse, and Upload — to locate image files that have not been uploaded to your Moodle directory.

The four Selection buttons — Delete, Move, Zip, and Rename — are actions you can take with the files that have been uploaded to your Moodle files directory.

Inserting a table

Inserting a table is simpler than inserting an image. Click the Insert Table icon, located next to the Insert Image icon. Moodle opens a new window with a number of fields to choose rows and columns, layout (the positioning of the table within your content), cell padding, and cell spacing.

Changing the editing field to HTML source

If you plan to paste HTML code, you need to change the editor to raw HTML mode. For example, when you need to embed YouTube into documents, you need to toggle to HTML source (using the Toggle Text and WYSIWYG tool) and paste the code, and then switch back. When you're viewing the source window, most buttons don't work. If you know HTML code and want to play with making changes to documents, this toggle feature will be your best friend.

Enlarging the editor

When you're working in the HTML window, selecting the Enlarge Editor tool enlarges the editing window. Working with HTML is much easier if your editor window is expanded. You will be less prone to errors when copying and pasting, and searching for bugs will be kinder on your eyes. You can return to the default size by clicking the icon again.

File formats: Tips and suggestions

You can employ a number of strategies to optimize your Moodle resources, allowing for quicker downloads, preventing broken icons, and ensuring your learners will be able to view all your resources. Here's a list of things to keep in mind when preparing resources for your learners:

- ✔ For learners to open specific files such as Excel, Word, PowerPoint, and ODS, they have to have the associated software installed on their computers. If you are unsure if all your learners have the appropriate software, it's safer to save the files in the PDF format. You can save text documents as RTF (rich text format) files, which most word processing programs can open.

- ✔ Reduce sizes of all files.

- ✔ If you have to scan articles, save them as text scans, not graphic images.

- ✔ Slide shows can become very large, so save them as PDF files. Alternatively, you can use SlideShare (`www.slideshare.net`) and link to slide shows.

- ✔ Save pictures as GIF or JPG files. PNG is also viewable in Moodle, but PNG files can be much larger than GIFs and JPGs.

- ✔ Sound and video files can be large, so using compression to minimize size is important. Make sure that the files are not larger than your upload capacity. Moodle supports the following formats: for audio, WAV, MP3, RAM, and MOV; and for video, MOV, WMV, RV, and FLV. Learners need media software to view these files. Most learners can play MP3 files and have QuickTime, Window Media Player, or RealPlayer. Check whether the videos you plan to upload can play with these media players.

- ✔ Embedding images in Moodle resources or activities is an efficient way to use images instead of uploading them as separate files (unless they're attached to wikis).

  Note that if the URL address of the file changes, the image can't be displayed, and you see the dreaded red X. If this happens, first try refreshing your browser. If the red X is still there, you need to do some sleuthing: Turn on editing, click the Insert Image editing tool, click the image to open the image editor, check the URL field, and go through the Browse option to check whether the file is still where it was when you first added it to the content. Sometimes when you back up your course and copy it to be reused, or copy it to another server, a link can be broken. Making a quick check and relinking the image can quickly solve the problem.

- ✔ If you and your learners use digital cameras for projects and then plan to embed those photos in resource files or attach them to specific activities, reduce the photo size. You will be able to view 72dpi. Many large photos quickly eat up allocated server space and can be slow to view.

Chapter 6

Adding Audio and Video to Your Course by Using Free Software

....

In This Chapter

▶ Using multimedia plugins

▶ Embedding YouTube video clips into a Web page

▶ Creating MP3 files and adding them to your course

▶ Creating a podcast and incorporating it in your course

▶ Understanding how real-time lectures can fit into your course

....

*T*o absorb what goes on around you, you must see, hear, read, and speak to others. You're immersed in and surrounded by all modes of media. This immersion has become more influential — and even needed and demanded by generations that have been exposed to it from a young age (a topic I discuss in greater detail in Chapter 2). Moodle meets the demand by encouraging and supporting the use of multimedia in Moodle courses.

Many tools are available that will help you integrate sound and video clips to add richness to your course. You probably don't want to spend too much money on software or developers to do the work for you, so all the tools I discuss here are available on the Internet for you to use. I also know time is precious, and you need to save as much time as possible when you're creating and using sound and graphics. This chapter encourages you to explore integrating sound and video to enhance your teaching goals and make you realize you don't need to develop very many new skills (or that much extra time) to be successful at it.

In fact, I have a shortcut that solves the problems often related to multimedia integration, and I start this chapter discussing it. You guessed it: integrating wonderful YouTube! If, however, you want to be more adventurous and have a video clip library, skip the YouTube section and continue on to the following sections on creating and uploading videos.

Using Moodle Multimedia Plugins

By default, most of the Moodle multimedia plugins are turned on. Before you start adding sound and video, either check with your system administrator, or if you have administrative privileges, check to make sure that all the required plugins are enabled. YouTube is one plugin that is not activated in Moodle's default settings. Chapter 13 covers the Administration block and plugins in more detail.

Enabling plugins

The plugins are located in the Administration block on the front page of the site. To check what settings are on and make changes, follow these steps:

1. **In the Administration block, click Module.**

   The list expands to show more options beneath Module.

2. **Click Filters.**

   The list expands again.

3. **Click Manage Filters.**

   Moodle takes you to the Multimedia Plugins page, as shown in Figure 6-1.

4. **Go down the list and select all the check boxes to ensure the filters are enabled.**

5. **Click the Save Changes button at the bottom of the page to return to your course.**

Figure 6-1: The Multimedia Plugins page.

When you add your multimedia resources, Moodle finds URLs in the Moodle files and replaces them with the required multimedia player. In Chapter 14, I include a table that lists all the multimedia formats that Moodle supports and recommends which to use that are most widely compatible with Web browsers.

Checking out YouTube services

YouTube provides a number of fantastic services, giving you a variety of options to use to meet your needs. The following services are offered by YouTube, free of charge:

- ✔ **Link to YouTube videos.** In Chapter 5, I cover how to use resources and link to external resources. Follow the instructions outlined in Chapter 5 to link to YouTube and TeacherTube.com as you would to other sites on the Internet.

  TeacherTube.com (`www.teachertube.com`) is a fantastic service for teachers and trainers; it provides free resources and enables you to upload your videos, as you would to YouTube, but you can protect them with a password making them available only to your learners.

- ✔ **Embed YouTube videos in Web pages.** Doing so prevents learners from accessing anything else on YouTube. I discuss how to do this in the next section.

- ✔ **Add a YouTube video (or any video file you have) to the HTML block.**

- ✔ **Upload your own video files to YouTube and then link or embed them.**

- ✔ **Use YouTube as a conversion tool to optimize your videos.** After optimization, you can download and add the videos to Moodle.

- ✔ **Create an account with TeacherTube.com and upload your instructional videos.** As I mention earlier, this is a password-protected service where videos are viewable only to learners who have the password. You can then embed videos or create links to them from your Moodle course.

Embedding YouTube video and uploaded video clips to a Web page

The process is fairly simple. The advantage to embedding a video in a Web page (you can set up by using the Add a Resource drop-down list discussed in Chapter 5) instead of linking to it is that your learners won't have to leave the Web page in your course to go to YouTube and be tempted to watch other, non-task–related videos. And yes, even adult learners, not just the young ones, are somehow drawn by the YouTube force field to start look-ing for their favorite songs. I discuss the procedure for linking to videos in Chapter 5 (in the section discussing the Web page editor).

To embed a YouTube video in a Web page, take these steps:

1. **From your course front page, click the Turn Editing On button in the top-right corner.**

   Editing tools are now available on the course front page.

2. **Go to the section or week to which you want to add the YouTube video.**

3. **From the Resources drop-down list, select Compose a Web Page, and then enter a name for the text Web page.**

   Anything marked with an asterisk is a required field.

4. **(Optional) Write a summary.**

   This summary is optional but useful to learners because they see it in the Resources Outline page. You and your learners can access the outline from the Activities block on the course front page, located right below the Participants block on the left

   Chapter 5 provides you with more information on how to add Web pages and content, and link to resources on the Internet.

5. **Go to www.youtube.com and find the YouTube video you want to use.**

   Notice the Share and/or Embed buttons under the YouTube video screen, as shown in Figure 6-2.

6. **Click the Embed button to select the code and then press Ctrl+C to copy the code.**

7. **Return to your Web page, look for the toggle icon in the editing menu (< >), and select it.**

8. **Delete the HTML code already there and then press Ctrl+V to paste the code into the window.**

9. **Choose the remainder of the settings and then click the Save and Return to Course button.**

   Moodle returns you to your course page with the Web page icon and title. Click it, and your YouTube video starts to play.

The nice thing about embedding the videos in Web pages in your course is that you can add titles, instructions, and any other content to the page. You can use Web pages to quickly develop interactive lecture notes that include embedded video and sound. For example, in a language course, you can embed a film clip or a recorded conversation, and then ask students to translate it. This can be used in the Quiz module with the essay question type.

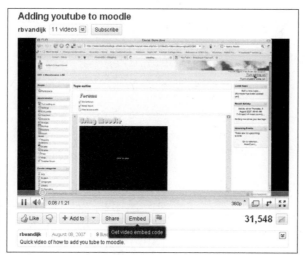

Figure 6-2:
Adding
YouTube to
Moodle.

You can embed any videos on the Internet that provide the source code. For example, many news networks and education sites include a link usually called Share or Embed, which provides you with the lines of code you need.

Adding a YouTube video to a block on the course front page

If you want to add a specific video clip to your course front page (perhaps an introduction to your course or a very important news segment relevant to your current topic), you can do so in few steps. Adding instructional video clips to a block makes it stand out more — it's in front of your learners every single time they log on to the course, so their excuses of "I missed it in the course listing" won't work! To embed the video in a block, follow these steps:

1. **On the course front page, click the Turn Editing On button in the top-right corner.**

   The editing tools become available on the page.

2. **Select HTML from the Blocks drop-down list.**

   By default, the Blocks menu appears under the other blocks on the right side.

The new HTML block appears with all the editing tools available for the block.

3. Select the editing tool (the hand).

Moodle takes you to the Configuring a HTML Block page, as shown in Figure 6-3.

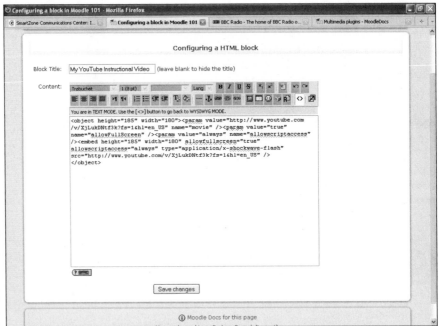

Figure 6-3:
The
Configuring
a HTML
Block page.

4. Give your video block a title.

5. Find your YouTube page, copy the code as described in the preceding section, and paste it into the large Content text box.

6. Click the Save Changes button.

Moodle returns to the course front page.

7. Click the Turn Editing Off button in the top-right corner.

You can see your video in a new block, as shown in Figure 6-4.

8. (Optional) To reposition the video block, turn editing back on and move the block using the arrows; when you're done, turn editing off.

Figure 6-4:
Course page
showing
video added
to the HTML
block.

A video uploaded to a block

Creating and Uploading Instructional Videos

Many departments have video files of whiteboard lectures that you may want to use in your Moodle course, or you may want to create some lecture or presentation videos to use for future online courses. Showing you how to create video for your course and optimize the video footage for online courses is outside this book's scope, but I can identify resources that will guide you to create what you need, and I advise you on the best tools to use. Many basic tools are bundled in your computer or can be downloaded for free. The following list is filled with advice, good ideas, and links to resources.

You don't have to be an expert to create videos and convert them to formats supported by Moodle and viewable by all browsers. The following Web sites demonstrate how to use various free video creation resources and download conversion tools:

✔ **Free Technology for Teachers** (www.freetech4teachers.com/p/video-creation-resources.html): Select the Free Downloads and Free Video Creation Resources links. Other than free downloads, you find tutorials and more — worth a visit.

✔ **Kioskea.net** (http://en.kioskea.net/faq/44-how-to-make-a-video-clip): An excellent tutorial.

✔ **Videomaker** (www.videomaker.com): Loads of help, ideas, and links to resources.

✔ **YouTube** (www.youtube.com/t/howto_makevideo): This is a great resource from YouTube on making and optimizing your videos. You can upload them to YouTube, optimize them in correct format, and then make them available on YouTube or download them and link to the video files in Moodle.

✔ **TeacherTube.com** (www.youtube.com/t/howto_makevideo): Has more instructional information and a link to optimize your video.

✔ **For Windows OS** (www.opensourcewindows.org)

✔ **For Mac OS** (www.opensourcemac.org)

✔ **PowerPoint conversion, if you use media files and animation** (www.ispringsolutions.com/products/ispring_free.html): This is a free PowerPoint Flash converter that keeps all sound and video and even compresses the files. You can use OpenOffice to create a presentation and then select Export from the OpenOffice File menu and have a Flash file. Simple!

After you save your videos as .flv or .swf formats, you can upload them to your Moodle course. The process follows the similar procedure of uploading other files to your course (which I discuss in detail in Chapter 5). Here are a couple extra steps that you need to take:

✔ **Upload video files to your Moodle Files folder:** The most efficient way to link to your files from the course resources page is to first create a folder in your Moodle Files folder and upload them there. You can upload Zip files, which Moodle unzips when they're needed. The Files folder is accessible from the Course Administration block.

✔ **Choose from three options to display the video:** Embed it in a Web page, link directly to it, or place it in the HTML block.

Incorporating Sound files into Your Moodle Course

As with video files, you can upload sound files to your course. Sound files may be useful for a number of teaching activities, such as translations (for a language course in which students are translating content) or pronunciation practice (for an ESL or a foreign language courses). You can also upload recordings of historic speeches, poetry recitation, and music (for interpretation or theory courses). No doubt you can find all kinds of uses for sound files.

The MP3 format is the sound file most compatible with Moodle. You can use any number of different conversion tools (which are usually bundled with newer computers) to create MP3 sound files. The following sound file formats are widely used:

- ✔ `.mp3 mp`
- ✔ `.aac`
- ✔ `.wma` (Windows Media Audio)
- ✔ `.ra` (Real Media)

A good program for creating and converting sound files is *Audacity* (`http://audacity.sourceforge.net`), a free, open source software for recording and editing sounds. It's available for most operating systems (Mac OS X, Microsoft Windows, GNU/Linux, and others). With Audacity, you can record your own lectures, readings, or music and then optimize those files for Moodle and save them in an MP3 format. Audacity also enables you to open other sound file formats and play with them and save them as MP3 files, or you can open an audio file in another format.

Audacity enables you to

- ✔ Record live audio.
- ✔ Convert tapes and records into digital recordings
- ✔ Edit Ogg Vorbis, MP3, WAV, or AIFF sound files.
- ✔ Cut, copy, splice, or mix sounds together.
- ✔ Change the speed or pitch of a recording.

You can see a complete list of features at the Audacity Web site. For Audacity tutorials, visit

```
http://wiki.audacityteam.org/index.php?title=Tutorials
```

 Moodle media filters use Flash to play back audio in the browser. Flash is a bit funny with audio; it requires fairly specific format ensuring that it's widely compatible with other players for iPods and cross platforms. Here are some settings to keep in mind when using software such as Audacity to create sound files for Moodle. For MP3 formats, use the following:

- A sample rate of 11.025, 22.05 or 44.1 kHz
- Constant Bit Rate (CBR) rather than Variable Bit Rate (VBR)
- Joint-Stereo rather than Mono or Full Stereo

 Sample rate or frequency, measured in kiloHertz (kHz), is not the same as *bit rate,* measured in kilobits per second (Kbps). The latter is a measure of file size and download time and also a rough measure of quality. Somewhere between 32 and 96 Kbps is appropriate with diminishing returns beyond 128 Kbps.

Incorporating Podcasts into Your Moodle Course

A *podcast* is an audio or a video file that is streamed media, theme driven, and downloadable. Podcasts emerged with developments of Web 2.0 technology and handheld devices like the iPod. Podcasts are especially useful in a Moodle course when students access Moodle files through handheld devices such as smartphones, iPads, and iPods. Students can use podcasts when creating interviews, for instance, and the completed podcast can then be uploaded to the Moodle course wiki, glossary, or database.

A number of free media software programs enable you to create podcasts:

- **Skype** (`www.ehow.com/how_2034834_podcast-with-skype.html`): A great tool for creating podcast interviews or for recording meetings and making them available. It's free, and many people are very familiar with Skype.

- **Audacity** (`http://wiki.audacityteam.org/wiki/Creating_a_simple_voice_and_music_Podcast_with_Audacity`): See the preceding section for details about Audacity.

- **Voicethread** (`http://voicethread.com`): Another application used widely within education. Moodle supports Voicethread.

Moodle for mobiles requires specific plug-ins. See `http://docs.moodle.org/en/Moodle_for_Mobiles`.

Many great resources can assist you with creating podcasts. A very good article published in 2005, which has been updated to keep current with technological changes, is "How to create a simple interview using a podcast" available at `http://onlamp.com/pub/a/mac/2005/10/10/how-to-podcast.html`. Also see *Podcasting For Dummies,* by Tee Morris, Chuck Tomasi, Evo Terra, and Kreg Steppe.

You upload a podcast to your course similar to how you upload video files. You can link to the podcast, embed it, or place it in a block. You can link to or upload media files by using Moodle activities (wikis, databases, and glossaries).

Adding Real-Time Instructions (Video Conferencing) to Your Moodle Course

If you've followed along so far, you know about all the various media possibilities. I know you're thinking, though: You want to hold real live meetings or lectures in front of your whiteboard to enable students sitting at different locations to ask you questions that you can answer and explain right away using your Web browser or that you want to set up a brainstorming session for your learners in real time — can you use Moodle and integrate your with my course?" The answer is "Yes, indeed!" Aren't you happy you asked?

Here are some of the perks:

- You can collaborate in real time like you were really there with any of your learners, located at different locations, anywhere in the world! *Hint:* Just get the times right — the Greenwich Mean Time (GMT) Converter can help you out in this situation (`http://wwp.greenwichmeantime.com/gmt-converter2.htm`).

- You can share documents, whiteboards, record your sessions — with no software to install! Just think of how much money you'll save in travel when these tools come bundled with video, voice, and phone conferencing.

- You can link to and/or integrate a number of third-party software. The one I recommend is the DimDim, which is open source software. There's no cost for small number of users, and if you use it within educational organizations, you have more options for larger groups for free.

  For a guide on setting up DimDim and integrating it with Moodle, go to `http://cvs.moodle.org/contrib/plugins/mod/dimdim/Install.pdf?view=co`.

A number of third-party software products also offer a similar service to DimDim. You may have heard of some of them:

- ✔ **Elluminate:** www.elluminate.com
- ✔ **GoToMeeting:** www.gotomeeting.com
- ✔ **Oovoo:** www.oovoo.com

The companion Web site includes hints and FAQs and links to other resources.

Chapter 7

Grading Learners' Progress and Knowledge

*M*oodle grades and the grade book are multifaceted tools for assessing student progress and recording achievement in a highly visible and interactive module. This module enables you to record scores; calculate grades for individuals, groups, and courses; and add feedback. I show you how to use those tools in this chapter.

Assessing progress, knowledge, and learning is a difficult task, and numeric grades aren't always suitable. The Moodle developers thought of this and provided a scale that uses nonnumeric, or qualitative, feedback, and Moodle has preinstalled a quantitative scale in addition to giving you tools to create your own.

In this chapter, I also show you how to use the *Choice activity,* which is a question with multiple choice replies. Instructors can use the Choice activity anywhere in the course to enliven a debate by asking a question, gathering learners' responses, and then making the results available to all learners. Choice is also used at the end of units to get learner feedback, vote on topics, or provoke learners to think about topics. After you start using Choice, you'll come up with variety of ways you can use it.

In the last section of this chapter, I explain how to use the Survey Activity module, which helps instructors collect data from learners about their course or their teaching methods. This data can help you analyze your course and teaching methods as well as improve specific areas that you may need to change. Alternatively, if your learners' surveys confirm that your course and your teaching are absolutely fabulous, you can just sit back and gloat in satisfaction.

Exploring the Grader Report Pages in Moodle

When you initially set up activities in Moodle, you can set up most of them to be graded; to do so, simply choose the grading option during setup. Moodle automatically records the activity in the grade book and records the grades after learners complete the work and you mark it. Or if it's a quiz, Moodle marks it automatically and pushes the grade to the grade book. You don't have to do a thing! See Chapter 11 to read more about the Quiz module. The Assignment module (see Chapter 10) is set up so you can create course-specific activities outside the scope of Moodle and enter the grades manually in the grade book, allowing for a complete record for your purposes. Your learners can access their grade books at anytime and see anything that will be evaluated with a grade or a scale. As soon as you add grades/comments, learners can see them.

Moodle has tools that calculate, aggregate, and display grades in standard formats that support most educational and training organizations' requirements. Moodle also includes exporting functionalities that instructors can use to export and upload grades to an organization's database. Before you start using this grading tool (which will save you from marking and calculating overall grades), you need to become familiar with the Grade module, so I start this chapter by giving you a tour of the tabs you find on the Grader Report pages.

Discovering the Grader Report tabs

From your course front page, locate the Administration block (on the left side, unless you moved it) and click Grades. Moodle takes you to the Grader Report page with the View tab selected, showing a grid with your students listed down the left and graded activities displayed in columns, as shown in Figure 7-1.

Depending on how the administrator set up the Grader Report, you see a view similar to the one shown in Figure 7-1 (with tabs across the top) or the Choose an Action drop-down list in the upper-left corner. Both offer the same choices.

To begin, I explain the tabs you see on the Grader Report pages and the information on each. The Categories and Items tab enables you to group specific activities (such as forums) and then change the grade setting for that group only, so I discuss that tab separately in more detail later in the chapter.

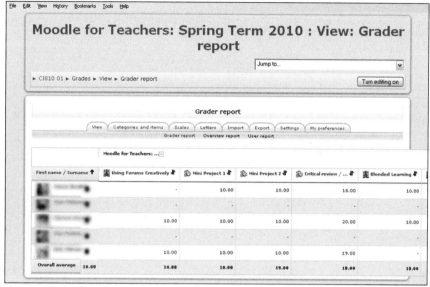

Figure 7-1:
The View
tab of the
Grader
Report
page.

View tab

If you aren't on the View tab already (the default tab when you first enter Grader Report), click the View tab, or from the Choose an Action drop-down list, select View Grader Report. Moodle displays the following information:

- The first column lists all your students, sorted by last name. You can change the sort order by selecting First Name at the top of the column and then clicking the sort icon (the black arrow). Each name is also a link that will take you to the student's profile page, where you can add notes, read blogs, send messages, and so on.

- The grade totals for each activity and assignment are listed, and you can view them in ascending or descending order. Click the small black arrows at the top of the columns to change the order.

- Each activity title is a link that displays the particular activity only, with the following columns (as shown in Figure 7-2):

    - *Grade*

    - *Comment:* This is your feedback.

    - *Last Modified (Student)*

    - *Last Modified (Teacher)*

    - *Status:* Brings up the grade window where you can enter or update a grade and/or feedback.

    - *Final Grade*

✔ The last column on the right displays the statistics for the course total. (You don't see this column in Figure 7-1 because there are many items. You have to use the horizontal scroll bar to see the last column.)

Figure 7-2:
The Grader
Report,
Submissions
page.

Scales tab

The Scales tab lists the Moodle scale provided and all the scales you set up. You also have editing capabilities from this tab. See the later section, "Creating Moodle Scales," for more information about setting up scales.

Letters tab

The Letters tab shows the settings for percentage ranges and letter grades from highest to lowest. For example, 100 to 93 percent = A, 92.99 to 90 percent = A–, and so on. You can edit the letter grade/percentage by clicking the Edit link located on the tab.

Import/Export tabs

Moodle provides you with tools for importing and exporting grades in various formats. For example, you can export to Excel by saving your exported files as CSV files. When your grades are saved as a CSV file, you have a backup if somehow your grade book is lost, and you can import the file and send it to your organization's grade database. You may also want to import grades from a spreadsheet into your grade book. Moodle enables you to export or import your grade book to or from an OpenDocument spreadsheet, a plain text file, or an XML spreadsheet. *Note:* If you upgrade grades for any particular activity, say for an assignment activity, after they're imported, you can't edit the grades on the Submissions page.

Settings tab

The Settings tab allows you to decide how the grade book appears to all learners in the course.

✔ **Aggregations Position:** Set this option to First if you want the Course Total column in the first column in the Grader Report, or select Last if you want the course total listed in the last column in the Grader Report. The default is Last. Set this option to First if you have many activities forcing you to scroll horizontally.

✔ **Grade Item:** Enables you to choose the grade display type: real numbers, letters (such as A, B, C, and so on), or percentage, in any combination. You can also choose the overall decimal point, which is the number of decimal points in the grade that Moodle displays. The default settings are Real and 2 decimal points.

✔ **Overall Report Displaying Ranking:** The default is Hidden, but you can choose to show rankings.

✔ **User Report:** These settings decide whether learners can view overall rankings and a percentage grade. The default is set to learners seeing the overall ranking; however, you can override it.

My Preferences tab

The My Preferences tab lets you set up how the Grader Report displays grades and other relevant information. You have to select options from a number of choices or leave the default settings. Here's a rundown of given options:

✔ **General Options:** Enables you to adjust display of the following:

   • *Aggregation View:* Choose from Report Default (set by an administrator for all courses on the site), Full View (displays grades and totals), Aggregates Only (displays only category and course totals), and Grades Only.

   • *Quick Grading:* If enabled, the Grader Report includes text boxes for each grade so that you can alter grades for a list of learners. This quickens the process of entering grades for many learners.

   • *Quick Feedback:* Same as for Quick Grading, but for feedback.

   • *Students Per Page:* This function enables you to set how many learners you want to see in each page of the Grader Report.

✔ **Show/Hide toggles:** This is a list of various display modes. I recommend leaving the default settings unless you specifically need one that is hidden.

✔ **Special Rows:** Options for displaying column averages.

I recommend leaving the default settings unless you need more information displayed.

Categories and Items tab

The settings on the Categories and Items tab are important if you want to group specific activities, such as forums, and then change the grade setting for that group only. For instance, if you're using the forums and giving extra credit to students who add discussion topics, the Categories function enables you to group all forums from one course together and then assign extra credit by setting weights. *Weights* determine how much the grade is worth in the overall total. For example, a grade can have a weight of 25 for participation, 50 for homework, 20 for quizzes, 30 for final exams, and so on. *Note:* The weights don't have to add up to 100.

You can also change the aggregations and a few other functions. Grouping the graded activities also makes it easier to view the Grader Report.

When you click the Categories and Items tab, you see the Simple view of the Edit Categories and Items page. In Simple view, you see only the Name, Aggregation, Weight, Max Grade, Actions, and Select columns. You can toggle between Simple and Full views. (Both links appear below the tabs, in the center of the page.)

In Full view, the Edit Categories and Items page expands to open all functionality, as shown in Figure 7-3, and you're ready to manipulate your grading options.

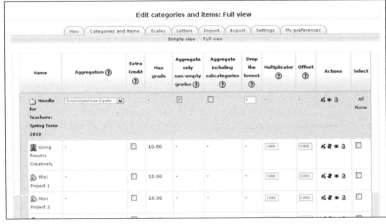

Figure 7-3:
The Edit Categories and Items page in Full view.

You see all your graded activities and assignments listed in chronological order. Categories are useful if you want to group a set of activities so you can manipulate them to add extra credit, weights, or curved grades. To group specific activities, select the check boxes in the rightmost column (under Select) or choose All from the top or bottom of the page. At the bottom, select the Add a Category by clicking it. Moodle groups the selected items, creates a folder, and highlights the row in light blue, as shown in Figure 7-4. Notice you have the standard editing icons to change settings or to delete the category. To make changes to the category, click the editing icon.

Figure 7-4:
A new
category.

The Edit Categories and Items page shows many columns (refer to Figure 7-3), which I detail in the following list:

✔ **Name:** This is the name of your item or category.

✔ **Aggregation:** The Aggregation table has a separate drop-down list, enabling you to choose the aggregation method you're comfortable with or required to use by your organization to calculate students' grades. Moodle converts to percentage values before the grade is aggregated and then uses the method you have chosen to convert it to the ranges. Explaining each grading option is beyond the scope of this book. Visit http://doc.moodle.org for a rundown on the choices. From the drop-down list, you can choose from the following options:

- Mean of Grades

- Weighted Mean

- Simple Weighted Mean

- Mean of Grades (With Extra Credits)

- Median of Grades

- Smallest Grade

- Highest Grade

- Mode of Grades

- Sum of Grades

- Available Aggregation Types

✔ **Extra Credit:** Enables you to set extra credit values.

✔ **Weights:** After setting up the categories, you can set specific weights. Moodle calculates weights as a percentage and adds it to a grade's total.

✔ **Max Grade:** What you set the activity grade for. Usually if this column is set for real numbers, you may have added anywhere between 5 and 100. In the example shown in Figure 7-3, all mini projects and forum contributions are worth 10 points.

✔ **Aggregate Only Non-Empty Grades:** Select the check box below this column heading to treat empty grades as minimal grades or not include them in the aggregation. For instance, if a specific assignment is set up to be graded between 0 and 100, and 25 percent of the students completed the assignment and received grades, Moodle ignores the grades if you've selected the check box; otherwise, Moodle counts the non-graded assignment and gives 0 in the aggregation.

✔ **Aggregate including Subcategories:** Subcategories of assignments are not included in the aggregation unless you select the check box. For example, a project may have a number of assignments associated with it, such as an outline, introduction, list of resources, and so on. You can choose whether these will be counted in the aggregation.

✔ **Drop the Lowest:** By selecting the check box, you can drop the lowest grade. For example, if your values are set 0–100, you can choose to drop anything below 20. You need to input the value next to the assignment or grouped assignments.

✔ **Multiplicator:** Allows you to change the value of a specific activity, multiplying the maximum grade with the maximum value you input.

✔ **Offset:** If you applied the multiplicator, this number is added to every grade. Moodle added these options to give you more flexibility and control over your graded assignments, tests, and quizzes. These settings can be adjusted anytime throughout the duration of the course.

- ✔ **Actions:** Notice a number of standard icons allowing you to edit, hide, move, and lock the category and assignment. If you choose the hidden option, Moodle removes a category for display and grade calculation.

- ✔ **Select:** Click this check box when selecting any of the listed activities you need to make changes to. For instance, if you're setting up a category, select the check boxes in the Select column to move to the category.

Moodle gives you the Grade Calculations tool to set up your own grade based on other graded items. Use this tool when you group together activities, such as forum contributions. To set up the grade calculation, you have to follow a formula-and-functions pattern found in most industry-standard spreadsheets like the ones in Excel. I recommend that you do *not* use this unless you experiment with the tool first. If incorrectly set up, this tool affects your whole grade book. You can easily make a small typographic error in the syntax when you're rushed to submit your grades before the deadline.

If you want to play with the Grade Calculations tool, click the Calculator symbol shown next to the group category, as shown in Figure 7-4, and you're taken to the Edit Calculations page. First visit Moodle's detailed explanation and have a look at the syntax (`http://docs.moodle.org/en/grade_calculations`). Then, find a bit of time (not the day before your grades are due), make yourself a cup of tea, and try it.

After you make any changes on the Categories and Items tab, make sure you click the Save Changes button at the bottom of the page.

Excluding from grades, and other exceptions

You can change various settings for assignments relevant to individual students. This can be useful if, for example, your student is ill during a specific assignment and you want to exclude the assignment from her grade calculations. To exclude a graded activity or an assignment, follow these steps:

1. **Click the View tab and click the Grader Report link among the links under the tabs.**

   Alternatively, after selecting Grades from the Administration block, you can use the Choose an Action drop-down list and select Grader Report under the View option.

2. **Find the student in the list on the left, and next to the assignment listing, click the editing icon.**

   Moodle has a nice feature: As you place your cursor over the editing icon, the name of the student and the assignment are displayed. This is very handy when you have a long student list and many assignments, forcing you to scroll horizontally.

Moodle takes you to Edit Grade page.

3. **Select the check box next to the Excluded option (the third one down).**

   Notice that you have many different grade options, such as overriding grades, dates, and so on. Also included is a feedback text box where you can communicate with your student regarding the particular assignment.

4. **Click the Save Changes button**

   Moodle returns you to the Grader Report page.

Displaying grades

Your learners can view their grades and the grade book anytime. Direct them to their Administration block, where they should have only two listings: Grades and Profile. When students click the Grades link, Moodle takes them to the User view and displays all the set work, their grades, and the course average for each listed work and overall. The Moodle default setting enables learners to view the course average. If you don't want learners to see the course average for overall assignments, you can change the setting by clicking the My Preferences tab (which I discuss earlier in the "My Preferences tab" section) and choosing No from the Show Column Averages drop-down list. Don't forget to scroll down and save your changes.

Creating Moodle Scales

Scales are a different way instructors can evaluate learners' performance instead of using traditional letter or percentage grades. For example, you may not want to give a numeric grade for contributions in a forum discussion or for adding comments to wikis, but you do want to evaluate the contribution in a qualitative way. Often, qualitative evaluations are more meaningful for learners and better for the learning goal you're trying to support. The Moodle developers have thought of this and created a scales tool that allows you to build your own scales. Moodle also includes a scale you can use if you don't want to create your own. The scales can be completely nonnumeric, or without values attached, or you can attach values. For example, you can create a scale for forum discussions.

Before you create the scale, think about the wording and how you want to explain it to your learners. The learners will be able to see the text associated with the scale when you evaluate their activity. If learners are unfamiliar with the meaning of the scales, they will be confused, and the evaluation exercise is counter-productive. Worse, yet, you will be inundated with messages, postings, and e-mails asking you to explain it.

Follow these steps:

1. **Click the Grades link in the Administration block on your course front page.**

   Moodle takes you the Grader Report page.

2. **Click the Scales tab, or if your Grader Report is set up with a Scales drop-down list instead of tabs, choose View.**

   Moodle takes you to the page shown in Figure 7-5. You see a table with the default scale and columns for Used and Edit.

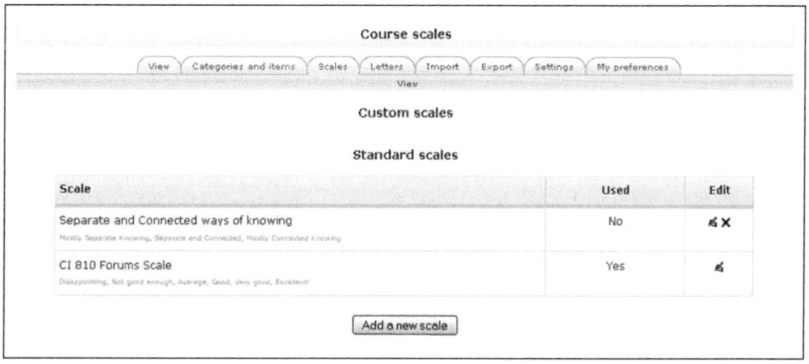

Figure 7-5: Moodle scales.

3. **Add your own scale by clicking the Add a New Scale button in the middle of the page.**

   Moodle takes you to the Scale window shown in Figure 7-6.

4. **Give the scale a name.**

   This is a required field (denoted by the asterisk). I advise you to choose a name that will identify the scale for you because it appears in the scale selection list, and over time this may become lengthy. In this example, because I'm setting up a scale for forums, I simply called it Forums.

5. **Select the Standard Scale check box if you want to make this scale available site-wide.**

   That means that other instructors can use it with their courses. If you want the scale to be used only for your course, leave the box empty.

6. **In the Scale text box, add your scale, starting from negative to positive.**

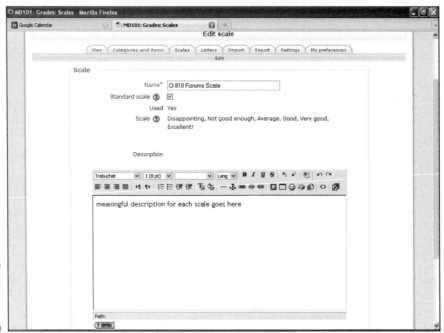

Figure 7-6:
The Scale
window.

Scales must be separated by commas only! If you don't use commas or you use other symbols and you try to save your scale, Moodle places a box around the field and gives you an error message stating `Please enter a comma-separated list of values (at least two values required.`

7. **In the Description text box, write a meaningful description explaining the scale and whether any value associated will count towards grades.**

   Learners have access to the description because they need to understand the scale.

8. **Click the Save Changes button when you're done.**

Moodle returns you to the Course Scales page, where you see your new scale listed in the table. You can edit the scale from this page by clicking the editing icon on the right. If you need to create more scales, select the Add a New Scale button and follow the procedure outlined here.

You can use the scales with any activity. You will find the scale in the grade option of all activity edit windows. The scales appear in the drop-down list with the grade values. To see the scales, scroll up — Moodle always adds the scales above the numeric values, and for the first time you use the drop-down list, it appears that the scales are not listed.

Moodle scale: Separate versus connected knowers

In case you don't have time to create your own scale, Moodle includes a default scale you can use to evaluate learners' performance. It's based on a theory that puts people into two large groups, based on how they approach the world:

✔ **Separate knowers** try to stay objective and avoid personal knowledge.

✔ **Connected knowers** learn by being socially connected in a more compassionate and sympathetic way. According to this theory, connected knowers don't like confrontation.

Moodle's default scale uses this method of how people approach the world and sets up the

scale using the following categories: Mostly Separate Knowing, Separated and Connected, and Mostly Connected Knowing. To find out more about this scale, the research behind it, and how the rating system is determined, follow these steps:

1. **Click the Grade link in the Administration block.**

2. **Click the Scales tab and then click the edit icon in the Edit column.**

   Moodle provides everything you need to know in the editing text box, including references where you can find more information.

Moodle.org provides you with a variety of example scales you can use. Visit `http://docs.moodle.org` and type **scales** in the search box.

Adding Choice to Your Course

Moodle *Choice* is a simple one-question survey you can use to get quick feedback from your learners about any course topic or activity. For example, instructors use Choice at the end of units to get student feedback on that particular unit. Used over a period of time with many courses, instructors have been able to collect valuable data about specific topics or units, for example, and what types of activities learners prefer or find useful.

The best part is that the Choice tool is quick to set up, and the results are easy to evaluate. Most learners do not mind spending under a minute on a poll. You have two restrictions when creating your informal Choice poll:

✔ You can ask only one question.

✔ The question must be in multiple choice format.

Creating a Choice activity

To add a Choice activity to your course, follow these steps:

1. **Click the Turn Editing On button in the upper-right corner of your course page.**

   The front page changes to show editing tools, allowing you to change the appearance and add functionality to your course.

2. **Click the down arrow next to Add an Activity and then select Choice.**

   You see the Adding a New Choice screen, as shown in Figure 7-7. The selections follow a similar format of other Moodle activities.

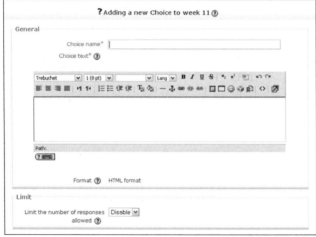

Figure 7-7: The General and Limit areas of the Adding a New Choice screen.

3. **In the General area, fill in the Choice Name (required).**

   It's useful to use descriptive names, especially if you will use Choices frequently.

4. **In the Choice text section (also in the General area), add your question.**

5. **Decide whether you want to limit the number of responses by selecting Enable from the drop-down list. (Disable is the default.)**

   By enabling a limit, you choose how many responses are allowed for each option available for learners to select; when the limit is reached, no other student can select the response. If you disable the limit, each of the responses can be selected by any number of students.

6. **Enter the responses in the Choice fields, and if you enabled a limit, enter the value.**

   Moodle provides five Choice fields by default.

7. **(Optional) If you need more than five Choice fields, click the Add 3 Fields to Form button shown in Figure 7-8 and repeat Step 6 for the new fields.**

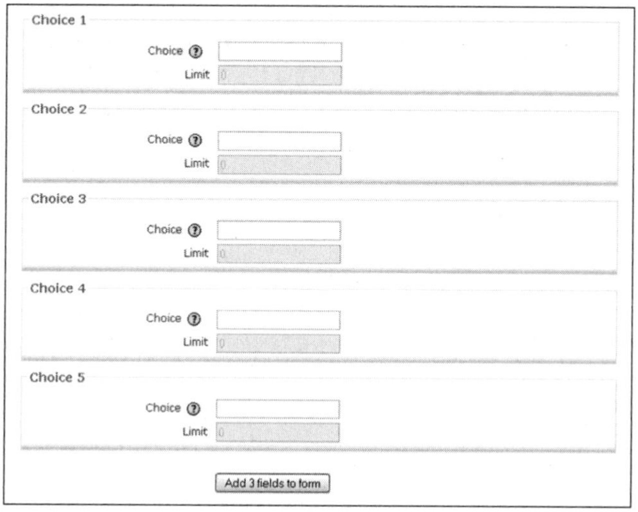

Figure 7-8:
If neces-
sary, you
can add
three
additional
Choice
fields.

8. **Select the Restrict Answering to This Time Period check box (shown in Figure 7-9) and enter dates and times if you want to limit the time the questions are available.**

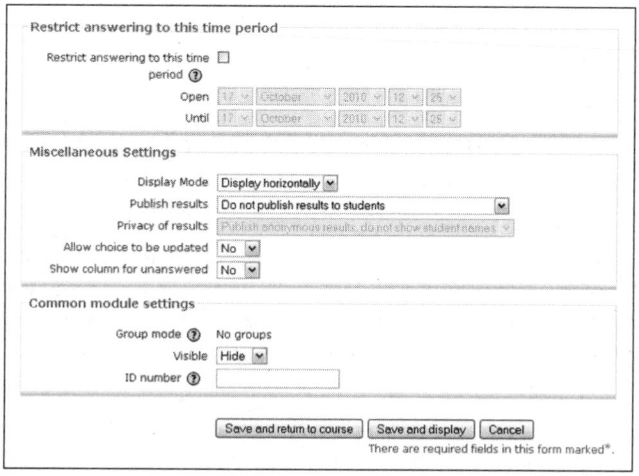

Figure 7-9:
Don't forget
to save your
changes.

9. **In the Miscellaneous Settings area, choose layout and display options.**

    Your choices are

    - *Display Mode:* From the drop-down list, select whether you want to display the responses horizontally or vertically. If you have very few responses, they look better horizontally displayed; a large number of and/or long responses look much better displayed vertically.

    - *Publish Results:* In this drop-down list, you have four options to display the results to the students: Do Not Publish the Results to the Student, Show Results to Students Immediately after They Answer, Show Results to Students Only After the Choice Is Closed, and Always Show Results to Students.

    - *Privacy of Results:* Depending on what you chose on your Publish Results setting, from the drop-down list select whether you want to publish results anonymously or with learners' names.

    - *Allow Choice to Be Updated:* Select Yes from the drop-down list if you want to allow your learners to change their minds.

    - *Show Column for Unanswered:* Select No from the drop-down list if you don't want to show names of learners who didn't answer the question.

10. **Choose the Common Module Settings as you would when you set up any Moodle activity.**

    See Chapter 3 for a rundown of the Common Module Settings.

11. **Click the Save and Return to Course button.**

Moodle saves your settings and returns to your course front page. Notice that Choice has its own unique icon, and it also appears in the Activities block, the Upcoming Events block, and the course calendar.

Administering choices

To keep track of Choice responses and gather feedback, Moodle has a View *[number]* Survey Responses link that appears in the top-right corner of the Choice page. Clicking the link takes you to a Responses page (shown in Figure 7-10) where you see the students, their replies, and tools to organize and maintain the responses. (You see the student names even if you selected in the Privacy of Results field the option to post anonymous results; the anonymity means only that participating students and guests cannot see other participants.)

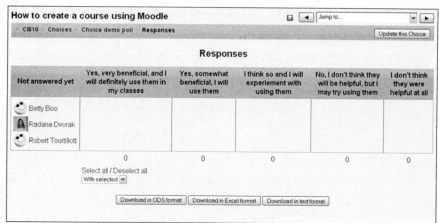

Figure 7-10:
Viewing
responses.

You can delete selected responses from the With Selected drop-down list. You also have links to Select All/Deselect All right above the drop-down list. This saves you from moving from student to student when you want to delete a large group of responses.

Moodle also features download functionality so that you can save data in industry-standard formats. You have three choices: Download in ODS (Open Document Spreadsheet) Format, Download in Excel Format, and Download in Text Format. Select the format you want to use to download your data, click the button, and follow the instructions.

Using Moodle Surveys

The Moodle survey module includes a set of questions installed in Moodle; you can't use it to create your own surveys. Moodle developers took care to install prepared, standardized survey instruments for teachers to use. The questions have been designed for use with online learning environments particular for educational purposes. If you want to create your own surveys, you can use the quiz tool as a questionnaire, which I discuss in Chapter 11.

Choosing the right survey

Moodle offers three types of surveys. Counting slight variations, you have five options when choosing a survey:

✔ **Constructivist On-Line Learning Environment Survey (COLLES):** This survey is made up of 24 statements asking learners about how they think the course is relevant and useful to their studies. It asks learners to comment on the interactivity nature of the course and involvement of other learners and the instructor. Moodle splits the survey into three different types:

- *COLLES Actual:* Ask learners how they're currently interacting with a course.

- *COLLES Preferred:* Asks learners how they *think* they would like to interact with a course.

- *COLLES Preferred and Actual:* Combination of the two with questions from both how they're currently interacting and how they would like to interact.

✔ **Attitudes to Thinking and Learning Survey (ATTLS):** This survey is based on how learners interact in a collaborative environment and apply it to online learning. The survey aims to measure the interactive nature of the course.

✔ **Critical Incidents:** This survey presents learners with recent events related to their online learning experiences and asks them to answer questions about how they relate to events.

A lot of research has gone into the development, testing, and use of these surveys. Visit the Moodle Web site for references to read more about the surveys, the metrics used, and the research methods that were used to develop these surveys.

Creating a survey

The actual procedure to set up the survey in your course is relatively simple because it's predetermined. All you need to do is choose the survey, a set of predetermined questions you want to use, add the introduction/explanation in the edit text box, and you're done. To add a survey to your course, follow these steps:

1. **Click the Turn Editing On button in the top-right corner of your course front page.**

   The front page changes to show editing tools, allowing you to change the appearance and add functionality to your course.

2. **Select Find Survey from the Add an Activity drop-down list from the section in your course where you want to administer the survey.**

   Moodle takes you to the Adding a New Survey page, shown in Figure 7-11.

3. **Fill in the survey Name, which is a required field.**

4. **From the Survey Type drop-down list, choose which of the five Moodle surveys you want to administer.**

5. **In the Custom Intro text box, explain the purpose of the survey and how you want to use it with the course.**

   Also let your learners know they'll be able to see the results.

6. **Choose the Common Module Settings as you would when you set up any Moodle activity**

   See Chapter 3 for a rundown of the Common Module Settings.

7. **Click the Save and Return to Course button.**

   Moodle saves your settings and returns you to your front page.

To view the survey, select it by clicking the survey name (next to the icon) on your course front page. When a participant completes the survey and submits it, Moodle returns a `Thank you [name]` message and provides a button to return to the course front page.

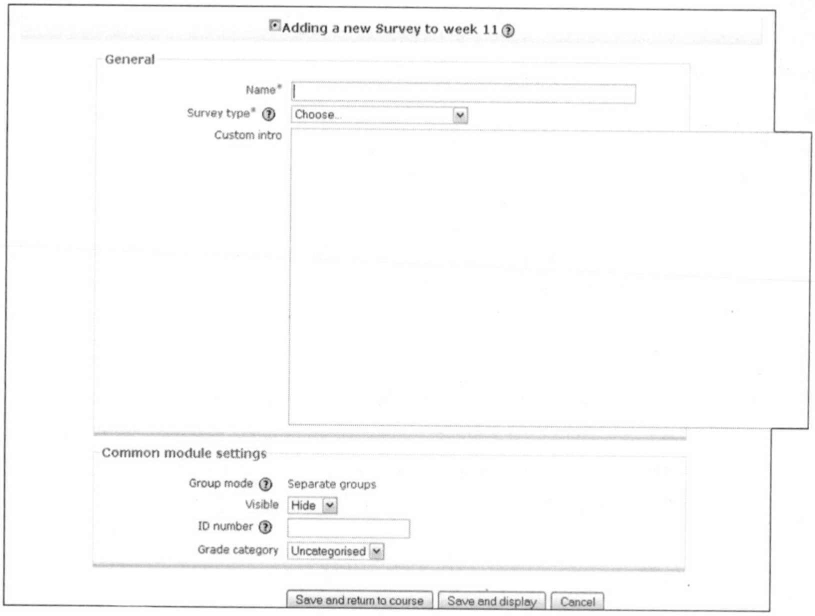

Figure 7-11:
Adding a survey.

Administering and managing surveys

Surveys will not take you too long to administer and manage. They are self-contained, and Moodle has tools enabling you to download the data into a spreadsheet or plain text file.

When selecting the survey from the front page, Moodle takes you to the summary of your results. See Figure 7-12.

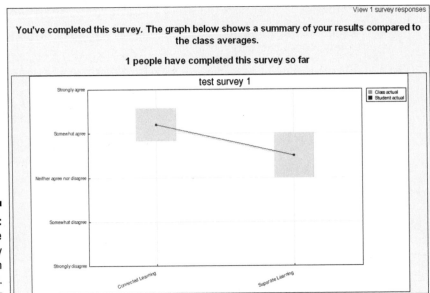

In the top-right corner of Figure 7-12 is a link that informs you how many people have completed the survey. Click that link — it reads View *[number]* Survey Responses — to see a summary report with five links in the upper left, as shown in Figure 7-13, that allow you to view the data in different formats and download the data. The following list details your choices:

✔ **Summary:** Takes you to a Moodle page that shows the survey responses against the average.

✔ **Scales:** Shows you a graphical representation of scale responses for the question type.

✔ **Questions:** Demonstrates all questions and student responses.

✔ **Students:** Lists the student, including a link to his profile and the date and time he completed the survey.

✔ **Download:** Takes you to a page with three buttons enabling you to download the data in three different formats: ODS, Excel, and Text. Select the format and click the appropriate button.

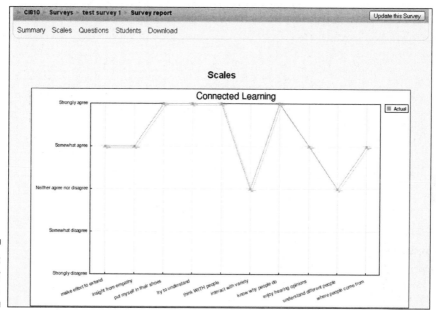

Figure 7-13:
Survey
report.

Although students or guest accounts can't see participants' results other than a general graphical report, the teacher, admin, and course creator accounts are able to view individual responses. I advise you to inform your students that the surveys are not completely anonymous, and if you intend to use the surveys for research purposes, you need to ensure anonymity.

Part III

Adding Activities to Your Moodle Course

The 5th Wave   By Rich Tennant

"This online course uses a football/math program. We're tackling multiplication, going long for division, and punting fractions."

In this part . . .

*B*efore you jump into the chapters in this part, you need to be comfortable with the Moodle layout. If so, you're ready to start Moodling and creating interactive content for your learners because the chapters here really show you how to

- ✔ Add forums, chats, and blogs
- ✔ Implement wikis and glossaries
- ✔ Pass out assignments and feedback
- ✔ Give and grade quizzes
- ✔ Collect, organize, and share searched resources through Moodle databases

Chapter 8

Adding Communication Modules

● ●

In This Chapter

▶ Using discussion forums to engage learners

▶ Creating and using chat rooms

▶ Using messaging and notes within Moodle

▶ Introducing your learners to Moodle blogs

● ●

Making use of Moodle communication tools allows you to use technology your learners are familiar with to enhance the course experience. Whether your course is completely online or part of a blended learning initiative, making use of Web 2.0 technology and communicating with your students support the nature of Moodle as a collaborative environment where instructors and students learn from and support each other. The strength of the tools is in the flexibility of how you use them to liven your training or teaching methods.

Adding Forums to Your Course

Also referred to as online message boards, *forums* are fabulous, powerful tools that can engage your learners in collaborative projects, such as out-of-class test reviewing, group project discussions/brainstorming (with all brainstorming documented), debating among classes, contributing to a topic discussion that's not in real time, role playing, inviting guests, and so on. Forums enable learners to practice skills not easily supported in traditional class settings. Studies have shown that learners participate in forum discussion more than they would in a traditional classroom setting. Educators have identified the following reasons for learners' increased participation in forums: Shyness is less of a factor, language barriers are less of a hindrance, and peer pressure is lessened. In addition, when learners discuss a topic in a forum, they can employ their computers' usability options to overcome disabilities that affect communication, and they have time to research and think through their answers before replying.

Before you create any forums, though, you need to choose what type of forum you want to create. To do that, you need to think about how to best integrate forums into your course. I discuss these issues before showing you how to actually create a forum.

Effectively using forums with your learners

Before you dive in and start creating stimulating forums for your course, take some time to think about the following issues:

- ✓ **Determine how the forum discussion will be related to the learning goals and topic.** Learners need to understand why they're asked to participate in an activity that can potentially be time-consuming.

- ✓ **Clearly explain your intentions of use and directions for your learners.** Understanding that the forum discussion is related to something and that each forum can have any number of new discussions with any number of replies can be confusing. If you don't clarify the structure and if learners don't understand that each new discussion topic needs to relate to the course activity, learners may create discussions on unrelated issues. Of course, this doesn't apply if it's your intention to open a discussion as a free form of expression.

  Monitor free-for-all threaded discussions. Topics can become hot quickly. Learners are known to be more forthcoming when not having to face others in discussing issues that ignite passionate feelings. You may find yourself having to bring white flags into your course and hold United Nation–style peace meetings.

- ✓ **Decide whether you want to assess learners' participation in forums.** Moodle forum activities can be graded by you or rated by you or other learners. If you decide to use ratings or any form of assessment, make sure your learners understand how their contributions will be evaluated. Watch out for quality versus quantity.

- ✓ **Establish classroom protocols for polite and positive replies.** Learners should not be made fun of, or made to feel small, for their contributions by other members of the class. Preparing guidelines regarding rudeness, vulgarity, and what is otherwise not acceptable will save you effort if such a situation should arise. If this is a concern, remind learners about school policy regarding student behavior and how it also applies to the online environment. If you assign points (set up forum marking or scales), for participation, often that's enough to deter negative behavior, and learners are more likely to participate.

After you've ironed out the preceding issues, get creative and make Moodle forums work for you. You can use different types of forums (which I discuss in the next section) to engage and encourage participation in discussion topics.

Getting a forum discussion going is probably the most challenging aspect of the activity. Unless your learners are forum-use savvy, you may need to start a discussion topic to get them going — which you may want to do anyway to keep topics in line with other course work and to keep your learners focused on learning goals. With that in mind, here are ideas to get you started with Moodle forums:

- ✔ **Use the News forum to make announcements to your students.** This is the only forum where students can't reply. Moodle sets up the discussion forum as a default, and it's displayed at the top of each Moodle front page. Instructors can use this forum for general announcements to all members in the course (for example, "Don't forget exam review in chat room") or topic-related announcements. Moodle sends each news forum to your learners' e-mail accounts, so you don't have to accept excuses like "I didn't know there was a new announcement on Moodle." The item is also added to the Latest News block on the course front page.

- ✔ **Invite guests to participate in an interview-style forum.** For example, an author, a politician, or some other notable person may be more willing to participate in a limited forum discussion than to visit a class. Organize your learners to post questions for the visitor and then let the learners rate the questions and choose the highest rated ones to use as topics to engage the guest in discussion.

- ✔ **Set up Q & A forums.** You and your learners can use these forums effectively for reviewing, debates, and problem-solving.

- ✔ **Encourage debate-style discussion by setting up a forum around topics.** Moodle is a great platform for topical issues that ignite passion. Use the same format for less-heated activities, such as reading groups.

- ✔ **Consider using role-play scenarios.** Assigning learners (or letting them choose) a character and its persona is fun. Learners have to post topics or replies based on knowledge of the characters they're portraying. This is an effective way for learners to investigate and think like the character. For example, choosing a historical figure to understand how decisions were made in a particular era can be a powerful learning activity and much more fun than just reading about the person and writing a report.

Choosing the right forum

Because Moodle is consistent in the layout and setup procedure of all activities and resources, setting up a forum is easy. The most important aspect of setting up the forum is first thinking about the type of forum you want to set up and then choosing correct options. Moodle supports four types of forums:

✔ **A single, simple discussion:** You post the main topic and instructions, and learners are allowed to post only replies to the discussion. This type of forum provides the instructor with the most control over the discussion topic. This forum type is useful if you want to post an issue/question and ask learners to reply.

✔ **Each person posts one discussion:** This forum type is useful if you want to restrict new discussion postings or require that each learner posts one discussion. Learners can post multiple replies. I use this forum type when I expect each learner to contribute a discussion to the topic and I plan to grade them for their efforts.

✔ **Question and answer (Q & A) forum:** This forum type is fabulous for many different activities. All learners are expected to post a discussion before they can see other learners' postings and replies. I've used this forum for guest interviews. I asked learners to post questions for our guest. After everyone posted a question, learners could reply to the questions and then rate them. Questions with the highest ratings were e-mailed to the guest. Q & A forums are also used in math and science. The instructor posts a problem to solve; each learner has to post a solution before they can see other learners' answers.

✔ **Standard forum for general use:** This is the simplest, most flexible forum for various activities. Your learners can post multiple discussions and replies. Keep track of discussion topics because heated replies can trigger new discussion postings not related to your course learning objectives.

Creating forums

Setting up a forum is simple after you decide what type of forum you want to use with your course and whether you want to assess the posting with grades or scales. To begin, follow these steps:

1. **On your course front page, click the Turn Editing On button.**

2. **Choose Forum from the Add an Activity drop-down list, as shown in Figure 8-1.**

   The Add an Activity drop-down list appears next to the Add a Resource drop-down list in the every week or topic on the front course page.

   Don't forget to first locate the week or topic set where you want to post the forum. Moodle takes you to the Adding a New Forum page for the course section selected.

3. **In the General area, type a name in the Forum Name field. (See Figure 8-1.)**

   Anything marked with an asterisk is a required field.

Figure 8-1:
The top
half of the
Adding a
New Forum
page.

Be descriptive with forum names — the titles will appear on your
Moodle front page.

4. **Choose what type of forum you want to set up from the Forum Type
drop-down list.**

   The preceding section explains each forum type.

5. **In the Forum Introduction text box provided, enter a brief explanation on how you want the forum to be used within the context of the
activity.**

   Describe how you'll be using this forum in your course and how it
   relates to the course learning goals. Use this space for specific instructions on how to use the forum, state whether you're planning to grade it,
   and explain your grading requirements.

6. **Choose whether you want to force everyone in the course to be subscribed to this forum.**

   Moodle sets the default to No. Click the drop-down list to choose one of
   the following options:

   • *Force Everyone to Subscribe:* If set to Yes forever, everyone will
     receive e-mail post when learners add a discussion topic or reply
     to any given topic. Posts are sent 30 minutes after they're added.
     This gives the learner/instructor chance to edit or change her
     posting, which is a good idea for those hotheads who are quick
     to reply and click the Post to Forum button, and later regret
     it. The 30-minute delay can be overridden by the Teacher or
     Administrator roles.

- *Selecting Yes Initially:* Choosing this setting subscribes everyone as above, but they can unsubscribe, and it's helpful to get your learners comfortable using forums and posting replies. It's also useful for learners who would rather read than write — make peer pressure work for you.

- *Subscriptions Not Allowed:* This setting restricts learners from subscribing and is useful if a forum is set up for teachers only, or if you want to restrict second-semester students or latecomers from joining the forum.

7. **Choose whether to track who reads which forum posts.**

   You have three options listed in the Read Tracking for This Forum drop-down list: Optional (the default), Off, and On. Moodle highlights unread forum posts. If you choose Optional, learners have a choice to turn this feature off or on. The Off or On setting does not give learners the options to override.

8. **Determine a maximum size for forum attachments.**

   This setting enables you to determine how large files can be uploaded to the forum in the course. Moodle enables learners to attach files or images to forum postings. I recommend that you select a smaller upload size from the drop-down list or restrict attachments altogether unless it's required by the learning activity. If the forum is active with many participants, learner downloading speeds can be affected, if they start uploading files, and you'll use up your allocated server capacity.

9. **Make your choices in the Grade area, as shown in Figure 8-2.**

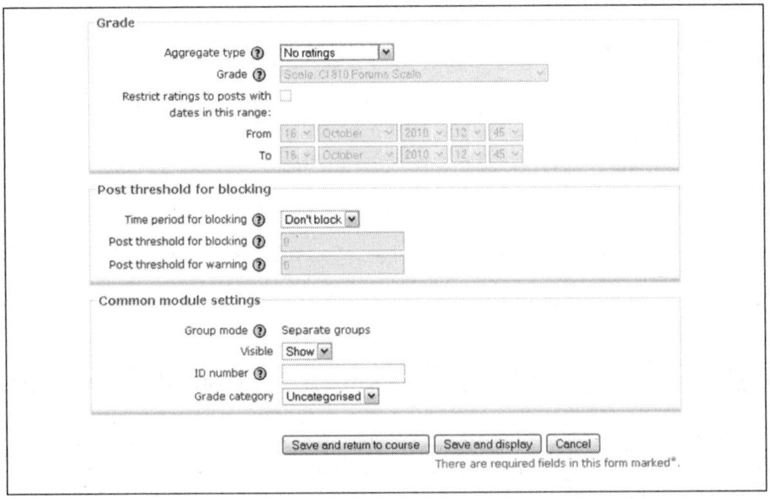

Figure 8-2:
Settings for
the second
half of the
Adding a
New Forum
page.

Moodle's default grading is set to No Ratings, with various grade options not activated. If you don't plan to grade or use scales for forums, skip this option. You will find that numeric or word scales are useful to give participation points to learners. Moodle automatically enters forum ratings in learners' grade books. To set up forum grades, select the following:

- *Aggregate Type:* From the drop-down list, select the type of rating. Your choices are Average Rating, Count of Rating, Maximum Rating, Minimum Rating, and Sum of Ratings. If you'll be using a descriptive scale, Moodle will ignore the aggregate.

- *Grade:* Depending on your aggregate choice, choose a numeric grade or a scale. I cover grades and scales in Chapter 7.

- *Restrict Ratings to Post with Dates in This Range:* Selecting this check box restricts rating to the specific time you select in the From and To dates. This option is useful if students are given permission to rate (see the next section), or if you want students to keep on task and participate in a given period.

10. **Restrict posting to encourage participation from every learner.**

    The Post Threshold for Blocking area gives you three options:

    - *Time Period for Blocking:* From the drop-down list, choose 1 Day to 1 Week. If you want to add restriction right away, choose 1 Day.

    - *Post Threshold for Blocking:* Enter the number of times a learner can post to the forum. This restricts the overactive and enthusiastic learners speaking out or doing work for others.

    - *Post Threshold for Warning:* Set the value to warn them. Quite simply, if you allow for three postings, you can set this value by entering **2**. When the learner post two discussions, Moodle informs her that she can post only one more.

11. **Choose options in the Common Module Settings area as you would when you set up any Moodle activity.**

    See Chapter 3 for a rundown of the Common Module Settings area.

12. **Click the Save and Return to Course button.**

    Moodle saves your settings and returns you to the course front page.

Managing and Administering Forums

 After you create your forum and when your learners are ready to post discussions, click the Forums icon from your course front page to access your forum. Click the Add a New Discussion Topic button, as shown in Figure 8-3, and you're taken to the Your New Discussion Topic page where you create a discussion.

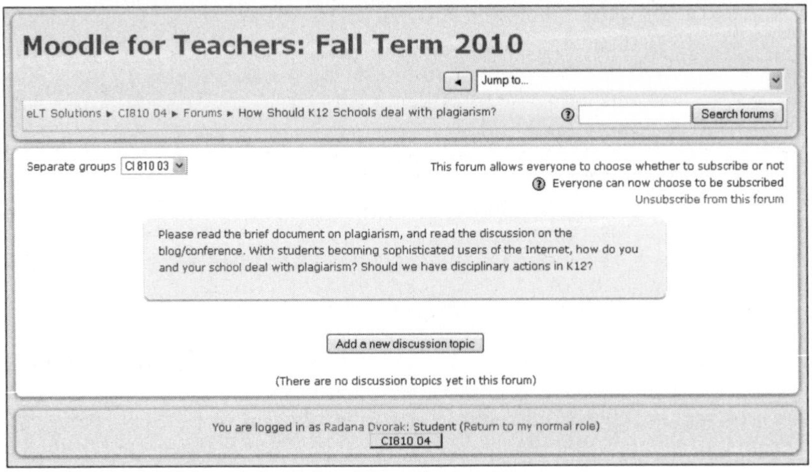

Figure 8-3:
Click the
Add a New
Discussion
Topic
button.

Moodle provides forum tools for you and your learners:

✔ **Subscriptions links:** Your learners see these links and have a choice to subscribe to the forum and receive all post in their e-mail. If you enabled learners to unsubscribe, they see a link in the same area on the forum page.

✔ **Forum instructions:** These appear in the center, followed by a button to add a discussion topic. You and your learners need to click this button to start the forum. When you use a forum for the first time, take the initiative and post the first discussion to get your learners familiar with the layout.

For instructors, this forum page has three extra options:

✔ **Update This Forum:** This button, located in the top-right corner, takes you back to the main editing page, where you can, for example, change the forum instructions.

✔ **Show/Edit Current Subscribers:** Located with the subscriptions links, this functionality allows you to make subscription changes, such as pushing the forum to e-mail, forcing all members to subscribe, and so on. Generally, you have at your disposal all the functionality you have when you set up the forum.

✔ **Separate Groups:** This drop-down list is located in the top-left corner and allows you to choose groups if you have group sets within your course.

Adding forum discussions

Beginning a discussion topic requires only a few simple steps:

1. **Click the Forums icon from your course front page.**

2. **Click the Add a New Discussion Topic button in the center of the page.**

   The Your New Discussion Topic page, as shown in Figure 8-4, appears.

3. **Fill in the following fields (anything marked with an asterisk is required):**

   - *Subject:* Give your discussion a name.

   - *Message:* Write what you want to discuss — identify the topic. It's useful to remind your learners to stay within the scope of the central theme or topic.

   - *Format:* When you're using text editing boxes in Moodle, they can come in a number of formats, of which HTML is the most widely used and is set as default. You can leave the default setting, and things will work as you expect. For instance, URLs will automatically become links and indenting or line breaks will be interpreted as new paragraphs. For more information on the formats, click the Help icon.

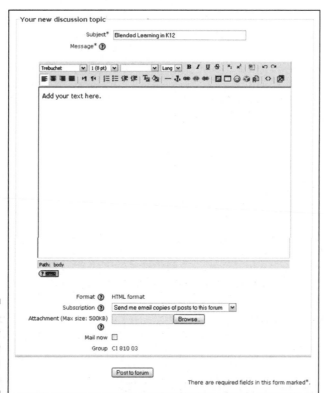

Figure 8-4:
The Your
New
Discussion
Topic page.

- *Subscription:* You and your learners can decide whether you want to receive e-mail copies of the posts.

- *Attachment:* Lets you attach a file to the forum.

- *Mail Now:* This field is available only to you. Student accounts cannot override this. Select the check box if you want to override the 30-minute posting delay.

- *Group:* Shows the group that's involved in this discussion. You set this group when you set up this particular forum discussion.

4. **Click the Post to Forum button.**

After you submit the discussion topic, Moodle tells you the post was saved and informs you that it will be posted in 30 minutes. After making a post, you (or your learners) have 30 minutes to go back and make changes. When the discussion is posted, your learners cannot make changes to it unless permissions are changed on students' profile settings. See Figure 8-5, which displays a learner's posting and a reply from another learner.

Figure 8-5: Example of a learner posting a discussion to the topic and a reply from another student.

Viewing, archiving, and searching forum discussions

The forum viewing pages offer you a few more forum capabilities and information about the postings. Figure 8-6 shows a standard list of discussions, who posted them, and the date and time of posting.

Figure 8-6:
Forum page
listing all
discussions
and replies,
by whom,
and when
posted.

Here are the most widely used tools:

- **Reply:** Clicking this link opens an editing window, allowing you and your learners to reply to a posting.

- **Edit/Delete:** These links take your learners back to their posting to edit it or delete it — as long as they do so within 30 minutes of posting. After 30 minutes, they can't make changes. There's no time limit for you to make changes.

- **Show Parent:** Shows the original discussion topic.

- **Split Discussions:** This option allows you to split the discussion to create new ones. This option is useful if a new topic is started in a reply that begins to generate discussions and you think it may be of more value to stand on its own.

- **Rate Posts:** Allows you to rate the postings. If you want users to be able to rate the postings, permissions need to be set in student profiles. Permission changes are beyond the scope of the book. Please visit `http://docs.moodle.org/en/Forum_permissions` for more details.

Above the discussion topics is a Display option drop-down list, which is useful for managing discussions. Moodle lets you view the discussions in four ways. The drop-down list gives you the following options:

✔ **Display Replies Flat with Oldest First:** All replies are displayed under the discussion topic with oldest first.

✔ **Display Replies Last with Newest First:** This option is the same as the preceding one except that newest replies display first.

✔ **Display Replies in Threaded Form:** The discussion is in complete form, but all replies post only headlines and author and date posted.

✔ **Display Replies in Nested Form:** My preferred viewing. You see all discussion topics and replies in full form with replies tabbed to the right. (Figure 8-5 displays the nested form.)

Moodle provides these extra tools that aren't seen by your learner:

✔ **Move This Discussion To:** Moodle lets you move the forum discussion to any other area in your course. If one of your forum discussions gets very long, you can use this utility to create a forum archive and then move all the entries there. The drop-down list enables you to move the forum discussion to any other forum listed in other units or weeks, or to an archive folder. This drop-down list is not available for learners.

Categorizing forum discussions and storing them in archive folders or combining them with other discussions keeps the current discussion easier to maintain, and makes the information available as a reference for your learners.

You can create an archive with few simple steps.

a. *Turn on editing, locate the unit or week in your Moodle course where you want to place the archive, and select Forum from the Activities drop-down list.*

I usually place the archive in the last week/unit.

b. *Set up the forum as instructed in "Creating forums" section, earlier in this chapter.*

I suggest you call the forum Archive and let learners know in the instructions let learners the title of the forum as it was listed prior to archiving.

c. *Go back to the forum you want to archive and click it.*

d. *Click the Move This Discussion To drop-down list and select Archive Forum, and then click the Move button.*

Archive Forum should be the last one in the list if you placed it at the bottom of your course.

Moodle moves the whole discussion to the Archive forum. You and your learners can view the archived discussion by clicking it from the forum listing accessed from the Activities block on the course front page.

✔ **Search Forums:** Searching a forum is useful if you or your students want to find certain terms or topics. Located on the front page, this tool can be handy if you use forums extensively and if the discussions become a resource for your students. It's also useful if you need to grade the forum. Enter the student's name in the forum search, and Moodle returns all forum contributions for that student.

You can enter a search term from the front page Search Forums block, or you can use the search feature within the discussion itself. The Search field is located in the top-right corner. If your search yields too many results, you can refine your search using the advanced search link, located in the right corner of your search results page. Clicking the link takes you to a detail search page where you can search your topic in any number of ways, such as by student name, date, and specific forums. You can use the standard advanced search options by clicking the advanced search link located below the search field. A new search page opens enabling you to enter details related to what you're trying to search. For example, if you're searching for a specific learner and dates he may have been active in the course, you have that option.

Adding a Chat to Your Course

A *chat* is synchronous communication, which is a way of describing how it allows you and your learners to hold a text-based discussion in real time. The Moodle chat room is different from the forum (which is asynchronous) because for forum discussions, the learners don't need to be logged in at the same time. In a chat room, students need to be logged in to the session at the same time and participate in a structured activity you can control. The Moodle chat room is similar to Google chat, AIM, MSN Messenger, and other chat rooms. However, the Chat module in Moodle is unique because it's tied to your course, and you have instant access to all the messages between learners, and between you and your learners. Having a record of the communication can be used in other activities, and you control how it's used within your course.

Effectively using chat with your learners

Although not as robust as some of the instant messaging found on the Internet, the Moodle chat room is an effective learning tool that instructors find useful. Here are a number of ways that instructors use the Moodle chat room:

✔ **Question and answer:** With online courses, you can use it as traditional online office hours, where students can ask you questions related to the syllabus. You can leave the past chat sessions available for students to re-read, and you can post some of the questions to the News forum.

✔ **Test reviews and preparation:** You can make yourself available before tests. You can use the questions and answers at a later date to create exam questions or prepare final exam reviews.

✔ **Study and project groups:** You can set up a number of chats for students to work in groups on projects or review for tests. You can set up chats for individual groups you've assigned for the projects, which restricts other learners from entering the chat room. See Chapter 4 on how to create groups.

✔ **Guests:** You can invite a guest to join a chat room and participate in a debate or answer learners' questions. For instance, a counselor set up a chat for a guest medical expert to answer questions related to his day-to-day work and his expertise. He was not able to take a day off work to visit the school, but happily agreed to spend an hour in a chat room.

✔ **Foreign language or ESL:** One of the most creative ways I've seen instructors use the chat is for students to hold an open discussion in their French and German courses. The teacher saved the transcripts from the chat and posted them as an assignment, asking the students to correct the grammar and spelling. It was an exercise everyone enjoyed.

✔ **For sick students:** A number of teachers have used the chat room when their students were ill and in the hospital for an extended period of time. Group work exam preparation and project feedback were completed by using the chat room.

Creating and entering into a chat session

The Chat module follows the same standard format as other Moodle activities. To set up a chat, follow these steps:

1. **On the course front page, click the Turn Editing On button.**

2. **Choose Chat from the Add an Activity drop-down list located in the course center sections.**

   Don't forget to first locate the section set where you want to post the forum. Moodle takes you to the Adding a New Chat page for the course section selected.

3. **Fill in the chat name.**

   I suggest using descriptive names — the title will appear on your Moodle front page.

   Fields marked with an asterisk must be filled in.

4. **Fill in the introduction text.**

   Use this space to tell the learners the purpose of the chat. If some learners are using chat for the first time, add instructions on how to use it. When I use the chat for the first time with a course or group, I usually say something like: "I will be in the chat room to answer questions related to the course. Click the Click Here to Enter Chat link. You will be taken to a chat window. Ask me questions by typing in the text line at the bottom."

5. **Enter the date and time you will hold the chat in the Next Chat Time field.**

   Depending on where your Moodle site is hosted, you may have a different time frame showing up in the chat. Ask IT whether the server time is the same as the time you are at; otherwise, when you enter the chat room, a different time may be displayed, which will confuse your learners.

6. **In the Repeat Chat Sessions field, determine whether you plan to hold regular chats scheduled at the same time.**

   Moodle publishes the chat in the Calendar, Latest News, and Upcoming Events blocks on the front course page. You have four options you can select from the drop-down list:

   - *Don't Publish Any Chat Times:* If you select this option, Moodle leaves the chat room open, and learners can enter it any time, which may not be ideal if you're using it for structured activities.

   - *No Repeat:* Select this option to create a chat on a specific date and time. This setting is useful if you don't hold regular chat sessions.

   - *At the Same Time Every Day:* Your course calendar will list the event for however long you specified.

   - *At the Same Time Every Week:* This option is the same as the preceding option, but on a weekly basis.

7. **Save the past session.**

   To do so, enter a specified amount of time in the field. The default is set to Never Delete. You can specify days by selecting them from the drop-down list.

8. **Decide whether everyone or teachers only can view past sessions.**

   If you want only teachers to view past sessions, select No from the drop-down list.

9. **Choose the Common Module Settings as you would when you set up any Moodle activity.**

   See Chapter 3 for a rundown of the Common Module Settings.

10. **Click the Save and Return to Course button.**

    Moodle saves your settings and returns you to the course front page.

When you and your learners first click the chat link from the front page, you'll enter the home page for the chat session. You see your description and purpose of the chat, information of the next chat session, and a Click Here to Enter the Chat Now button. If this is the first session, nothing else is displayed on the page.

If you set up the chat session so that messages are saved and if you're returning to the chat, you see a View Past Chat Sessions link in the top-right corner. You can click the link to see a transcript of the chat. To enter the chat, click the Enter Chat Room button, and a new, smaller window opens.

Figure 8-7 shows the Chat screen, which is divided into two frames. The left frame displays the chat messages, including the name and profile picture of the person who entered each message. The right frame lists all the people who are currently participating in the chat session, displaying each participant's profile picture, name, and the time he or she entered the chat. To enter messages, type in the text field at the bottom and press Enter. If you don't want the chat window to auto-scroll, you can disable it by deselecting the Auto Scroll check box below the text input field. The auto scroll places a scroll bar in the text window when text fills it. Scrolling up may be useful if you need to return to a question a student may post.

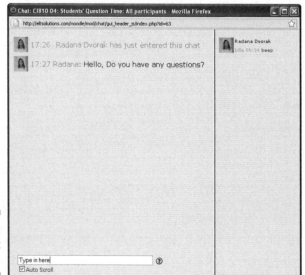

Figure 8-7:
A basic Chat
screen.

Managing and administering a chat

Moodle provides a number of features that enable you to manage your chat session.

✔ **Refresh:** Chat refreshes every five seconds, so don't worry if you don't see your message right away. You may hear a sound every time it refreshes.

✔ **Beeps:** To get someone's attention, you can click the Beep link on the right next to her name, and she'll hear a beep (if her sound is turned on).

If you want to beep everyone, enter **beep all** into the text field. If you want your learners to respond to the beep, ask them to turn on their sound. You can also ask everyone to turn off sound if it becomes annoying.

✔ **Internet addresses:** Typing in any standard Internet address results in a link and opens a new window with the Web page you wanted.

✔ **Smileys:** You and your learners can type any emoticon supported by Moodle, and it shows up as an appropriate smiley.

✔ **HTML:** If you're familiar with HTML, you can insert images, change text color, or add sound to chat session.

You may want to limit how many students can enter a chat room. Working with a large number can be difficult and time-consuming. Small groups work best if you use the Chat module with your course, you may think about setting some protocols to manage sessions.

If several students are on Chat and a large number of replies come in within seconds, Moodle Chat is known to freeze up. If you will use chat with large groups, one option is to build a server daemon that takes the load off the database. For discussions and solutions, see `http://moodle.org/mod/forum/discuss.php?d=2947`.

I post the following rules on the front page in the first week of every new Moodle course:

✔ Wait for the teacher/moderator to ask for your questions.

✔ Do not use the beep unless you feel someone is not paying attention or an answer/question you posted is directed at the specific person.

✔ If you just can't wait to answer your questions (if you're the student who stands up and jumps up and down with a hand up), send a question mark in the chat.

✔ If you have an observation or a comment or you think something is important, send an exclamation point in the chat and wait for the speaker to acknowledge you.

✔ Uppercase letters usually indicate shouting. A combination of upper- and lowercase is difficult to read.

✔ Give others time to respond. Don't send a set of rapid messages. Often it's difficult to tell which response goes with which message. This is very important if more than two people are using chat. I often enter the learner's name first and then answer his question, especially if several questions come in before I can answer them.

✔ Ask learners to not judge typing skills and typos and spelling errors. Everyone makes errors, and you don't want to set a standard where others feel they have to be as careful in a chat as a forum. Some students won't be active if judgment is used.

✔ Think before you press Enter. This is important if students use this as an in-class reward activity for finishing work. Chat transcripts are saved for a long time. Tell your students to be polite to their classmates.

✔ Use humor and sarcasm carefully. Humor and sarcasm are very difficult to interpret when people can't see facial expression. Use smileys for emotions. (You can use the standard smiley supported by Moodle. Entering the characters into the text bar results in the smiley appearing in the chat window — for example :-) makes the smiley.)

The protocol you devise varies with the age group you teach; however, some of the suggestions are relevant to all learners.

Using Moodle Messaging

When you want to send private communications, Moodle messaging may be the tool for you. Users can send private messages between instructor and learner, between instructors, or between learners. Messages are not specific to a Moodle course. If your organization has a Moodle site with many different courses, all the people registered with the Moodle site can send messages to each other. If you want to avoid clogging up your e-mail, this is a fantastic alternative because Moodle messaging enables you to have all Moodle course-related messages held within it.

Creating messages

You can send messages to other Moodlers from their profiles or from the Message block. I recommend enabling the Message block to encourage learners and instructors to send messages through Moodle because you can track all messages from one place, and you know when the message has been read.

Messages are sent via a pop-up window, which saves you time because you don't have to open another messaging utility or e-mail. However, if some of your learners avoid visiting the Moodle course, the messages are still sent to their current e-mails registered with their student accounts. Your learners won't find an excuse for lack of notification and communication.

To send a message, follow these steps:

1. **Open a message window.**

   You can access the message window from your own profile page, the button on the bottom Messages page, or the Message block. Each learner has the Message button on their profile and can access the Message block from the course front page. To enable the Message block, refer to Chapter 3 for instructions.

2. **Click the Search tab and enter the name of the person you're sending a message to.**

3. **If the learner is in your course, select the Only in My Courses check box and then click Search.**

   A message box opens with the name you entered in Step 2.

4. **Type your message and click the Send Message button.**

   Moodle copies the message, and it appears above the text field.

You can also send messages to a group of learners by selecting any number of participants from the Participants block on the front page.

1. **Click the Participants link.**

2. **Select which participant you want to send a message to by selecting the check box next to the profile or clicking the Select All button at the bottom.**

3. **From the With Selected users drop-down list, select Add/Send Message.**

4. **In the text box, type your message and click the Preview button.**

   Moodle shows the message.

5. **Edit the message by clicking the Update button or send it by clicking the Send button.**

Managing and administering messages

Three tabs on the message window offer a few cool message features. One of these is the Search tab, which I discuss in the preceding section. The other two tabs are Contacts and Settings:

- ✔ **Contacts tab:** After you send your first message to another Moodler, you can add him to your contact list. Click the Add Contact link, and Moodle creates a contact list and adds him. As well as adding a contact, you can block a contact by clicking the round green button. You can also use your contact list to remove contacts or see the history.

- ✔ **Settings tab:** Enables you to select a number of options to manage your messages and contacts.

  - *Automatically Show Message Window When I Get New Messages:* Make sure your browser needs are set so it doesn't block pop-ups on your Moodle site.

  - *Block All New Messages from People Who Are Not on My Contact List*

  - *Beep When a New Message Comes*

  - *Use HTML Editor*

- *Version without Frames and JavaScript*

- *Email Messages When I Am Offline: Offline* means not on the Moodle site. You can set up the time you are away and determine the e-mail address where you want messages sent. Don't forget to save your changes.

Adding Notes about Your Learners

Notes are a useful tool that instructors can use to keep memos on learners' performance, illness, or achievements. You can also use notes to share information about learners with the Moodle instructors of other courses. Notes are *not* visible to learners; they are visible only to you, and you have the control to make your note available to other instructors.

Creating notes

You can access the Notes page and create notes anywhere that you can click a learner profile or from the Participants link on the front course page. To create a note, take these steps:

1. **Click the Participants link in the People block on your course front page.**

2. **Select the check box next to the desired learner.**

3. **From the With Selected Users drop-down list, select Add a New Note.**

   You can also find the Notes section on an individual student profile, Notes tab. See Figure 8-8.

   Moodle takes you to a new page with the learner's name, a text box for your note, and a drop-down list on the right of the note to select who gets to view the note.

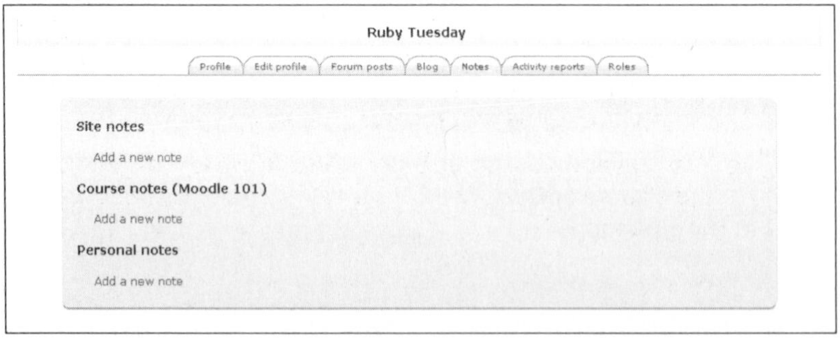

Figure 8-8:
Ready to
add a new
note on the
Notes tab.

Ruby Tuesday

Profile | Edit profile | Forum posts | Blog | Notes | Activity reports | Roles

Site notes

Add a new note

Course notes (Moodle 101)

Add a new note

Personal notes

Add a new note

4. **Write your note.**

5. **Set privacy for your note by choosing an option from the drop-down list next to your notes.**

   Your choices are

   - *Personal:* The note will be visible only to you.

   - *Course:* The note will be visible to other teachers' accounts that have access to your course.

   - *Site:* The note will be visible to other teachers in all courses on the organization' Moodle site.

6. **Click the Save Changes button.**

   Moodle returns you to the participants list.

Student accounts or guest accounts don't have access to the notes. The tab does not appear on their profiles.

Using notes

Notes help you keep tabs on your learners and can be useful when you are assigning projects, grading, or setting up groups. Do think carefully about making a note available to a whole site. For example, if a school Moodle site has 300 courses, the note you placed on the learner's profile will be available to all the teachers. This functionality is useful only if you want to share something with many instructors that interact with the student (for example, if your student won a scholarship or was in the hospital for an extended length of time).

To look at your newly added note, select the learner profile, and you see a number of tabs appear across the screen. The following list briefly describes their functionality:

- Click the Notes tab to go to the notes functionality. Under Personal is the newly added note. See Figure 8-9.

- From this Notes page, you can edit or delete the note by clicking the blue link. For instance, you may want to make it available to the course. From the Edit link, you have the drop-down list that allows you to change the status of the note.

- You can add new notes to Personal, Course, and Site. Notice that by the Course option, you have a list of which courses the student is registered for.

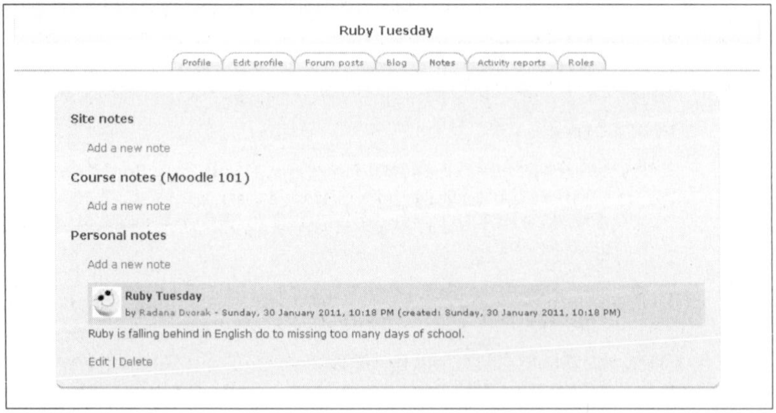

Figure 8-9:
Looking
at added
notes.

Adding Moodle Blogs to Your Course

Moodle blogs provide yet another way to enable you to creatively engage your learners in self expression. The term *blog* comes from what now is an ancient term *Web log* coined in the late '90s. Moodle blogs — which can be written and read by instructors and students alike — have replaced the Moodle journal, which is still available but is no longer a default application. (If you want to use Moodle journals, you have to ask your administrator to enable the feature. I recommend sticking with blogs, which your learners are likely to think are a lot cooler than old-fashioned journals.)

Don't worry that the Moodle blog will be available to the whole world. Moodle developers are very clever and have installed tools that enable you to choose who views your blog entries. Also of note, each Moodle user can have only one blog.

Effectively using blogs with your learners

As with all other projects and activities that you use with your learners, Moodle blogs need to have a clearly defined learning goal, and you must convey that to your class. Here are a few examples of how instructors and teachers have found versatile uses for blogs:

- ✔ **Encouraging creativity:** Writing about their personal experiences or interests can be related to a project or left open-ended.

- ✔ **Enhancing reviewing and critical analysis:** You can set up reviewing and analysis around a lecture or presentation, and ask your learners to briefly blog about the presentation. Present the class with a film and/or issues — give them five minutes to blog.

✔ **Supporting writing skills:** With younger learners, encouraging writing about topics they're interested in enhances all aspects of their education. They can keep a diary about their learning or any other topics. The blog can be shared only between you and your student to keep personal entries confidential.

✔ **Encouraging individual research projects:** Students can use blogs to collect information and keep a log of project work. You and your learner can keep track of progress. This can take shape similar to a fieldwork journal.

✔ **Encouraging group work:** Learners working together can each keep a blog on their part in a group project. It allows them to share and keep track of each others' work. Peer pressure helps to keep everyone on track. For example, you can require each group member to write two blog posts per week.

Blog tags

One cool feature of Moodle blogs is the use of *blog tags,* which are relevant keywords and/or terms used within a blog. These tags are one way to identify a blog theme or find information in a blog. An instructor can enable blog tags to be displayed on the course front page.

To keep learners focused on what they're blogging about, ask them to identify keywords (tags) that'd draw readers to their blogs. You can present it to them by suggesting, "If you were looking for your own blog, what keywords would you put into a search engine like Google?" Learners are very Google-savvy; they're sure to understand this analogy. I discuss tags a bit more in the following section.

Creating blog posts

If you plan to ask your learners to blog, I recommend you use your own blog as an example. For instance, you can blog about topics like how to start blogging in Moodle and your expectation of blogging, ground rules for the blogs, and how you will evaluate them if they're part of an assessment exercise. Your blog can be sort of a meta blog.

Unlike other Moodle resources or activities, blogs are user-based and found on all participants profiles. To set up your blog, here's what you do:

1. **On your profile page, click the Blog tab.**

   Moodle takes you to a new page.

2. **To add a new entry, click the Add a New Entry link (in the center of the page or from the Blog menu on the right).**

   See Figure 8-10.

   You're taken to the blog editing page.

3. **Give your blog post a title (see Figure 8-11).**

   This is a mandatory field, as denoted by the asterisk.

4. **Write your content or copy and paste it.**

   Don't forget that if you're pasting from Word, use the Word clean functionality feature. Alternatively, copy from Notepad.

5. **Click the Browse button to attach a picture or other file.**

Figure 8-10:
Click the
Add a New
Entry link.

Figure 8-11:
The blog
editing
page.

You should be familiar with the Browse and Add documents or Pictures tool. This attachment functionality is that same used throughout Moodle and other applications, such as e-mail applications that allow attachments.

6. **Use the Publish To drop-down list (shown in Figure 8-12) to set who gets to read your blog.**

   You have three options:

   - *Yourself:* It's good to start with restricting the blog for only you to read. This allows you to draft it and to choose your keywords (which I discuss in the next step). When you're happy with it, you can change this setting to share the blog.

   - *Anyone on Your Site:* Your blog will be visible to all classes on the organization's Moodle site. Restrictions can be set to only groups, teacher, and course through the Admin options. You need to have administrative permissions or ask your IT to make the changes for you. The changes are made in the site Administration block in the security section.

   - *Anyone in the World:* You don't see this third option in the drop-down list because by default, it's disabled. Moodle blogs aren't available to be accessed by anyone on the Internet unless permissions are changed in the site Administration blog. Most administrators don't allow this because it can pose security risks. If you want your learners to have their blogs available on the Internet, you can use Google's Blogger (www.blogger.com) or Edublog (http://edublog.org) and link to the blogs from your course front page.

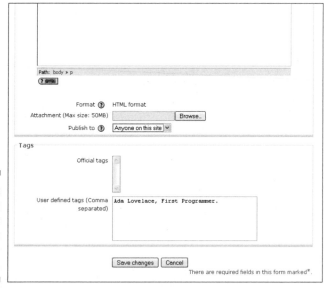

Figure 8-12: Choosing options from the Publish To drop-down list.

7. Enter tags (keywords) so others can find your blog in searches.

Each blog post should have one or two tags linked to it. Tags are useful for search term retrieval and grouping blog entries by subject matter. Two types of tags exist:

- *Official tags:* These tags are site wide, so they show across all courses on a Moodle site. The system administrator needs to enable official tags.

- *User-defined tags:* Learners can create their own individual tags. Try to minimize tags to no more than two because if you have many learners blogging, and enable Blog Tag block on the course front page, the list becomes too long and can look sloppy. Make sure you use a comma to separate the tags.

8. Click the Save Changes button.

Moodle takes you to your blog page (see Figure 8-13). Your blog post is in the center, your blog tags are on the left, and your tags for the site are on the right.

Figure 8-13:
Your blog page.

Administering blog posts

Moodle provides you with a number of editing tools to manage your blog and blog tags from the Blog Menu block, in addition three links that under blog posts: Edit, Delete, and Permalink.

Notice the four editing tools in the Blog Menu block in the upper-right corner (refer to Figure 8-13):

  ✔ **Add a New Entry:** I explain this in the preceding section.

  ✔ **View My Entries:** See all your blog entries if you're in your own blog. From the Blog Tags block, you can view particular entries based on the tag.

  ✔ **Blog Preferences:** Clicking this menu item takes you to a new page where you select how many blog entries are shown on a page. Moodle sets the default to ten.

  ✔ **View Site Entries:** Clicking this link lists all blogs on the Moodle site, listed by most recent entry. If there are more than ten, you see a link to page numbers and a Next button at the bottom of the page. All tags associated with the blogs are shown in a menu on the right.

Under each of your blog posts are three more tools that help you manage your blog (refer to Figure 8-13):

  ✔ **Edit:** Takes you back to the same editing page where you created the blog post. You can add or change tags, edit text, or change the title.

  ✔ **Delete:** Clicking this link removes the post and all tags associated with it. Moodle asks you to confirm the delete before it is removed.

  ✔ **Permalink:** Clicking the Permalink link places the Web address of your blog in your browser address bar, allowing you to copy the link and send it to someone via e-mail. Remember that the person must have a Moodle account to view the blog.

The Blog Tags block

If blogs are an important part of the learning goals you set out for your class, you can encourage learners to read the blogs by placing their blog tags on the front page. The blog tags are listed for all the blogs in a cluster known as a *tag cloud,* and the most frequently accessed blog tag appears in a large font.

Tags are course wide, so if blogging is a one-to-one activity between you and your learners, you do not want to use the Blog Tags block.

To add a Blog Tags block to your course's front page, follow these simple steps:

  1. **On the course front page, click the Turn Editing On button in the top-right corner.**

  2. **Find the Add Blocks block, located on the right side, and select Blog Tags from the drop-down list.**

     The drop-down list has a number of operations for you to play with; for instance you can edit the Blog Tags block, move the whole block, hide it, and so on.

3. **Click the Edit link to configure the Blog Tags block.**

   Moodle takes you to the editing page. Both the Blog Tags block and the editing page are shown in Figure 8-14.

4. **Adjust the settings to your liking.**

   You can change the following settings:

   - *Blog Tags Block Title:* Instead of Blog Tags, you can call it the name of your course or activity.

   - *Number of Tags to Display:* The tags are displayed on your course front page and on the blogs; I usually change the default 20 to 10.

   - *Display Tags Used within This Many Days:* Select from the drop-down list how many days you want to leave tags on the front page.

   - *Sort the Tags Display By:* The drop-down list has two options: Tag Text and Date Tag Was Last Used. Choosing the Date Tag Was Last Used option quickly shows you which blog is getting the most viewing.

5. **Click the Save Changes button.**

Have fun blogging!

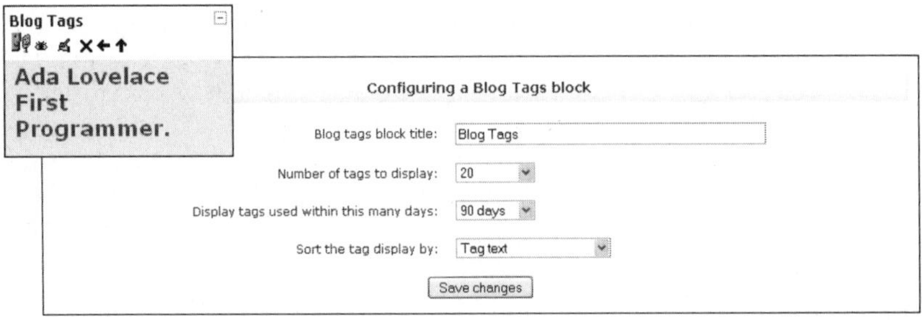

Figure 8-14:
The Blog
Tags block
(with editing
turned on)
and the edit-
ing page.

Chapter 9

Adding Collaborative Modules

・・

In This Chapter

▶ Using wikis to foster learners' involvement

▶ Crafting glossaries into learning modules

▶ Providing lessons that engage and challenge

▶ Making effective use of Moodle's collaborative offerings

・・

Adding collaborative modules to your Moodle course supports the educational philosophy of learning by doing activities with other learners. That philosophy simply says that people learn from each other by sharing information and constructing projects for all to use.

In this chapter, you find out how to create specific Moodle modules for the learners in your course to use with you and/or other learners. For example, this chapter shows you how to create and manage a wiki that the course participants can use to learn about a chosen topic. You also discover some interesting uses for glossaries and use the Glossary module for collaborative project work. You set up lessons that lead your learners to follow a guided or branched path through information supporting their learning strategies. When you incorporate these modules, you can turn passive learners into active participants in your course.

Adding Wikis to Your Course

Wiki-wiki is a Hawaiian word meaning *quick*. In Moodle and other learning content management systems (LCMS), a *wiki* is a collection of collaboratively authored Web pages that are set up to be easy to add to and edit. The most famous wiki is *Wikipedia* (www.wikipedia.org); you and your class are most likely familiar with this online encyclopedia.

Wikis can be powerful modules for collaborative activities because their structure includes Web page–editing capabilities that help you coordinate information between any number of class members. As a teacher, you can decide whether the entire class can edit a wiki together, or you can create group wikis that are editable by specific class members. Moodle ensures that wikis are easy to set up and even easier to use, which makes them a great resource for any type of course project.

Effectively using wikis with your learners

Use your imagination and make wikis work for you and your class. Teachers and trainers use wikis in various ways: with a whole class, with multiple classes, with groups (subdivisions of courses), or with specific learners for individual research projects.

Here are a few ways that using a wiki can benefit your learners:

- **Encouraging creativity:** Use wikis to encourage learners to upload images, link to resources, use graphical editing options, and add sound and/or video clips as appropriate for the course. For example, a wiki designed for an introductory fashion design course can allow class members to get more creative by posting their fashion designs, linking to fashion shows, adding designs by famous designers, and planning and staging a show.

- **Encouraging group work:** Use wikis to encourage learners to work in groups on activities such as sharing lecture notes. For instance, you can set up a group wiki for each topic or lecture to encourage learners to share notes, add concrete examples, and decide what's valuable to review for exams.

- **Managing group projects:** Assign a group project and give each group a specific topic to post research, link to resources, create outlines and presentations, or design and develop a product. For example, a graduate student in my course, a teacher, who was reading the book *The Outsiders* (by S. E. Hinton) with her class set up group wikis around various '60s themes, such as hairstyles, music, culture, fashion, art, TV programs, movies, and significant political events in the United States and around the world. The kids loved it and had lots of fun creating the wiki pages (and learning while doing so).

✔ **Enlivening individual research project work:** Use the wiki to supervise individual project work that's shared only between you and your learner. Encourage your learner to use multimedia presentations, video, sound, text, readings, debates, interviews, and reference lists to create a project for assessment. You can use the wiki to observe and guide the learner from the beginning stages starting with an outline.

Just think of how *green* you and your learners will be as you save mountains of paper when you don't require your learners to hand in paper-based project work.

Choosing the right wiki structure

You have standard information to fill in and choices to make when you set up a wiki for your course. Preparing standard information for your wiki — such as a name and a descriptive summary — may seem simple, but giving a little thought to making these items informative, engaging, and intuitive for the class is important. Some choices you make affect the overall wiki configuration and determine who has access to read, edit, and add to the wiki materials. Other options you must choose are more technical in nature and relate to the level of complexity you want to incorporate.

The wiki name and summary description are required information in Moodle. Give your wiki a name that ties it closely to the course outcomes, learning objective, or specific project. In the summary field, describe the purpose of the wiki and how it will be used as part of your course, or if it's a wiki for a project, describe how you expect participants to contribute to it and how you'll assess it.

After naming your wiki and adding a summary, you need to determine how your wiki will be used with the course and set the appropriate permission in the Type field. This field is important because the setting determines who has editing permissions and can add to or help maintain the wiki, as follows:

✔ **Teacher:** Choose this option if you're the only one with editing permission.

✔ **Groups:** Select the Groups setting if the group has editing and/or viewing permissions.

✔ **Student:** If students have editing permission, select this choice.

Table 9-1 gives you a comprehensive explanation about setting options.

Table 9-1	Wiki Types and Permissions		
Wiki Type	**Group Mode - No Groups**	**Group Mode - Separate Groups**	**Group Mode - Visible Groups**
Teacher or Trainer	Only one wiki is created, and only the teacher can edit it. Students can view the wiki and all contents.	One wiki is set up for every group, but only the teacher can edit the wikis. Students from other groups cannot view the page.	Each group can create one wiki, but only the teacher can edit the wiki. All groups can view the wiki.
Groups	One wiki for the whole course is set up. The teacher and all students can edit the wiki.	One wiki per group is set up. Students can edit the wiki in their group only. Other groups can't view the wiki.	Each group has its own wiki, which the group members can edit. Other groups can view the wiki but can't edit it.
Student (Individual Learner or Trainee)	The wiki is student-teacher–based. Only the student and teacher can view and edit this wiki.	Each student has her own wiki, which only the student and you can edit. The wiki can be viewed by other students in the group.	Each student can have her own wiki, which only the student and teacher can edit. The wiki can be viewed by all students in the course.

Creating wikis

Creating and setting up a wiki are relatively simple processes. Moodle follows the same editing procedure that you use when setting up other Moodle modules. (See Chapter 3 for the discussion on basic editing procedures.) After you've decided where you want to add the wiki, follow these steps:

1. **Click the Turn Editing On button in the upper-right corner of your course front page.**

The front page changes to show editing tools, allowing you to change the appearance and add functionality to your course.

The editing tools are listed in Chapter 3 and on the book's Cheat Sheet at Dummies.com. (See the inside front cover for more details about the Cheat Sheet.)

Note the question mark icon next to certain features. Clicking this icon opens a help window that explains Moodle specifics about that feature.

2. **Find the section or week in your course where you want the wiki to appear. In each section, you should see two drop-down lists, one for Add a Resource, the other for Add an Activity. Click the down arrow next to Add an Activity and select Wiki from the list.**

   Moodle takes you to the Adding a New Wiki page, shown in Figure 9-1, which has a similar layout to the pages for other activities — such as setting up a forum, as outlined in Chapter 8.

   The top portion of the Adding a New Wiki page is shown in Figure 9-1; you have to scroll down to see the rest, which is shown next in Figure 9-2.

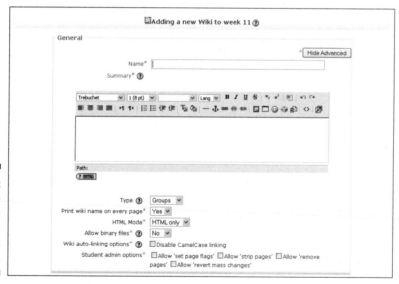

Figure 9-1: The settings on the Adding a New Wiki page.

3. **Fill in the Name and Summary fields, which are required.**

   In the Summary description, if the wiki is meant to be used by learners for a project, you may want to add requirements and state whether you'll use any assessment to evaluate class members' work on the wiki. Be as clear and concise as possible. Bullet points may help here.

4. **Select what type of wiki you want to set up from the Type drop-down list.**

   Your choice here sets the editing permissions, which I describe in the preceding section.

5. **From the Print Wiki Name on Every Page drop-down list, select No if you don't want the name showing on every page; alternatively, leave the default, Yes.**

6. **Select the HTML setting from the HTML Mode drop-down list.**

   Usually, the default setting is HTML Only, which means you don't see the HTML tags.

   Make your selection based on the technical skill level you have and the skill level you expect from your wiki participants. Unless you and your class are very familiar with HTML and want to add or change the look and feel of the page, you may want to stick with the default HTML Only setting and rely on the Moodle wiki editor, which allows you to view and edit HTML source code using the toggle editing tool. (See Chapter 5 for instructions on how to use the WYSIWYG editor.)

   The other two settings are No HTML, which shows all HTML tags, and Safe HTML, which shows only certain tags.

7. **Continue selecting options that define the wiki's allowable features.**

   Make choices for the following:

   • *Allow Binary Files:* Select Yes if you want to have the option of uploading graphics, audio, video, and other nontext resources. Your learners will have much more fun creating and viewing the wiki if you allow them to add media. Text-based-only wikis are boring!

   You always want the option to upload various types of media (other than text) unless your IT support puts a tight cap on space allowance. To combat this situation (should it arise), get your picket signs out and march with your class to the IT office and demand more space. Or picking up the phone or sending the IT folks an e-mail may work also.

   • *Wiki Auto-Linking Options:* Select the check box next to Disable CamelCase Linking if you don't want Moodle to automatically create a new wiki page when it sees a word with a capital letter at the beginning and another capital letter somewhere in the middle. For example, the name *GeorgeWashington* (no space between the first and last name) creates a new wiki page.

If you don't disable CamelCase linking, you must make sure there's no space between the words you're using to link! I tend not to use CamelCase — it's prone to causing errors whenever students type text or copy and paste text into the wiki editor.

You can disable this feature because Moodle provides you with another way to create new pages — by putting brackets around the words. For example, if you discuss the [first moon landing], putting brackets around these words, Moodle recognizes this as an instruction to create a new wiki page, with the text in the brackets becoming a link to the new page. I go into further detail on this in the upcoming "Checking out a new wiki page" section.

8. Select the check box next to the desired student admin options.

Moodle gives students specific editing and administrative privileges, which you control. I cover each of these options in the next section.

9. Type a name in the Page Name text box, shown in Figure 9-2.

Adding a name here is important only if you want the name of the first page to be different from the name of the wiki.

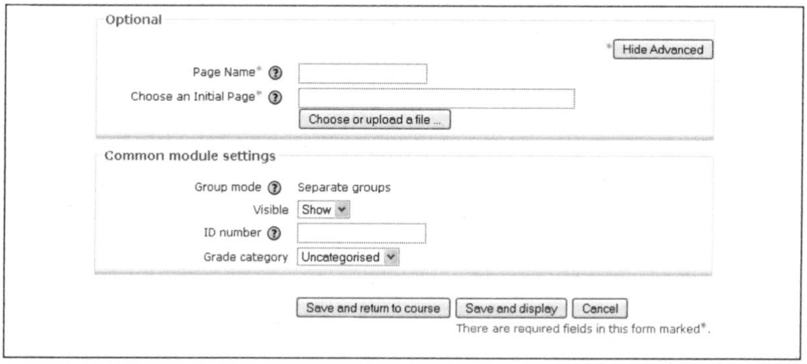

Optional

Hide Advanced

Page Name* ⑦ [   ]
Choose an Initial Page* ⑦ [   ]
[Choose or upload a file ...]

Common module settings

Group mode ⑦ Separate groups
Visible [Show ▾]
ID number ⑦ [   ]
Grade category [Uncategorised ▾]

[Save and return to course] [Save and display] [Cancel]
There are required fields in this form marked*.

Figure 9-2:
Scroll down
to make all
your wiki
settings.

10. Choose the Common Module Settings as you would when you set up any Moodle activity. Then click the Save and Return to Course button.

Moodle saves your settings and returns your new wiki-editing page, as shown in Figure 9-3. See Chapter 3 for a rundown of the Common Module Settings.

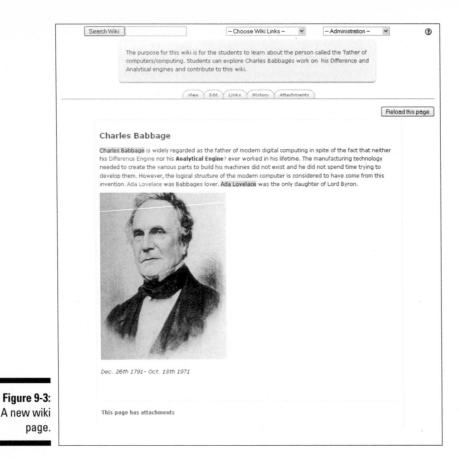

Figure 9-3:
A new wiki
page.

Managing and Administering Wikis

After you set up a wiki for your class or individual learners, you can start creating new wiki pages. As you start using the wiki, you and your learners will be inspired to find creative ways to present and use wiki content. This is where the fun begins!

Checking out a new wiki page

Your new wiki page includes a number of features you and your learners need to familiarize yourself with. Looking at your wiki page, Moodle first displays the summary located above the tabs, as shown earlier in Figure 9-3.

Above the main text area are five tabs you and your learners can click to interact with your wiki. Here are descriptions for the tabs and what they do:

✔ **View:** You and your learners see this tab when browsing the wiki. It is the page you and your learners first come to when you click the wiki from the front course page or when you first create the wiki. The View tab includes a link to all the attached files for the wiki page.

✔ **Edit:** From this tab, you can change content, attach files, and create new wiki pages, as shown in Figure 9-4. Notice that I place brackets around [Difference Engine], [Ada Lovelace], and [Charles Babbage], which tells Moodle to create new wiki pages.

Figure 9-4: Editing a wiki page and setting up new wiki pages using words in brackets.

✔ **Links:** The Links tab displays a list of all the titles of wiki pages that link from the page. Each title is a link to that particular wiki page.

✔ **History:** Check out the History tab to see the complete activity of the wiki page. Every time learners click the Save button, they save a new version of the wiki page, and the History tab shows you the changes, who made them, and the date and time, as shown in Figure 9-5.

The History tab also offers three more cool functions:

- *Browse:* Allows you to view every version of a wiki page.

- *Fetch-back:* Fetches an old page for editing. Once changes are made, it becomes the newest version of the page.

- *Diff:* Highlights the differences between two consecutive versions of the same wiki page. The additions have a plus sign (+), and deletions have a negative sign (-).

✔ **Attachments:** On the Attachments tab, you can attach any type of file to your wiki page, add a comment in the comments box, and give the image a name that is different from the saved image file. The Attachments tab also shows you who attached the file and the date it was attached. You can link straight to the learner's profile by clicking the name. Figure 9-6 shows the upload field, a linked image, and the name of the user who added the image to the wiki page, a text box for comments, and a field to enter the name.

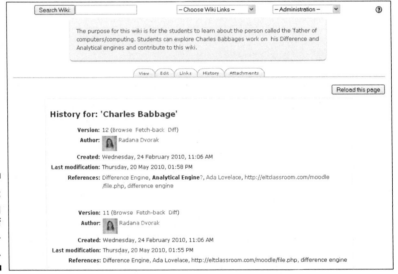

Figure 9-5:
Displaying
the layout of
a wiki his-
tory page.

Each time you see a profile picture and name of a learner's activity, you can access his or her full profile by clicking the name.

Creating wiki pages

Accessing your wiki is simple. Moodle takes you right to your first page when you set up the wiki, or you can go to it by clicking the wiki icon from your front page. Then you're ready to take these steps:

Figure 9-6:
The Attach-
ments tab.

1. **Add content to your first wiki page by typing in the editing box.**

   You can copy and paste text from Notepad or another plain-text document into the editing box, or use the Clean Word function in the editing box, as described in Chapter 5. But you can't copy and paste text
   straight from Word or other word processing software because you will
   copy HTML code, which will make your page look messy.

2. **Place brackets around any words or phrases you want to act as links
   to generate new wiki pages.**

   For example, earlier in the chapter in Figure 9-4, I placed brackets
   around the words [Difference Engine], [Analytical Engine], and [Ada
   Lovelace]. (*Note:* I highlighted the words in yellow so they are visible in
   the figure. Moodle software does not highlight the text.)

3. **Click the Save button under the text box.**

   Moodle refreshes the page and thanks you for your contribution.

   In the center, you can see your new text with a red question mark next
   to the word or phrase you enclosed in brackets. This is a link to your
   new wiki page.

4. **Click the red question mark, and Moodle takes you to the new editing
   view page.**

   You or your learners can add content and create as many new links and
   wiki pages, from every new page, as you need.

Assigning wiki admin duties

For the successful evolvement of your wiki, and so that you and your learners can experience the wiki as a fun and collaborative activity, you need to assign administrative duties to your learners. A lot of learners will get a kick out of being "wiki wardens." If you use wikis in your course or in groups, choosing group leaders with specific tasks will help manage the wiki. Administrative tasks include monitoring new wiki pages, keeping an eye on most updated pages, testing links between wiki pages and to external resources, and removing wiki pages (called *stripping* pages). For example, you will want one of your learners to help with removing old versions of all wiki pages, or the database can quickly fill up. Every time someone adds a link, attachment, or any other file to a wiki page, Moodle saves the old version.

There are three wiki management tools you will want to familiarize yourself with. They are the Search Wiki, Choose Wiki Links, and Administration tools located under the Moodle navigation bar. Each is described in more detail here.

✔ **Search Wiki:** Allows learners to find wiki pages that include specific search terms. The search results list every page, as a specific link, where the search term is found. For example, I entered *Ada Lovelace* into the wiki search engine, and the search page returned five links. See Figure 9-7.

✔ **Choose Wiki Links:** Click the down arrow next to Choose Wiki Links to explore your wiki in different formats. This is useful when looking for information by means other than a search. These tools are also useful to assist you or your learners to view wiki page activities. Wikis need to be monitored to identify errors and whether you need to delete old wiki pages or alter any content. You can view the wiki pages in the format listed here:

Figure 9-7: Search results.

- *Site Map:* Moodle displays all the wiki pages by name, starting with the first wiki page. Each name is also a link to that particular wiki page.

- *Page Index:* Lists all the pages in the wiki alphabetically. Each page is a link.

- *Newest Pages:* List most recently updated and created pages.

- *Most Visited Pages:* Generates a number of most-visited wiki pages with the *hits* (number of times it was visited). If you set up learners to create individual wiki pages, you can give an award to the winning page based on visits. Alternatively, you may just want to keep a check on high-traffic pages just in case learners swayed away from the original task and decided to add something resembling entertainment value to distract learners in the course.

- *Most Often Changed Pages:* Keep an eye on a page that may be constantly changed. You may find a wicked wiki battle is happening between a few learners and clogging up your database.

- *Updated Pages:* Displays wiki pages by time and date of last edit.

- *Orphaned Pages:* These are standalone pages that were created but all the links to them have been deleted.

- *Wanted Pages:* These are pages that have not been created, but identified by learners by placing brackets around text.

- *Export Pages:* Moodle allows you to select your wiki pages and export them as HTML files to a Zip folder you can download or save in one of your Moodle directories.

- *File Download:* Allows you to download all files that you or your learners attached to wiki pages.

✔ **Administration:** Click the Administration drop-down list to find tools that you and your learners can use to keep your wiki running effortlessly.

For instance, you may want to look for orphaned pages using the Search Wiki links tool discussed earlier, and delete them or reconnect them. *Orphaned pages* are wiki pages that are not linked to or from another page, or have no links in them to go to another wiki page — they are stand-alone pages that no one would find. Learners may leave orphaned pages if they frequently update and add files to wiki pages. Too many orphaned pages can quickly take up database space, and you may find your Moodle course using up your allocated server space.

- *Set Page Flags:* Allows you to set specific permission for each wiki page. See Table 9-2, which explains each flag.

Table 9-2	Setting Page Flags Permissions
Page Flags	*Page Flag Properties*
TXT	Allows the wiki page to contain text.
BIN	Allows binary (graphics) content.
OFF	Short for *offline*. The page is there but can't be read if learners don't have editing permissions.
HTM	Allows HTML content instead of wiki default text.
RO	Short for *read-only*. Learners can read the wiki page but can't make changes.
WR	Means read-write or writable. Allows anyone in the course to make changes.

- *Remove Pages:* Allows you and your learners to remove orphaned wiki pages. You need this tool because orphaned pages can't be reached through the wiki View or Edit tabs.

- *Strip Pages:* The wiki keeps track of all changes and stores old versions in the database. It's important you check the history and occasionally delete all the old versions so the database doesn't get cluttered.

- *Revert Mass Changes:* No need to panic. This tool allows you to roll back the clock and restore an older version of the wiki if learners make a mess of many pages in the wiki. You don't need to share with your learners that at a click of a button you can restore everything and clean up their catastrophic mess. Letting them stew about their mistakes for a few minutes may be satisfying. Keep paramedics on hand though.

Note: Students can work simultaneously on the same wiki but not on the same wiki pages. Moodle informs students if a wiki page is being used (it is locked), and they'll have to try later.

Be sure your learners know that it's important to save after editing because if they open a page and forget to save the changes, the opened wiki page is locked, and no one else can view or edit it. You or IT support can change permissions, allowing learners to override locked pages. See Chapter 13 for advice and information on how to change permissions.

Adding a Glossary to Your Course

The Moodle glossary is a neat module for activities involving gathering resources and sharing information. The glossary is simpler to use than the wikis and lessons, and you can use it collaboratively with your learners, encouraging your learners to find and present information. Be sure your learners know that it's important to save after editing because if they open a page and forget to save the changes, the opened wiki page is locked, and no one can view or edit it. You or IT support can change permissions, allowing learners to override locked pages. See Chapter 13 for advice and information on how to change permission and how to bribe your IT staff to do it for you.

A structure such as the glossary can be fun. Moodle enables you to create a course glossary, or allow groups or individual learners to create their own. The glossary will assist them in understanding the terms in context of the assignment, project, or unit and will act as a resource for others.

Effective ways to use your glossaries

Use your imagination to add the Moodle glossary to your learning activities. Learners can use it just like a dictionary, but the Moodle glossary is much more than a word list your learners may need for your course. The features allow you and your learners to share the glossary lists, add comments to individual glossary entries, and link the glossary terms. Moodle allows you to enable the glossary terms to be highlighted whenever they appear throughout the Moodle site or in individual courses. The highlighted terms become links to the entry in the glossary. You can use the Random Glossary Entry block to show the glossary entries on your main course page — similar to Blog Tags, explained in Chapter 8 — or set up a Question/Answer format. The possibilities are endless if you forget the old definition of a glossary and start using the Glossary module. You will quickly discover how flexible and extensible it is.

Here are a few successful uses of the glossary:

- **Collaborative glossaries:** Learners work together to create a glossary of unfamiliar terms related to the topic studied or project work.

- **Developing review questions for exams:** Learners create glossaries around questions and answers. They can link and enable note functionalities to add depth to the topic.

- **Project work:** A collaborative research project allows learners to create a resource for each topic, sharing it with others in the class.

✔ **Creating course directories:** Learners can create a glossary entry for themselves and add content. This can become a sharing and learning activity if learners add resources to their entries. For example, a summer trip to Rome can include links to places visited, local culture, music, art, history, local cuisine, and so on.

Creating glossaries

Setting up a glossary is simple. Moodle follows the same process you find when setting up other Moodle activities (such as forums, as described in Chapter 8, and the wikis described in this chapter).

1. **Click the Turn Editing On button in the top-right corner of your course front page.**

   The front page changes to show editing tools, allowing you to change the appearance and add functionality to your course. The center of the front page displays two drop-down lists in every week or unit of your course: Add a Resource and Add an Activity. The editing tools are listed in the Cheat Sheet and explained in Chapter 3.

2. **Click the down arrow next to Add an Activity in the section of the course where you want the glossary to appear, and select Glossary from the drop-down list.**

   Moodle takes you to the Adding a New Glossary page, shown in Figure 9-8. The page has similar layout to the pages for other activities you may have set up — such as the wiki, as outlined in the earlier in the chapter. If you've already created wikis, you will find creating a glossary easy going!

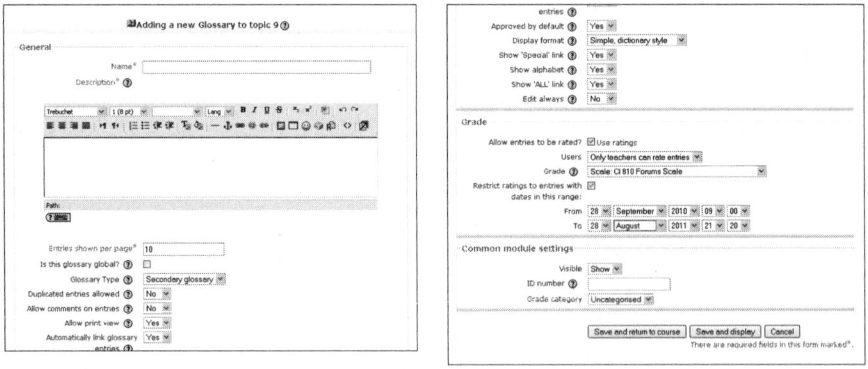

Figure 9-8: The settings on the Adding a New Glossary page.

3. Fill in the glossary Name and Summary fields, which are required.

In the Summary field, you may want to add instructions on how the glossary should be used and state whether you'll use any assessment to evaluate learners' work on the glossary. Be as clear and concise as possible. Bullet points may help here.

4. Continue selecting the general options defining the glossary's allowable features.

Make choices for the following options:

- *Entries Shown per Page:* Decide how many words and definitions will be displayed to learners at any one time. The default is 10.

- *Is the Glossary Global?* It is usually decided by administrators of the Moodle site. As a teacher, you may not have permission to activate this setting. If the permission is set, glossary terms appear for every course on the Moodle site.

- *Glossary Type:* Decide whether the glossary is main or secondary. You can export entries from a secondary glossary to a main glossary. The default is Main.

- *Duplicated Entries Allowed:* Select Yes if you want to allow for more than one definition for any term.

- *Allow Comments on Entries:* Selecting Yes enables learners to add comments to any definition. Moodle makes the comments available through links at the bottom of the definition section.

- *Allow Print View:* Selecting Yes allows learners to link to a printer-friendly page.

- *Automatically Link Glossary Entries:* If you select Yes, Moodle highlights and links all words in the course to the glossary definition.

  To be able to automatically link glossary entries, the autolinking feature needs to be enabled in the Site Administration Block in the Modules section, in the Filter sub-section. Your system administrator needs to enable this if you don't have administrative privileges. See Chapter 13 for more information on how to do this.

- *Approved by Default:* Decide if you will allow learners to add entries with or without your approval required.

- *Display Format:* Decide how you want the glossary to appear to your learners. I recommend that you figure out how you want to use the glossary and then choose a style. It's fun to experiment. Remember that you can easily delete any module you are not 100-percent happy with. Click the drop-down list and select one of the following.

You are familiar with *Simple Dictionary Style*, where authors are not shown and attachments appear as links only. *Continuous without Author* displays all entries and editing icons. *Encyclopedia* is similar to the Full with Author format, but attached images are displayed. *Entry List* style displays terms and concepts as links. *FAQ* is a very cool format showing a list of frequently asked question. Moodle automatically attaches a term as a Question and displays the concept and definition as an Answer. *Full with Author* is similar to a forum format, showing attachments as links. Finally, *Full without Author* is the same as Full with Author but doesn't display authors' data.

- *Show 'Special' Link:* Select Yes as prompted if you want to enable your learners to browse the glossary by selecting the first character of a word. Special Link shows characters like $, #, @, %, &, and ?.

- *Show Alphabet:* Select Yes to allow your users to browse the glossary with ease, using the alphabet displayed as tabs.

- *Show 'ALL' Link:* Select Yes if you want to allow your learners to view all glossary entries at once. I usually select No because the alternative browsing options are familiar to most learners.

- *Edit Always:* Selecting Yes assigns editing permissions to you and/or your learners for all entries.

5. **Choose the Grade options as you would when you set up any Moodle activity allowing grading.**

   For example, you can set up glossary grading scales as you set up the forum grading, as outlined in Chapter 8.

   Make choices for the following:

   - *Allow Entries to Be Rated:* If you select the check box next to User Ratings, the grayed-out choices become highlighted.

   - *Users:* This option allows you to grade or enable learners to grade the entry and definitions. Select Only Teachers or Everyone from the Users drop-down list.

   - *Grades:* Select the down arrow next to Grades to choose a grading scale.

   - *Restrict Ratings to Entries with Dates in This Range:* Select the check box if you need to restrict when learners can grade, and then select the down arrows next to From and To.

6. **Choose the Common Module Settings as you would when you set up any Moodle activity and then click the Save and Return to course button.**

   See Chapter 3 for a rundown of the Common Module settings.

Moodle saves your settings and returns you to the course front page. You can see the newly added glossary icon with its title in the week or unit where you first set it up.

This book's Cheat Sheet at Dummies.com has all the Moodle icons. For more information about the Cheat Sheet, see the inside front cover.

Managing and Administering Glossaries

After you create your glossary for your class or individual learners, you can start populating it with entries. I suggest you add a few entries and attach an example file when you first introduce the glossary to your course.

Checking out a glossary page

When you and your learners first view the newly created glossary page, it may look baffling because it appears quite busy with many features. It's actually easy to use, and your learners will have a lot of fun populating it when you start adding entries.

Click the glossary icon from the course front page. (It's located in the week or unit where you set up the glossary.) Moodle opens the glossary, as shown in Figure 9-9.

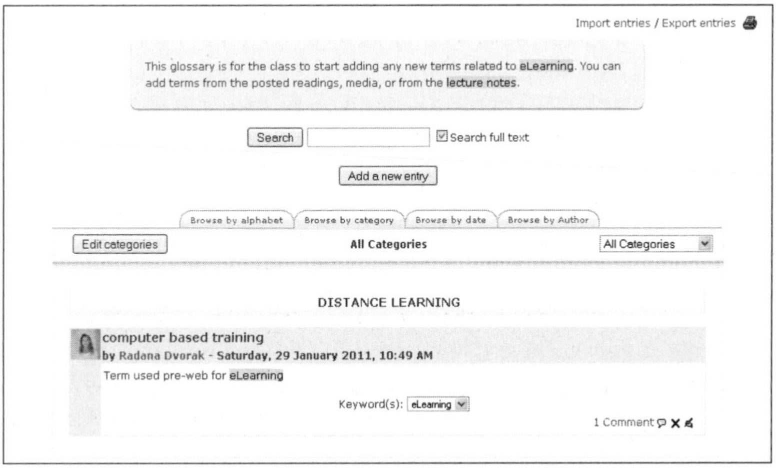

Figure 9-9:
A new glossary page with an entry.

✓ **Browsing the glossary:** Notice the four large browsing tabs in the center.

   • *Browse by Alphabet:* Learners are able to look up words by its first letter.

   • *Browse by Category:* You can create categories for your glossary and then learners can use them when looking for specific words. For example, you can create categories for each unit topic and add related entries. To learn how to set up categories, see the next section.

   • *Browse by Date:* If learners will add content to the glossary, browsing by author is useful to keep track of who is participating in the assignment.

✓ **Import Entries and Export Entries:** In the top right under the Update This Glossary button, you see two links allowing you to import and export glossaries. You can import a glossary from another course, or this course, and you can export a glossary to a file that you can download to your computer or another Moodle course. Importing and exporting are outside the scope of this book; if you need details, visit `http://docs.moodle.org`, or access the Moodle forums at `http://moodle.org`, or go to this book's companion Web site at `www.dummies.com/go/moodlefd`.

✓ **Waiting approval:** If you set the Approval default to No when you set up the glossary, after your class begins to add entries you see an additional link with a number, in brackets, telling you how many words are waiting for your approval before they can be added to the glossary. When you click the link, you're taken to a page with a list of these new entries, and a check box next to each.

✓ **Printer icon:** If you set Allow Print View to Yes when you set up the glossary, you see a small printer icon right under the Import Entries/Export Entries links. Your learner can click the printer icon to print the entries and definitions in a printer-friendly format.

✓ **Search:** You and your learners can search for terms by entering the key term in the field located right above the browsing tab. If you want to search for an entry anywhere in the text, select the check box next to the text entry field.

When you understand the layout of the glossary page, you can start adding terms to your glossary. If you plan to use the glossary as a collaborative exercise, add a few terms, definitions, and notes to demonstrate to your learners how the glossary looks. I advise you to take your students through a short tutorial, emphasizing how the activity is related to the learning goal or the course or project. If you use one glossary across a number of units or topics, you may want to think about categorizing the terms, enabling your learners to search by categories.

To add a new glossary entry, take these steps:

1. **Click the Add a New Entry button located in the middle of the glossary page. (The earlier Figure 9-9 shows the button.)**

   Moodle takes you to the Add a New Entry page. Notice the name of your glossary at the top of this page.

2. **Fill in the new word or concept in the Concept field.**

3. **Fill in the definition and/or explanation in the text box.**

4. **If you have set up categories for your glossary, choose the category where the new term belongs by highlighting the category name in the selection box.**

   See the upcoming "Adding categories" section if you need to know how to add categories.

5. **If it would be useful to your course members, add synonyms in the field next to Keyword(s).**

   If you have more than one synonym, enter one word per line in the text field.

6. **Click the Browse button next the Attachment field to add a file to your glossary term.**

   The file can be any type, text, graphics, sound.

7. **If you or your learners require the term to appear as a link, select the check box next to This Entry Should Be Automatically Linked.**

   Activating the automatically linked functions enables you to choose from the following options:

   - *This Entry Is Case Sensitive:* Select this option if correct case is a requirement for the word(s).
   - *Match Whole Words Only:* Select this option if you want to match whole words (concept) or part of a word.

8. **Click the Save Changes button.**

   Moodle saves the new term and returns you to the main glossary page.

Commenting on entries

If you selected Yes for the Allowing Comments on Entries option when you first set up the glossary, you and your learners can see small icons at the bottom right of the glossary for each term added. (You can see the icons in the earlier Figure 9-9.)

✔ *Speech bubble icon:* Click the icon, and a text box appears for comments. As with all editing additions and changes in Moodle, you have to click the Save button for Moodle to make changes and return to the term with the new comment right below it.

✔ *Editing and delete icons:* You and your learners can edit and delete the comments.

The comment will appear right under the term and next to the bubble icon. Moodle tells you how many comments are associated with the term. (Figure 9-9 shows one comment.) If you enabled the author details to show, you can link to the author's profile.

Adding categories

To add a category, here's what you do:

1. **On the main glossary page, click the Browse by Category tab.**

   Moodle takes you to the Edit Categories page.

2. **Click the Edit Categories button.**

   Moodle refreshes the screen, taking you to the Categories page, where you can add and edit categories. Click the Add Category button to get to the Add category page shown in Figure 9-10.

Add Category

Name: Learning Styles

Automatically link this category: No ▾ ⑦

Save changes   Back

3. **Give the new category a name and decide whether you want to link the category as well as the term.**

   I recommend against linking the category name because any occurrence of the words will be linked, and when your learners click the link, they're taken to the Browse by Category page instead of the main glossary page. This may be confusing.

4. **Click the Save Changes button, and Moodle returns you to the Add Category page.**

If you don't want to add another category, click the Back button, and Moodle returns you to the Browse by Category page. Notice you can see your new category in the drop-down list located in the right side under the tabs (as shown in Figure 9-11).

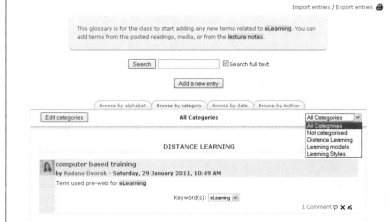

Figure 9-11: Find your category in the drop-down list.

Adding Lessons to Your Course

In Moodle, a *lesson* is an activity that's structured to adapt answers to questions and send learners to different pages of the lesson based on their answers. Moodle adapts to the learner so content can be interesting and ever-changing. Lessons are most useful (and fun) when you're presenting branched or guided content or an assessment activity because these types of lessons enable learners to follow their own paths through the information.

Unlike other activities in Moodle, creating lessons is more complicated, but if you spend time planning them, you will quickly find they aren't as tricky as they may first appear. Taking extra time thinking and organizing your content will benefit the lesson's success and usefulness. Go on; jump in and have fun!

Effectively using lessons with learners

Classroom activities can support various learning styles that involve remembering, understanding, applying, analyzing, evaluating, and creating new knowledge. One of your main goals as an educator is for your learners to put to use new knowledge and be creative. The unique aspect of a Moodle lesson activity over other Moodle activities is that you enable your learners to drive the lesson. Structuring is tied to a learning objective based on the choices learners make on each page. Here are a few examples of how you can use Moodle lessons for instructional and/or assessment purposes:

- ✔ **Branched assignment or quiz:** Set up questions where each correct answer allows the learner to continue; if the learner answers incorrectly, Moodle loops back to display more information before allowing the learner to answer the question again. Question types can be multiple choice, matching, true/false, and essay, though the essays require you to correct them.

- ✔ **Flashcards:** You can set up lessons to test knowledge or for review, like a stack of flashcards (which most learners are familiar with). Vocabulary, multiplication tables, sign language, geography, new policy, quotations, anatomy, periodic table elements — these are just few examples of successful uses of lessons.

- ✔ **Case studies:** Learners are presented with a real-life situation and, as they proceed through the lessons, they need to decide what to do next. For example, case studies have been used with CPR training, where learners need to learn and understand a sequence of steps to save victims from choking or heart attacks.

- ✔ **Role play:** By using simple role play, your learners can take on the persona of a literary character (such as Hamlet or Huck Finn) and answer a set of multiple choice questions leading them to scenarios where they have to demonstrate they have read the material. If the learner chooses an incorrect answer, you can structure the role play to take her back to an explanation, or refer her to specific parts in the book. As stated previously, you need to structure the lesson and decide what type of feedback you use for incorrect answers.

Choosing the right lesson

Before you start building your lesson, you need to decide which type of lesson page style you want to use. Only you will be able to view the page structure; your learners will see only the questions. They will not see that the way they answer the questions determines what they are presented with next, such as the path through the lesson.

- ✔ **Branching page:** Give your learners choices to select an option from a branch presented as a chain of questions. Because there is no correct or incorrect answer for each response, the choices are not graded. When learners complete a chain, they're returned to the branch table and choose another one or end the lesson.

✔ **Question page:** You can set questions requiring your students to provide a correct answer. Depending on the answers you have set up, the learners are taken to another question or looped back. The question page allows you to include information, instructional content, and graphics before displaying the question. You can set scoring for question pages.

Creating lessons

Structuring and organizing your content are the most challenging parts of creating a lesson activity for your learners. Before you start, I recommend drawing a flowchart after deciding which type of lesson you want to set up. The flowchart should include the following:

✔ How you will represent the first page

✔ The number of options you have and where each option leads the learner

✔ Where you want to give feedback or hints

More than one option can lead to the same information. Wherever it makes sense to do so, be sure to reuse pages! Reusing pages keeps your page numbers smaller.

When Albert Einstein was asked about the most difficult part of his work on the theory of relativity, he replied, "thinking about the problem." To assist you with planning and structuring a lesson activity, you can download a template from this book's companion Web site at www.dummies.com/go/moodlefd.

The general settings that come first are similar to settings for other activities (such as the wiki and glossary outlined earlier in this chapter). Dive right in and create a lesson by following these steps:

1. **Click the Turn Editing On button in the top-right corner of your course front page.**

   The front page changes to show editing tools allowing you to change the appearance and add resources and activities to your course. The editing icons are listed on the Cheat Sheet and in Chapter 3.

2. **Locate the week or unit in your course for which you want to add the lesson, click the down arrow next to Add an Activity, and select Lesson from the drop-down list.**

   Moodle takes you to the Adding a New Lesson to Week page, shown in Figure 9-12, which has a similar layout to pages for other activities you may have set up.

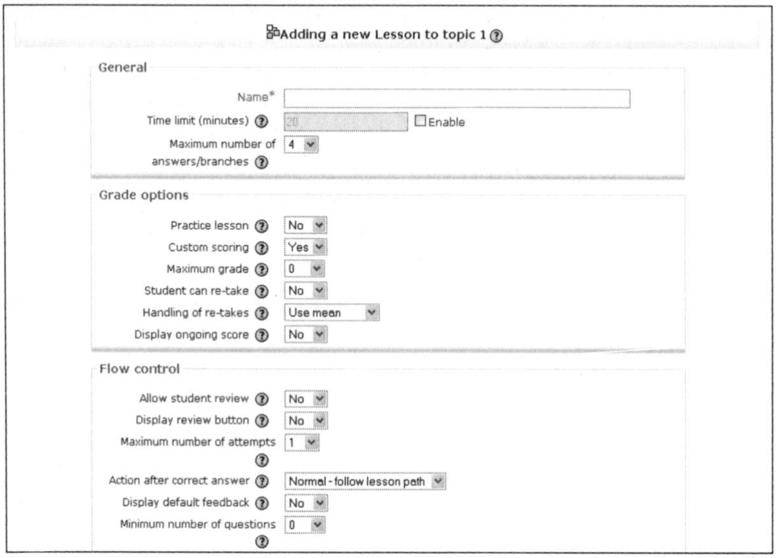

Adding a new Lesson to topic 1 ⑦

General

Name*	
Time limit (minutes) ⑦	20 ☐ Enable
Maximum number of answers/branches ⑦	4 ▾

Grade options

Practice lesson ⑦	No ▾
Custom scoring ⑦	Yes ▾
Maximum grade ⑦	0 ▾
Student can re-take ⑦	No ▾
Handling of re-takes ⑦	Use mean ▾
Display ongoing score ⑦	No ▾

Flow control

Allow student review ⑦	No ▾
Display review button ⑦	No ▾
Maximum number of attempts ⑦	1 ▾
Action after correct answer ⑦	Normal - follow lesson path ▾
Display default feedback ⑦	No ▾
Minimum number of questions ⑦	0 ▾

Figure 9-12:
Add a new
lesson.

Don't let the long list scare you away — I promise most settings can be left as default and updated later. Play, test, get your hands dirty, and have fun!

3. **Fill in the Name field, which is required.**

4. **(Optional) Select the check box next to Enable if you want to set a time limit for the lesson. The field and text come to life. Add the time limit in minutes.**

   By setting a time limit on the lesson, if learners run out of time, Moodle allows them to finish the lesson, but questions are not counted.

5. **Select a number from the Maximum Number of Answers/Branches drop-down list.**

   I advise to choose a higher number so you don't limit yourself. For example, if you put only 4, you're limiting yourself to only four multiple-choice or matching answers or four branches. You can always change the settings later on.

6. **Fill in the Grade Options section if the lesson will be used for assessment.**

   - *Practice Lesson:* Select Yes if you want the lesson to be only used for practice. The scores won't be recorded in the grade book.

   - *Custom Scoring:* Select Yes if you want to score each question independently.

- *Maximum Grade:* Select a value from the drop-down list. I tend to set the grading to 100 unless I know I have a set of 10 or 20 questions and then assign each to be worth 10 or 5 points. Working with 100 gives you the most flexibility. If you leave this setting at 0, Moodle knows you aren't using the lesson for assessment.

- *Student Can Re-Take:* Selecting Yes allows students to go through the lesson questions and re-enter answers. If you set this to Yes, you need to decide how you want Moodle to handle the scoring, which is what the next option is for.

- *Handling of Re-Takes:* From the drop-down list selecting Use Mean or Use Maximum tells Moodle how to assess learners at the end of the lesson if they retake the lesson. If you selected No for the preceding option, Moodle ignores this setting.

- *Display Ongoing Score:* Selecting Yes shows learners how they're doing as they progress through the lesson.

7. **Fill in the Flow Control section (shown at the bottom of Figure 9-12).**

These settings allow you to set how learners will move through the lesson. Learners can move at different paces depending how you set up the reviews, attempts, and feedback in the lesson settings.

- *Allow Student Review:* Selecting Yes allows your learners to move through the lesson again from the start or back and forth to check answers.

- *Display Review Button:* If you select Yes, a review button is displayed under incorrectly answered questions. The learner will see "Yes, I'd like to try again" and "No, I just want to go on to the next question." The learner is given another chance to answer a particular question before a penalty is given.

If you're using essay questions, leave the default setting for Review button set to No because it isn't compatible with this type of assessment.

- *Maximum Number of Attempts:* If you allowed your learners to use the review functionality, you now need to set how many attempts they're allowed before a penalty is set. For example, if you set a matching question with eight different matches, you may set the penalty to 3, meaning the learner can choose three different options before he is penalized for an incorrect answer and moved to the next page.

- *Action after Correct Action:* Select from the drop-down list what you want the learners to see after they answer a question.

Normal - Follow Lesson Path: You want to direct learners to a page following the correct answer.

Show an Unseen Page: You can direct your learners to a randomly selected new page they have not seen before if they answer the question incorrectly. You will find this setting useful with flash-card-type questions and exercises.

Show an Unanswered Page: You can set this option if you want to see the page again, but it will be shown only if they have not answered the question correctly. This setting is most useful with flashcard exercises to give your learners another chance if they did not get a correct answer.

- *Display Default Feedback:* If you don't want to set up your own feedback, leave this setting to Yes. Moodle's default feedback is `That's the correct answer/That's the wrong answer.`

- *Minimum Number of Questions:* Leave the default 0 unless your lesson is set for grading. Learners are told how many questions they have attempted and how many they are expected to attempt before their work is graded. Each learner will have to answer the minimum number generated to receive a grade. If the learner answers fewer questions, his grade will be based on the value at which you set it.

- *Number of Pages (Cards) to Show:* You use this setting only if you're using a flashcard lesson. Select the number of cards you want your learners to view. Once the student sees all the cards, the lesson ends. See the next section for instructions on how to effectively set up a flashcard lesson.

8. **Fill in the Lesson Formatting section.**

   You have to scroll down to see this section, as shown in Figure 9-13.

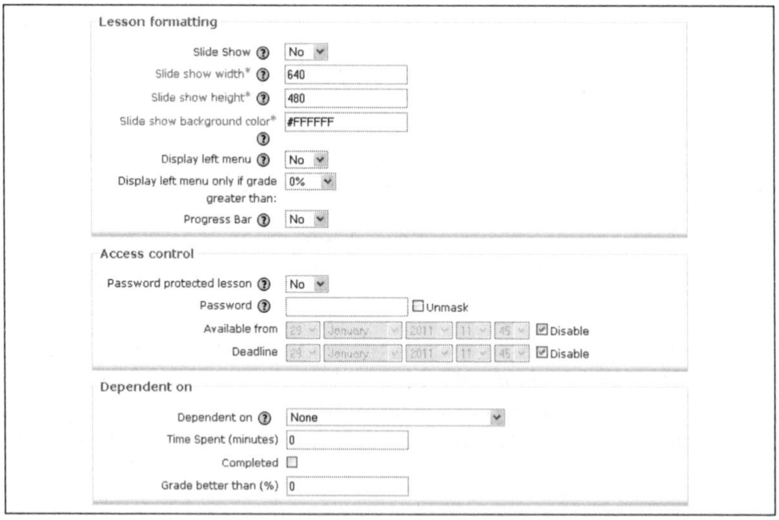

Figure 9-13:
Set your
lesson-
formatting
preferences.

Moodle lets you present the lesson as a slide show. The default is No. If you leave it set to No, you don't need to worry about the following settings.

Selecting Yes from the drop-down list activates the slide show and a few options for customizing it.

- *Slide Show Width and Slide Show Height:* The default settings are same for all the pop-up window options used with the resources. You can make this window smaller or larger, though I recommend you do not make it much smaller than the default.

- *Slide Show Background Color:* The Moodle default is white. Choose a different HTML color code if you want to change the background of the lesson.

Changing the color requires you to enter an HTML character color code reference. Remember to use the six-character HEX value in the field.

- *Display Left Menu:* Selecting Yes displays a navigation bar on the left side allowing your learners to jump slide to slide. Without this bar, learners have to proceed through the slide show in order and exit only when they finish. You can set a percentage grade for learners to achieve before allowing them to jump freely reassuring you they've completed the lesson to an acceptable standard before you allow the freedom to roam.

- *Progress Bar:* Selecting Yes from the drop-down list enables learners to view their progress at the bottom of the lesson page.

9. **Fill in the Access Control section.**

Selecting these settings gives you options to place various restrictions on the lesson.

- *Password Protect Lesson:* If you select Yes, you're required to enter a password. Your learners need to enter it before they can begin the lesson. If you forget your password, selecting the Unmask check box shows you what you've entered.

- *Available From and Deadline:* Entering dates and times in which learners have to complete the lesson.

10. **Select the Dependent On settings.**

These settings allow you to set conditions on the lesson activities preceding the lesson.

If you've set this lesson as a practice lesson or if this is your only lesson, you cannot set dependency values, and Moodle defaults to None. If you have more than one lesson, select the lesson that this one is dependent on from the drop-down list and then make the following selections:

- *Time Spent:* Requires your learners to spend a specific time on the previous lesson. Enter a value in minutes or leave it at 0.

- *Completed:* Requires your learners to have completed the lesson selected.

- *Grade Better Than %:* Setting a required percentage restricts the learners to achieve a certain grade to access the lesson.

11. **Fill in the Pop-Up to File or Web Page section.**

    This section is at the bottom of the Adding a New Lesson page. The options are shown in Figure 9-14.

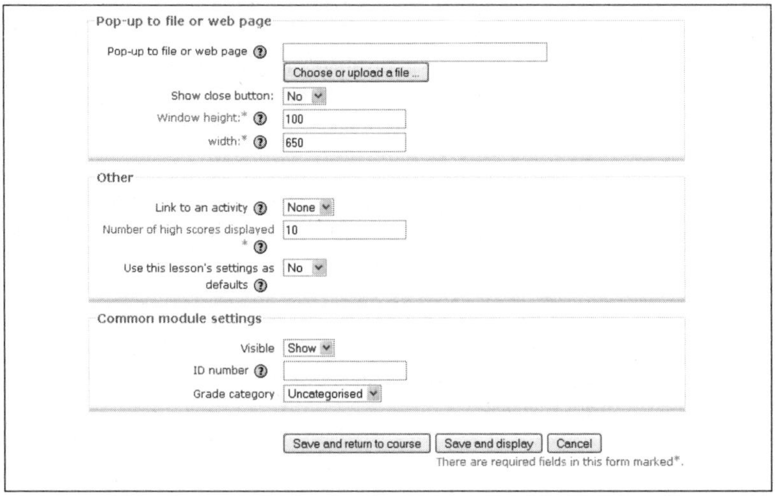

Figure 9-14:
Adjust how windows display.

Click the Choose or Select File button, which is standard to most software and discussed in Chapter 3. The file or page will be displayed in a separate window at the beginning of the lesson.

Enabling a file or a Web page is useful if you want your learners to see, read, or hear a file or Web site before or during the lesson. For example, you can show your learners an image (such as a map) that they can use to answer specific questions. Or you can use a sound file of spoken words for any language course if part of your lesson is built around oral comprehension.

- *Show Close Button:* Default setting No restricts learners to close the window. Selecting Yes allows learners to close it.

- *Window Height and Width:* Change the default settings if you require a different size. You can always go back and change the window after viewing the lesson. Notice that these are required fields.

12. **Review the Other option settings, which give you more flexibility and save you time when creating the next lesson.**

    - *Link to an Activity:* Selecting an activity from the drop-down list will display it at the end of the lesson. All activities you have created will be listed. If you don't choose anything, Moodle will return the learner to the front page.

    - *Number of High Scores Displayed:* This is a required field and ignored if the lesson is set as a practice lesson. Choose a high score, and the learners achieving the highest score will be able to enter their names.

      This feature is useful for igniting the competitive nature of your students, or if they're an inactive bunch, bribery can work.

    - *Use This Lesson's Settings as Defaults:* Selecting Yes will save all your settings for the next lesson you'll be preparing. This is a very useful feature if you need to prepare a series of similar activities, such as flashcards or case studies.

13. **Choose the Common Module Settings as you would have when you set up any Moodle activity and then click the Save and Return to Course button.**

    Chapter 3 describes the Common Module Settings.

    Moodle saves your settings and returns you to the course front page. You can see the newly added lesson icon with its title in the week or unit where you first set it up.

Managing and Administering Lessons

After you set up the core structure of the new lesson for your learners, you can start populating it with content and questions. It isn't as difficult as you may think, but because it's an activity enabling you to create instruction and assessment, it's more time-consuming than some of the other activities — but well worth it!

Checking out a lesson page

After you first create a new lesson, click the lesson icon on the course front page, and Moodle takes you to a How to Add Lessons to Your Class page, with the Edit tab open. (See Figure 9-15.) Here you have four options:

✔ **Import Questions:** Allows you to import from different formats such as Microsoft Word, Hot Potatoes, Blackboard, and Examview, creating a question for each.

✔ **Import PowerPoint:** Slides from a presentation are imported as branch tables, including previous and next answers.

✔ **Add a Branch Table:** Creating a branch table provides your learners with a method of moving through pre-order pages where you create branches or paths. The main difference between branch pages and question pages is that branch pages enable learners to choose their own paths through the information. They don't receive page responses, and moving through the lesson doesn't impact their grade. If you want students to move through the information in a specified order, there's no reason for you to use branch table lessons; instead use the question page.

✔ **Add a Question Page:** Question pages are similar to branch pages but with more exciting functionality. Your learners see content, which is followed up by a response. Answering the question makes Moodle respond with a response and a Continue button that takes them to the appropriate page. You can use question pages for assessment, and the results will show in the learners' grade book.

Figure 9-15:
An editing page for a newly created lesson.

If this is the first time you're creating a lesson, I recommend you start with a question page.

Creating a question page lesson

Question page lessons are ideal for delivering content and a follow-up question or response, ensuring that your learners are assimilating and understanding the content.

To begin, click the Add a Question Page link from the editing page shown earlier in Figure 9-15. It's the last link under Moodle's question, "What would you like to do first?" Moodle takes you to a new Add a Question page (see Figure 9-16), showing six tabs, one for each question type — multiple choice, true/false, short answer, numerical, matching, and essay.

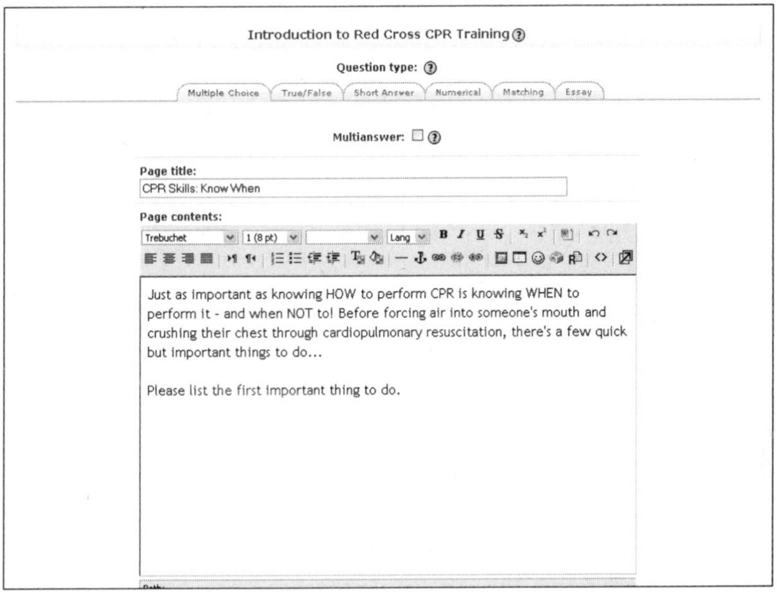

Introduction to Red Cross CPR Training ⑦

Question type: ⑦

| Multiple Choice | True/False | Short Answer | Numerical | Matching | Essay |

Multianswer: ☐ ⑦

Page title:
CPR Skills: Know When

Page contents:

Trebuchet | 1 (8 pt) | | Lang | **B** *I* U S ×₂ ×¹ | | ↶ ↷

Just as important as knowing HOW to perform CPR is knowing WHEN to perform it - and when NOT to! Before forcing air into someone's mouth and crushing their chest through cardiopulmonary resuscitation, there's a few quick but important things to do...

Please list the first important thing to do.

Figure 9-16:
Choose
the type of
question
you'd like
to add.

1. **The Multiple Choice tab should be opened. If not, click the Multiple Choice tab.**

2. **Select the Multianswer check box if your multiple-choice questions require students to choose more than one answer.**

3. **Fill in the Page Title field.**

   Giving the page a descriptive title is useful for you and your learners. You can organize your questions by titles. Your learners can see the title after completing the lesson.

4. **In the Page Contents field, add the page content including your first question.**

   If you're creating a flashcard, entering a question is all you need to do in this part.

5. **In the Answer 1 box, enter a possible answer to the question, as shown in Figure 9-17.**

Answer 1: [Use editor: ☐ ⑦]

> Check the Scene

Response 1: [Use editor: ☐ ⑦]

> Well done! That is the first thing you need to do.
> Make sure it is safe for you to help the person. Don't become a victim
> yourself by rushing to help someone without being sure you will be
> safe. Some examples of this are victims in contact with electric wires,
> victims in traffic, or victims in fires.

Jump 1: Next page ▾ ⑦ Score 1: 100

Answer 2: [Use editor: ☐ ⑦]

> Check the person.

Figure 9-17:
Entering
answer
choices and
responses.

Response 2: [Use editor: ☐ ⑦]

> Important, it's the second thing to do, but not the first. You are
> close, try again.

Jump 2: This page ▾ ⑦ Score 2: 0

Response 3: [Use editor: ☐ ⑦]

> Important, the third thing to do, but not the first. Try again.

Jump 3: This page ▾ ⑦ Score 3: 0

Answer 4: [Use editor: ☐ ⑦]

> Check the airway.

Response 4: [Use editor: ☐ ⑦]

> Very important - it's the 4th thing to do, not the first. Try again

Jump 4: This page ▾ ⑦ Score 4: 0

[Redisplay page] [Save page] [Cancel]

6. In the Response 1 box, enter a response for the answer.

In my example, it's useful to place the first answer as the correct one, so I entered **Well done!** and then gave further explanation. Moodle shuffles the questions and answers every time it displays them to learners.

7. (Optional) Select an option from the Jump 1 drop-down list, which determines what page the learner sees next.

By default, for the Jump 1 drop-down list, Moodle takes the learner to the next page and question. This jump assumes that the first answer was the correct one. You can change the setting to take learners else-where if they make an error.

By default the Jump 2–4 drop-down lists have Next Page selected, assuming answers 2–4 are incorrect.

8. Enter the score for the answer in the Score field.

9. Continue to fill in the following Answer boxes, Response boxes, Jump drop-down lists, and Score fields.

This may sound silly, but be sure you create a correct answer.

10. When you finish, click the Add a Question Page button at the bottom to go to a new lesson construction page.

The four tabs shown in Figure 9-18 allow you to manage your lesson.

- *Preview:* Selecting this tab enables you to view the questions.

- *Edit:* Shown in Figure 9-19, this is your main workspace. Notice right under the Edit tab, two links: Collapsed View and Expanded

View. Collapsed View shows your questions in a table format, allowing you to edit the question, and it has a drop-down list for action functionality.

The Expanded view (shown in Figure 9-20) shows details of the question and offers a number of further options:

Import Questions: Allows you to import questions from your computer's hard drive without having to go back to the main page.

Add a Cluster: You can add specific questions to a cluster, and Moodle randomly chooses the questions. You may find this useful if you want different questions to pop up for different students. Selecting the Random Question within a Cluster option, from the Start Cluster menu enables most options.

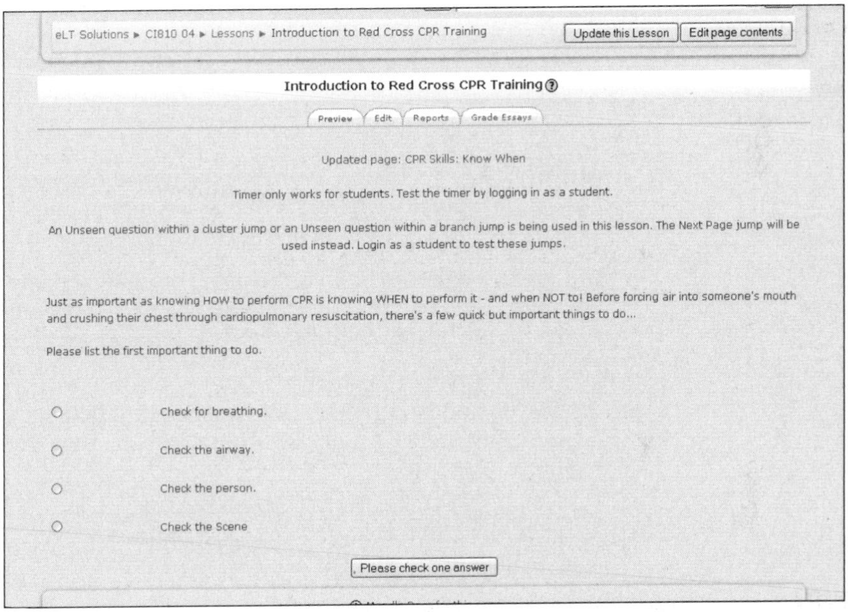

Figure 9-18:
Lesson construction pages with your first question.

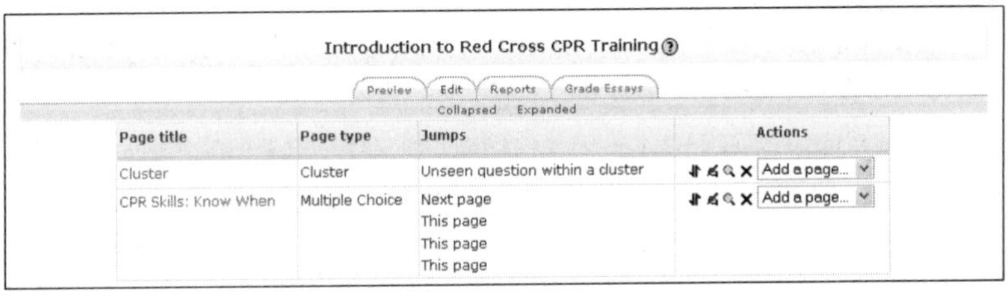

Figure 9-19:
Your main workspace.

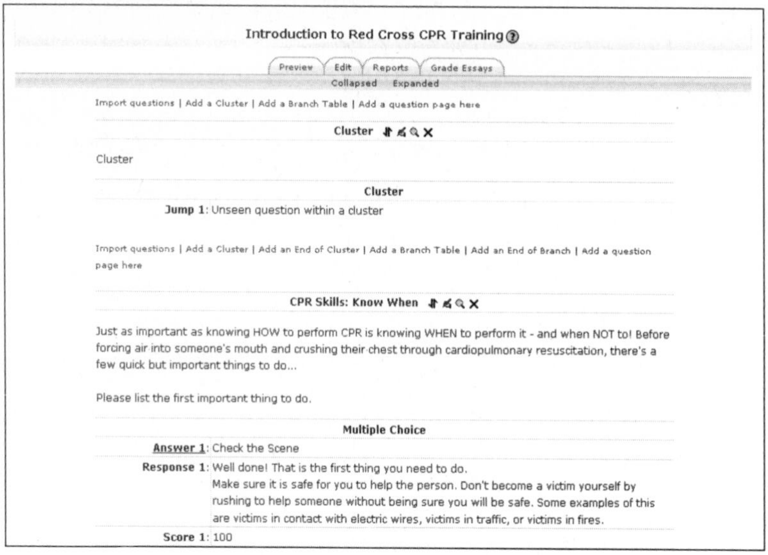

Figure 9-20:
Additional
editing
options.

Add an End of a Cluster: One cluster question has to be designated as an end of a cluster, acting as a jumping point to direct learners to more questions or information pages.

Add an End of Branch: If you're using branching pages and tables, you should end each branch with an *end page,* which directs learners to the last branch table so they can choose another branch or activity.

- *Reports:* Click this tab to see an overview or a detailed report of individual learners' activity within the lesson. The overview is the default setting.

- *Grade Essays:* Clicking this tab leads you to options to grade essay questions. If you didn't set essay questions in the lesson, nothing is displayed under the tab.

The lesson module has many more cool features, functionality, and options such as creating flashcards. Because I don't want to scare you off with too many pages, I offer more instructions with accompanying examples on this book's companion Web site at www.dummies.com/go/moodlefd.

Go on. Start planning your first lesson and have fun. Your learners will think you're the coolest instructor!

Chapter 10

Creating Assignments

● ●

In This Chapter

▶ Using the Assignment module

▶ Constructing online and offline assignments

▶ Managing submissions

● ●

*T*he Moodle Assignment module provides you with means to grade and give feedback on learners' work created online or created offline and then uploaded. The work is not graded automatically, like the Quiz module, though once assigned, you can input the grades and feedback in Moodle, and your learners can view the grades and feedback in their grade books. The Assignment activity module has two broad categories:

✔ **Offline:** Learners can complete work on their computers and then upload the files from their hard drives, or you can present the material offline, in a traditional classroom setting.

✔ **Online:** Learners can complete the assignment requirements online.

You can think of this activity module as a catch-all for anything that you want to set and record in the course Moodle grade book that cannot automatically be marked by the Moodle Quiz module.

Effective Ways to Use Assignments

Instructors can be very creative when selecting and assigning work to their students. You may not necessarily like evaluating performance with a test only. The Assignment module is designed to support you in setting any type of work, and Moodle lists it in a number of places such as the calendar, grade book, and Activities block on the front page. You can give feedback and add grades to the posted assignments. The Assignment module allows learners to do the following:

✔ **Upload content for grading:** This content can include essays, presentations, Web pages, audio or small video clips, spreadsheets, and photograph portfolios that students have completed and saved to their hard drives.

✔ **Complete work online:** Students can write essays and reports and answer questions online.

✔ **Take part in case studies:** Case studies usually have a more entailed process and are completed over time. They usually have several distinct parts, are like puzzles to solve, and are an excellent learning tool that you can use with the Assignment module. A case study usually comprises basic information that defines the problem, a method to resolve the issue, and data that supports the results/conclusion. For disciplines like math, statistics, and engineering, this format may differ and have more distinct parts than medical, law, or business case studies. For example, I set up a case study for my graduate school learners; it involved setting up a scenario of students taking a course online, giving the graduate learners some information about the makeup of the class (student demographics), and asking them to look at different learning styles and how they can be supported in an online environment. Next, I asked them to set up a demo course online and then test it with a few students. Finally, I asked my learners to report their findings and write a summary.

✔ **Participate in project work:** For example, when I teach Moodle courses, I assign mini projects requiring learners to set up various Moodle activities. These are set and listed as assignments, and I mark them offline, and then give a grade and feedback to the learners in Moodle online, and the grades are published to the grade book along with the feedback.

The Moodle Assignment module is set up with four assignment types that give you flexibility to set work, review and mark the work, and then later add feedback to the assignments. The four types are

✔ **Upload Single File:** Learners can upload a file in any format, including a Zip file.

✔ **Offline Activity:** This can be any activity performed outside of class that cannot be viewed or assessed by Moodle. An offline activity may be, for instance, a presentation, debate, play, or a physical creation (such as a model of something a learner had designed).

✔ **Online Text:** Learners add text online; for example, writing an essay. You can view it online, grade it, and add inline comments. Clearly outline your objectives in the syllabus and instructions online, and then guide your learners to meet the requirements. For instance, if a student is expected to write an essay online, either instruct her to prepare in advance and to not leave the Moodle session for more than half an hour or inform her about Moodle timing. If learners need to leave the session, they can add a note, submit the assignment as-is, and then return later to finish. Online text assignments are often used for reflective work, with or without instructor feedback, and can be a useful learning activity. They tend not to be used for exams. (The essay question in the Quiz module is better suited for this type of assessment because you can control the timing and security settings.)

✔ **Advanced Uploading of Files:** This type of assignment permits learners and instructors to enter notes and upload new versions. For example, a learner can upload a draft with comments and questions, the instructor can comment on the draft, and then the student can access the feedback and upload a final version. The instructor then enters the assignment grade and adds feedback.

Creating Assignments

After you decide what type of assignment you're going to set, the procedure is not very complex. Follow these steps:

1. **Click the Turn Editing On button.**

   The front page changes to show editing tools, allowing you to change the appearance and add functionality to your course.

2. **From the Add an Activity drop-down list, choose an assignment.**

   Note the four types of assignments, described in the preceding section, are listed here. Make sure you choose the drop-down list in the section (or week) you want it to appear in your course.

   Moodle takes you to the Adding a New Assignment page, as shown in Figure 10-1.

3. **In the General area, fill in the fields accordingly.**

Figure 10-1: The Adding a New Assignment page, General settings.

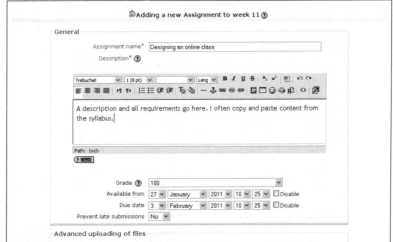

Anything marked with an asterisk is required.

- *Assignment Name:* Give the assignment a descriptive name.

- *Description:* In the Description text area, you can explain the assignment in detail, add requirements, and state how you will assess the work.

  Be as clear and concise as possible. Bullet points may help here. I usually copy and paste from my syllabus so there's no confusion.

  Don't copy straight from Word or any other type of file; you'll copy the code, which will make your content look sloppy, filled with code characters. Use Notepad or the Clean Word tool located in the text box's toolbar).

- *Grade:* Select the grading scale from the drop-down list.

- *Available From and Due Date:* Add the date and time by using the drop down-lists. You set when you plan to make the assignment available and when it's due. If dates are not important, select the Disable check boxes.

  Notify your students that the Upload box doesn't appear on the assignment listing until the date from when the assignment is available. Not seeing an Upload box may cause confusion when students look at the assignment and don't see the usual field with a Browse button and an Upload button. I usually explain how the uploaded process works in the description text area when I set the assignment.

- *Prevent Late Submissions:* If you will be accepting late submissions after the due date specified, leave the default No; otherwise, choose Yes from the drop-down list.

4. Select the appropriate options for the type of assignment you chose in Step 2.

Note, General settings and Common Module settings are the same for all four types of assignments. Sections below explain unique option setting for each.

If you chose Advanced Uploading of Files (see Figure 10-2), make these choices:

- *Maximum Size:* The maximum course upload, listed at the bottom of the drop-down list, is set by Moodle admin. You can make changes to this in your course settings. If your learners will be uploading video or sound files, make sure you allocate enough space.

- *Allow Deleting:* Decide whether students can delete uploaded files before they're due.

- *Maximum Number of Uploaded Files:* From the drop-down list, choose how many files learners can upload for the assignment. The Moodle default is 3, but you can choose up to 20. Note that learners don't see this number. If you require a number of different uploads for the assignment, to avoid confusion, inform your learners in the description and syllabus that they can upload the required number of assignments.

- *Allow Notes:* If useful to the learning goals and assignment, you can enable notes, which allow your learners to add notes in a text box when they upload the assignment. Notes can be useful if students want to add any instructions, have questions, or want to bring your attention to any aspect of the assignment. Another good communication tool!

- *Hide Description before Available Date:* Select Yes if you want the students to be able to see the description of the assignment. I usually leave the default No, unless it affects the assignments.

- *Email Alerts to Teachers*: Select Yes if you want to be alerted every time a student uploads a file. The default setting is No.

- *Enable Send for Marking:* Decide whether you want to be alerted by an e-mail when your learners are ready for the assignment to be marked. The default is set to Yes.

If you chose Online Text Assignment, select the same options as for Advanced Uploading of Files Assignment, except the following choices.

- *Allow for Resubmitting:* Select Yes, if you want to allow students to resubmit assignments after they've been graded. The default setting is No.

- *Comment Inline:* Select Yes if you intend to comment inline or edit the original text. Moodle will copy the submissions into a feedback comment field when you're grading. The default setting is No.

For the Upload a Single file assignment, all the options are the same as in the two previous assignments.

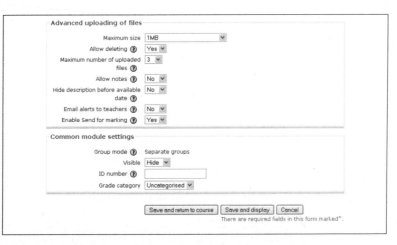

Figure 10-2:
The Adding a New Assignment page, Advanced Uploading of Files and Common Module Settings sections.

Offline Activity is the simplest assignment type to deal with, in terms of selecting options. All functionality is explained in the first two assignments. If you choose to grade the activity, it's listed in the grade book, and you can enter the grades and comments just as with the other three assignment types.

   5. Choose the Common Module Settings. (See Figure 10-2.)

   Make choices here as you would when you set up any Moodle activity.

   6. Click the Save and Return to Course button.

   Moodle saves your settings and returns to your course front page. Notice that the assignment has its own unique icon, and it also appears in the Activities block, the Upcoming Events block, and the course calendar. Note, if you click the Save and Display button, Moodle shows you the Assignment page instead of taking you to the course front page. This is useful if you want to verify how it appears and to check for errors. If you're happy with it, use the navigation bar to return to your course front page, but if you want to make changes to the Assignment, click the Update the Assignment button located on the right side in the navigation bar.

Administering Assignment Submissions

Only a few administrative tasks are involved with assignment submissions and upkeep. Moodle adds useful functionality for you to view submissions. When you're ready to mark and/or comment on students work, the following tools make your job easier.

   ✓ **Viewing students' submissions:** You can view student's submissions in two ways. You can click the Assignment link in the Activities block, and Moodle takes you to a table that lists all the assignments by week/topic assigned, tells you what type the assignment is, states the due date, and tells how many were submitted and what the grades are. (See Figure 10-3.) This is a very useful overview. Each assignment name is a link that takes you to that specific assignment. If you click the View *X* Submitted Assignments link, Moodle takes you to an Assignment Submissions page like the one shown in Figure 10-4.

   Another way to access the assignment is from the course front page. By clicking the name of the individual assignment, Moodle takes you to new page listing the assignment description and another link in top-right corner informing you how many assignments have been submitted. Select this link by clicking it. Moodle takes you to the Assignment Submissions page like the one shown in Figure 10-4. Notice this page is set up as a table with headings First Name/Surname; Grade; Comment; Last Modified (Student); Last Modified (Teacher); and Status. You can sort the list by clicking the heading.

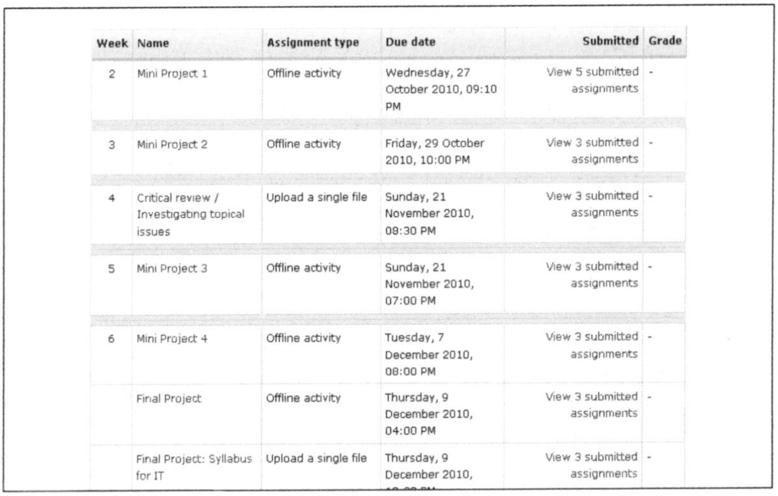

Week	Name	Assignment type	Due date	Submitted	Grade
2	Mini Project 1	Offline activity	Wednesday, 27 October 2010, 09:10 PM	View 5 submitted assignments	-
3	Mini Project 2	Offline activity	Friday, 29 October 2010, 10:00 PM	View 3 submitted assignments	-
4	Critical review / Investigating topical issues	Upload a single file	Sunday, 21 November 2010, 08:30 PM	View 3 submitted assignments	-
5	Mini Project 3	Offline activity	Sunday, 21 November 2010, 07:00 PM	View 3 submitted assignments	-
6	Mini Project 4	Offline activity	Tuesday, 7 December 2010, 08:00 PM	View 3 submitted assignments	-
	Final Project	Offline activity	Thursday, 9 December 2010, 04:00 PM	View 3 submitted assignments	-
	Final Project: Syllabus for IT	Upload a single file	Thursday, 9 December 2010,	View 3 submitted assignments	-

Figure 10-3: A table that details all assignments.

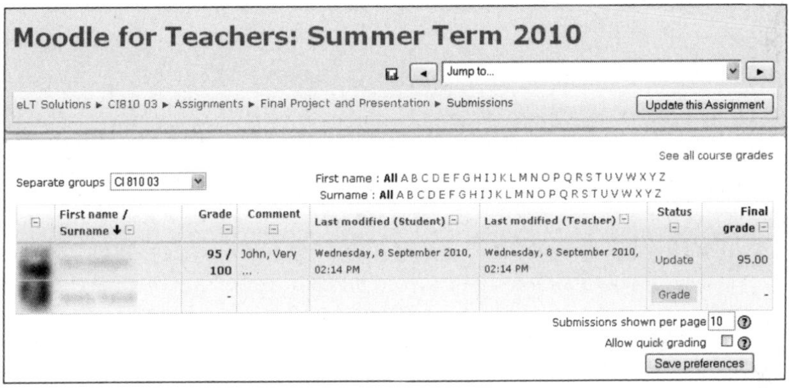

Figure 10-4: The Assignment Submissions page.

- **Grading students' submissions:** To grade a submission, click the Grade button in the Status column on the right. (See Figure 10-4.) Moodle takes you to the Student's Assignment Grade and Feedback page, as shown in Figure 10-5. The look and feel of the feedback page and links are identical for all assignment types with slight differences to compensate for the diversity of functionality.
  - *Upload a Single File and Advanced Uploading of Files:* The main difference is that you have a link to access the uploaded document located in the bottom-right corner. If it's a Web page, you can open it in the browser. A Word document also opens, but if you want to make comments, you need to save it to your hard drive. For Advanced Uploading of Files, you also can use a response file to give students feedback. When students are finished with the final document, they click Submit for Marking.

- *Online Text:* You can view the submission in a separate box with the word count located above. If you've enabled the inline comment option when setting up the assignment, Moodle copies the text into the feedback comment box.

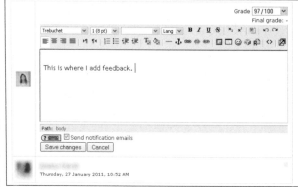

Figure 10-5:
The
Assignment
Grade and
Feedback
page.

When you finish reviewing and commenting on the assignments, choose the grade from the drop-down list located in the top-left corner, add comments in the comments box, and select the Save Changes or Save Changes and Show Next button.

Two more neat functionalities are located in the grade window. If you want to grade multiple assignments, all on the same page, select the Allow for Quick Grading check box in the bottom left of the assignment Submissions page. All you need to do is add grades and make comments and then click the Save All My Feedback button. Remember that you can access students' profiles by clicking their names, which may be useful if you want to add a note, as discussed in Chapter 8.

All assignment types have the Grade drop-down list located in the top-right corner. Below the drop-down list, Moodle tells you whether the grade is final. The textbox is very useful for feedback and to highlight any aspect of the project or assignment. Below the feedback text area, select the check box if you want the learner notified by e-mail that the assignment has been graded. This is useful if you're giving feedback on drafts of an assignment. At the bottom, you have four buttons: Save Changes, Cancel, Save and Show Next, and Next. The first two buttons are self-explanatory; the latter two each take you to the next learner in your class list.

Chapter 11

Quizzing and Testing in Moodle

In This Chapter

▶ Using assessment creatively to give learners a positive experience

▶ Crafting the Quiz module to create worksheets, quizzes, and tests

▶ Setting up various question formats that you can reuse

▶ Adding, editing, and previewing questions

▶ Collecting data on all aspects of your assessment activity

Some form of assessment is important in training and education. Instructors spend time evaluating performance and even more time giving feedback to learners. As an educator, you may not like using quizzes and tests to measure performance, but often they're required by the organization providing a certificate of accomplishment or a degree. In an online learning environment, if you aren't interacting with your learners, then setting quizzes, tests, and assignments is the only way you can validate that your learners are remembering, understanding, and demonstrating they are able to apply what you're teaching them.

With Moodle's Quiz module, you can set up a variety of assessment activities to accomplish course outcomes and requirements. Moodle computerized assessment is designed to take marking off your hands and enables you to add feedback for each question or overall feedback for a series of questions. Imagine, writing feedback only once! Moodle can also manipulate questions to randomly shuffle multiple-choice answers and matching questions within the question, and you can control questions to be shuffled between attempts. Possibilities seem endless when you start using this module.

Looking at the Testing Features

The Moodle Quiz module is slightly more complex than some of the other modules. It comprises of two separate parts: the *quiz body*, what your learners see and interact with in your Moodle course, and the *question bank*, which holds all the questions you create. The question bank is like a wardrobe for all your questions. Your wardrobe contains shelves (question categories), where you group questions depending on topics, themes, units, semesters, or any other category you currently use to organize your courses.

The Question Bank module is separate, allowing you to create, hold, reuse, and combine your questions in any combination. Your question bank can comprise multiple-choice, true/false, short answer, numerical short answer, matching, random short-answer matching, calculated, essay, and embedded answers (Cloze).

If you're wondering about that last one, the Cloze question type comprises a piece of text from which a number of words have been removed. A learner is required to insert the missing word(s). In some cases, the missing words are supplied as a single list, from which the student has to select, which in effect is matching a word with the space where it belongs. It's just a matching question.

Moodle also includes *description* questions, which are really just holding spaces for you to add instructions, pictures, or anything else between a set of questions. Moodle added this functionality, enabling you to include notes or instructions in some of the question types or between question types, because the question setup features don't leave space for instructions.

The neat aspect of populating your categories with questions is that you can reuse them as many times as you like and in as many courses as you like. As your question bank grows, it becomes a valuable, time-saving resource.

The Quiz module has considerable flexibility, allowing you to use it for more than just setting quizzes and tests. Here are few examples of how instructors use Moodle quizzes:

- ✓ **Worksheets:** Although Moodle calls this module a quiz, you can set it up with any assignment title. For example, if you're creating practice worksheets for foreign language courses, you can call it "French nouns worksheet 1." Creating worksheets is one way you and your learners can ease into using the module before using it for formal quizzes and test. Moodle marks your worksheets and records them in the grade book. You can exclude worksheets from the grade book if you prefer not to add scores to the final course grade.

- ✓ **Self assessment:** Setting up quizzes for learners to measure their knowledge is easy. You can set the quiz settings for repeat practice at specified time intervals. You have the option of showing learners correct answers and feedback, or you can choose to hide the correct answers and just provide feedback. Like the worksheets, you can exclude self-assessment quizzes from the grade book.

✓ **Timed and secured tests:** Moodle enables you to time your tests and to set them for specific dates. Moodle includes security provisions that prevent learners from accessing the Internet. You can also use IP addresses and secure individual computers.

✓ **Short quizzes or test to evaluate topics:** Quiz tools allow you to set frequent, short quizzes. You can use a combination of all question types or stick with one style (for example, multiple choice).

✓ **Graphical enhancements:** Moodle lets you import graphics into your questions. This feature is very useful for basic identification exercises. For example, you can upload a map and ask learners to identify countries and cities, or upload a picture of a skeleton and ask learners to identify bones.

Creating a Quiz Body

Setting up the quiz body requires you to choose a number of settings and create parameters for how your learners will interact with the quiz. You're creating a repository for your questions, which are stored somewhere else in the Moodle engine. (See the later section, "Creating a question bank.")

To create the quiz body, follow these steps:

1. **Click the Turn Editing On button in the upper-right corner of your course front page.**

   The front page changes to show editing tools, allowing you to change the appearance and add functionality to your course. The editing tools are listed on the book's Cheat Sheet at Dummies.com and in Chapter 3.

2. **Click the down arrow next to Add an Activity in the section/week where you want the quiz to appear, and select Quiz from the drop-down list.**

   Moodle takes you to the Adding a New Quiz setup page, shown in Figure 11-1.

3. **In the Name text box, fill in the quiz name.**

   Use descriptive names that will make sense to your learners. If you're using the Quiz module to set a worksheet, name it just that (for example, "French Verbs Set 1").

4. **In the Introduction text area, explain the quiz in detail, add requirements, and state how you will assess the work.**

   Be as clear and concise as possible. Bullet points may help here. I usually copy and paste from my syllabus so there's no confusion.

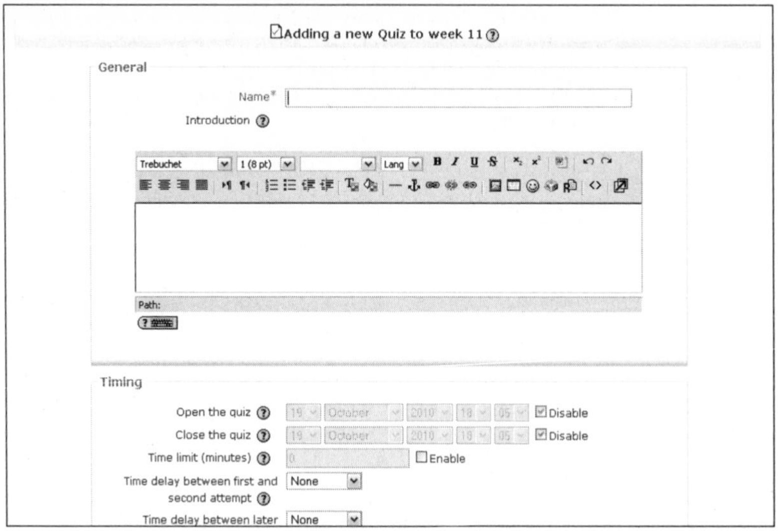

Figure 11-1:
Adding
a quiz.

5. **Set the following Timing preferences if you intend to place a time limit on when the quiz is opened and closed and how long the learners have to take the quiz:**

    • *Open the Quiz and Close the Quiz:* Dates when the quiz will be available to take and when it closes. To activate the date entry boxes, deselect the Disable check box, and the fields are made available for editing.

    • *Time Limit (Minutes):* Selecting the Enable check box permits you to set a time limit for your quiz. Enter the time in whole numbers. Remember that you're setting the time in minutes.

    • *Time Delay between First and Second Attempt:* Set the time for how long your learners have to complete the quiz between the first and second attempt. From the drop-down list, select the time. (Your options are from 0 to 7 days.) If you don't want to enable more than one attempt, leave the default, None.

    • *Time Delay between Later Attempts:* Set the time for how long your learners have to complete the quiz after the second attempt. Select the time (your options are from 0 to 7 days) from the drop-down list. If you don't want to enable more than two attempts, leave the default of None.

6. **In the Display section, shown in Figure 11-2, specify how questions will be displayed to your learners.**

    • *Questions per Page:* Decide how many questions you want to be displayed on each page. Select the number from the drop-down list. I suggest you shoot for higher numbers so you aren't limited if you decide to add more. If the questions exceed the page size, a default navigation button appears at the bottom.

- *Shuffle Questions:* Decide whether you want questions shuffled between attempts.

- *Shuffle within Questions:* Decide whether you want answers within questions shuffled between attempts (only for multiple choice and matching).

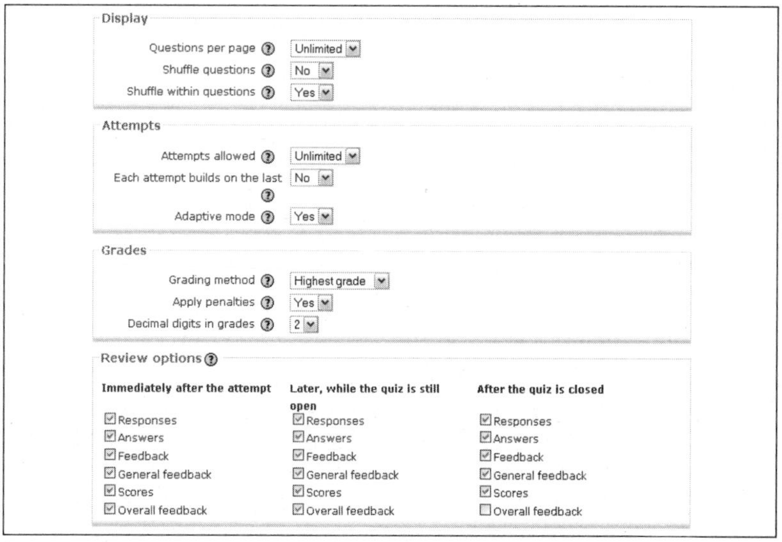

Figure 11-2:
Choosing
quiz
settings.

Display

Questions per page ⑦	Unlimited ▾
Shuffle questions ⑦	No ▾
Shuffle within questions ⑦	Yes ▾

Attempts

Attempts allowed ⑦	Unlimited ▾
Each attempt builds on the last ⑦	No ▾
Adaptive mode ⑦	Yes ▾

Grades

Grading method ⑦	Highest grade ▾
Apply penalties ⑦	Yes ▾
Decimal digits in grades ⑦	2 ▾

Review options ⑦

Immediately after the attempt	Later, while the quiz is still open	After the quiz is closed
☑ Responses	☑ Responses	☑ Responses
☑ Answers	☑ Answers	☑ Answers
☑ Feedback	☑ Feedback	☑ Feedback
☑ General feedback	☑ General feedback	☑ General feedback
☑ Scores	☑ Scores	☑ Scores
☑ Overall feedback	☑ Overall feedback	☐ Overall feedback

7. **In the Attempts section, set the number of attempts you like to allow, along with grade penalties. You have these three different settings to consider:**

- *Attempts Allowed:* From the drop-down list, select how many times you will allow learners to take the quiz. The default is set to Unlimited. Your options are 1–10 attempts.

- *Each Attempt Builds on the Last:* This option is useful if you're using the quiz as a practice exercise. If you set the drop-down list to Yes, learners can see their incorrect responses when they retake the quiz.

- *Adaptive Mode:* Set this option to Yes if you want to let the learners try to answer the question again, but want to apply a small penalty to the score. Moodle provides an extra button for the learner to submit the answer. The learner sees the result right away with the score and can try again immediately. The learner has a choice of whether to take a chance at a penalty or keep the original incorrect answer.

8. **In the Grades section, these settings enable you to decide on grade settings:**

   - *Grading Method:* If you allow your learners to take the quiz more than once, select an option from the drop-down list to determine how Moodle records the grades. Your options are Highest Grade, Average of All Attempts, first Attempt, and Last Attempt. If learners have only one shot at the quiz, Moodle ignores this setting.

   - *Apply Penalties:* From the drop-down list, select No if you don't want penalties applied if you're running Adaptive mode.

   - *Decimal Digits in Grades:* Moodle calculates grades to the number of set decimal points. The default is 2, but you can choose 0–3.

9. **In the Review Options area, Moodle provides you with a number of options to control when and how learners receive feedback. They can receive feedback during these timeframes:**

   - *Immediately after the Attempt:* Usually within one to two minutes after clicking the Submit All and Finish button.

   - *Later, after the Quiz Is Still Open:* Within a few minutes if the quiz is still opened. If there's no ending for the quiz, learners can see feedback anytime.

   - *After the Quiz Is Closed:* Immediately after.

   For each timeframe, you also have a series of choices on what information you include in the feedback.

   - *Responses:* What the learner entered for each question.

   - *Answers:* The learner is shown the correct answers to each question.

   - *Feedback:* Learners see the feedback you added for each response to each question — it's question-specific.

   - *General Feedback:* Not specific to learners' responses. One response is given for the question. This feedback may be useful to give extra information, such as links or references, to increase learners' understanding of the topic.

   - *Scores:* Moodle displays the scores that the learner collects for each question.

   - *Overall Feedback:* Displayed to learners after they complete the whole quiz, and feedback depends on the overall score received. The feedback is part of this setup. (Instructions are available in Step 12.)

Make sure you select check boxes in only one set of timeframes; otherwise, the learners may not be able get back in the quiz again. For instance, if you're choosing for learners to see feedback immediately after the quiz, don't select the Later, While the Quiz Is Still Open check box or the After the Quiz Is Closed check box.

10. **In the Security section, shown in Figure 11-3, you have a set of browser and computer security settings preventing students from cheating on the quizzes by venturing off to the Internet, copying and pasting, accessing thumb drives, and so on. Here are the areas you can control:**

Figure 11-3:
Modifying
security
settings.

- *Browser Security:* From the drop-down list, select Full Screen Pop-Up with Some JavaScript Security. Learners need a JavaScript-enabled Web browser. (Most browsers are JavaScript enabled unless that functionality has been turned off.) Moodle brings up the quiz in a new, full-screen pop-up window without any navigational features such as an address bar, forward and back buttons, and so on.

- *Require Password:* You can assign a password in the field, which learners need to input before they can take the quiz. Requiring a password is useful if you want different groups of learners taking the quiz at different times. A Moodle feature I love is the Unmask check box next to the password entry field. It allows you to view the password you entered by simply selecting the check box. No need to keep a record of all your Moodle passwords!

- *Require Network Address:* If you want learners to take a test in a lab and/or you need to set proctored tests, this feature allows you to restrict the test so that it's available only on a set of computers that have a range of IP addresses. For example, if you want to make it available on 30 computers with an IP range from 125.125.125.25 to 125.125.125.55, in the field enter **125.125.125.25/55**.

You may require your IT administrator's help identifying the IP numbers. Moodle allows you three options: Full IP Addresses, which specifies individual computers on a network; Partial Addresses, which matches computers with the first two sets of numbers; and CIDR, which allows you to use only an IP prefix.

11. **In the Common Module Settings section, choose the Common Module Settings as you would when you set up any Moodle activity.**

I discuss Common Module Settings in Chapter 3.

In the next section, Overall Feedback, you can specify what feedback is shown to learners after they finish the quiz.

12. **In the Grade Boundary text box, enter the grade as a percentage, and in the Feedback text box, enter the text that you want to appear onscreen.**

If you run out of fields for boundaries and feedback, click the Add 3 More Feedback Fields button at the bottom of the page, and Moodle opens the new fields.

Your feedback is based on overall scores received by individual learners. Moodle sets up fields for grade boundaries starting with 100%. (The 0% and 100% are added automatically by Moodle, although you add your own feedback. Remaining boundaries are up to you.) For example,

- Grade boundary: 100%

- Feedback: "Absolutely fabulous."

- Grade boundary: 90%

- Feedback: "Well done; showed you studied."

- Grade boundary: 40%

- Feedback: "See me as soon as possible."

The grade boundary feedback is based on the % and better. So in the preceding example, learners with 90% to 99% would see the "Well done; showed you studied" comment. Learners with 40% to 89% would see the "See me as soon as possible" comment. I recommend setting these boundaries in increments appropriate for your grading scale.

If you want to enter more feedback than the fields shown, click the Add 3 More Feedback Fields button. You can do this several times, setting up a detailed range.

If you're getting an error message such as "boundaries must be between 0% and 100%" (and they are), first check that the Maximum Grade for this quiz is set to something greater than zero. (I tell you how to adjust that setting later in the chapter in the "Questions in this quiz" section.) If that is entered correctly, check what you have entered into the Grade

Boundary fields, making sure you enter only one % grade in each, such as 50%. It's very tempting to add a range such as 65–70%, but that will cause the error message. If you want specific feedback for 65% to 70%, just type **71%** into one Grade Boundary field, enter **65%** into the Grade Boundary field below it, and add the appropriate feedback for both. Moodle gives the feedback for the 65% to 70% range.

13. **Click the Save and Return to Course button.**

   Moodle saves your settings and returns to your course front page. Notice that the Quiz module has its own unique icon that appears in the Activities block, Upcoming Events block, and the course calendar.

Creating Quiz Questions

After you've finished setting up the quiz body, as described in the preceding section, you're ready to start adding questions to your quiz. Before you can add questions, you need to set up your question categories and then the question bank. Be sure to start by setting up categories in which to organize your questions even if you're just playing around. Over time, the categories will help you find specific questions to add to your quizzes, tests, and worksheets.

Setting up categories

Think of a question category as a folder you have set up on your computer. When creating questions, you can store them in these categories similar to the way you store files in your folders. You can set up subcategories as your question bank grows.

Setting up categories is purely for you to keep a potentially very large bank of questions organized, making it easier to search when adding the questions to your worksheets, quizzes, or tests. Each category must have a name, and you can include a short description. You can create a hierarchy and specify a parent category for each set of questions. This enables you to separate categories into categories, subcategories, sub-subcategories, and so on.

Before beginning, think of a naming convention that's intuitive to your courses and topics. You can set up categories any which way that works for you. For example, you name a Parent category Chemistry 101, and subcategories by theme: Science of Chemistry, Matter and Energy, Atomic Structure and Electron Configuration, and so on. This way, you will have a set of questions in each subcategory from which you can pull questions for quizzes, tests, reviews, mid-term, and so on. Another Parent category can be AP Chemistry, with similar subcategories. This will then enable you to choose easy and harder questions for various assignments.

To set up a category, you need to go to the editing page of your quiz.

1. **If this is your first time setting up a category and questions, select the quiz you just created from your course front page.**

   Alternatively, you can select Questions from the Administrative block on your course front page.

   Moodle takes you to the Editing Quiz page shown in Figure 11-4. Note that if you click the Questions link from the Administration block, the page looks slightly different, but tabs and functionality are the same. More frequently, teachers use this process to create questions after setting up categories.

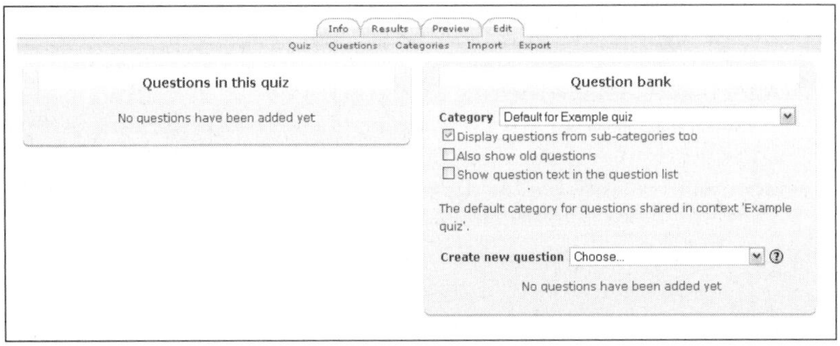

Figure 11-4:
The Editing
Quiz page.

2. **From the Edit tab, click the Categories link.**

   Moodle takes you to a list of default categories, as shown in Figure 11-5. You see headings for the quiz, course, category for your course, and system. Aim to store your categories either under the default course category or create your own categories.

3. **Scroll down until you see the Add Category section shown in Figure 11-6. From the Parent drop-down list, select the parent category that will contain your new category.**

   I recommend that you use your course name as the parent.

4. **In the Name text box, give the category name.**

   For example, enter **Moodle for Teachers**.

5. **In the Category Info box, describe the category.**

   I usually state the courses that will use questions from this category.

6. **Click the Add Category button to save your new category.**

   Notice that when Moodle saves the category and returns you to the category lists, you can edit, delete, and move the categories. Clicking the icons to the right of the name allows you to make any changes.

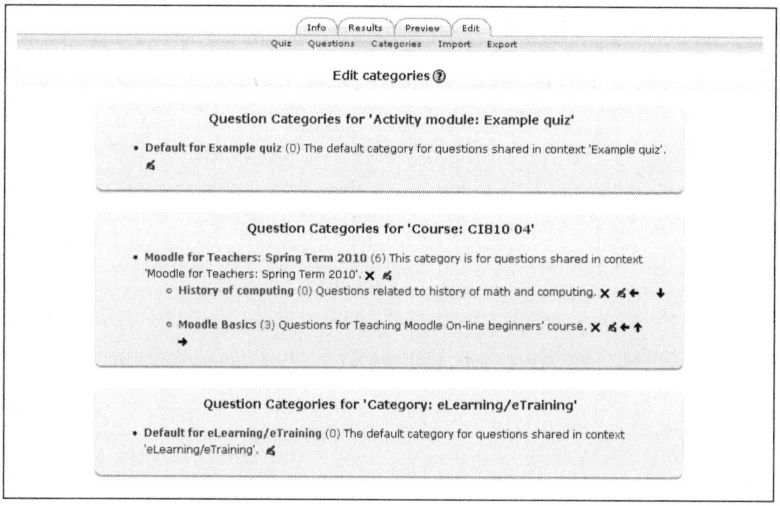

Figure 11-5:
The Edit
Categories
page.

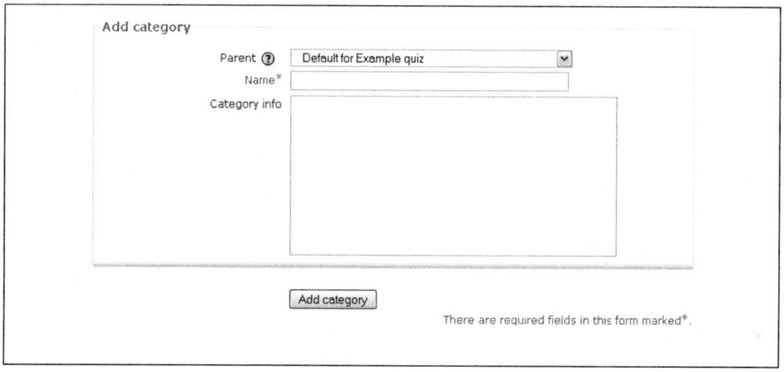

Figure 11-6:
Adding
question
categories.

Creating a question bank

After creating categories, you're ready to start creating questions to populate the categories and then add them to your quiz. Moodle has ten types of questions you can create and add to your quizzes. You can mix and match them however you want when adding them to the quiz. There is no predetermined order, question number, and question type required by Moodle. You're in complete control of your quiz's questions and structure.

The question types in the Moodle drop-down list are as follows:

✔ **Calculated:** These types of questions are used for mathematical equations. You set up holders for specific mathematical values that are listed in the Moodle dataset. For example, you can ask students to calculate the area of a triangle by inputting 1/2 * {base} * {height}.

✔ **Description:** This is actually not a question type. It is purely a text box you embed between questions so that you can add instructions. For instance, when you come to a new set of questions that require extra information, you can add instructions for the new set, or you can add a few paragraphs and ask students to read the text and then answer a series of questions. You can also embed graphics. You will find Description useful, as most of the question types don't have input fields for instructions.

✔ **Essay:** Use essay questions for short answers; I advise no more than two paragraphs. You need to mark each essay question and assign the grades manually. If you require your learners to write a longer essay, use the Online Text Assignment module.

✔ **Matching:** This question type is represented by two columns, where text from one column must be matched with content in the other. For example, a line from a poem should be matched with the poet. I suggest that you enter the longer statement in the left column and the shorter statement in the right column, as the matches appear in a drop-down list. So in the poetry example, the line from the poem would be on the left, and authors on the right.

✔ **Embedded Answers (Cloze):** This question type allows you to embed answers such as multiple choice, short answer, and numerical answers in the text. You can embed more than one answer type and any combination. Language and math teachers like this question type.

You need to embed the syntax for the question type in the text in order for the Moodle engine to recognize it, or you need to use third-party quiz software, such as Hot Potatoes, to embed answers. Detailed explanation of the syntax is beyond the scope of this book. Check `http://docs.moodle.org/en/Question_bank` for a detailed explanation and examples.

✔ **Multiple Choice:** This is a familiar question type bundled with a few extras. Moodle can shuffle answers within the question. Moodle lets you select multiple answers, you can add feedback for every answer, and you can assign positive or negative grades, which discourages guessing or if you allow for your learners to take the test more than once.

✔ **Short Answer:** This question type requires learners to type in a word or phrase. Moodle allows you to choose case sensitivity, a wildcard answer (described in the upcoming "Short answer" section), and feedback. I advise you to keep answers short and add several acceptable answers. The only way Moodle can mark this is by matching text exactly. You do have an option to override the answer, though that defeats the purpose of Moodle automatic grading taking that workload off your shoulders.

I tend to go back to short answer questions only if too many students are getting them wrong, or if a student has a borderline grade.

✔ **Numerical:** This is just like the short answer question with extra functionality allowing you to set an accepted error range for each answer. For example, if the answer is 50, you can set up the accepted error of 3, meaning that 47, 50, and 53 would be evaluated as correct.

✔ **Random Short-Answer Matching:** For learners, this question looks just like matching; however, you provide several answers for each subquestion. So instead of two long lists as in the matching question, each subquestion has two to three possible choices. See Figure 11-7 for an example of how this question looks when presented to learners. Notice that the question has three subquestions and a drop-down list for each.

✔ **True/False:** Learners are given two choices for each question, true or false. The format for setting this question type is similar to multiple choice, though simpler.

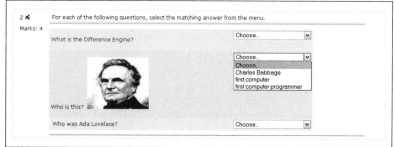

Figure 11-7: A short-answer matching question.

When creating your questions, you're following a similar format to setting up some of the other activities. Moodle provides you with a form with various options for each question type. The form is consistent in layout, and you need to input each question, the answers, and the feedback. It does take some time to create a complete bank of questions. But remember, you have to do this only once. Start small; for example, add one quiz or worksheet. Moodle marks and pushes the grades to the grade book. Don't get discouraged. It may be a slow process until you get the hang of it. Remind yourself that you can reuse the questions over and over.

Setting Up Various Types of Questions

The following sections explain, in detail, how to set up various questions types in Moodle.

The order in which I list the explanations follows the popularity of use. For instance, Multiple Choice, Matching, and True/False are more popular with instructors than Random Short-Answer Matching and Embedded Answers (Cloze).

Note that after you give your question a name, you don't have to state what type of question it is because as soon as you save the question, Moodle lists it with a specific icon representing the question type. The icons make it easier for you to organize and identify the question type, giving you the freedom to name them as you wish. Table 11-1 lists all the questions with the corresponding icons. The icons help you identify the questions when you view or move them into your quiz (discussed later in the chapter). If you need more assistance, visit `http://docs.moodle.org/en/Question_bank`.

Table 11-1 Question Types and Icons Used in the Question Bank

Question Icon	Question Type
2+2 =?	Calculated
	Description
	Essay
	Matching
	Embedded answers (Cloze)
	Multiple choice
	Short answer
12	Numerical
?	Random short-answer matching
	True/false

Multiple choice

 Multiple-choice questions enable you to set up single and multiple-answer questions, upload images, and give specific answers weights to calculate grades. To create a new multiple-choice question, follow these instructions:

1. **Click the Questions link in the Administration block on your course front page.**

   Moodle takes you to the Question Bank page, shown in Figure 11-8.

2. **From the Category drop-down list, select your category, and from the Create New Question drop-down list, select Multiple Choice.**

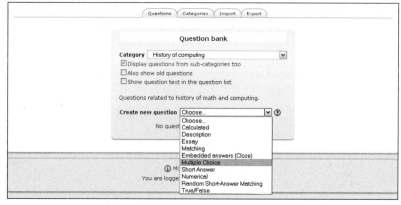

Figure 11-8:
Adding a
question to
the Question
Bank.

Don't forget to change the category where you want to store the questions. Moodle leaves the default category unless you select yours from the drop-down list.

Moodle takes you to the Adding a Multiple Choice Question setup page, shown in Figure 11-9.

3. **In the Question Name text box, give the question a name.**

   I suggest you use a descriptive name to identify your question. Naming the question by topic, unit, theme, class, and so on will be helpful as your question bank grows. Setting a generic name like Question 1 or Intro 1 won't help you when you have several hundred questions in your question bank. Moodle adds an icon to the question to identify its type. Refer to Table 11-1, which lists all the icons.

4. **In the Question Text field, add your question.**

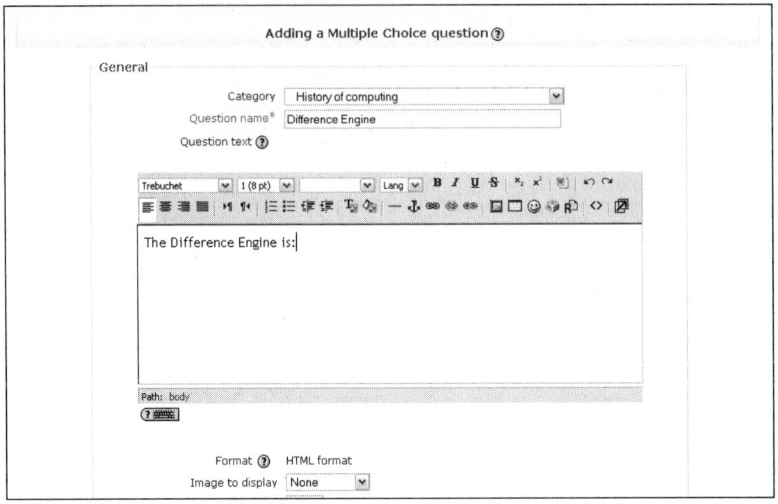

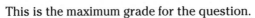

Adding a Multiple Choice question ⑦

General

Category | History of computing

Question name* | Difference Engine

Question text ⑦

The Difference Engine is:

Path: body

Format ⑦ | HTML format

Image to display | None

Figure 11-9:
Adding a
multiple-
choice
question.

5. If you want to include an image with your question, select your image from the Image to Display drop-down list.

In the Image to Display drop-down list, Moodle lets you choose from all the images saved in your directory. You need to have images uploaded to Moodle in order to be able to add them to questions. You don't have the option to browse your hard drive. Refer to Chapter 5 for details on how to upload images.

6. In the Default Question Grade text box, shown in Figure 11-10, enter a whole number, and the percentage will be calculated based on this.

This is the maximum grade for the question.

The fields with asterisks are required fields.

For simplicity, each of my questions tends to be worth 1 unless it has several parts, such as the matching short answer, where I may allocate it 4 or 5 (25/20% for each answer).

7. In the General Feedback field, add the general feedback that your learners will see when they complete the question.

This isn't based on the response and isn't necessary if you're giving feedback per correct or incorrect answers. You can leave this field blank, if you'd like. Learners see general feedback only if you selected the Feedback option in the Immediately after the attempt column of the Review Options are when you set up the quiz. See the "Creating a Quiz Body" section for more information on adjusting feedback settings.

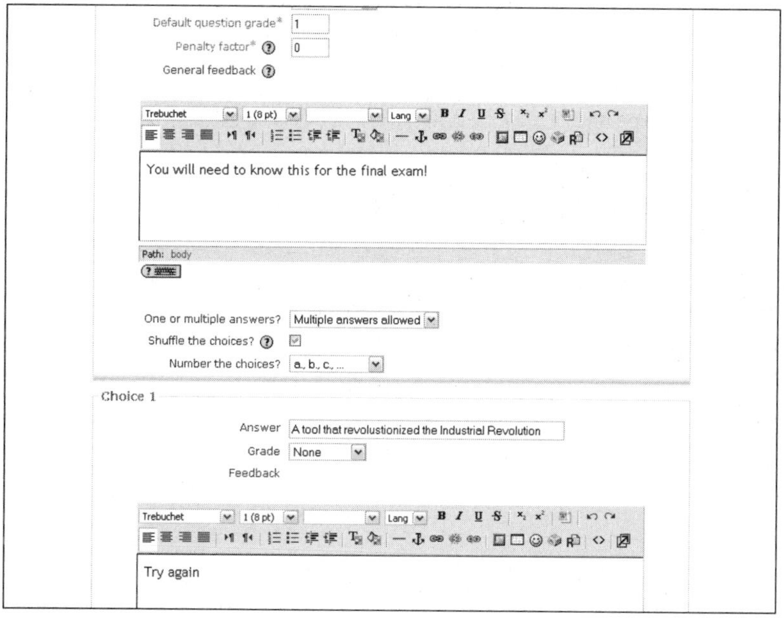

Figure 11-10:
Choosing
multiple-
choice
question
options.

8. **From the One or Multiple Answers drop-down list, select an option to determine whether your question will have only one correct answer or multiple answers.**

9. **Select the Shuffle the Choices check box if you want the choices shuffled on each new attempt.**

10. **From the Number the Choices drop-down list, you have an option to choose the style of numbering for the answers.**

    The default is lowercase alphabet (such as a, b, c).

11. **For the sections labeled Choice 1–Choice 5, compose the choices for your question. Specify the following information for each choice:**

    - *Answer:* Write your answer.

    - *Grade:* If this choice is incorrect, leave the default, NONE, or from the drop-down list select the percentage mark for the particular question. If you have only one correct answer, select 100%. If multiple answers are correct, divide 100% by the correct answers. For instance, if two answers are correct, each grade would be 50%.

    - *Feedback:* Add your feedback for the choices, if you're using the feedback options, telling students why their answers are incorrect (for each incorrect answer) or providing a positive statement for the correct one.

12. **If you need more choices, click the Blanks for 3 More Choices button.**

13. **In the General Feedback section, you can indicate what feedback to display For Any Correct Response, For Any Partially Correct Response, and For Any Incorrect Response.**

    This feedback feature is useful if you have more than one choice.

14. **Click the Save Changes button.**

    Moodle takes you to a busy question and category page. I refer to this as my Questions workspace page. See Figure 11-11 depicting the new question on the right. All the functionality in this workspace is described in the later section "Viewing, Editing, and Adding Questions to Quizzes."

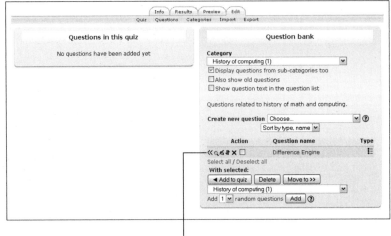

Figure 11-11:
Questions
workspace
page.

New question

Matching

Matching questions provide learners with a drop-down list to a question. They're useful for many different assessment activities such as memorizing, visual identification, and language understanding. See Figure 11-12. To set up a matching question, follow these steps:

1. **Follow Steps 1–7 in the preceding section. In Step 2, select Matching from the Create New Question drop-down list. (Refer to Figure 11-8.)**

    I entered **Match the Moodle Tools with the Description** as the question.

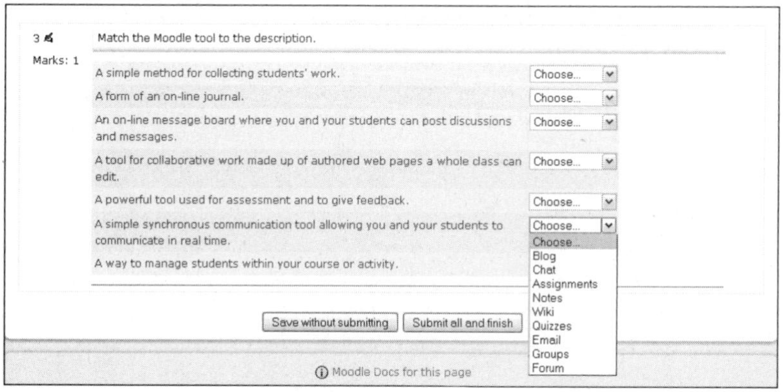

3	Match the Moodle tool to the description.	
Marks: 1	A simple method for collecting students' work.	Choose...
	A form of an on-line journal.	Choose...
	An on-line message board where you and your students can post discussions and messages.	Choose...
	A tool for collaborative work made up of authored web pages a whole class can edit.	Choose...
	A powerful tool used for assessment and to give feedback.	Choose...
	A simple synchronous communication tool allowing you and your students to communicate in real time.	Choose...
	A way to manage students within your course or activity.	

Choose...
Blog
Chat
Assignments
Notes
Wiki
Quizzes
Email
Groups
Forum

Save without submitting   Submit all and finish

ⓘ Moodle Docs for this page

Figure 11-12:
A matching
question.

2. **If you want to shuffle the questions (if you allow for multiple attempts — that's when this feature is useful), select the Shuffle the Choices check box.**

3. **In the Question boxes for Questions 1–3, add the questions with the answer below.**

You need to add at least three questions in order for Moodle to accept the matching question, and you must include up to three answers. You can leave one or more blank questions, with extra answers so that you don't have one answer to each question. For example, you can add seven descriptive questions and have 10 answers in the drop-down list.

4. **Click the Save Changes button.**

Moodle returns you to the Question Bank editing page, where you can preview the question and add it to your quiz.

TIP

When you're creating a series of questions of the same type, you don't need to go through this process each time if the only thing you're doing is changing the question and the answers. To save yourself time, here's what you do: Open an existing question of any type; keep all the same settings; change the Name (such as Moodle basics Q2); add the new question and answers; and at the bottom, instead of clicking the Save Changes button, click the Save as New Question button.

True/false

The true/false question is a very familiar format that is simple to implement. (See Figure 11-13.) The only thing you need to remember when you're setting up feedback for this question type is that the first answer, whether true or false, is the correct answer.

Figure 11-13:
The Preview
question
page.

Follow these steps to create a True/False question.

1. **Click the Questions link in the Administration block on your course front page.**

   Moodle takes you to the Question Bank page shown earlier in Figure 11-8.

2. **From the Category drop-down list, select your category, and from the Create New Question drop-down list, select True/False.**

   Moodle takes you to the Adding a True and False Question setup page.

3. **From the Question Category drop-down list, choose the category where you want the question to be stored.**

   The Adding a True/False Question page appears, as shown in Figure 11-14.

Figure 11-14:
Adding a
True/False
question.

4. **Follow Steps 3–7 in the section "Multiple choice," earlier in this chapter.**

5. **From the Correct Answer drop-down list, shown in Figure 11-15, choose True or False.**

   Notice Moodle prompts you that the first answer has to be the correct one. Add feedback for the True answer if you think it may be helpful.

6. **(Optional) Enter feedback for the False answer.**

7. **Click the Save Changes button.**

   Moodle returns you to the Question Bank editing page, where you can preview the question and add it to your quiz.

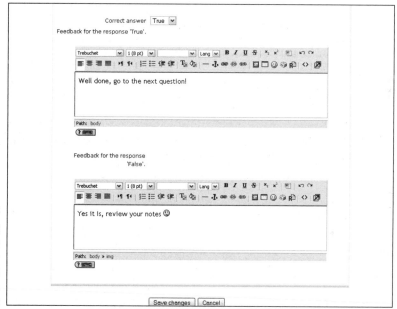

Figure 11-15:
Choosing
the answer
and adding
feedback.

Short answer

The setup for a short-answer question is similar to the setup of the questions discussed previously in this chapter. The most important thing to remember when setting up the short-answer question is to keep answers as short as possible. The Moodle quiz engine evaluates whether the answer is right or wrong by exact matching, character for character, in the order you specify. Warn your learners about spelling errors. There is no implied intelligence that can deduce an answer if the wording is correct in context but phrased differently. Think about possible acceptable answers, enter them, and use a *wildcard* as a space holder for text when appropriate.

Moodle uses the asterisk character (*) to indicate a wildcard allowing any sets of characters between words, within words, before a word, or after a word. Table 11-2 shows how you can use a wildcard with a two-word answer (Paris and London in this example) and how Moodle would grade it.

Here are some things to remember when working with wildcards:

✔ Standard practice for using the wildcard is to place the wildcard answer last in the list of questions/answers so that Moodle knows what to do if nothing else matches.

✔ Wildcards are needed because Moodle finds the answers by comparing characters exactly to your answers. So spell the words correctly — and tell your students to spell them correctly, or the answers will be marked incorrect.

Table 11-2	Using the Wildcard
Paris*London	100%
Paris or *London*	50%
*	0%
"Paris London", "Paris, London", "Paris; London", "Paris & London", "Paris and London", "Paris or London", "Paris not London"	All acceptable, so you need to be careful

To set up a short-answer question, follow these steps:

1. **Follow Steps 1–2 in the section "Multiple choice," earlier in this chapter.**

   Be sure to select Short Answer from the Create New Question drop-down list in Step 2.

2. **In the Question Text box, add the question.**

   If you want to leave a blank space, use the underscore character, as in, "_____was the first American president."

3. **In the General Feedback field, add feedback your learners will see when they complete the question.**

   Include feedback if it would be useful to the goals of the assignment.

4. **From the Case Sensitivity drop-down list, you have an option to decide whether case is important in the answer. The default is No, Case Is Unimportant. Select Yes if case is important.**

If you change the setting to Yes, think carefully about when this is important. For example, if a learner types **george Washington**, and case sensitivity is set, Moodle would mark this answer incorrect.

5. **In the Answer 1–3 fields, fill in the following information:**

   • *Answer:* Enter the answers you will accept. Don't forget about the wildcard and that it should be used as the last answer.

   • *Grade:* Assign a percentage grade. If a word is frequently misspelled, you can allocate partial credit.

   • *Feedback:* Add feedback for any answer or leave it blank.

   If you want to add feedback for all wrong answers, use the wildcard (the asterisk, *) as the only answer, and leave None as the grade. If you need to add more possible answers, click the Blanks for 3 More Choices button under the Answer 3 field.

6. **Click the Save Changes button.**

   Moodle returns you to the Question Bank editing page, where you can preview the question and add it to your quiz.

The bottom portions of Figures 11-16 and 11-17 show how the quiz looks with one correct and one incorrect short answer.

Numerical

You will quickly see that numerical questions are much like the short-answer questions discussed in the preceding section; the difference is that you can set answers in an error range you specify. You can also accept answers in multiple units (such as metric and imperial). For your learners, the look and feel are identical to short-answer questions.

To set up a numeric question, follow these steps:

1. **Follow Steps 1–2 in the section "Multiple choice," earlier in this chapter.**

   Be sure to select Numerical from the Create New Question drop-down list in Step 2.

2. **In the Question Text box, add your equation and/or the Question.**

   This can include an equation, text, or an image of a formula if the Algebra filter or TeX filter is not enabled. See Chapter 13 and the companion Web site, `www.dummies.com/go/moodlefd`, for more information on how to enable the filters. You need administrative privileges. Enabling these filters allows you to use mathematic notations. These filters enable math functions to be added to the WYSIWYG editing bar.

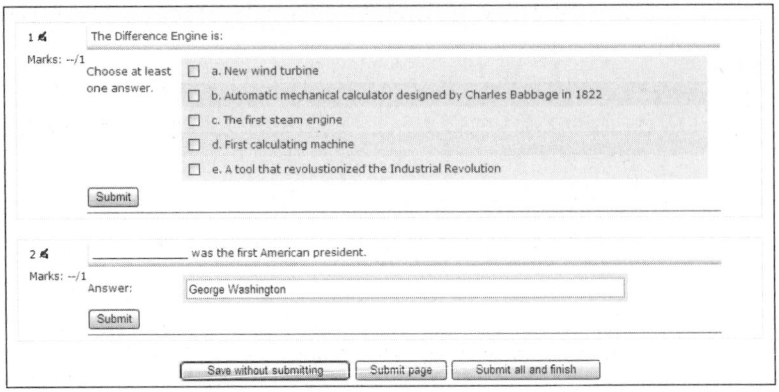

Figure 11-16:
Previewing
the
question.

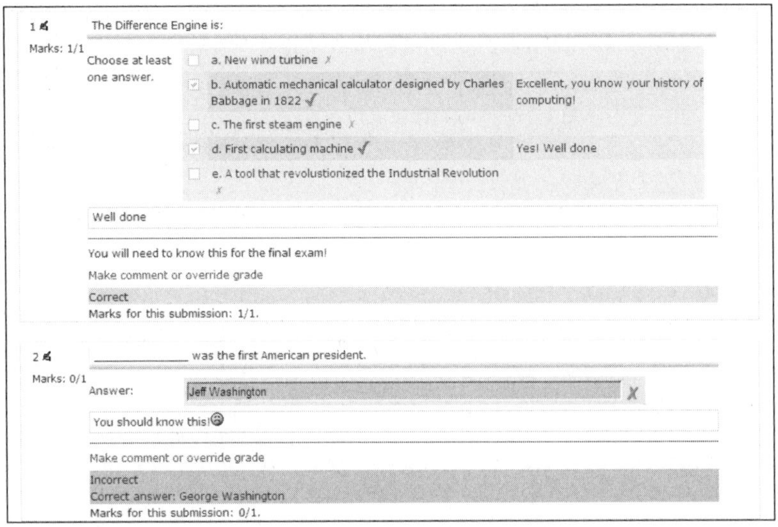

Figure 11-17:
The results
of a submit-
ted quiz.

3. **If you want an image, select it from the Image to Display drop-down list.**

   You have to upload the image to your Moodle folders first. Moodle displays the image right after the textual question and before the answer field.

4. **In the Default Question Grade field, enter the maximum grade/points for the question.**

   For example, enter 1 point for each question.

5. **The Penalty Factor field is applicable only if you set up the question in Adaptive mode only. You can add 0 or just leave as is.**

   Moodle ignores the setting if it isn't set in Adaptive mode.

6. **If feedback would be useful, add general feedback that will appear when the learner answers the question.**

   The general feedback is not based on the answer.

7. **In the sections Answer 1–3, fill in the following information for each answer:**

   • *Answer:* Enter the answer.

   • *Grade:* Select the default grade from the drop down list.

   • *Accepted Error:* Enter the accepted error range for the answer. For example if the answer is 10, and you will accept 9.5 or 10.5, enter **.5** as your accepted error range. Add feedback for the accepted answer. This is what the learner will see if she got the question correct.

   You also have to specify incorrect answers using the wildcard (the asterisk character, *) as the answer and setting the grade to NONE. If you need more choices, click the Blanks for 3 More Choices button, and Moodle adds three more answer fields.

8. **In each of the Unit fields, add the unit and, if needed, add the multiplier.**

   You can specify metric and imperial units. For example, if the answer is 5, accept 5cm or add .01 as the multiplier for cm to m. Moodle will accept 5, 5cm, and .05m as correct answers.

9. **Click the Save Changes button.**

   Moodle returns you to the Question Bank editing page, where you can preview the question and add it to your quiz.

Random short-answer matching

The random short-answer matching questions are very easy to set up, and they add variety to your quiz, test, or worksheet. Your learners will just think it's another matching question. To set it up, you give an introduction to the set of matching questions, and Moodle randomly selects short-answer sub-questions from the current category (make sure the short questions are included in the category), creating a drop-down list of all correct answers. Moodle shuffles the questions and answers, selecting different question for each new attempt at the quiz.

The topic has to be the same, or the answers in the questions won't make sense. For example, categories of capital cities and countries should include questions/answers on only capitol cities and countries. If you include questions about French verbs, the answers will be mixed up and not make sense. This is when subcategories become useful. Remember that each question is weighted equally to generate overall points.

To set up a random short-answer matching question, take these steps:

1. **Follow Steps 1–3 in the section "Multiple choice," earlier in this chapter. Be sure to select Random Short-Answer Matching from the Create New Question drop-down list in Step 2.**

2. **In the Question Text box, inform the learners of what they're matching and the learning goals, or use Moodle's default text.**

3. **In the General Feedback field, add feedback if it would be helpful.**

4. **From the Number of Questions to Select drop-down list, select how many questions you want to add to the matching questions.**

It's important you don't add more than the number of short-answer questions you have in the question bank under the category.

5. **Click the Save Changes button.**

Moodle returns you to the Question Bank editing page, where you can preview the question and add it to your quiz or edit it.

Essay

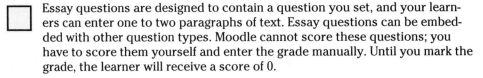

Essay questions are designed to contain a question you set, and your learners can enter one to two paragraphs of text. Essay questions can be embedded with other question types. Moodle cannot score these questions; you have to score them yourself and enter the grade manually. Until you mark the grade, the learner will receive a score of 0.

If you use essay with other question types in a quiz, Moodle will correct all the other questions and push the grade to the learner's grade book. Learners can see their grades right away, so I advise that you include in your instruction a note that Moodle will record a 0 mark because it is waiting for you to mark the essay.

To grade an essay in a submitted quiz, select the Results tab from the Editing Quiz page, and then under the tabs, click the Manual Grading link, which takes you to a page where you can read and score the essay and add comments.

To set up an essay question, here's what you do:

1. **Follow Steps 1–3 in the section "Multiple choice," earlier in this chapter. Be sure to select Essay from the Create New Question drop-down list in Step 2.**

2. **In the Question Text field, write your question and, if necessary, any instructions.**

If your question has few parts, then bullet points or numbers can help the learners to structure the essay.

3. In the General Feedback box, add general feedback.

Adding Moodle-generated feedback in most circumstances is helpful, though for essay questions you have options to add comments when you mark the essays, so you can leave the fields blank

4. Click the Save Changes button.

Moodle returns you to the Question Bank editing page, where you can preview the question and add it to your quiz or edit it.

Calculated

2+2 =? The main purpose of using the Calculated question type is if you're teaching math and you want to create multiple questions by using a specific formula with different numerical values. Moodle will randomly pull the numbers from a dataset you can specify. For example, to set up a worksheet to practice division problems, creating two placeholders and a division sign, such as {a} / {b}, tells Moodle to select values for a and b automatically. Each time the test is taken, different values will be added, and your learners will be presented with a new practice activity each time. Just think all the time this will save you marking practice work sheets!

To set up a calculated question, take these steps:

1. Follow Steps 1–3 in the section "Multiple choice," earlier in this chapter. Be sure to select Calculated from the Create New Question dropdown list in Step 2.

2. In the Question Text box, shown in Figure 11-18, add the question your learners need to answer.

Make sure you use at least one wildcard and add the values Moodle will randomly assign in curly brackets. For example, you could enter {x} * {y} /{a}.

3. Fill in the Default Question Grade and Penalty Factor fields, if necessary.

Penalty factor is necessary only if you are using Adaptive mode.

Moodle ignores the penalty factor if you did not select Adaptive mode in the quiz setup page.

4. Add general feedback if needed.

5. In the Answer section, shown in Figure 11-19, enter the following information:

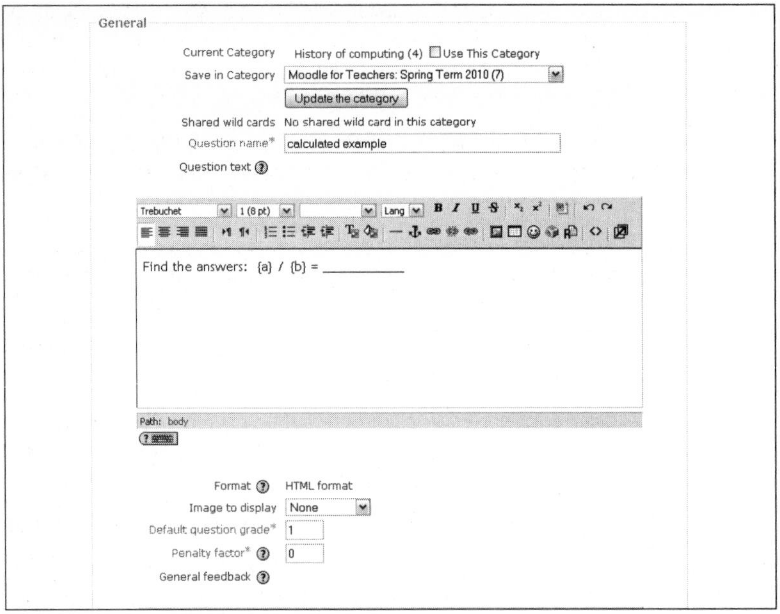

General

Current Category	History of computing (4) ☐ Use This Category
Save in Category	Moodle for Teachers: Spring Term 2010 (7)
	Update the category
Shared wild cards	No shared wild card in this category
Question name*	calculated example
Question text ⑦	

Trebuchet | 1 (8 pt) | | Lang | **B** *I* U̲ S̶ ×₂ ×² 🖼 ↶ ↷

Find the answers: {a} / {b} = _____

Path: body

Figure 11-18:
Setting
up the
Calculated
question.

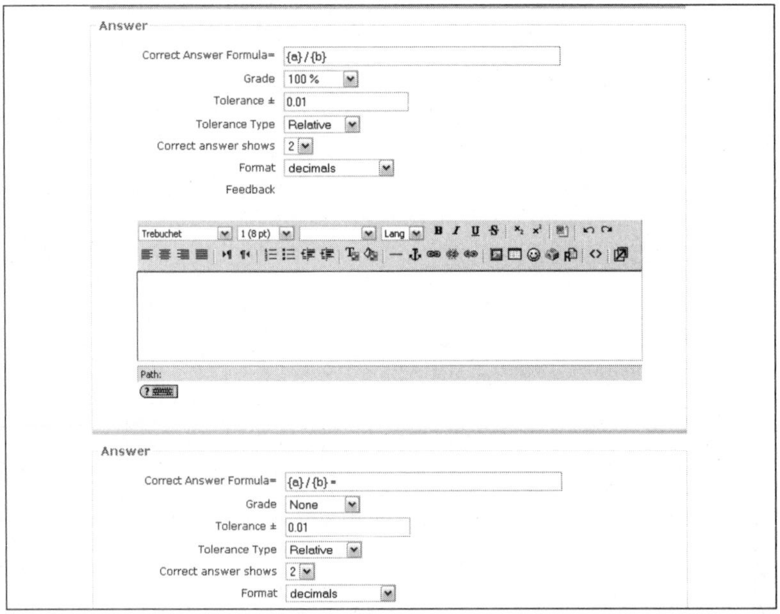

Format ⑦	HTML format
Image to display	None
Default question grade*	1
Penalty factor* ⑦	0
General feedback ⑦	

Answer

Correct Answer Formula=	{a}/{b}
Grade	100 %
Tolerance ±	0.01
Tolerance Type	Relative
Correct answer shows	2
Format	decimals
Feedback	

Trebuchet | 1 (8 pt) | | Lang | **B** *I* **U̲** S̶ ×₂ ×² 🖼 ↶ ↷

Path:

Figure 11-19:
Setting
acceptable
answers.

Answer

Correct Answer Formula=	{a}/{b} =
Grade	None
Tolerance ±	0.01
Tolerance Type	Relative
Correct answer shows	2
Format	decimals

- *Correct Answer Formula:* Add the correct answer formula. Moodle needs to recognize a formula, such as {a}/{b}, in order to set up the question. See the correct syntax formula at `http://docs.moodle.org/en/Question_bank`.

- *Grade:* From the drop-down list, select 100% grade value for the correct answer. You need to select 100% unless you set up the quiz at a different percentage.

- *Tolerance:* Select the tolerance of error you will accept. For example, choosing a relative error of .05 could be acceptable for my preceding division example.

- *Tolerance Type:* From the drop-down list, select the type of tolerance (relative, nominal, or geometric).

- *Correct Answer Shows:* Decide on the precise number of significant figures or decimal places you will accept for the correct answer. Moodle sets 2 as the default.

- *Format:* From the drop-down list, choose the option that indicates decimals or significant figures.

6. **In the Feedback field, add answer feedback as appropriate.**

7. **If required, add units for the correct answer (meters, oz, kg, and so on), as shown in Figure 11-20.**

   You can add both metric and imperial.

8. **Click the Next Page button.**

   Moodle opens another page for you to complete, as shown in Figure 11-21.

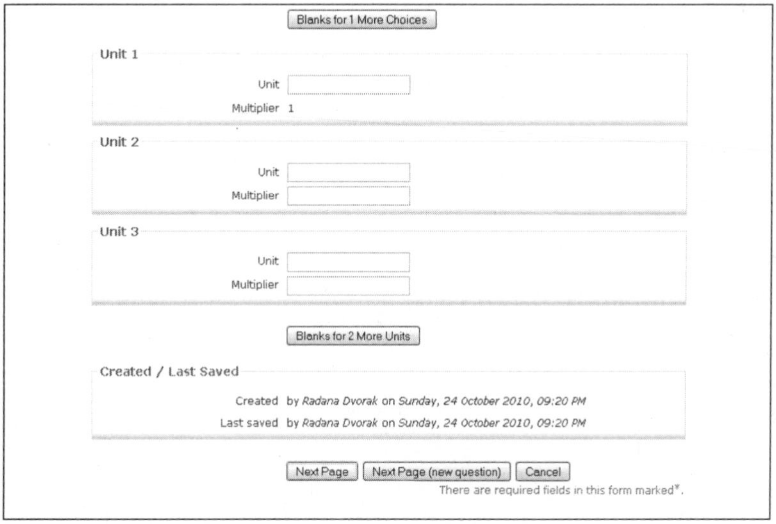

Figure 11-20:
Indicating
units.

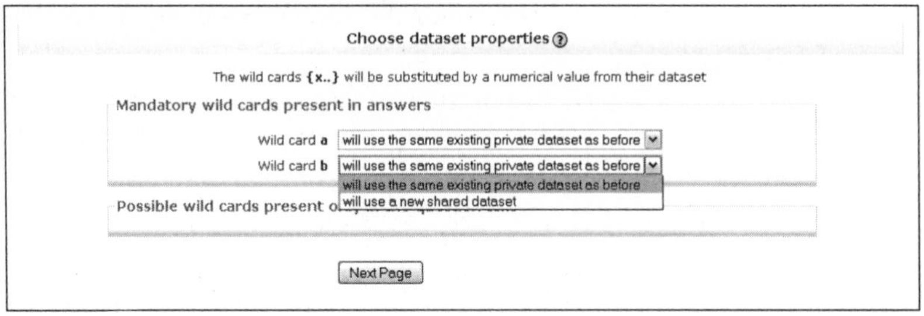

Figure 11-21:
Choosing
wildcard
options.

9. **In the Mandatory Wild Cards Present in Answers section, decide whether you want to use the same existing private data set as before or use a new shared data set. These are your choices:**

   - *Private:* If you select this option, you're restricting Moodle to use it with this question only.

   - *Shared:* If you select this option, you allow Moodle to share it with other calculated questions within the same category. This option will save you time.

10. **Click the Next Page button.**

    Moodle takes you to page 3, shown in Figure 11-22.

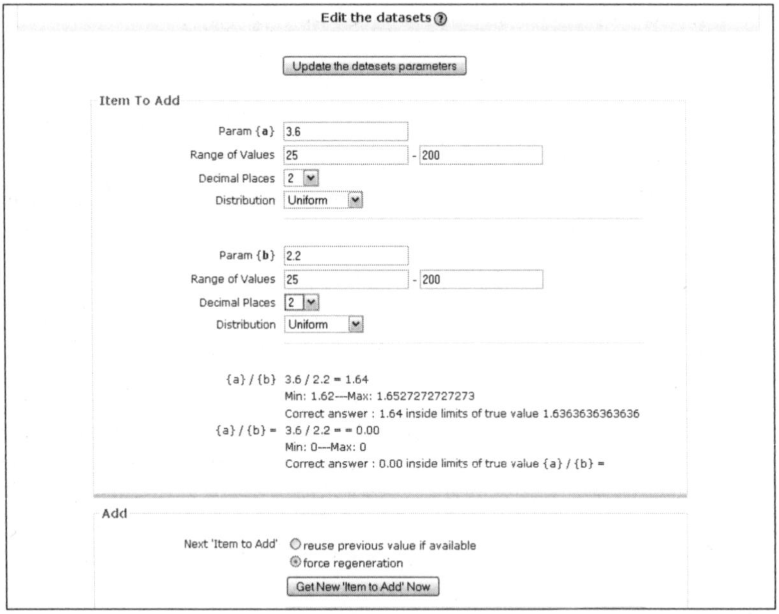

Figure 11-22:
Creating a
dataset.

11. **Create a dataset for questions(s) in the category.**

All you need to do is generate a series of values for the placeholders. It's better to shoot for generating more values because Moodle will not have to repeat values. For simplicity, I let Moodle create values. Here's the information you need to fill in:

- *Param:* Add the value you want to start with.

- *Range of Values:* Enter the range of values in the fields and enter the lower and upper limits for the values you would accept.

- *Decimal Places:* Choose a number of decimal places for the value.

- *Distribution:* Choose the distribution of values between the limits. *Uniform* means any value between the limits is equally likely to be generated; *Loguniform* means that values toward the lower limit are more likely.

12. **Scroll down to the Add section and select the Force Regeneration option.**

13. **Click the Get New Items to Add Now button.**

14. **Click the Save Changes button.**

Moodle returns you to the Question Bank editing page.

Embedded answers (Cloze)

 If you want to set questions within text, use the embedded answers (Cloze) question-type. Often, instructors like to take a passage from text and embed short-answer, multiple-choice, or fill-in numerical questions right into the passage. This question type is often used with language instruction. A Cloze question comprises a piece of text from which a number of words have been removed. A learner is required to insert the missing words. In some cases, the missing words are supplied as a single list from which the student has to select, which, in effect, is matching a word with the space where it belongs. Simply, it's just a matching question embedded in text and can be represented as a selection in a drop-down list of possible answers.

 You cannot use a graphical interface for this question type, and you need to use specific syntax to embed the format. Using third-party software, such as Hot Potatoes, is the simplest way to design these types of questions, and then you can import them right into Moodle.

To create an embedded answer, follow these steps:

1. **Follow Steps 1–3 in the section "Multiple choice," earlier in this chapter. Be sure to select Embedded Answers (Cloze) from the Create New Question drop-down list in Step 2.**

2. **In the Question Text field, shown in Figure 11-23, add the question text with the embedded answers using the specific syntax.**

   See the bullets at the end of this list for a summary of the syntax. You can find more information on how to use the syntax on the Moodle.org Web site (`http://docs.moodle.org/en/Embedded_Answers_%28Cloze%29_question_type`).

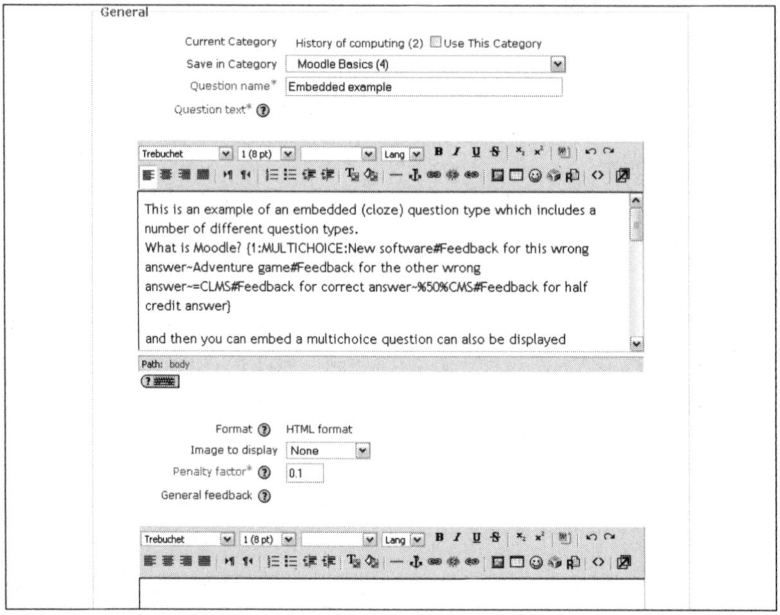

Figure 11-23: Setting up an Embedded Answers (Cloze) question.

3. **Fill in the default Question Grade and Penalty Factor text boxes (if in Adaptive mode).**

   The Penalty factor is important only if you set the Adaptive mode in the Quiz. If you did not set it, the Penalty factor will be ignored.

   Note: You will be adding the weight value for the grade inside the Cloze questions – it's part of the syntax.

4. **In the General Feedback field, add feedback if is useful to the learning goals.**

5. **Click the Decode and Verify the Question Text button.**

   Moodle gives you a preview of the questions, answers, and points to test if you entered the correct syntax.

6. Click the Save Changes button.

Moodle returns you to the Question Bank editing page.

Here's the syntax you can use with Cloze questions:

- ✔ All question type items are coded inside curled braces { }.

- ✔ The number that appears between the opening brace and the colon, such as 1 in {1:, is the weighting of that item; if it's set at 1 for all the items, you don't need to specify it, so you can have {:.

- ✔ After the colon, you have the item question type: MULTICHOICE, SHORTANSWER, NUMERICAL.

- ✔ If you've installed the REGEXP question type plugin, you can also use the REGEXP question type.

- ✔ The syntax for MULTICHOICE and SHORTANSWER is nearly the same; the only difference is in the way the item displays to the student.

- ✔ The order of the various answers is indifferent (except if you want a catch-all for wrong answers; see the next bullet point).

- ✔ In the SHORTANSWER type, you may want to put a catch-all (wrong) answer in order to send "wrong, try again" feedback; you can do this by inserting an asterisk (*) as the very last expected answer in your formula.

- ✔ A correct answer is preceded with the equal sign (=) or a percentage (usually %100%). *Note:* The equal sign doesn't seem to work with SHORTANSWER.

- ✔ A wrong answer is preceded with nothing or a percentage (usually %0%).

- ✔ You can allocate points between 0 and 100 to some questions if you put the appropriate percentage in your quiz setup.

- ✔ All answers except the first one are separated from one another by a tilde (~).

- ✔ Answers can be followed by an optional feedback message, preceded with the pound sign (#). If there is no feedback message, # can be present or absent — it does not matter.

- ✔ The feedback message and correct answer are displayed in a small Feedback pop-up window upon mouse hovering (if and when the correct answer and/or feedback have been declared accessible to the students in the Quiz settings). You can use HTML tags to format your feedback. It can help not to have the form fields for the answers too close to each other.

- ✔ Unfortunately in MULTICHOICE MODE, you can't have the answers scrambled. In SHORTANSWER mode, it is not possible to make the answers case-sensitive.

Description

 Description is *not* a question type. Moodle developers have added this option to the question bank because a number of individual questions do not allow for instructions, and you may need to add content between questions. This tool works similar to the label resource: All it does is allow you to add text (or graphics) to instruct learners. For example, instructors have used the description option to present a map to students and then present a series of multiple choice questions. Another example is language teachers using it to display a few paragraphs in a foreign language, and then they can check whether learners can understand the passage by asking them to read it and answer a series of following questions. Use this functional utility creatively to support your quiz activities as you find need.

The description option is quite simple to set up. Follow the same procedure as for other question types. There is no grade allocation. After adding your content and/or image, you can add general feedback in a text box provided, but most likely you won't have any use for feedback here. Like with all the other question types, make sure you choose the correct category and don't forget to save your changes.

Viewing, Editing, and Adding Questions to Quizzes

The Moodle Question Bank editing page has a number of different tools that enable you to add the questions to your quiz, preview them, edit them, and move them between categories and quizzes. Moodle uses icons to depict the questions and functions. Refer to Table 11-2 for the icons and their explanations. (To access the Question Bank page, click the Questions link in the Course Administration block, located on the left side of the course front page.)

Editing the question bank and quiz

The Quiz Question page is divided into two parts: Questions in This Quiz and Question Bank.

Question Bank

The Question Bank section is on the right (see Figure 11-24) with a number of different tools to manage your questions and categories. You have three drop-down lists:

✔ **Category:** This drop-down list enables you to display your questions stored in specific categories you created. You also have options to include various questions by selecting the check boxes, Display Questions from Sub-Categories Too and Also Show Old Questions. If you create a very long list of questions, and the question names are too generic and don't give you enough information to identify specific questions, select the Show Question Text in the Question List check box to add the text above the question in the list.

✔ **Create New Question:** This drop-down list offers all the question types. Use this list when you need to add a new question.

✔ **Question sorting:** Moodle allows you to sort your questions by type, name, or date created.

Sort

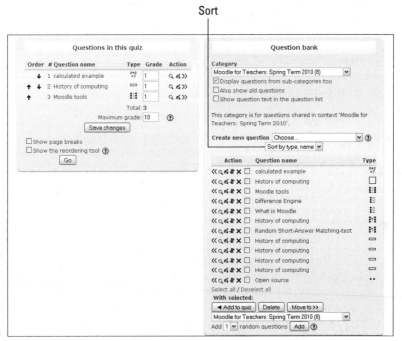

Figure 11-24:
Adding
questions
to a quiz.

Below the drop-down lists are your questions with certain tools to view, edit, delete, and move them. Table 11-2 shows all the icons and their functionality. Below the list of questions, you have four operations you can carry out with selected questions. Notice that you can select individual questions by using the check box in front of the questions or by clicking the Select All or Deselect All links. Furthermore, you can use the following buttons:

✔ **Add to Quiz:** Selected questions are moved to the quiz question list located on left side of the page. Note you can move the question only once.

✔ **Delete:** Selected questions are deleted.

✔ **Move To:** Selected questions are moved to a different category that's selected using the drop-down list.

✔ **Add:** Click this button to add random questions. Select from the drop-down list how many questions you want randomly added to the quiz. Each attempt results in different questions.

Questions in this quiz

After moving questions to the left section titled Questions in This Quiz, you have more tools to help you organize, structure, edit, and preview your quiz. Refer to Figure 11-24; starting from the left, here are the columns in the table of questions:

✔ **Order:** Order the questions by clicking the up and down arrows next to the questions.

✔ **Question Name:** Lists the name of the question.

✔ **Type:** The icon depicts the type of question.

✔ **Grade:** In the input box, set the number of points for each question. Think about the type of question and the points you will add. For example, you may want to give a matching question, requiring 10 matches, more points than a True or False question. Moodle weighs each question to match the total points possible that you allocated the quiz when you set it up. Below the total points, you can set the Maximum Grade for the whole quiz. This number can be larger than the total — Moodle simply rescales the grades out of a maximum grade.

✔ **Action:** You can preview each question by selecting the magnifying glass icon. A new window opens with options to complete the question and several buttons: Submit the Page, Submit All and Finish, Fill with Correct, Start Again, and Close Window. The options allow you to see correct and incorrect answers with the feedback you've added.

Below the table of questions, you find these two check boxes:

✔ **Show Page Breaks:** If you want to add page breaks, after several questions, select the check box, and Moodle adds a Next button. I recommend you do add page breaks if you have many questions; otherwise, your learners will have to scroll.

✔ **Show the Reordering Tool:** Selecting the reordering tool allows you to increase line numbers between questions, starting at the top. Moodle increases lines in a factor of 10, leaving you room to insert new questions.

You can leave the default or increase by a factor of 10 (recommended). Using line numbers and changing line numbers by the questions are ways to reorder the questions. If you added page breaks, the new pages are also given line numbers. However, if you remove the show page breaks, the line numbers aren't displayed, and only gaps show. I don't use the line numbers because they're a bit cumbersome. I find that by ordering question using page breaks and Moodle's own numbering system, the quiz is displayed well and efficiently.

When you're finished, don't forget to click the Save Changes button!

Previewing the quiz

After previewing your individual questions and adding them to your quiz, you need to preview and take the quiz yourself to make sure the layout, feedback, and points allocated for each question are all correct. From your Editing Quiz page, select the Preview Tab, and Moodle takes you to the quiz.

To get to the Editing Quiz page, click the quiz from the Activities block on the course front page, and then select the Edit tab. Table 11-3 shows the icons you see on the Editing Quiz page.

Table 11-3	Moodle Editing Quiz Page Icons
Icons	*Description or Question Type*
≪	Moves the question to the quiz
🔍	Allows you to preview the question
✍	Allows you to edit the question
↑ ↓	Moves question up or down in the list
✗	Deletes the question

(continued)

Table 11-3 *(continued)*

Icons	Description or Question Type
	Allows for a number of questions to be selected and moved to a quiz
2+2 =?	Calculated
	Description
	Essay
	Matching
	Embedded answers (Cloze)
	Multiple choice
	Short answer
12	Numerical short answer
??	Random short-answer matching
	True/false

If you set a keyword for the quiz, you need to enter it. Take the quiz, submit the answers, and finish. When you submit the finished quiz, Moodle returns a page with the results, as shown in Figure 11-25. Notice all the information Moodle gives to learners just below the name of the quiz: You see the date and time when the quiz was taken and completed, the time it took, the total points scored out of the maximum, the percentage grade, and general feedback.

Below the scores, Moodle displays the answers. In this particular example, if the answer is incorrect, the correct answer is not displayed because the teacher set up the quiz to let each student take it four times. If the student's answer is incorrect on the last try, the correct answers are displayed.

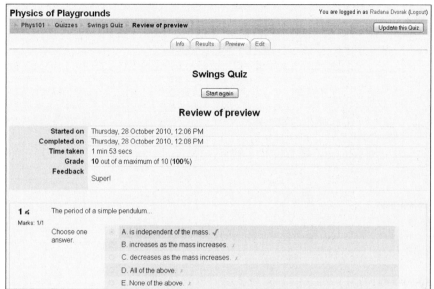

Figure 11-25:
Reviewing
a submitted
quiz.

If you allowed for shuffling within multiple-choice questions and have a com-
bined answer (such as a, b, and c are all correct but answers d and e are not),
shuffling doesn't work because the answers don't combine the same way the
next time the student takes the quiz. (a, b, and c may include d as a, b, or c.)
In this case, I recommend you use All or None as one of the multiple-choice
options instead of a, b, and c. Be careful about using All of the Above as an
answer because this answer may appear as a. You can, of course, choose not
to use shuffling within multiple-choice questions and then not worry about
inconsistencies if you have more than one answer correct and/or use All of
the Above.

Managing Quizzes and Data

Moodle collects data on all learners' activities, which is discussed in Chapter
14. Within the Quiz module, data is collected on individual learners, including
results for individual responses and itemized analysis for each question.

Viewing the results

On the Editing Quiz page (refer to Figure 11-25), click the Results tab. This
action opens the Overview quiz reports page, shown in Figure 11-26. There
are four links right under the tabs: Overview, Regrade, Manual Grading, and
Item Analysis.

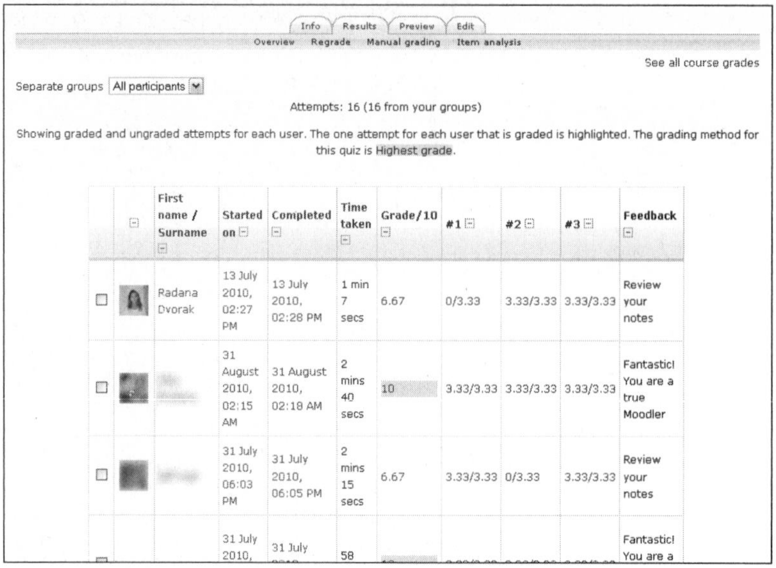

Figure 11-26:
Looking at
the Results
tab.

✓ **Overview page:** This page displays detailed information about learners' attempts, including dates when the quiz was taken and completed, time taken, overall score, score per question, and the feedback. If more than one attempt is allowed, you see the follow-up attempt(s) under the learner's name. The check box to the left of each attempt allows you to delete it. *Note:* If you want to add questions to the quiz, you need to delete all the attempts before Moodle allows you to make any changes.

At the bottom of the list, Moodle provides the overall average score as well as Select All and Deselect All links, which select all the attempts on the quiz or deselect the selections. (See Figure 11-27.) To remove the attempts whether they're all selected or just individual selections, click the Delete Selected Attempts button.

- *Downloading data:* Moodle provides you with tools to download the data into industry standard formats. Located right under the Delete Selected Attempts button, you can click a button to download the data in ODS format, Excel format, or text format. Just click the appropriate button and follow the simple instructions.

- *Preferences for the page and the report:* Moodle default setting displays information about all attempts on the quiz. The drop-down list below the download buttons lets you select All Attempts, which includes students in the current class and all past students who attempted the quiz who are no longer enrolled. The All Students option selects everyone whether or not they attempted the quiz. The other two options — Students with Attempts Only and Students with No Attempts Only — are self-explanatory. Below the drop-down list is a check box further allowing you to show or download only the attempts that are graded for each user for the highest grade.

You can also select how many students you want to be displayed on each page and if you want to show or download marks for each question — the default is Yes. Click the Save Preferences button.

Below the Save Preferences button, Moodle shows you a graphical display of a number of students achieving grade ranges, as shown in Figure 11-28.

✔ **Regrade page:** This link takes you to a report listing all quiz answers that you've altered when you were regarding. Moodle recalculates the grade only if you change the point value for a question or a quiz. Selecting the Regrade tab automatically starts the regrade process. Please note that this tab triggers the process and highlights those student answers that have been changed through the regrading process.

✔ **Manual Grading page:** This link is for manually grading questions that cannot be marked by Moodle, such as the essay questions, and for manually overriding and adding comments. For instance, you may find learners answer a specific short-answer question correctly, though Moodle marks it wrong. You can manually change the grade until the quiz is closed. I would then suggest that you add the acceptable answers to the question or alter the question.

✔ **Item Analysis page:** This tool is fabulous for evaluating the repeatability of the questions in the quiz. Moodle displays this report in a table, as shown in Figure 11-29. The basic info you want to see is comparing how the highest scores from students compared with the lowest on individual questions. Table 11-4 explains the table headings and how you can use them for your analysis.

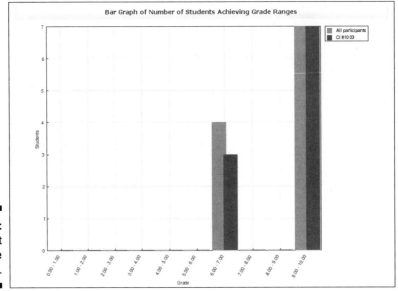

Figure 11-28: Student grade ranges.

Figure 11-29: The Item Analysis Table.

Bar Graph of Number of Students Achieving Grade Ranges

Item Analysis Table ⑦

Q#	Question text	Answer's text	partial credit	R. Counts	R.%	% Correct Facility	SD	Disc. Index	Disc. Coeff.
(25)	What is Moodle : Moodle is	a content management system (CMS)	(0.00)	0/11	(0%)	73%	0.467	0.86	0.74
		a learning managament system (LMS)	(0.00)	3/11	(27%)				
		a virtual learning environment (VLE)	(0.00)	0/11	(0%)				
		a moodle world adventure game	(0.00)	0/11	(0%)				
		a, b, c	(1.00)	8/11	(73%)				
(27)	Moodle tools : Match the Moodle tool to the description.	**An on-line message board where you and your students can post discussions and messages.: Forum**	(1.00)	10/11	(91%)	84%	0.303	0.55	0.42
		A simple synchronous							

Separate groups: All participants

See all course grades

Info Results Preview Edit
Overview   Regrade   Manual grading   Item analysis

Table 11-4	Understanding the Item Analysis Table
Column Name	**Description**
Q	Displays question ID number, icon depicting type of question and a preview icon allowing a pop-up to appear with the questions
Question Text	The questions
Answerer's Text	Individual learners' answers
Partial Credit	Score for each answer
R. Counts	How learners selected a particular answer an the total number of attempts
R. %	Percentage of learners who selected the particular answer
% Correct Facility	Percentage of correct answers for a particular question.
SD	Standard deviation; measures the variation of selected answers
Disc. Index	Discrimination index
Disc. Coeff.	Discrimination Coefficient

Below the table, you can choose a number of analysis options and use the three buttons to download the table in ODS format, Excel format, or text format.

Importing and exporting questions

If you have a repository of questions from various resources or use third-party software such as Blackboard or Hot Potatoes, Moodle has built-in tools and default formats enabling you to import questions and answers.

Often the method isn't straightforward with some of the software. It all depends on the database and on how it is set up. I found that it takes me longer to edit and check everything than using the Moodle interface and creating my questions. If you have hundreds of questions, I recommend experimenting; some good third-party tools can aid the process if you don't have success with the importing tools within Moodle.

You can also export your questions to a text file and make them available for reuse for other applications.

Links to Import and Export Questions pages are found on the Edit Quiz page, right under the tabs. (Refer to Figure 11-7.) Clicking these links takes you to the Import Questions From File page, from which you choose formats and make selections such as the category you want to import questions to or from, file format, and nearest grade. You can find more detailed explanation on the companion Webs site as well as links to resources on the Web.

Moodle supports a popular quiz format called Hot Potatoes and TexToys quizzes. Teachers create the quizzes on their computers and then upload them to their Moodle courses. The Hot Potatoes module called hotpot module plugin is hidden within Moodle by default until you or your system administrator turns it on. If you have an administrative user account, go to the site front page Administration Block. From the subcategories, click Modules, and then click Activities. Enable the plugin by selecting the eye icon hide/show column. You can find more information about administrating Moodle in Chapter 13.

Chapter 12

Using Databases to Share Resources and Adding the Latest News via RSS

In This Chapter

▶ Understanding the reasons to use the Moodle database

▶ Building a database, adding fields, and editing the interface

▶ Exploring what your database looks like to you and your learners

▶ Managing your database and ensuring the quality of entries

▶ Adding RSS feeds to your front page and Moodle Activities

*T*he Moodle Database module is a simple database that you can quickly set up and is easy to use for general purposes. The database has been embedded in Moodle to serve as a tool for collaborative development that introduces your learners to the structure and function of databases as well as their usefulness.

The Moodle database isn't meant to be as powerful as MS Access or MySQL. Rather, it's a tool that you and your learners can use for projects, galleries, portfolios, and resources. In this chapter, you find out how to set up a database, add your own fields, and tweak the interface. You can have your learners help structure the database and learn an important skill. If that would be too much to ask of your learners, you can set it up for them, and they can populate it with data such as text, links, photos, graphic files, sound, and/or video.

In addition to databases, this chapter also introduces you to RSS feeds and how to set up an RSS feed block on the course front page as well set up RSS in other Moodle activities (such as a forum, wiki, and database). I can hear you thinking, "Why is she introducing newsfeeds in a chapter on databases?" Great question! The answer is twofold. First, I think it's a great tool, and I struggled with where to put it. You can add newsfeeds in a number of different places in your course (such as your front page, forums, glossaries, wikis, and databases) to inform your learners about the latest topical issue and give them information they need. The reason you chose to bring this information to your learners is because you thought it has some value. Sharing valuable information and resources is exactly what databases are for, just like newsfeeds.

Harnessing the Power of Databases

The Database module enables instructors and learners to build, make available, and search a large storage space of information in a variety of formats. This information can be on any topic, and you or your learners choose what to add. You can add multiple databases to a course.

Exploring how Moodle databases work

You can set up the database in one of three ways:

- ✔ As a **course database,** where everyone in the course contributes and/or uses it
- ✔ As a **group database,** used for group projects that can be shared with other groups of the course or the whole Moodle site
- ✔ As an **individual project database,** between you and your learner, or for your own use, which is limited only by your imagination

Your learners can use the database for storing images, files, videos, sound files, Web addresses, numerical data, contact data, and so on. The Moodle database also enables you and learners to rate and view entries, write comments to entries, and set up an approval option so that you can safeguard the database entries. For instance, you can set up a group of students with permission allowing them to approve what's entered and viewable by the other course members.

The Moodle community provides good examples of how to use a Moodle database. See the database in action at `http://moodle.org/buzz`. This site is made available through Moodle.org and uses the database to store news and publications about Moodle from around the world, as shown in Figure 12-1. You can find other examples on the Moodle.org demo site, `http://demo.moodle.net`.

The Database activity module is a collaborative activity within your course; it should not be confused with the MySQL Moodle database that stores all your course data for the modules in the Moodle site.

Figure 12-1:
An example
of how the
Moodle
database is
being used.

Finding creative ways to use a database

As you familiarize yourself with Moodle activities and experiment with using the database, you will find many uses for it. After you teach your learners about its capabilities and set up a few simple databases for group or individual projects, you'll be surprised at the creative uses your learners will come up with.

The Database module isn't just for learners, though. Instructors can also collaborate and develop a database that they can share among themselves. For example, several teachers of different subjects created a college information database pertaining to their areas of expertise. They involved the students and created a repository of study programs in computer science, arts, science, math, social sciences, literature, and languages. Students collected information on local and out-of-state colleges and categorized them so they could be searched by size, requirements, fees, rankings, contact person, scholarships, and so on.

Here are few other ways that you can use the Database module:

✔ Storage for content and images so that learners can upload files and then download them from other places

✔ Private student storage for project

✔ Contact database for teachers or students (personal, business, or academic)

✔ Scholarship repository

✔ Research repository (articles, URLs, references, experts, and students own research data)

✔ Image gallery

✔ Subject database that can include a collection of data such as links to resources, experts, citations, and so on

✔ Arts competition: database created by style and medium, such as pottery, oils, watercolors, poetry, musical pieces, drama, and so on.

If the competition is within the school, consider letting the students be the ones to review entries and decide the winner, or if it's an outside competition, let them pick which piece will represent the school.

✔ Summary of course activities, including lectures, problems solving, and so on

Students can use this summary for reviews for tests or to catch up after an absence. Students can ask to contribute after each class, lab, or lecture. This summary will take some organization skills, but it'll be a great resource to populate information.

Adding a Database to Your Course

The Moodle database is slightly more complex than the Quiz module, but less so than the Lesson activity. If you have set up a database or are used to structured information, you'll find this database quite simple to use. If you haven't had any experience, don't worry: Find a chunk of time and follow the instructions at your own pace. There are no risks involved. You can easily change settings at a later date. The database is a standalone module and has no impact on anything else you've done in your course prior to adding the database. That's one of the strengths of Moodle: All activities are independent of each other.

In the simplest form, a database has two parts:

✔ **Fields** are the tables where you store data in the form of text, dates, files, images, URLs, and so on.

✔ **Templates** are what you and your learners see. Templates are the front end, whereas the fields are the back end of the database. Templates enable you to control the layout of information when you're adding to, editing, or viewing the database.

Before you dive in to adding a database, spend few minutes thinking about what information you want it to contain. Planning ahead will save you time in the long run because you need to make these decisions when you're setting it up. To help you with your planning, here are few questions to ask yourself:

- ✔ What will I be using the database for?

  Knowing vaguely is okay for the first time you create a database. Don't worry; you don't have to be precise. Sometimes it's good to play and get your hands dirty.

- ✔ What type of information will the database contain? Will it contain one topic (a single entry) and data related to the topic? Or will it contain multiple entries with detailed information related to each entry?

- ✔ How will I and others want to view the information?

- ✔ Will learners be adding and editing the database?

The companion Web site has a number of examples of databases and a flow chart and template that will help you plan your database.

After you've answered some of the questions in the preceding list, you're ready to create the database. You set up the database in two parts, similar to the way you use the Quiz module to set up quizzes. You first set all the settings for the database as you did in the quiz. Then you create the fields and set and/or edit the template.

Setting up your database

To set up the first part, the database, follow these steps:

1. **Click the Turn Editing On button in the upper-right corner of your course front page.**

2. **From the Add an Activity drop-down list, in the week or topic section of your course, select Database.**

   Moodle takes you to the Adding a New Database page, shown in Figure 12-2.

3. **Enter a name for your database as well as a short description of the purpose of the database.**

4. **Select the following General options as they relate to your course and project:**

   - *Available From/To Dates:* This availability is for both viewing the database and adding entries to it.

   - *Viewable From/To:* Setting these dates enables the database to be available only for viewing. It's closed for adding any data.

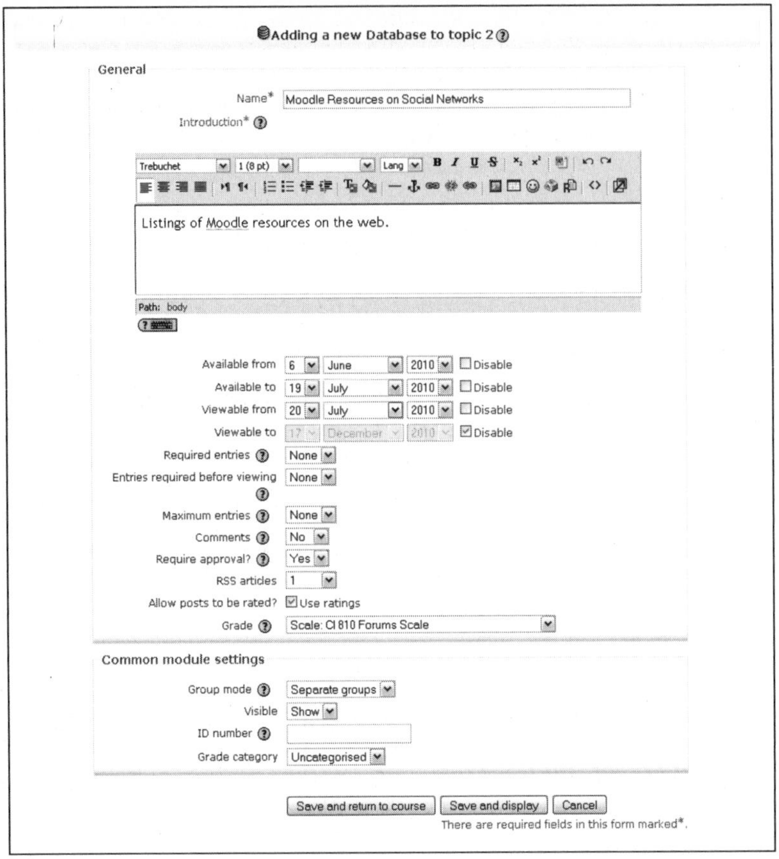

Figure 12-2: The Adding a New Database page.

The figure shows the "Adding a new Database to topic 2" form with the following fields:

General

Name*: Moodle Resources on Social Networks

Introduction*: Listings of Moodle resources on the web.

Available from: 6 June 2010 ☐ Disable
Available to: 19 July 2010 ☐ Disable
Viewable from: 20 July 2010 ☐ Disable
Viewable to: 17 December 2010 ☑ Disable
Required entries: None
Entries required before viewing: None
Maximum entries: None
Comments: No
Require approval?: Yes
RSS articles: 1
Allow posts to be rated?: ☑ Use ratings
Grade: Scale: CI 810 Forums Scale

Common module settings

Group mode: Separate groups
Visible: Show
ID number:
Grade category: Uncategorised

Save and return to course   Save and display   Cancel
There are required fields in this form marked*.

- *Required Entries:* You can make this a required activity, meaning students have to enter a certain number of entries before it will be considered complete. From the drop-down list, select the number of entries required of each student. Moodle will send reminder messages to the students who haven't completed the required entries. You can require up to 50 entries. The Moodle default is None.

- *Entries Required before Viewing:* You can set the number of entries each student is required to submit before they get to view other entries in the database. If they haven't completed the required entries, they can see only the entry page and not the pages with complete data.

If you set up the database to require entries before viewing, make sure you or your system administrator disables the database autolinking filter. If it isn't disabled, Moodle can't determine whether a learner has submitted the required entries. You can disable or enable autolinking from the Site Administration block. From the block, click Modules, then Filters, and then Manage Filters.

(This is discussed in Chapter 13.) Remember that you need to have an Administrator user account or privileges to access the setting. Alternatively, get very friendly with your system administrator. It's always a good idea to become his good friend. Overworked and unappreciated, bring them Coke and Skittles and tell them how wonderful they are — doesn't take much, really.

- *Maximum Entries:* This setting allows you to put a limit on how many entries students are allowed to enter into the database before they're blocked. This has been added to help prevent spamming. Most of the time you don't have to worry about this problem. Place a requirement if you feel some students will get so carried away and "data happy" that they may do the work for others.

- *Comments:* Enabling this function by selecting Yes from the drop-down list allows for comments to be added to each entry and viewable as a drop-down field in the template.

- *Require Approval?* If you set this functionality to Yes, each entry will require approval before it's added to the database. You can set up a role for an assistant that approves the data entries, or you can enable this capability to specific learners. See Chapter 4 for details on how to set permissions to activity capabilities.

- *RSS Articles:* Select the number of articles you want to be automatically added to your database. Note that you need to enable the RSS feed in the Site Administration block. If you don't have the privileges on your user account, ask your system administrator to enable this module. (See the discussion on RSS newsfeeds in the last section in this chapter.)

- *Allow Posts to Be Rated?* If you enable this setting, it allows you to rate entries, and the score will be added to the grade book. It's one way to get your learners involved. For example, you can ask them to add three entries, each worth five points. Receiving points that go toward their final grade or may be an incentive to add more quality entries. This is more of an incentive for younger learners in secondary schools than for learners attending training sessions or college levels.

- *Grade:* If you allow for posts to be rated, the grade functionality is enabled. From the drop-down list, select a scale or a numeric value. See Chapter 8 for details on how to set up scales and grades.

5. **In the Common Module Settings section, choose the following functions as required for the course:**

- *Group Mode:* If the group mode is forced at the course level, the setting within individual activities is ignored. If you created groups, you can choose No Groups; Separate Groups, where students only work within their groups; or Visible Groups, where students see other entries but cannot add to the database if they aren't assigned to the group. I discuss groups in detail in Chapter 4.

- *ID Number:* This option is useful to set if you're grading the activity, and it will appear in the grade book and/or exported to a CSV file. The grade book ID numbers keep the tables shorter, which means less horizontal scrolling.

6. **Click the Save and Display button.**

   Moodle takes you to the database editing page, where you can create the fields for entries, as described next.

Adding fields to your database

The next step is to create fields for your data. You can either create your own fields or use *presets,* which are fields you've created earlier in another application or within Moodle database. The purpose of the presets functionality is to save you time so that you don't have to create the fields more than once if you're replicating the database entries.

Figure 12-3 shows the Database field design and editing page. Notice the tabs across the page. You're going to be working in the Fields tab, which opens by default when you first define your database by following the steps in the preceding section. If you were to use presets, you would import them from the Presets tab, as described in the section "Viewing Your Database — What You and Your Learners Will See," later in this chapter.

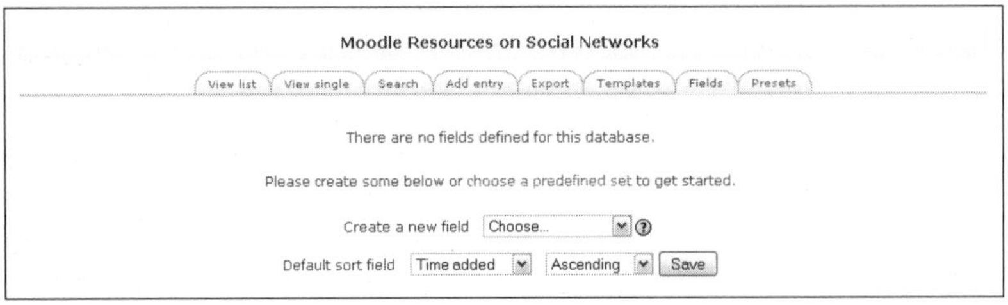

Figure 12-3:
A newly
created
database.
The Fields
tab is
opened.

Exploring the types of fields

Fields define the basic structure of your database and the information your learners will be entering. Individual fields are units of information. You create your database by selecting the different units that you need for your information related to something you've chosen to support your teaching unit. You can have any number of fields defining different types of information. For example, in the Moodle demo Resources for Social Networks shown in Figure 12-3, I can have a date field for my Moodle social network resources, used for listing the date when specific entries were posted. Table 12-1 lists the specific field choices as well as a brief explanation of how you can use them.

Table 12-1	Types of Database Fields
Field Type	*Description*
Check Box	Enables check boxes. Each new line represents a new check box. Text will appear next to the check box. Multiple check boxes enable users to select more than one entry. For example, if you were listing after school activities, you would need more than one check box to enter, sports, music, work, and so on. If you want to limit the entry to only one selection, use the Radio Buttons field.
Date	Allows learners to enter a date. Moodle offers a drop-down list for selecting a day, month, and year.
File	Learners can upload any type of file to this field. If they're uploading a graphic file, advise them to use the Picture field.
Menu	Enables learners to use a drop down menu. Each listed option needs to be added on a different line.
Menu (Multi-Select)	Same as Menu, though this option enables learners to select more than one of the choices from the drop-down list by holding down the Ctrl or Shift key as they select.
Number	Learners can enter any number, whether it's positive, negative, or zero, and the number can include decimal notations.
Picture	Used to upload any image file from learners' computer.
Radio Buttons	Used to require a student to choose one option from a range of options. If the learners don't select any of the options, Moodle prevents them from submitting the entries and prompts them to select an option. You can use this field with Yes/No or True/False questions.
Text	A text box field enabling learners to enter text up to 60 characters in length. Formatting options are not available.
Text Area	Allows users to enter text over 60 characters with formatting options (similar to forum posts).
URL	Enables learners to enter a Web address (URL). They're given an option to select autolink, which automatically makes the URL an active link to the address. If you force a name of the link, the name will be used for the displayed hyperlink.
Latitude/ Longitude Number	Enables learners to enter geographic locations by entering the latitude and longitude. When learners view the entry, Moodle automatically provides links to geographic data services such as Google Earth/Maps, OpenStreetMap, GeaBios, Mapstars, Multimap, and so on. (***Note:*** The teacher can choose which of those links appear or choose not to use any at all.)

I suggest you inform your learners about the capabilities and restrictions of the specific fields, such as the Text field.

Defining your fields

Open the Fields tab of the database field design and editing page (refer to Figure 12-3) and then follow these steps to define the fields you need for your database:

1. **From the Create a New Field drop-down list, select the type of field you need.**

   The Text Field editing page appears. The options that appear on this page depend on what type of field you selected from the list. For example, if you selected Text Field, you see the page shown in Figure 12-4.

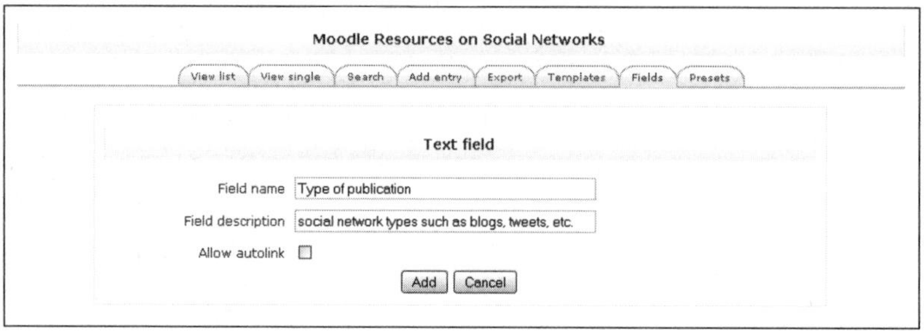

Figure 12-4: The Text Field editing page.

2. **Enter the field name.**

   All the field names in the database need to be unique and short because they will be displayed in the template. Intuitive names are good.

3. **Add a short description of the field.**

4. **Add and/or select other settings as required by the type of field.**

   For example, in Figure 12-4, adding a text field requires only Steps 1 through 3 and then clicking the Add button. Other fields, such as a Text Area field, require you to enter the width and height of the text box and offer you some default settings that you can alter. All the different types of fields are straightforward, but if you need more information, visit the Moodle docs at `http://docs.moodle.org/en/mod/data/field`.

5. **Click the Add button.**

   Moodle takes you back to the Fields page and shows the field you just added, as shown in Figure 12-5. Notice the Default Sort Fields drop-down list options. I left the default settings. These fields enable you to determine how new fields are organized in the database. You can make changes to them any time.

Figure 12-5:
A database
showing
newly
created field
and field
positioning
options.

6. **Repeat Steps 1 through 5 to add more fields.**

In the example shown in Figure 12-6, notice how Moodle builds your fields, giving you options to edit, delete, and sort each.

When you're finished adding all the fields you require, you're ready to start editing your templates, as described in the next section.

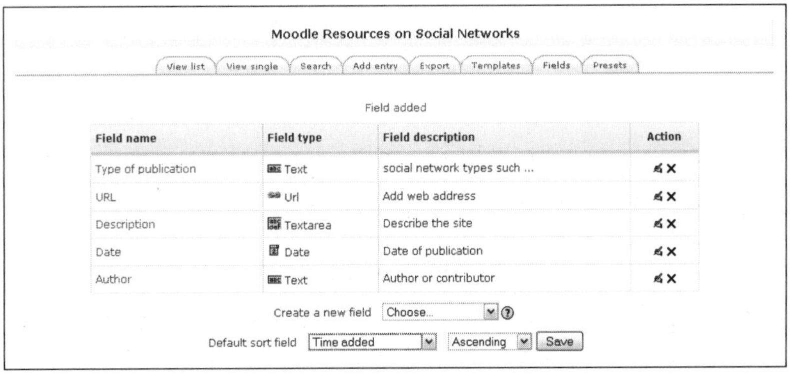

Figure 12-6:
The Field
Added page.

Editing your database interface

After setting up all the fields you need for your database, Moodle creates a default template that determines the *front end,* also referred to as the *interface.* This template enables you and your learners to view, list, and edit the database entries.

The templates are all HTML pages (Web pages) with a specific set of tags for the Database module. When you first select the Templates tab, Moodle takes you to the Single template, as shown in Figure 12-7. You can select another template by clicking one of the template links directly below the tabs.

Template links

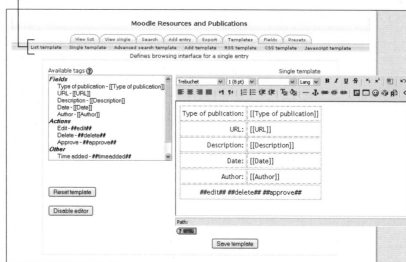

Figure 12-7:
Adding a
Single
template
to the
database.

Editing the Single template

The Single template is used to display a single entry instead of a list of
entries. This template gives you more space for text or images. Think about
how you will organize the information if you have a number of entries in a
single-entry template.

All the tags available for the single template are listed on the left side of the
editing page. (Refer to Figure 12-7.) Moodle reads the tags by looking at the
information between the square brackets [ ], which define data tags, meaning that when you enter data (text or numbers) in the fields, the Database
module knows to replace the generic description you entered (for instance,
replacing [URL] with the actual URL). So what you are doing is editing the
entry instead of creating a whole new one.

Tags represented by ## mean that the text currently in the template will be
replaced by a link or an icon/button to enable a particular action. These tags
are specific to actions such as

- ##edit##, which creates an icon you can click enabling you to edit an entry
- ##delete##, which creates a clickable icon enabling you to delete an entry

There are a number of these tags, such as More, Approve, Comment, and
User. You can create more icons by just adding #icon# to the editor. See
the Moodle.org online documentation for more information on tag usage at
http://docs.moodle.org/en/Database_templates#Tag_usage.

Under the available tags list, you see two buttons that give you additional editing options:

- ✔ **Reset Template:** Allows you to revert to the original template created when you set up the fields. So don't worry; go and play. It's okay to make mistakes. You'll learn from them, and you can always go back to the original — nothing is lost.

- ✔ **Disable Editor:** This option is useful if you want to work in raw HTML code instead of toggling between the editor text box and the code. If you click the Disable Editor button, Moodle provides you with pure text window to alter the HTML tags, as shown in Figure 12-8. Notice the button name changes to Enable Editor so that you can return to the editing window to see the results of your clever changes.

Figure 12-8:
A Single Template editing page showing the HTML code for the fields.

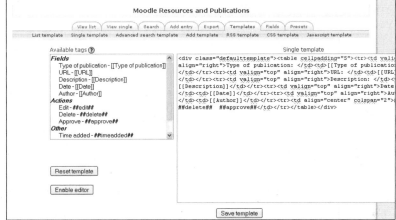

After you make changes to your database template, make sure you click the Save Template button.

Exploring other templates

In addition to the Single template, you can choose from six other possible templates based on your database requirements. Here's a rundown of the other templates you can use:

- ✔ **List template:** This template is the first thing students see when they access the database. The default template generated after you select your fields isn't very exciting, and you may want to lay it out so it looks less bland and boring. You're provided with three fields and given an option to add a header (an overview), a body, and a footer. The header can be used in the tables identifying each row, the body for the data, and the footer to end the table. The overview is useful when you are exporting the database as a CSV file. HTML tag knowledge is useful. For example, if you want to use the footer to end the table, all you need to do is add the `</table>` tag. With a little tweaking, you can make the whole List template into one table, which looks a lot neater. Visit the companion Web site for the coding and examples or visit `http://moodle.org/buzz` to view an example.

✓ **Advanced Search template:** This template is useful if you want to add an advanced search in your database. It's especially useful if you have many fields and your database will grow quickly. Users need to be able to narrow a search when exposed to a large amount of data.

✓ **Add template:** Use this template when you want to add or edit entries to the default template. Using this template, you can create an interface form enabling learners to enter data quickly in one form than specific fields. This is useful if you have lots of data to fill in.

✓ **RSS template:** This template enables you to structure how the newsfeed is presented to the learners. (I discuss RSS feeds in more detail later in the chapter.) Remember that the database will publish the entries right into the field, without your having to do anything. Just imagine choosing a topic and having all the news fed into your database without spending hours searching the Internet or going through your favorite journal articles and Web sites to gather the information for your students. Quite brilliant.

✓ **CSS template:** If any HTML templates require CSS to enhance styles, you can add them to the CSS template. Using CSS, you can change fonts, colors, spacing, alignment, and other display features that may be limited by the HTML tags. You need some knowledge of CSS in order to use this template.

✓ **JavaScript template:** Same as with the CSS template — if you know JavaScript, you can add JavaScript routines in this template. The JavaScript will be defined when the page loads. For example, you can run scripts around names and how many times they're displayed, or define the size of images and sound files. Knowledge of JavaScript, run-time routines and HTML is essential. If you have no idea what I'm talking about, forget this template.

Adding an entry

After you've edited the template and saved your changes, click the Add Entry tab located above the template links. Moodle takes you to the interface to add or edit an entry. In Figure 12-9, I entered the information into the fields specified in the template shown earlier in Figure 12-7.

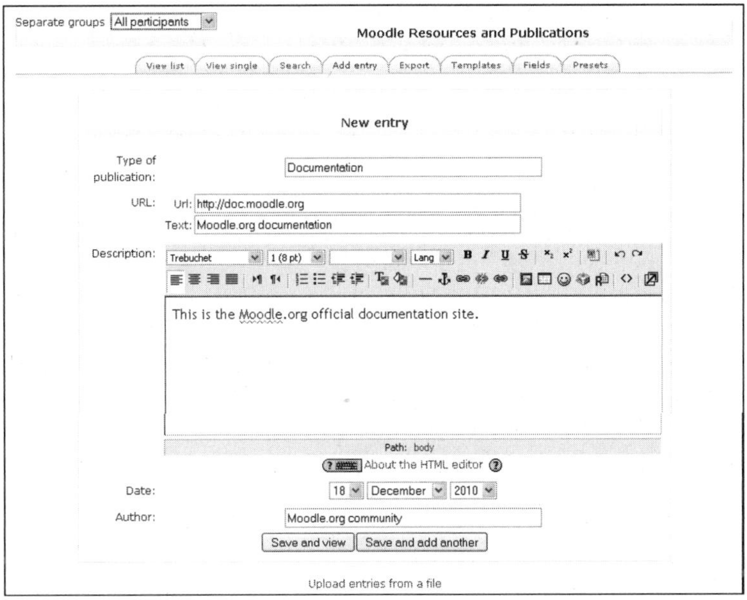
Separate groups All participants
Moodle Resources and Publications
View list
View single
Search
Add entry
Export
Templates
Fields
Presets
New entry
Type of publication:
Documentation
URL:
Url: http://doc.moodle.org
Text: Moodle.org documentation
Description:
Trebuchet
1 (8 pt)
Lang
This is the Moodle.org official documentation site.
Path: body
About the HTML editor
Date:
18 December 2010
Author:
Moodle.org community
Save and view
Save and add another
Upload entries from a file

Figure 12-9: Adding a new entry into a database URL field.

After you complete your entry, click the Save and View button at the bottom of the page. Moodle informs you that the entry was saved and then displays the entry, as shown in Figure 12-10. Notice that the tab switched to the View Single page, with editing and deleting icons at the bottom of the screen.

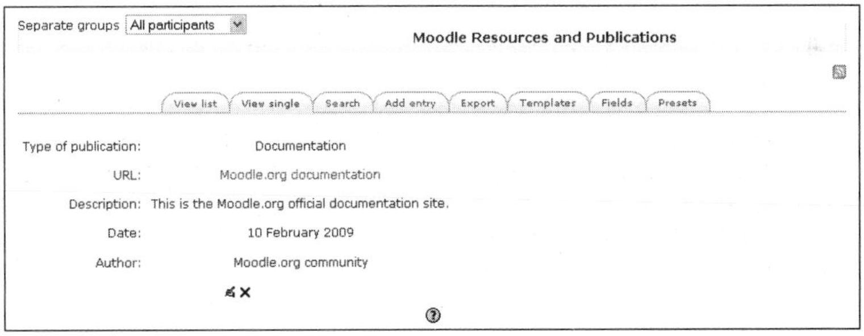
Separate groups All participants
Moodle Resources and Publications
View list
View single
Search
Add entry
Export
Templates
Fields
Presets
Type of publication: Documentation
URL: Moodle.org documentation
Description: This is the Moodle.org official documentation site.
Date: 10 February 2009
Author: Moodle.org community

Figure 12-10: Moodle confirms the new entry.

Viewing Your Database — What You and Your Learners Will See

When you or your learners select the database from the course front page, Moodle displays the main database page with a number of tabs. Each tab has a specific function. Student roles, by default, see only three tabs, as shown in Figure 12-11. In this list, I describe all the tabs shown in Figure 2-12:

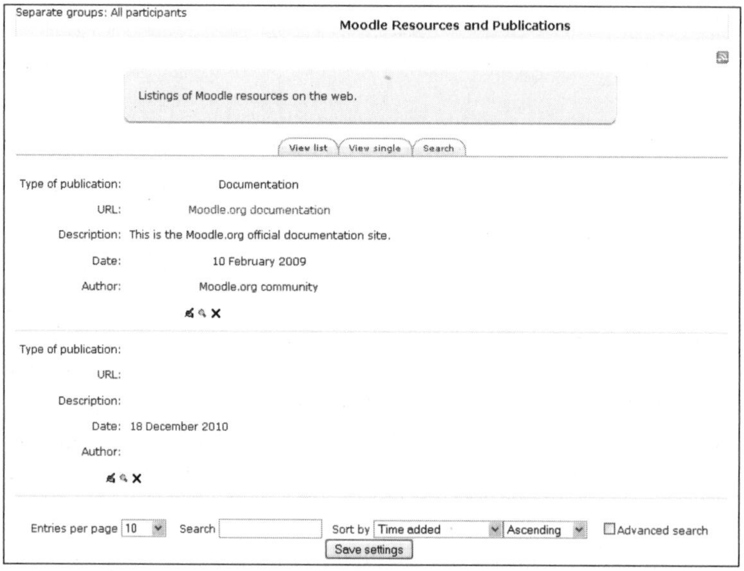

Figure 12-11:
The learners' view of the database from the View List tab.

✔ **View List tab:** This is the first page you and your learners see when you select the database from the course page. The page lists the entries that you and your learners have added. You decided how many entries can be viewed in the list when you set up the database. Note that you see the same view; the only difference is that you see more tabs.

✔ **View Single tab:** Only one entry is displayed. If you enabled users to add comments, the comment feature is available here.

✔ **Search tab:** Enables you or your learners to search for specific entries.

✔ **Add Entry tab:** Allows you and your learners (if you enabled student entries) to add entries to the database by filling in the form you created. I give an explanation on how to add entries earlier. The front end, the interface is decided on the templates you have chosen and possibly edited. *Note:* Your learners can see this tab only if you enabled the Student role to add entries to the database.

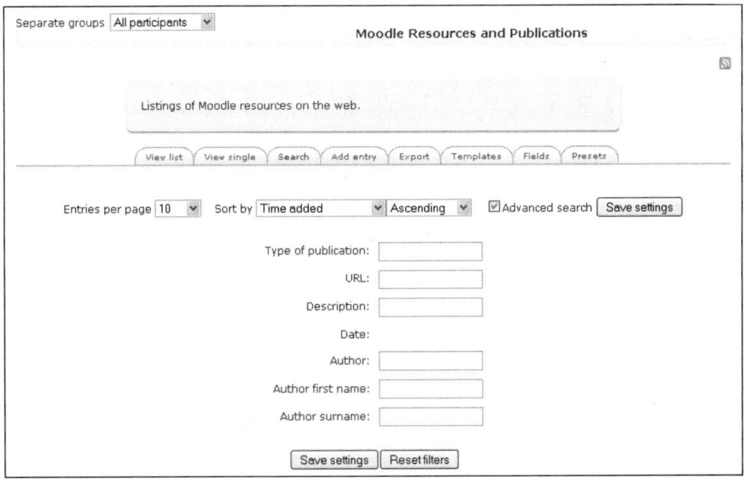

Figure 12-12:
The main
database
page
showing
all the tabs
available.

✔ **Export tab:** You can export your data to a CSV file with a choice of delimiters, Excel, or ODS. This is a required field. One format must be chosen in order for Moodle to proceed with the export. You can also choose which fields you want to export. They're all listed with a check mark in the check box. If you don't need a particular record of the entry, deselect the check box and then click the Export Database Records button. This tab is not seen by your learners.

✔ **Templates tab:** The template controls how you enter and edit the data into your database. For the lowdown on the individual templates, see the section "Editing your database interface," earlier in this chapter. This tab is not seen by learners.

✔ **Fields tab:** This is the tab where you define what type of data you want to enter into your database. (See the earlier section "Adding fields to your database" for more on this tab.) This tab is not seen by learners.

✔ **Preset tab:** A *preset,* in the Moodle database, is an ingenious functionality that allows you to reuse the database you created, saving you valuable time. Similar to the quiz question pool, the motto is "create once, reuse many times." For example, if you set up your course in groups and you want each group to have its own database, you can replicate it by using this functionality. Similarly, you can share the database (referred to as *preset*) with your colleagues, just as the Moodle community has shared its most popular databases with you. For example, the ever-so-popular image gallery preset is bundled in the Database module to help you learn how to use this tool and get you started creating quickly. Check out the companion Web site for more presets!

To import a preset, follow these steps:

1. **Click the Presets tab.**

   The Presets page appears, as shown in Figure 12-13.

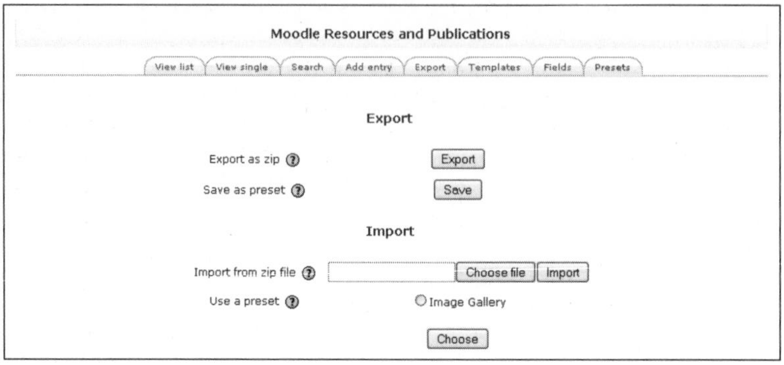

Figure 12-13:
The
importing
and
exporting
settings of
the Presets
page.

Moodle Resources and Publications

View list | View single | Search | Add entry | Export | Templates | Fields | Presets

Export

Export as zip ⑦   [Export]

Save as preset ⑦   [Save]

Import

Import from zip file ⑦   [　　　　] [Choose file][Import]

Use a preset ⑦   ○ Image Gallery

[Choose]

2. **In the Import section, click the Choose File button, locate the Zip file on your computer, and then click the Import button.**

3. **After the preset is imported, you can alter the fields and the template, and start to add entries.**

   Note that after you've imported and/or created a number of databases, you will have an option to choose a previously loaded preset.

   Quite simple, don't you think? All the tedious work is done for you — marvelous!

If you've developed an absolutely fabulous database and it has become a marvel to all your colleagues and learners, share it! You will be loved by all. What better way is there to become popular in your department, organization, and even an international star than by sharing your creation through the Moodle.org community?

To export your database preset, click the Presets tab and then do one of the following:

✔ **Select the Export as Zip option** by clicking the Export button. Follow the steps to save your file as a zipped file on your computer so that you can import it to another course or Moodle site.

✔ **Select the Save as Preset option** by clicking the Save button. Moodle takes you through a few steps, and Moodle publishes the database for other teachers on the site to use. When you save your database as a preset, it appears in the preset list, and you can reuse it.

Managing Your Database

Making sure users enter quality information into the database is an important aspect of developing a collaborative tool that can be used as a valuable teaching resource. Be sure to educate your learners about entering quality data instead of just populating it willy-nilly. Structure is only one aspect of a database. Learners often enter information based on their knowledge and understanding of the purpose of the database and its goals. Don't be shy about going over organization, accuracy, and interpretation — grasping those elements can become a learning exercise. However much you introduce the concept, as the database grows, you need to track the information to ensure the information's consistency and accuracy.

Moodle has added a number of tools that help you manage the information and ensure the quality of the entries. (You can either set these options when you first create your database or go back later and enable them.)

✔ **Comments:** By adding comments, you can guide students, give them feedback, and let them know you're watching and reading what they've entered. I can hear what you're thinking: "How can I possibly find time to add comments to entries, especially if I have more than 90 students in my three Moodle courses!" You don't have to do this alone. Remember that you can set permission to specific student accounts, guest accounts, or create a new database monitor role. Why not get an assistant? You can ask a previous student, trainee, or a group leader to take the burden off your shoulders.

✔ **Require Approval:** Moodle hides entries from the learners in the course until you, or someone with the capability approves the new entry. Requiring approval helps you ensure that the entries are valuable and accurate before they become available to learners. Note that this is not a default setting: You need to select the option for it when you set up your database.

✔ **Ratings:** If the preceding two tools seem like too much work, one way to ensure quality and quantity is to assign grades for entries to the database. You can set up a simple point system or use a scale. Rewarding students for their contribution is most likely the best method to ensure quality. Students like to be rewarded, and they can view creating entries as a simple way to bring up a grade. Rating in the database doesn't provide you with a feedback field as in the Assignment or Quiz modules. However, you can combine rating with comments, and this becomes a powerful learning and assessment tool, even more so if you involve groups.

Enabling students, guests, student teachers, or any other user account to rate, comment on, or even approve entries can save you time. You select the setting options for enabling comments when you set up the database. You need to enable the other capabilities by giving the roles specific permissions.

If you didn't set the rating, comment, and approval functions when you set up the database, follow these steps:

1. **Click the Update This Database button on the database viewing page, located in the top-right corner.**

   Moodle takes you to Editing Database page. You see three tabs as with all activities. Moodle defaults to the Settings tab, where you can update and change any of the options and settings.

2. **Scroll down the page. From the drop-down lists next to Comments and Require Approval?, select Yes.**

3. **Next to the question Allow Posts to Be Rated?, select the Use Ratings check box. Select the grade or scale from the drop-down list.**

4. **Click the Save and Display button.**

To allow for specific capabilities on different roles, follow these steps:

1. **Repeat Step 1 in the preceding step list.**

2. **Select the Override Permissions tab by clicking it.**

3. **From the Role to Override drop-down list, select the role you want to override.**

   For example, in Figure 12-14, I selected Student.

4. **From the Capability list, select the Allow radio button for the Write Comments feature and the Rate Entries feature. (See Figure 12-14.)**

5. **Click Save Changes button at the bottom of the screen.**

Your students in the course now have the abilities to rate and comment on entries. If you want only specific learners to have permission, you need to override the permission capabilities from their profiles. *Note:* You can create a new role (such as Student Teacher) and assign the role the capabilities discussed in this section, and then give specific students this role. Refer to Chapter 4 for more information and examples on roles and setting permissions.

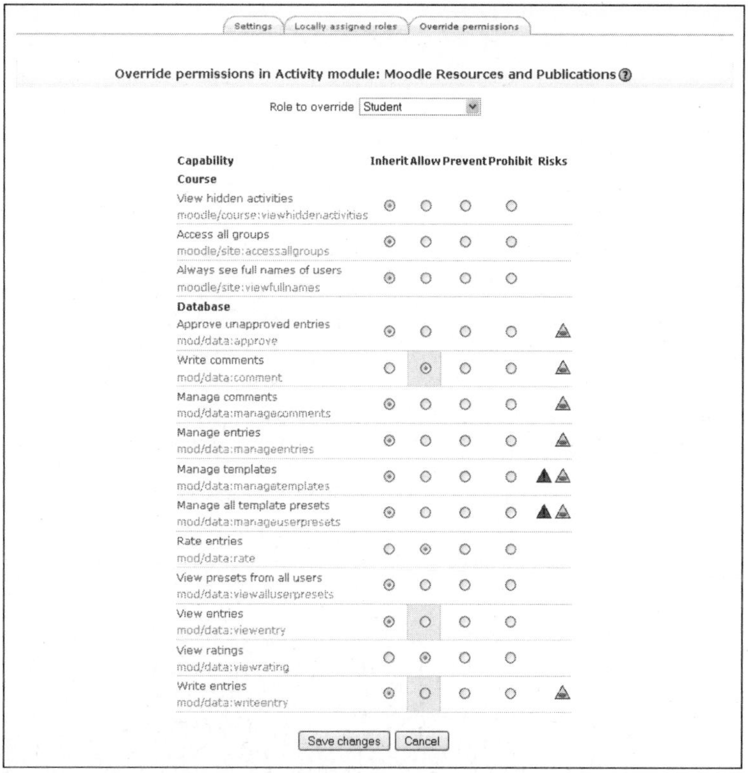

Figure 12-14:
The
Override
Permissions
page.

Adding RSS to Your Course

I know you have been itching to learn how to add a newsfeed to your course and to finally understand what RSS stands for so you can impress all your friends. RSS is a geeky term standing for Really Simple Syndication (also referred to as Web feed, feed, or channel). What this means is that when you subscribe to a site on the Internet, the news is brought to you so that you spend less time looking for updated information in blogs, e-zines, news headlines, audio, or video. The short summary in the RSS includes publishing dates and a link to the source.

"Fantastic," I hear you thinking! Before I take you through the steps on how to add it to your course, I need to give you a little more information.

Moodle enables you to bring feeds (information) to various activities in Moodle. You can use RSS with

✔ Forums

✔ Glossaries

✔ Databases

✔ The course front page (blocks)

For you to be able to use RSS, it needs to be enabled in the Administration block in the Server subsection. If you don't have administrative privileges, ask your system administrator to enable it. It will also have to be enabled in the Forum activity. When you're making this request, ask the administrator to enable administrative and teacher submitters in the Blocks section. If you need instructions on how to make these changes, see Chapter 13, which provides a brief rundown on many of the Moodle administrative tasks.

Including RSS on the course front page

The RSS feeds block allows you to bring feeds to a block on the course front page. The block will automatically update to bring in the latest feeds. You can add one or more RSS feeds to your course front page. You create a list of the Web sites and then you can select from the list how many you want to arrive to your activity or course front page block at any one time. Site and course front pages are common places for an RSS feed block(s).

To set up an RSS feed block, follow these steps:

1. **Click the Turn Editing On button in the top-right corner of your course front page.**

2. **Find the Blocks block on the front page (you may have to scroll down to find it) and select Remote RSS Feed from the drop-down list.**

   The Remote News Feed block appears, as shown in Figure 12-15.

3. **Click the edit icon on the Remote News Feed block.**

   Moodle takes you to the default page, Configuring a Remote RSS Feeds Block, shown in Figure 12-16.

4. **Set the following options to configure the block feeds:**

   • *Display each link's description?* Select Yes or No from the drop-down list. If you select Yes, the block shows the description of each article as it appears on the Web; select No, and the block displays only the title. Both are generated by the feed — you have no work here.

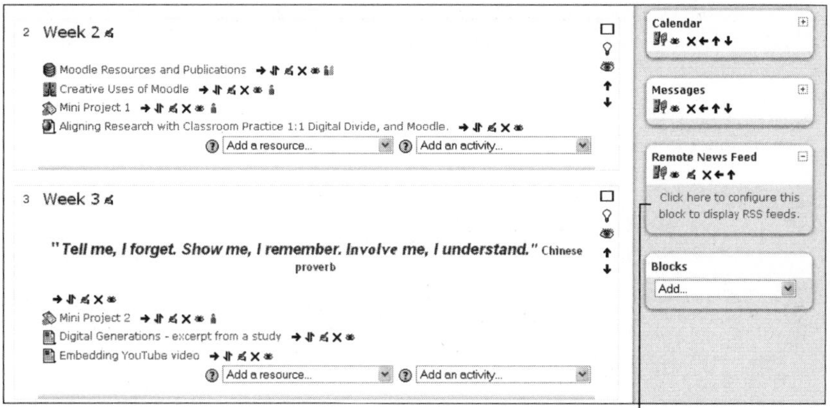

Figure 12-15:
The course
front page
showing the
RSS block.

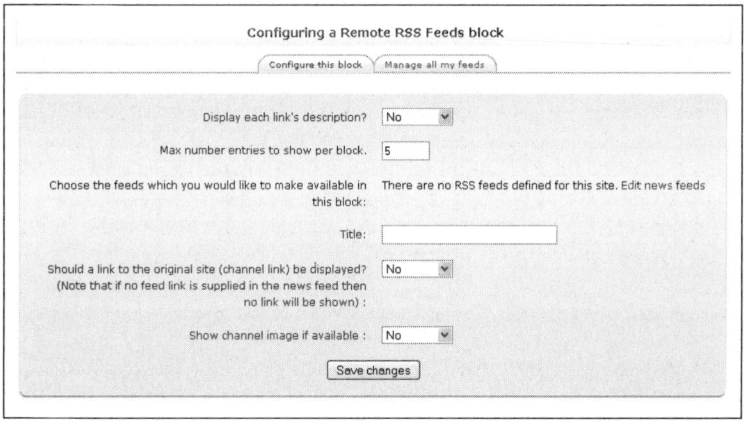

Remote News Feed block

Figure 12-16:
The
Configuring
a Remote
RSS Feeds
Block page.

- *Max Number Entries to Show per Block:* The default is 5. Moodle displays the most recent first.

- *Choose the Feeds . . .:* After you select a number of feeds, you see a check box next to them and you can select each feed by selecting the check box. You can break up the feed block by having more than one.

- *Title:* Make sure you add a title, or Moodle takes the title from the newsfeeds, which can be messy if you have more than one feed.

- *Display a Link?* If you select Yes from the drop-down list, Moodle provides you with a link to the full article and the original site from where it was first published. This link is useful if your learners will want to reference the information in their projects, essays, and so on.

- *Show Channel Image?* Newsfeeds have images and logos and display them with the feed unless you leave the default as No.

    Allowing for images and logos can eat up your Moodle space, which is particularly problematic if you're on a restricted space budget. I recommend leaving the default No if you need impressive negotiating skills to get more space for your course.

5. **Click the Save Changes button.**

    Moodle returns you to the course front page. You see the title of your newsfeed in the block.

6. **From the RSS block, click the Add/Edit link located right under the editing icons.**

    Moodle takes you to the Configuring a Remote RSS Feeds Block page again, this time with the Manage All My Feeds tab selected, as shown in Figure 12-17.

Figure 12-17:
The
Configuring
a Remote
RSS Feeds
Block page.

Configuring a Remote RSS Feeds block

Configure this block   Manage all my feeds

Nothing to display

Add a news feed URL:

http://www.moodlenews.com/

Custom title (leave blank to use title supplied by feed):

Moodle News

☐ Shared feed

Add   Validate feed

Unless you get the privilege to add the feeds, which I strongly recommend, only the administrator has this privilege but can be easily changed to Administrator and Teacher. Bring your system administrator a soda and chocolate ask for this privilege.

7. **Fill in the following information about the feed you want to add:**

    - *Add a News Feed URL:* Copy and paste (or type) the URL address of the RSS feed in the field provided. Moodle generates the RSS page address.

    - *Custom Title:* In the field provided, add your title. Moodle tells you that if you leave it blank it will use the one supplied by the feed, which means the generating site.

    - *Shared Feed:* Select this check box if you want to make the feed available to all the courses in the Moodle site. This option can be useful, for instance, for an announcements feed in college publications.

Remember that even if you select this option, courses that don't have the RSS block enabled will not display the RSS block. Don't rely on sharing the RSS feed block as a main means of communicating important news.

- *Validate Feed:* Before clicking the Add button, Moodle provides a validation feed tool to confirm the feed URL is accurate. Click the Validate Feed link. Wait a few seconds, and Moodle returns a validation page congratulating you, as shown in Figure 12-18.

FEED Validator

FOR ATOM AND RSS AND KML

| http://www.moodlenews.com/feed/ | Validate |

Congratulations!

VALID RSS ✔ This is a valid RSS feed.

Recommendations

This feed is valid, but interoperability with the widest range of feed readers could be improved by implementing the following recommendations.

- line 108, column 0: content:encoded should not contain object tag (5 occurrences) [help]

    `<div class="prezi-player"><!-- .prezi-player ( width: 550px; ) .prezi-player ...`

- line 230, column 0: style attribute contains potentially dangerous content: position [help]

    `<content:encoded><![CDATA[<p><span id="wylio-flickr-image-2475580517" sty ...`

Source: http://www.moodlenews.com/feed/

```
01.     <?xml version="1.0" encoding="UTF-8"?>
02.     <rss version="2.0"
```

Figure 12-18: The output of Moodle's feed validator.

8. **Click the Add button to submit the feed.**

   Moodle confirms the addition and returns you to the Manage All My Feeds tab, where you can edit it and add another feed. (See Figure 12-19.)

   Note that it will take a little time before the server refreshes, and you will see the new news feed in your newly created Remote News Feeds block.

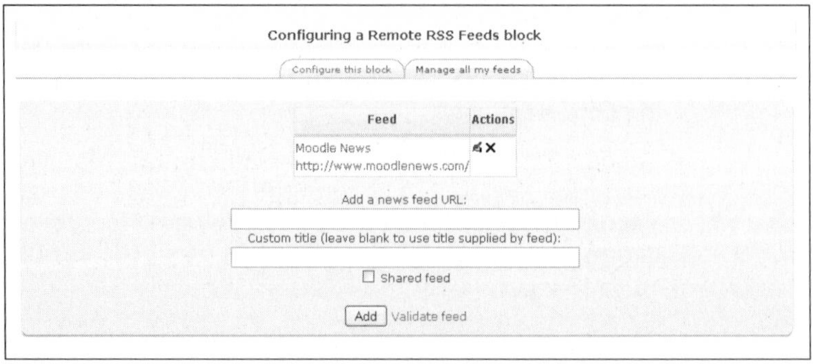

Figure 12-19:
The
Configuring
a Remote
RSS Feeds
Block page
with a new
feed added.

Configuring a Remote RSS Feeds block

Configure this block | Manage all my feeds

Feed	Actions
Moodle News http://www.moodlenews.com/	✍ ✗

Add a news feed URL:

Custom title (leave blank to use title supplied by feed):

☐ Shared feed

Add | Validate feed

Add RSS to forums

If you set up a forum discussion around a specific learning goal topic, a debate, or a project, you and your learners may find it very useful to enable newsfeeds to be brought to the forum. Forum newsfeeds can generate further discussions and debates. Even though RSS is enabled, it also has to be enabled in the Site Administration block, located in the Modules subsection in Activities under Forum. When you enable RSS, the Forum Editing page includes an RSS section with two extra settings. If you already have RSS enabled for your activities, you don't have to worry about pleading with your system administrator.

To set up RSS in your forum, follow these steps:

1. **Add (or select update) a forum in the section where you want the forum to appear. If you already have a forum set up, click the Forums link in the Activities block, select the particular forum, and click the Update This Forum button located in the top-right corner.**

   If this is a new forum discussion, complete all the fields to set up the forum. See Chapter 8 for details on how to set up a forum.

2. **In the RSS section, specify these two settings (see Figure 12-20):**

   • *RSS Feed for This Activity:* From the drop-down list, select Posts if you want the feed to send any news post to subscribers. Select Discussion if you want the fee to send new discussions to subscribers. Leaving the default None disables the RSS.

   • *Number of RSS Recent Articles:* From the drop-down list, select the number you would like. Five is a good, manageable choice. Moodle is quite generous, enabling you to set up to 50 newsfeeds. This would be an extraordinary number to allow and would quickly use up your allocated space if the topic could generate this much info. Your system administrator may have tweaked this option so that you only have choices up to 5.

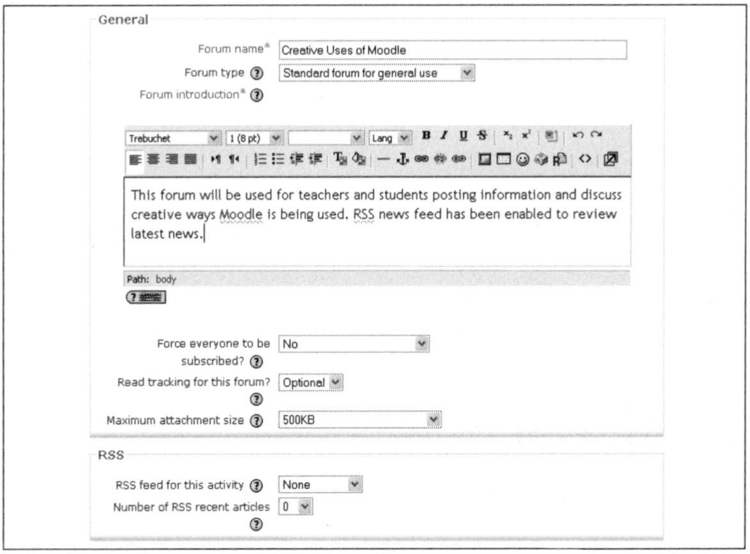

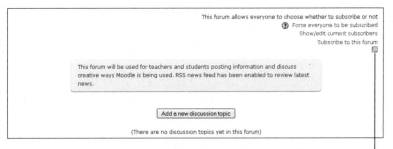

General

Forum name*	Creative Uses of Moodle
Forum type ⑦	Standard forum for general use
Forum introduction* ⑦	

[Text editor toolbar: Trebuchet | 1 (8 pt) | Lang | **B** *I* U S x₂ x² 🖉 ↩ ↪ / ≡ ≡ ≡ ≡ | ¶ ¶ | ≔ ≔ ≔ ≔ | ⸺ 🔗 ∞ ∞ ∞ | ⬜ ⬜ ☺ ✿ 🔌 <> 🖉]

This forum will be used for teachers and students posting information and discuss creative ways Moodle is being used. RSS news feed has been enabled to review latest news.

Path: body

[? HTML]

Force everyone to be subscribed? ⑦	No
Read tracking for this forum? ⑦	Optional
Maximum attachment size ⑦	500KB

RSS

RSS feed for this activity ⑦	None
Number of RSS recent articles ⑦	0

Figure 12-20:
The Forums
set-up page
showing
RSS options.

3. **Click the Save and Return to Course button.**

Moodle returns to your course front page.

Click the new or updated forum, and Moodle takes you to it. Notice the RSS icon shown in Figure 12-21. Whenever you see this icon, a newsfeed is enabled for the activity.

You can add RSS to your glossary, wiki, and database by using a similar procedure as described in the Forum section. You don't have to enable filters in these modules as you have to in the Forum module. When RSS in enabled in your course, it's available to use in the modules.

This forum allows everyone to choose whether to subscribe or not
⑦ Force everyone to be subscribed
Show/edit current subscribers
Subscribe to this forum

Figure 12-21:
A forum
discussion
with RSS
enabled.

This forum will be used for teachers and students posting information and discuss creative ways Moodle is being used. RSS news feed has been enabled to review latest news.

Add a new discussion topic

(There are no discussion topics yet in this forum)

RSS icon

Part IV
Moodle Management

The 5th Wave   By Rich Tennant

"It was the hardware requirement for my online bartending class."

In this part . . .

This part empowers you to manage your content. In Chapter 13, I show you how to optimize your files for smooth running, how to back up your data, and how to replicate your course with a quick shortcut so that you don't have to start from scratch. It's a techy chapter, and you can skip it if you aren't responsible for administering the Moodle site. Chapter 14 guides you in the collection of user reports to keep on top of your learners and demonstrate impressive statistics in your annual report.

Chapter 13

Administering Moodle Courses

*Y*our Moodle installation comes complete with default settings that enable you to get your courses up and running without too many system tweaks. You have many options for customizations, performance, and enabling or restricting various module filters. Many of the administrative options are located and accessible by Teacher roles from the course Administration block, as discussed elsewhere in the book. I also make frequent references throughout the book to administrative permissions and the Site Administration block located on the site front page.

In this chapter, I introduce most of the administrative functions that enable Moodle to run smoothly. I also explain, in more detail, several functions that you need to understand. Moodle has too many settings for me to cover all of them in this chapter, and most often, many settings are taken care of by the system administrator or by IT support staff members who are given the task of looking after Moodle. It may be that you end up wearing multiple hats: site administrator, course creator, and teacher. If this is the case, you need to pay special attention to this chapter. If you have IT support in your organization, it's useful for you to know what is in here so that if your system administrator is new to Moodle, you can inform him that there are ways you can get what you need with few tweaks. Believe it or not, often IT staff are given the job to support new software without any prior experience — that's why they require mass quantities of caffeinated beverages and walk around blurry eyed.

The structure of this chapter follows the categories listed in the Moodle Site Administration block, shown in Figure 13-1. This structure is also followed by the help files at Moodle.org. Each item in the Site Administration block is a link that takes you to the particular section or displays more subsections.

Note: You need to have an administrator user account or administrative privileges in order to be able to view the Site Administration block.

Site Administration block

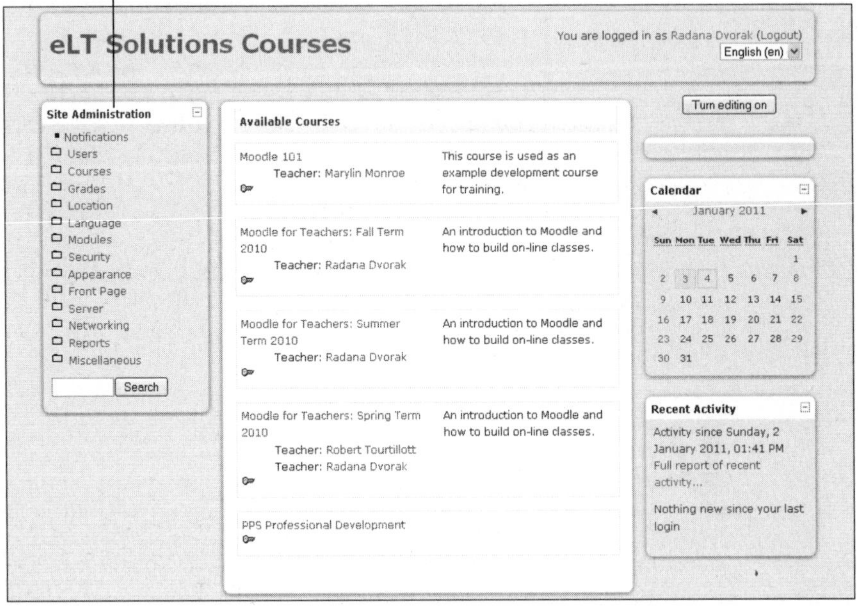

Figure 13-1:
The Site
Admini-
stration
block.

This chapter touches only the surface of information for the IT administrator, so if you need additional information on a particular setting, click the Moodle Docs for This Page link located at the bottom of the page. This link takes you to the Moodle documents written and updated by Moodle.org developers.

Notifications

The Notifications page has useful details, including the version of Moodle you're using, which you may need if you want to report a bug to Moodle.org (http://tracker.moodle.org). This page may also include a warning that your site may not be secured if the *cron* (the time-based job scheduler that runs predefined tasks) has not been run. Most often, you don't need to worry about this, because the cron is run automatically.

This page also displays a Moodle Registration button with a statement above the button, Please register your site to remove this button. You or your system administrator would have registered with Moodle.org when you first downloaded Moodle; however, it's a good practice to update your registration (I update quarterly) to help Moodle.org keep accurate Moodle global statistics, which you can visit at `http://moodle.org/stats`. (By the way, keeping on top of registering the site doesn't remove the button.)

Users

User, in Moodle, is an account that has a particular role, and each role has a permission status assigned to it. The main default user roles are Administrator, Teacher, Student, Non-Editing Teacher, and Guest. User management is the most time-consuming administrative job because unlike the other utilities, registering and maintaining users, roles, and permission for courses is an ongoing process throughout the lifecycle of courses. Moodle has a number of tools that can make the process easier, depending on how you and/or your organization decide to register students. There are three main sections in the Site Administration block under the Users category: Authentication, Accounts, and Permissions.

Authentication

Authentication is all about creating accounts for learners and anyone else who needs access to courses, enabling learners and others to log in to Moodle courses. Creating student accounts is covered in Chapter 4, where I suggest that the most efficient way for new learners to acquire a Moodle course account is through self registration. Self registration may not always be possible, for any number of reasons, such as the way an organization is structured and the server architecture; however, Moodle provides you with alternative authentication (the Moodle word for creating accounts) methods.

From the Site Administration block, click Users to open three subfolders, each of which is a link. Click the Authentication folder to view the following authentication options:

✔ **Manage Authentication:** This page, shown in Figure 13-2, enables you to choose the authentication method (plugin) for your organization. Click the closed-eye icon in the Enabled column and then click the Settings button located to the right of the plugin. You can select more than one plugin. I recommend you order them using the up and down arrows, placing the plugin that will handle most registrations at the top.

In Moodle 2.0 onwards, the Authentication link has been dropped, and you access this page by clicking Access Administration, then Plugins, and then Authentication.

You can take a few more actions in the Common Settings section of the page (see Figure 13-3):

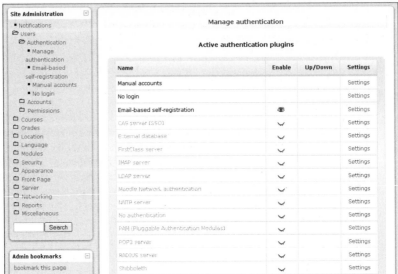

Figure 13-2:
The Manage
Authen-
tication
page for
plugins.

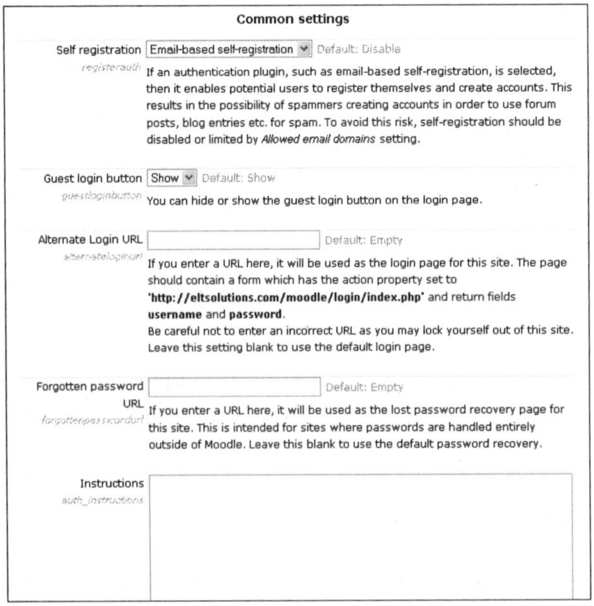

Figure 13-3:
The
Common
Settings
section
showing
registration
plugins.

• *Self Registration:* If you include e-mail–based self-registration, select Email-Based Self-Registration from the Self Registration drop-down list.

• *Guest Access:* If you need to set up guest access, select To Show from the Guest Login Button drop-down list. Moodle places a guest login button on the login page. Note, by default, this setting is set to Show the guest login button. It may have been disabled by someone with admin privileges, in which case you would have to select the Show option from the drop-down list.

This page offers a number of other options, and I recommend you leave the default settings unless configuration is necessary to meet the requirements of the department's system architecture.

When you're finished making changes, click the Save Changes button.

✔ **Email-Based Self-Registration:** These permission settings enable learners to create their own accounts using their e-mail to register. There are a number of options your learners are required to input and select in order to complete the registration process, otherwise the registration will fail. Chapter 4 shows the New Account page that learners need to complete and submit. Required fields are highlighted by the asterisk (*). Self registration is covered in more detail in Chapter 4.

After learners complete the self-registration process, they receive a confirmation and a default welcome message. Learners' profiles are created with the information they were required to provide. They can, at any time, update their profiles, change their passwords, upload their pictures and add to their profiles when they have access to the course.

I recommend that you open self registration for a limited time only and then disable it. Disabling it prevents spammers from accessing forum posts, blog entries, and so on. Another way to minimize site spam is to limit self registration to specific e-mail domains, which can be set from the Manage Authentication page. (Refer to the preceding bullet.)

✔ **Enable reCAPTCHA element:** This is a setting you want to enable because it's a small program that tests whether a user trying to register is really human. Because bots still can't read distorted text like humans, they can't access a site that's protected by CAPTCHA, so the CAPTCHA successfully prevents programs from entering and generating spam.

✔ **Manual Accounts:** The system administrator needs to create all the user accounts manually. Locking the default removes the ability for self registration. See the following section for more information on manual accounts.

Accounts

The Accounts settings are related to all the individual user accounts in the Moodle site. The Accounts folder has a number of subcategories, each a link with various options:

✔ **Browse List of Users:** This page lists all users and provides links to their profiles.

If you have a large number of courses, you may want to filter this list by course, dates first or last accessed, and so on. To do so, click the Show

Advanced button to see a list of fields to select from, as shown in Figure 13-4, which shows the Hide Advanced button because Show Advanced has been clicked. This page also enables you to add a new user by clicking the Add User button at the bottom of the page, which takes you to a registration page that's identical to the self-registration page discussed in Chapter 4.

- ✔ **Bulk User Actions:** This link takes you to a page where you can perform a variety of actions for registered users, such as adding or sending a message, deleting users, or forcing a password change, as shown in the drop-down list in Figure 13-5.

- ✔ **Add a New User:** This page enables you to set up a new user account. You need to complete a number of required fields in order for Moodle to set up the account.

Users can update this page from their profiles, so keep the info to the minimum required. If a student forgets her password, you can reset it from this link by clicking the Update Profile button at the bottom of this page.

You can set up a test account and use a secondary or spare e-mail address for it.

- ✔ **Upload Users:** If you need to register a large number of learners at once, this page (shown in Figure 13-6) enables you to do just that using a simple CSV file.

Click the Moodle Docs for This Page link at the bottom of the page for more information about bulk registration.

Before you set about this task, I advise that you check out the other authentication options, as this task can be time consuming. For example, letting users self register or connect to your organization's external database will be much easier than registering each user individually. For alternative ways to manage authentication, see `http://docs.moodle.org/en/Manage_authentication`.

- ✔ **Upload User Pictures:** Enables you to upload pictures and assign them by name or user ID.

- ✔ **User Profile Fields:** You can alter and create new user profile categories and fields. You can set up any type of field, such as a menu of choices, text area, or check box.

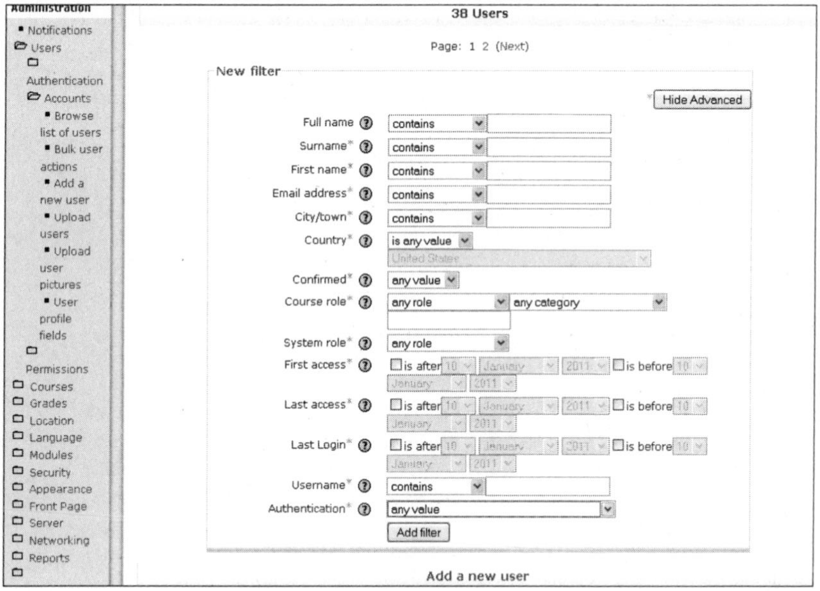

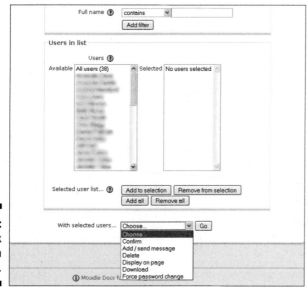

Figure 13-4: The Browse List of Users page with Show Advanced settings enabled.

Figure 13-5: The Bulk User Action page.

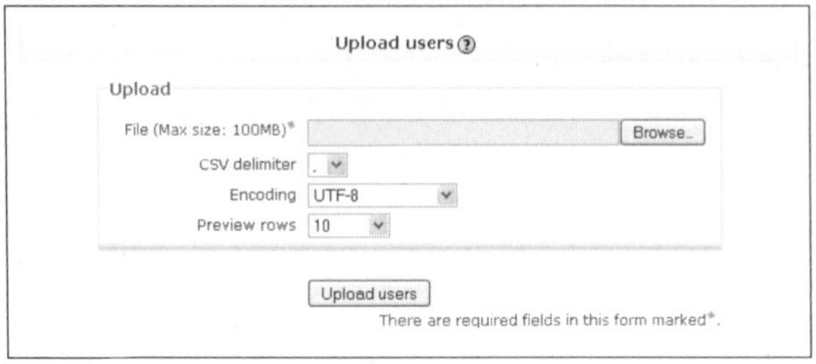

Figure 13-6:
Uploading
a CSV file
page.

Permissions

I touch on roles and permissions in several chapters, including a more detailed explanation in Chapter 4. New roles and permissions utilities equip you with a variety of options to manage how different user accounts (Student, Teacher, Guest, and so on) interact with Moodle activities, resources, and other user accounts. For example, a teacher can give a student permissions to help with approving what's added to wiki pages and with monitoring forums. However, before a teacher can do this, you need to enable certain permissions. You need to understand three utilities: Define Roles, Assign System Roles, and User Policies.

Define Roles

The Define Roles page has three tabs:

- ✔ The *Manage Roles tab* is the first page you see. (See Figure 13-7.) All roles currently assigned to the Moodle site are displayed with editing capabilities in the far right column. You can move the roles up and down and rename them or enable particular capabilities. If you want to change many of the permissions and capabilities, it's easier to create a new role. The Add a New Role button under the defined roles takes you to a page enabling you to do just that. Adding a New Role is discussed in more detail in Chapter 4.

- ✔ The *Allow Role Assignments tab* (shown in Figure 13-8) enables you to assign roles (permissions assigned to the role) from user accounts holding the role in the left side to the roles in the columns. Just select the check boxes and then click the Save Changes button.

- ✔ The *Allow Role Overrides tab* enables you to choose which role(s) you can override by each of the roles in the left column. (This page is similar to the Allow Role Assignments tab in Figure 13-8.) For example, it may be important for you to enable teachers to set role overrides so that students can have specific permission when they use certain activities (such as forums, chat, or wikis).

  To enable teachers to set role overrides, you need to first allow the capability to override roles and then set which role(s) teachers can override.

Figure 13-7:
The Roles
editing
page.

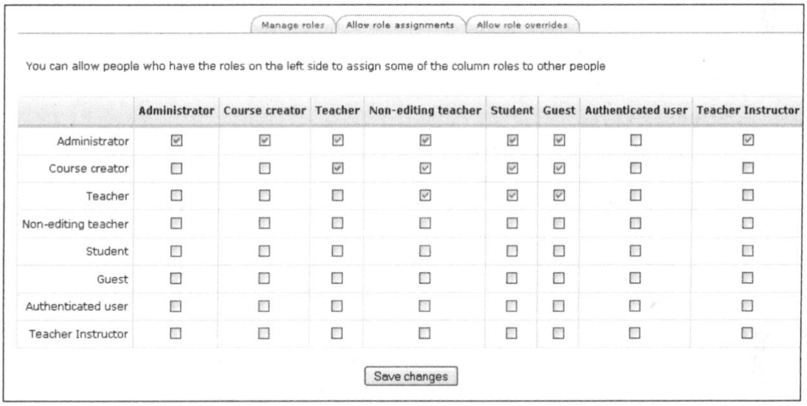

Figure 13-8:
The Allow
Role
Assign-
ments tab.

1. Go to the Manage Roles tab. (Refer to Figure 13-8.)

2. Click the Teacher role on the left.

   Moodle takes you the role's detail page.

3. Click the Edit button at the top.

4. Scroll down to permissions until you see the capabilities and then change the capability moodle/role:manage (or moodle/role: safeoverride in some older versions) and select the Allow option.

5. Click the Save Changes button.

6. Select the tab Allow Role Overrides.

7. Select the check box(es) in the teacher row for the role(s) they need to be able to override.

It's useful for teachers to be able to override Non-Editing Teacher, Student, and Guest roles. You wouldn't want them to be able to override the admin.

8. Click the Save Changes button.

The role changes take effect only after the person holding that particular role logs in again.

Assign System Roles

I cover adding students to your course in Chapter 4 (that is, assigning the role of a student). You can do the same for Teacher, Guest, Course Creator, and any other predefined user account in the course. You can also create a new role, which is explained in the same chapter.

Any role you assign from the Site Administration block is a global role, meaning the user will have access to every course unless a key is set. Note the Teacher role does not need a key. For example, if you add a user to a Teacher role, the user is registered as a teacher in every course instead of just the one or two courses he's teaching.

User Policies

This page enables you to change various policies for roles and accounts to help with authentications and registration. If you're linking to a database to register in bulk, you need to review these settings.

Courses

Teacher, Course Creator, and Administrator roles are all responsible for adding courses to a Moodle site. Although teachers are an integral part of the process, they don't have permissions on the Teacher role to add courses unless the administrator changes the capabilities. If you're an administrator, and depending on the organization and how involved you are with the site, you may want to give the Teacher role the capability to add courses to save you time.

You can find a number of links within the Courses folder: Add/Edit Courses, Enrollments, Course Default Settings, Course Request, and Backups.

Add/Edit Courses

It's good practice to define a number of categories before you start adding courses. Moodle provides you with one category, Miscellaneous. You can name your categories anything you want, though it makes sense to follow either departmental listings or a logical and descriptive format that instructors and students will be able to easily understand.

To add a category, follow these steps:

1. Click Courses in the Site Administration block and then click Add/Edit Courses.

You see the Course Categories page, shown in Figure 13-9.

Figure 13-9:
The Course
Categories
page.

2. Click the Add New Category button.

The Add New Category page appears, as shown in Figure 13-10.

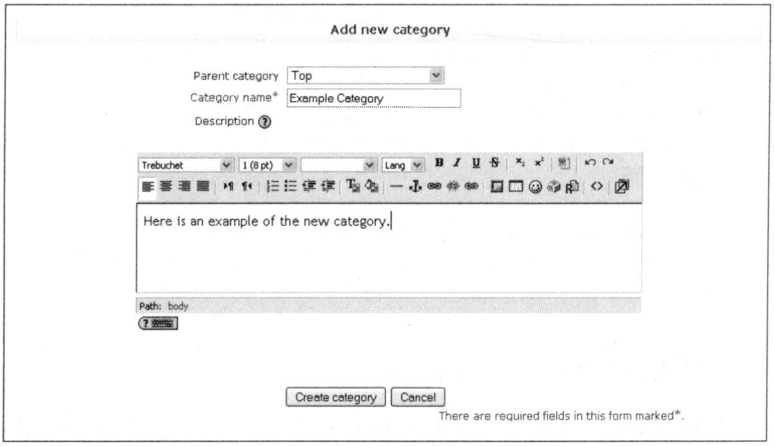

Figure 13-10:
The Add
New
Category
settings
page.

3. **In the Category Name text box, give the category a name and, if useful, add a short description in the Description box.**

4. **Save the category by clicking the Create Category button.**

   Moodle takes you to a page where you can add courses, as shown in Figure 13-11.

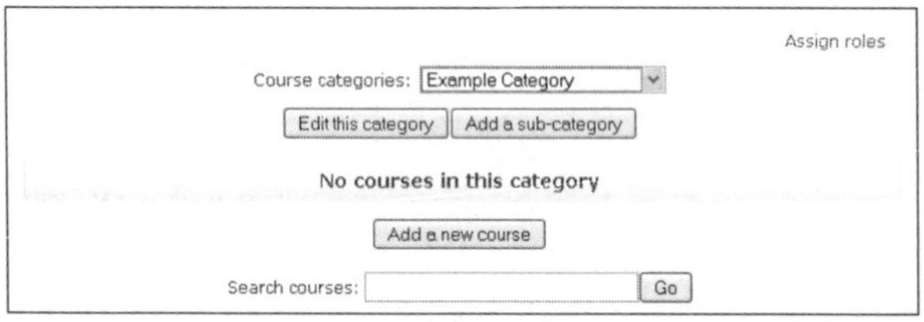

Figure 13-11:
The Add/
Edit Courses
page.

> Assign roles
>
> Course categories: [Example Category ▼]
>
> [Edit this category] [Add a sub-category]
>
> **No courses in this category**
>
> [Add a new course]
>
> Search courses: [_____] [Go]

5. **If you want to add a new course, click the Add a New Course button and then fill in the information about the course.**

6. **When you finish, click the Save Changes button, and Moodle takes you to Assigning Roles in Your Course page.**

7. **Add a Teacher role and then click the Click Here to Enter Your Course button.**

8. **Return to the Add/Edit Courses page by clicking the link in the Site Administration block.**

   This page provides you with a number of options to edit and move the categories around. (See Figure 13-12.)

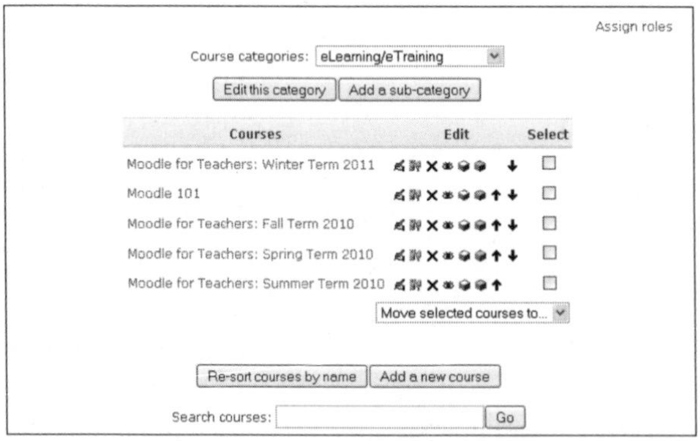

Figure 13-12:
The
Add/Edit
Courses and
Categories
page.

> Assign roles
>
> Course categories: [eLearning/eTraining ▼]
>
> [Edit this category] [Add a sub-category]
>
> | Courses | Edit | Select |
> |---------|------|--------|
> | Moodle for Teachers: Winter Term 2011 | ☞ 🏫 ✕ ⊛ ◉ ◉ ↓ | ☐ |
> | Moodle 101 | ☞ 🏫 ✕ ⊛ ◉ ◉ ↑ ↓ | ☐ |
> | Moodle for Teachers: Fall Term 2010 | ☞ 🏫 ✕ ⊛ ◉ ◉ ↑ ↓ | ☐ |
> | Moodle for Teachers: Spring Term 2010 | ☞ 🏫 ✕ ⊛ ◉ ◉ ↑ ↓ | ☐ |
> | Moodle for Teachers: Summer Term 2010 | ☞ 🏫 ✕ ⊛ ◉ ◉ ↑ | ☐ |
>
> [Move selected courses to... ▼]
>
> [Re-sort courses by name] [Add a new course]
>
> Search courses: [_____] [Go]

Selecting one of the categories in the Course Categories drop-down list brings you to a list of courses (see Figure 13-12), and you have the same editing capabilities as with the categories, including a drop-down list to move the courses to a different category, Add a New Course button, and Re-Sort Courses by Name button. You can hide the course and category by clicking the eye icon.

You can edit the default Miscellaneous category — just select the editing tools and rename it to meet your requirements. Click the Edit This Category button to make changes.

Enrollments

Authenticating and enrolling users are discussed in the Users category in this block, explained earlier in this chapter. In this section, Moodle gives you options to set up course enrollment.

Exploring the Enrollment plugins

The default setting enables users to self enroll by selecting a course name and then selecting Yes when the question "You are about to enroll yourself as a member of this course. Are you sure you want to do this?" If you don't want self enrollment or you want to set up a payment method, Moodle enables you to set up other methods to manage enrollment by using plugins. Figure 13-13 shows the Enrollments page with the following plugins:

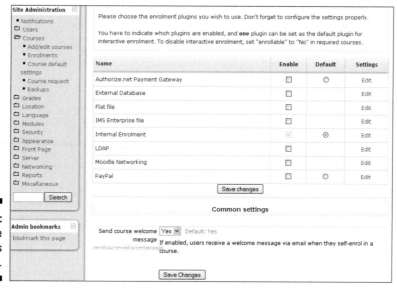

Figure 13-13:
The
Enrollments
page.

✔ Authorize.net Payment Gateway

✔ External Database

✔ Flat File

✔ IMS Enterprise File (from 1.6 onwards)

✔ Internal enrollment (default method)

✔ LDAP

✔ Moodle Networking

✔ PayPal

The Moodle documentation (you can find a Moodle Docs for This Page link at the bottom of the Moodle page, as shown in Figure 13-13) explains each of these methods in detail. When you know the type of enrollment method you want to use, your next step is quite simple — all you need to do is select the check box in the Enable column and then click the Edit link. Remember to click the Save Changes button.

Setting up automatic payments

Moodle provides you with two different plugins to set up automatic payment methods for your learners: Authorize.net Payment Gateway and PayPal. Here's how to set up those modules:

✔ **Authorize.net Payment Gateway module:** This module enables you to set up a payment method by third-party merchants. You may have to pay a fee for the service, which you can add to the cost of the course. There are many different merchant options, including the usual, major credit-card merchants.

    1. In the Site Administration block, click Enrollments.

    2. On the enrollments page (refer to Figure 13-13), select the check box for Authorize.net Payment Gateway.

    3. Click Edit in the Settings column.

       Moodle takes you to the plugin page shown in Figure 13-14.

    4. Follow the instructions, and if you need more information, Click the Moodle Docs for This Page link.

    5. Click the Save changes button when you're finished.

For security reasons, you need to turn on security filters. These can be found in this Site Administration block: Click Security and then click HTTP. Select the first check box next to HTTPS.

✔ **PayPal:** This module enables you to set up a payment method through PayPal (www.paypal.com). You need to set up a PayPal account before you enable Moodle to take payments. PayPal provides you with links and icons that you can add to your Moodle page.

To enable PayPal plugins, follow the procedure in the preceding bullet, but instead of selecting Authorizing.net, select the PayPal check box from the Enable column, and then click the Edit link. This action takes you to the PayPal plugin module, where you select options for the course. (See Figure 13-15.) Make sure you click the Save Changes button.

Figure 13-14:
Setting
up an
Authorizing.
net pay
gateway.

Figure 13-15:
The PayPal
settings
page.

Course Default Settings

The default course settings determine how the course appears to all learners or any other user. The basic settings define the course front page that teachers access to start developing their courses. Teacher roles have a number of options to make minor changes to the course front page, which is discussed in Chapter 3; however, you can make changes here to give the teachers and course creator other layout options.

Course Request

In case you want any user account to be able to request new courses, Moodle enables you to set up the functionality. Just follow these steps:

1. Click the Course Request link.

Moodle opens a Course Request page, as shown in Figure 13-16.

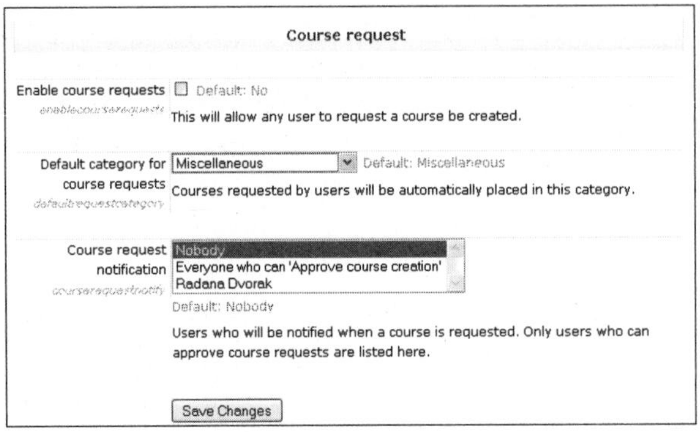

Figure 13-16:
The Course
Request set-
tings page.

2. Select the Enable Course Requests check box.

3. From the Default Category for Course Requests drop-down list, select the category.

4. From the Course Request Notification drop-down list, select who should be notified.

Note that only accounts with permission to register courses will be listed.

5. Click the Save Changes button.

Moodle places a button for all users on the All Courses page. You can see the course requests on the Courses Pending Approval page. You need to check this page regularly.

Backups

The Backup page is the same as the backup from the course Administration block, which I cover in Chapter 14. Please refer to that chapter for a detailed explanation. It is covered in the course sections because teachers are able to back up without having administrative privileges.

There's one difference in the Backup on the Site Administration block: You can set automatically scheduled backups for all courses.

Grades

The Grades and Gradebook modules have been revised in Moodle versions 1.9+ and include a number of vital differences. The changes are good and make it easier for you and your students. *Note:* If you're using an older version, you should either update or go to `http://docs.moodle.org` and find documentation for your version.

The Moodle Grades module is made up of two parts:

- ✔ **Grades:** The scores you or Moodle assigns for work in the Moodle course.

- ✔ **Gradebook:** A repository for all grades for every learner in your course. The Gradebook module is a tool for you to use with your course and every student, and it's available for all learners so they can see their own grades and course averages (if you enable that functionality). The links in the Grades section of the Site Administration block enable you to make changes to the default settings.

From the Grades section, you can access the links described in the following sections.

General Settings

General grade settings enable you to change the defaults and create a set of defaults for your site courses. You can enable or disable the graded roles, outcomes, scales in aggregated grades, publishing grades, or a number of different grades features. There are too many to list here and explain each. The Moodle Grade Settings page, shown in Figure 13-17, provides a brief explanation for each setting. If you need more help, click the Moodle Docs for This Page at the bottom of the page to find a more detailed explanation.

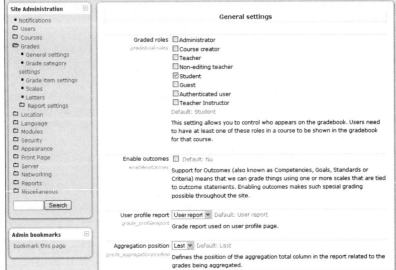

Grade Category Settings

The category settings allows you to choose which options teachers can view and use when adding or editing a grade category in their course grade books. This also sets the default values. Note that making any changes affects all courses on the site.

You can find two important check boxes next to most features on this settings page:

- **Force:** Selecting this check box removes options the teacher can view. (For instance, the teacher can see "mean of all grades" only as an aggregation.)

- **Advanced:** Selecting this check box hides the specific feature until the teacher clicks the Show Advanced button. Teachers quickly familiarize themselves with the Hide and Show buttons. This functionality reduces the initial menu choices for teachers but provides them a button to see the choices if they want.

Grade Item Settings

The Grade Item Settings page provides you with options to edit settings for all grade books used by teachers. Modifying the default settings changes what items are displayed for each grade. Turning the setting on or off would require teachers to input data. See the Grade Item Settings page for an explanation of each option available. Under each option, Moodle briefly explains each function.

Scales

I discuss scales at great length in Chapter 7. On the Scales setting page, you can see all the scales that have been added, and you can change the site-wide scale that came with the Moodle setup files as a default. Moodle's default scale uses categories that include Separate and Connected ways of knowing, also discussed in Chapter 7. Here you have the option of renaming it, altering it, or deleting it altogether. You can also set up a whole new site-wide scale that the teachers have an option to use with their courses.

Letters

The Grade Letters page is important because it lists all the letter grades. You have the option of making changes to the default settings. For example, you can change the letter grade boundary for A. Current default setting lists the grade A as 93% and above, with A– given the boundary 93–90%.

Report Settings

The grade book report settings determine the appearance of grade book reports in all courses on the site. The site administrator can find the default and enabled/disabled settings in the administration area.

- ✔ **Grader Report:** Settings enable you to decide how the grades will be presented. The default settings are a good start if you're unsure.

- ✔ **Overview Report:** Just one option for you to decide whether you want the report to display the position of the user in relation to the rest of the learners in the class, for each graded item.

- ✔ **User Report:** This setting enables you to set what the learners see in their grade books. The teacher can override any setting in the User Report in the course setting section located in the Administration block on the course front page.

Location

Moodle has two separate Moodle pages for location: Location Settings and Update location time zone.

Location Settings

You have three options to make changes on the Location Settings page:

✔ **Default Time Zone:** The first drop-down list is for the default time zone. It's set for where the server is located. You can change this.

✔ **Force Default Time Zone:** You can enable users to choose the time zone or force one for everyone.

✔ **Default Country:** The default allows users to choose their country. If you choose the country, it will become the default for all new user accounts, site-wide. I recommend letting users choose.

The remainder of this page is related to IP settings and IP address lookup and includes a short explanation for each choice.

Update Time Zones

The Update Time Zones page enables anyone with administrative privileges to update their local database with information about world time zones. This option is useful because you may need to make changes to accommodate Daylight Saving Time.

Language

Moodle is available in 82 languages and widely used around the world. You can give users a choice of language, or you can force a language for a course. The Language category offers three different settings.

Language Settings

The Language Settings page gives you a number of options, such as setting the default language, enabling users to set a language for their browser, display menu for language options, and so on. Each selection is explained on the Moodle editing page specific to the particular selection, with a link at the bottom of the page to Moodle docs for more detailed explanation.

Language Editing

The Language Editing page provides you with a tool to change any word or phrase used on the site. You may, for instance, want to change the word *Assignments* to *Offline Activities*. The Language Editing link takes you to a new Moodle page with three links under the main tab, as shown in Figure 13-18:

 ✔ Check for Untranslated Words or Phrases

 ✔ Edit Words or Phrases

 ✔ Edit Help Documents

Each link takes you to an editing page with a number of options for changing the default settings.

Figure 13-18:
The
Language
Editing
page.

Language Packs

Moodle has more than 75 languages that you can install on your Moodle site. To add a language pack, follow these steps:

1. **Click the Language Packs link (under Language) in the Site Administration block.**

   Moodle takes you to the selection page, shown in Figure 13-19.

2. **Select the languages you need from the Available Language Packs list on the right and then click the Install Selected Language Pack button to move them to the left column.**

Figure 13-19:
The
Language
Packs page.

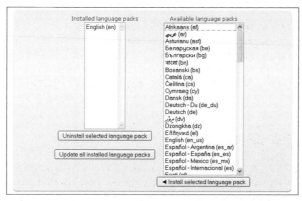

Modules

The Modules link enables you to manage activities, blocks, and filters. In programming terms, *modules* are separate objects. In Moodle, modules are small separate activities that you and your learners can interact with. They are separate, in terms that they can be saved, updated, and reused. You can import other modules and plugins from Moodle.org. If you're an IT administrator, I encourage you to visit and explore what's available. For example, Moodle.org has a lot of cool themes you can download as separate plugins.

Moodle.org plugins are safe to use. Be very careful when adding third-party modules or plugins because they may cause difficulties if not installed properly. Check the Moodle.org forums and ask about a third-party module or plugin that you'd like to try. When you post within 24 hours, you'll get replies from developers and/or users who may have some experience with the particular plugin.

Activities

When you click the Activities link in the Site Administration block under Modules, and then Manage Activities, Moodle takes you to the page shown in Figure 13-20. This page lists the various activity modules in table format. Here's the lowdown on the individual columns in this table:

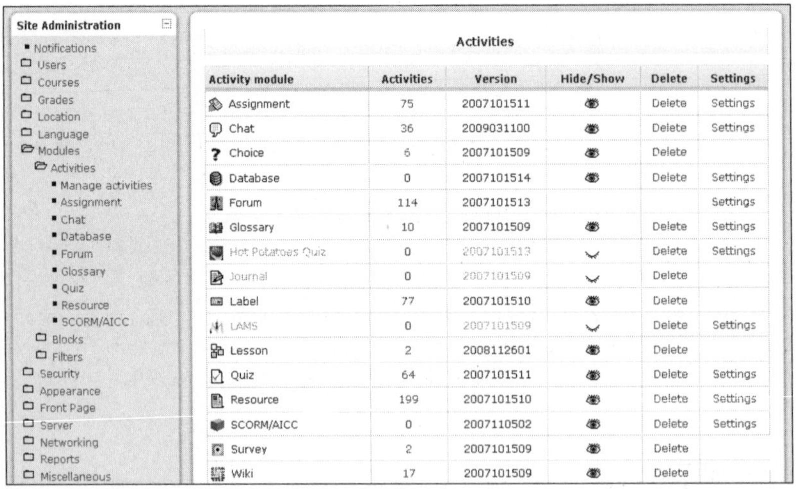

Figure 13-20: The Manage Activities page.

Activity module	Activities	Version	Hide/Show	Delete	Settings
Assignment	75	2007101511	☻	Delete	Settings
Chat	36	2009031100	☻	Delete	Settings
Choice	6	2007101509	☻	Delete	
Database	0	2007101514	☻	Delete	Settings
Forum	114	2007101513			Settings
Glossary	10	2007101509	☻	Delete	Settings
Hot Potatoes Quiz	0	2007101513	⌄	Delete	Settings
Journal	0	2007101509	⌄	Delete	
Label	77	2007101510	☻	Delete	
LAMS	0	2007101509	⌄	Delete	Settings
Lesson	2	2008112601	☻	Delete	
Quiz	64	2007101511	☻	Delete	Settings
Resource	199	2007101510	☻	Delete	Settings
SCORM/AICC	0	2007110502	☻	Delete	Settings
Survey	2	2007101509	☻	Delete	
Wiki	17	2007101509	☻	Delete	

The Site Administration block shows: Notifications, Users, Courses, Grades, Location, Language, Modules (Activities — Manage activities, Assignment, Chat, Database, Forum, Glossary, Quiz, Resource, SCORM/AICC; Blocks; Filters), Security, Appearance, Front Page, Server, Networking, Reports, Miscellaneous.

✔ **Activities:** Lists how many activities are currently on your Moodle site. If you click the number next to the activity, the courses that include the module are displayed.

✔ **Version:** Shows which version of the module you're running. This option is useful if you want to report bugs.

✔ **Hide/Show:** You can click the eye icon to close it so that the module is not enabled. Remember that in doing this, all courses on the site are unable to use the module. By default, some modules are hidden. Opening Hot Potatoes Quiz is useful because it allows teachers to import question. Some of the other modules are hidden because Moodle no longer supports them, although they're still available to use. For example, Journal is hidden because it's very similar to Blogs.

✔ **Delete:** You can delete any module other than the forum. You have no reason to delete any modules unless a specific upgrade requires you to do so. If you need to delete a module, you also have to delete the module folder called moodle/mod located in the system settings. You have to delete this from the server.

✔ **Settings:** The Settings link takes you to individual activity settings that you may need to set up. The following list gives a quick rundown on the more useful and important settings. You can also access the settings from the individual module in this block under the Modules link.

- *Assignment/Forum:* You can set the maximum file upload. This feature is useful to keep the database from getting clogged up. This setting is also available in other modules, though the Teacher role can adjust upload sizes for individual courses. It may not be necessary to restrict the maximum file upload site-wide. For example, if you restrict the Database module and a course needs to use this module to create a database of pictures, the course would be restricted.

- *Chat:* If courses use the Chat module frequently, encourage the teacher to clear chat data. This setting enables you to use a server *daemon* (a program that runs in the background and handles service requests) to reduce the load.

- *Database, Forum and Glossary, and RSS:* If your teachers need to use RSS, enable the filter in each individual activity.

- *Resource:* These settings enable you to allow teachers to create links to files on your organization's local fileserver or devices such as CD drives, network drives, and external devices, such as USB sticks.

- *Quiz:* Please be very careful making any changes to this setting — it affects every quiz in every course on the site. These options can be set for individual quizzes in each course.

Blocks

The Blocks section gives you editing tools to make changes or enable filters for all blocks in the site. Clicking the first subsection, the Manage Blocks link, takes you to a page similar to the Activities page (described in the preceding section).

Here are a few of the columns you may want to use on the Blocks page:

✔ **Hide/Show:** Using the Hide/Show column, you can hide any block so it does not appear in any course's Add a Block drop-down list and cannot be used in any course. This option is useful to save space if certain blocks won't be used. (For example, the Global Search block is rarely used at course level.) In the Instances column, you can view instances of blocks occurring in the courses.

✔ **Multiple:** This column enables you to restrict multiple uses of the block in a course. Not all blocks have the capability. The HTML block is such an example. Unless you have a server space issue, you have no reason to restrict this option for all courses on the site.

✔ **Settings:** Some blocks have extra settings, which you can access by clicking the Settings link.

One block that you may want to configure on the Blocks page is the RSS Feed block. (You can get to this page by clicking the Manage Blocks link.) Newsfeeds are very useful for teachers, and unless you enable it in this module, you will be inundated with requests. To enable RSS, follow the steps:

1. **On the Blocks page, click the Settings link next to RSS.**

   You can also get there directly from the links in the Site Administration block: Just click Modules and then Blocks.

   The Remote RSS Feeds page appears, as shown in Figure 13-21.

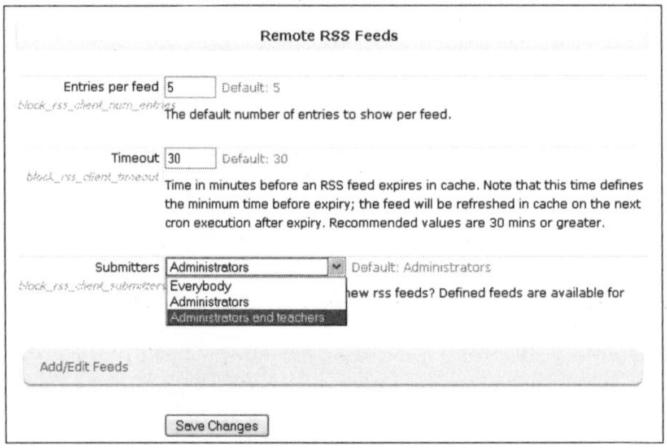

Figure 13-21:
The Remote
RSS Feeds
settings
page.

2. **Fill in the following fields:**

   • *Entries per Feed:* This is the number of news items to show for each newsfeed.

   • *Timeout:* Select a timeout period in minutes. Below the option is an description of what a *timeout* is.

- *Submitters:* Select who can set up RSS. Notice I highlighted Administrators and Teachers. You don't want to give everyone the capability to add RSS, even though students may have editing capabilities for glossaries and wikis. Instructors need to monitor what newsfeeds arrive in the course.

3. **When you're finished, click the Save Changes button.**

Sticky blocks seem to pop up in various places and can add confusion, so here's a little detail on the subject: A *sticky block* is a block you can set up on the whole Moodle site, and it forces the block to appear in every course and/or users' front page. For example, the Participants and Administration blocks are sticky blocks because they appear on every course front page.

Filters

Filters enable you to set up automatic-change text on the front page into different forms, such as hyperlinks. For example, titles of resources can automatically become hyperlinks that take you to the relevant resource. There are many options and extensions, and you can download special filters from the Moodle.org site's Modules and Plugin database.

You can enable a number of filters for the site. These filters are all listed on the Manage Filters page, shown in Figure 13-22. They're all important for the complete functioning of the activities. Pay particular attention to the following filters:

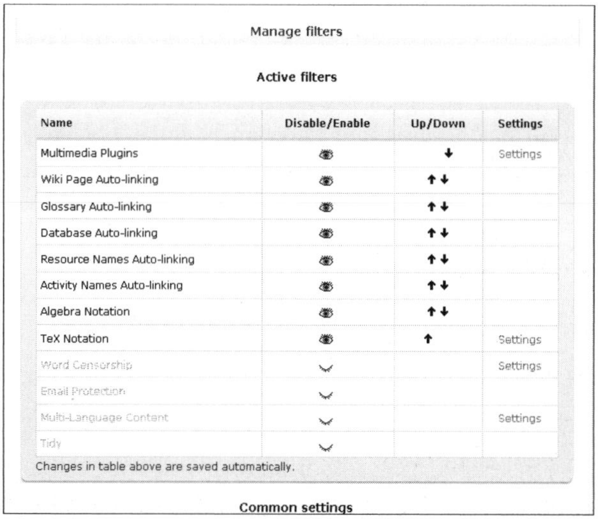

Name	Disable/Enable	Up/Down	Settings
Multimedia Plugins	👁	↓	Settings
Wiki Page Auto-linking	👁	↑ ↓	
Glossary Auto-linking	👁	↑ ↓	
Database Auto-linking	👁	↑ ↓	
Resource Names Auto-linking	👁	↑ ↓	
Activity Names Auto-linking	👁	↑ ↓	
Algebra Notation	👁	↑ ↓	
TeX Notation	👁	↑	Settings
Word Censorship	⌄		Settings
Email Protection	⌄		
Multi-Language Content	⌄		Settings
Tidy	⌄		

Manage filters

Active filters

Changes in table above are saved automatically.

Common settings

Figure 13-22: The Manage Filters settings page.

✔ **Multimedia:** Click the Settings link to see a list of many different filters. All are selected, by default, except the last one in the list, which is the YouTube filter. If your instructors want to be able to embed YouTube in Web pages or link to YouTube, you need to enable this filter. Make sure you click the Save Changes button at the bottom of the page.

✔ **Algebra Notation and TeX Notation:** These filters both need to be enabled in order for code to be converted to GIF images. TeX Notation enables you to display math notations correctly. You can find many plugins to enable easy use of mathematical functions and notations for more advanced math and engineering courses. Click the Moodle Docs For This Page link at the bottom of the page, which includes a link for Algebra settings listing resources for additional mathematics filters. The companion Web site, `www.dummies.com/go/moodlefd`, also has a link to resources for plugins for mathematic notations.

The Multimedia and TeX Notation filters both have separate links on the Filters submenu. Clicking these links also takes you to the settings pages for these filters.

Security

Moodle developers take security very seriously. Moodle is widely used at universities, so you can be reassured that security is in place to protect courses, user accounts, and data, Like with all software, hackers get in, and developers set up patches. As you know, there's no such thing as complete security.

Moodle.org provides a list of basic recommendations to keep your site as secure as possible. The following list summarizes the recommendations:

✔ Carry out regular Moodle updates

✔ Make *sure* you disable Register

✔ Use strong passwords for admin and teachers

✔ Trust the users who get Teacher role privileges

You can find more information at `http://docs.moodle.org/en/Security`.

Check out the following sections to discover more about the settings that help you manage security and enable users to link to resources.

Site Policies

Site policies settings determine what users can access and see as well as who can enter your site. Click the Site Policies link to go over the default settings (which provide the required security), though you may want to enable others. Each setting has check box and a short description.

You can trust the defaults, which I highly recommend, and go through the page to see all the available settings when you're comfortable with Moodle.

HTTP Security

The HTTP Security page allows you to choose a number of security options, such as using HTTPS to encrypt user login details, enabling cookies, and using the required Flash version that is known not to pose a security risk as some versions have known security risks. I recommend using the default settings unless you have HTTPS on your server. For example, if you enable HTTPS for logins in Moodle and you don't have HTTPS set up on your server, you will lock yourself out of your site.

Module Security

Use the settings on the Module Security page, shown in Figure 13-23, to disable any activity for all user accounts other than the administrative account. For example, you can disable the Chat activity across the whole site or for specific courses. Notice each option is explained, and if you don't understand the implications, don't change the default settings until you investigate them thoroughly.

Figure 13-23:
The Module
Security
settings
page.

Notifications

You can set up Moodle to inform you if someone is trying to steal student or teacher logins. If you enable the Display Login Failures option, a link is added to the site front page after you log in, informing you of the number of failed logins. Click the link to access the login error page.

If you worry about logins failing, you can set up e-mail notification to inform you about failed attempts.

Anti-Virus

Moodle includes an antivirus feature you can enable. It's an open-source virus scanner called ClamAV, and you need to install it on your server first in order to enable the capabilities in this page. See www.clamav.net for further information. If you have antivirus running on your server, you don't need to worry about it and can leave the default settings.

Appearance

Moodle has a number of editable features that enable you and your users to change the look and feel of the course front page. There are also options for some of the blocks, calendar, and HTML editor. I explain each main functionality briefly. You can use customized modules to spice up your course front page — if you need to change the appearance and customize the look and feel of your site and/or courses, you can find plugins and information within the International Moodle support group. Read on; you'll enjoy these sections.

Themes

Themes are a popular topic in Moodle. You, as an administrator, can choose a theme for the site, which will be carried through all the site's courses. Setting a Moodle theme is similar to setting up your desktop on your computer; you can choose background colors, fonts, sizes, and so on. You can also set permissions to enable teachers (and students if the students have the capability) to choose their own theme for their course. Changing the theme does not affect any functionality within Moodle.

Many companies using Moodle integrate their corporate branding so the site matches with the corporate identity.

All this is possible from few pages and selections. You have two options:

✔ **Theme Settings:** This page is a list of options where you decide whether other users can change themes and choose and hide blocks.

✔ **Theme Selector:** Moodle bundles a number of theme templates that you can choose from. Each theme provides you with a small screen shot and preview and information links, as well as a Choose button to select a new theme.

You can download many themes and instructions on how to edit your front page theme at `http://docs.moodle.org/en/Themes`.

Calendar

The Moodle calendar can display events for the whole site, course, groups, and individual users. A number of settings and options pertain to the organization of the calendar and capabilities for other roles. Click the Calendar link (under Appearance) in the Site Administration block to make changes to the default settings.

HTML Editor

I discuss the HTML editor in Chapter 3 in detail. This administration page enables you to change the look and feel of the editor, and you can add or hide extra buttons. For instance, you can add a spell checker button, include a math function button, and hide emoticons. Note that the spell checker plugin takes up space and may slow down your system. To access the HTML editor page, click the HTML Editor link under Appearance in the Site Administration block.

HTML Settings

This option enables you to remove all HTML tags from all activity and resource names.

Moodle Docs

The Moodle Docs for This Page link that appears at the bottom of each Web page leads administrators and teachers to a fantastic resource: documentation maintained at Moodle.org. The Moodle Docs settings page enables you to remove this link or have the link open a new pop-up window when clicked. By default, the link is enabled, and clicking it takes you to the page. You need to use the browser Back button to get back to your Moodle page. If you prefer a pop-up window, enable the setting.

My Moodle

The My Moodle utility enables a customizable front page displaying a user's links to all the site courses and specific activities. For example, if the user has unopened assignments or unread forum posts, Moodle provides links to them. You can enable this functionality by selecting the check box next to Force Users to Use My Moodle. You can also decide how many courses to display by typing the number in the field. Don't forget to save your changes.

Course Managers

The Course Managers setting empowers you to decide who is listed in the course description. By default, the teacher's name is listed. If there are a number of Teacher roles, they are all displayed.

AJAX and JavaScript

Moodle provides you with the ability to enable the use of AJAX (advanced client/server interfaces using JavaScript) across the complete Moodle site. With this setting enabled, users can still make a choice in their profiles; otherwise, AJAX is disabled for everybody.

Manage Tags

The Manage Tags setting displays all the tags created in the courses and the user who created them, including how many times they were used. If inappropriate tags are used, they appear tagged and in red font.

You have an option to add Official tags, which are displayed to every user on the site. Official tags are useful so that many duplicate tags are not created around a topic or a theme creating a long list. I discuss tags in detail in Chapter 8.

Front Page

The site front page is similar to the course front page. You can make changes and edit the site front page by simply clicking the Turn Editing On button located in the top-right corner.

Front Page Settings

Enables you to give the site a name to appear on every page above the navigation bar, a short name that appears in the navigation bar, a front page description that you can use for your general organization introduction or anything else relevant, and a number of other options. Leave the default settings if you aren't sure about the purposes they serve.

Front Page Roles

You can set up front page roles and overrides the exact same way you set up roles in Chapter 4. If you decide to use a front page forum, you need to assign a Student role to everyone on the site on the front page in order for them to receive e-mail copies of the forum.

Front Page Backup and Restore

Moodle enables you to back up the site front page the same way you back up courses, as discussed in Chapter 14. All the settings follow the same format.

Front Page Questions

The Front Page Questions link leads you to the question pool for all the quizzes in the site. You can make any changes to the quiz categories or create new quizzes. You can limit the questions to be used on the site, course, or within a quiz.

Site Files

The Site Files link takes you to a list of all the backup files for all courses on the site. These files are similar to the site files for each course. All actions and buttons work in the same way discussed in Chapter 3. This storage area can be accessed by anyone who has access to the URL or can guess the URL. To ensure security of backup files, they should be stored in the secure backupdata folder.

Server

The Site Administration block includes many settings for adjusting how Moodle relates to the server and the server settings. Most of the default settings should be left as they were configured by Moodle on installation; however, you need to be familiar with a couple that involve setting permissions for teachers to be able to use certain tools:

✔ **System Paths:** Server information. Leave the default settings.

✔ **Email:** Options to change hosts and usernames, e-mail forwarding, and so on. Leave the defaults unless you have difficulties with e-mails.

✔ **Session Handling:** Server information related to database, timeout on users logged in to the system, and cookies. Leave the default settings.

✔ **RSS:** You need to enable the RSS feed by selecting the check box. This page has only one selection.

✔ **Debugging:** If errors occur or users experience problems with any aspects of Moodle installations, debugging is useful for developers and anyone helping you. If you post questions to the Moodle help forums, a developer may ask you to turn debugging on and e-mail the report. Leave the default settings.

✔ **Statistics:** You need statistics enabled if you want graphical representations of user activities and summaries, as discussed in Chapter 14.

✔ **HTTP:** These options are for developers who want to make changes to frames, slash arguments, and so on. Leave the default settings unless you know what you're doing.

✔ **Maintenance Mode:** The settings enable you to secure your site while maintenance is taking place. If registered users attempt to access their courses, they will receive a message stating that that Moodle maintenance is taking place.

✔ **Cleanup:** Enables you to tidy up the sites by unsubscribing users from courses after they've completed those courses. You can also delete unconfirmed users and clean up the log files.

✔ **Environment:** This is a system check so you can ensure your server meets all the requirements to run the Moodle version you plan to download and any future Moodle updates.

✔ **PHP Info:** Provides info about the version of PHP being used. Leave the default setting.

✔ **Performance:** Information on memory status, cache, and so on. Leave the default settings.

Networking

You can set up networking options to share resources among Moodle sites. For your server to be able to be networked to other Moodle sites hosted on different servers, you need specific extension. Setup and requirements are outlined in Moodle docs for the specific setup pages. By default, all networking settings and capabilities are disabled.

Reports

Similar to how teachers can get reports and logs of all activity that happens in their courses, you can view log files and reports of the complete Moodle site with information related to course(s) use, security risks, space, and so on.

- **Backups:** This page enables you to set up scheduled backups and logs related to back up.

- **Course Overview:** To view the course overview information, you need to enable statistics, as discussed in the earlier section "Server."

- **Logs:** Moodle provides you with an option to choose any combination of course, site, participants, date, activity actions, and so on by using filters as in the course reports. You can choose whether they're displayed on the log file page or downloaded in text, ODS, or Excel format.

- **Live Logs:** Provides a link to a report of live logs for the past hour

- **Questions:** This page reports problems in your question database. You should see a statement `No problems found in your question database.`

- **Security Overview:** A list of the security status of your Moodle site, with a list of possible security risks, giving you status report of OK, Warning, Serious, or Critical. This is good to check once in awhile. Note that if you enable `.swf` filters, you will see a Critical message that this poses a security risk.

- **Spam Cleaner:** This page will start a program that enables you to search all user profiles for certain strings and then delete anything that was created by spammers. You can also search for inappropriate words by using multiple keywords strings with commas (such as *casino, porn*). See the Moodle docs for more information about reducing spam in Moodle.

- **Statistics:** This page enables you to collect statistics on all activities. This page is available through a number of different links in the Site Administration block. The page follows the same format as course statistics that you find by going to the course Administration block and clicking the Reports link.

- **Unit Tests:** This page enables you to run a test on your Moodle site to look for possible errors. A report is generated and displayed.

Miscellaneous

Miscellaneous is a catch-all category for extra information a Moodle system administrator may find interesting.

Experimental

This page lists all options that are experimental and in beta testing. They aren't necessarily stable, and they require testing and bug fixing. Leave all the default settings unless you're a developer and want to contribute to developing any of the tools and features listed.

XMLDB

This tool enables developers to edit various Moodle options and tools such as tables, field, keys, indexes, and so on. Leave the default settings unless you're a developer.

Finding Support

I can't guarantee you won't have any problems. However, when you do come across a problem, you may be surprised that often you can solve the problem by simply doing a little digging for information. The satisfaction is worth the try.

However, you may come across some issues that truly stump you. No need to ever panic! Moodle support is available for free. Also, because Moodle is used across the whole world, someone is up 24/7, will read your plea for help, and help.

Here are all your options to get more support:

- ✔ Go to this book's companion Web site, www.dummies.com/go/moodlefd.

- ✔ Check out the Moodle documentation that I have made numerous references to throughout this book, found at http://docs.moodle.org.

- ✔ Head to the Moodle community discussion forums. You can search for all kinds of answers to every problem imaginable. If you can't find your answers, don't be too shy to ask questions; someone is always ready to help. That's the wonderful thing about the Moodle community. With almost 50 million users worldwide, spanning 210 countries, you never have to feel alone. http://moodle.org/forums.

Chapter 14

Managing Course Data, Reports, Logs, and Statistics

. . . .

. . . .

*T*he content that you upload to your course and the activities you and your learners create and populate with information are the knowledge data, the value, in your course. The job isn't done when your term, semester, or training is completed — managing the knowledge is a key to your continued success as an online instructor. You need to make sure that the information you upload is kept up-to-date, ensure you optimize your files before uploading, and clear old material so that you don't use up your allocated space too quickly.

When you have an effective and efficient course running smoothly, your learners love it, and you're the envy of all your colleagues. Of course you don't want to have to re-create a course like that. This chapter shows you how to duplicate your whole course, rename it, and reuse it.

Because you created and made available a lot of content, you may want to see whether your learners are accessing it and how long they spend with various activities. This chapter introduces a number of Moodle tools you can use to keep track of your learners.

Managing Your Course Data and Staying Up-to-Date

After creating content, uploading it to your course, setting up various activities, and getting your course running successfully, you may feel very pleased with yourself. Well done. But you have more to do: Now you need to be able to handle the updates and maintenance of your course. One of the most important aspects of keeping your learners engaged is keeping your course current by updating your files, deleting old files, and linking to new sites.

Learners are tech savvy: They can download a document and view the date when it was last updated. Recently, one of my students told me how grateful she was that I kept the course fresh and interesting. She told me that one of her online courses had material dated 2003, broken links to sites that did not exist, and a recycled syllabus dated 2000. She learned all of this within the first week of the course, and she withdrew from the course and demanded her money back. Rightly so!

Moodle has added tools in the course Administration block to help you manage and keep your files updated. To view the Files tools, go to your course front page, locate the Administration block (by default, Moodle displays it on the left side, as shown in Figure 14-1), and click the Files link.

Figure 14-1: The Administration block on the course front page.

Moodle then takes you to the Files editing page, shown in Figure 14-2. Here you find a number of tools to help you manage your course. All the files you've uploaded are listed with a check box on the left. At the bottom of the list, you find the following four buttons, which enable you to work with these files:

Name	Size	Modified	Action
☐ 🗀 Week_3_notes	3.6MB	27 May 2010, 06:46 PM	Rename
☐ 🗀 backupdata	148.4MB	29 September 2010, 09:27 PM	Rename
🗀 moddata	1.4MB	15 July 2010, 03:55 PM	
☐ 🗀 week5_notes	3.4MB	27 May 2010, 06:46 PM	Rename
☐ 🗀 week_3	7.3MB	27 May 2010, 06:46 PM	Rename
☐ 🗀 week_6	325.5KB	27 May 2010, 06:46 PM	Rename
☐ 📄 Assignments_grades.pdf	69.3KB	21 June 2010, 06:31 PM	Rename
☐ 📄 Assignments_grades_Spring2010.doc	38.5KB	27 May 2010, 06:46 PM	Rename
☐ 📄 Bb_K12_09_TrendsUpdate.pdf	368.8KB	27 May 2010, 06:46 PM	Rename
☐ 📄 Bb_K12_ParentsReport.pdf	7MB	27 May 2010, 06:46 PM	Rename
☐ 📄 Bb_K12_WP_BlendedLearning.pdf	920.6KB	27 May 2010, 06:46 PM	Rename
☐ 📄 Choice_notes_CI810W10sum10.pdf	603.7KB	25 August 2010, 01:34 PM	Rename
☐ 📄 Choice_notes_CI810W10sum10.ppsx	911.9KB	25 August 2010, 01:36 PM	Rename
☐ 📄 Course_syllabus_06_22_2010.doc	54.5KB	21 June 2010, 06:33 PM	Rename
☐ 📄 Course_syllabus_06_22_2010.pdf	81.7KB	4 July 2010, 09:34 AM	Rename
☐ 📄 Course_syllabus_March_2010.doc	56KB	27 May 2010, 06:46 PM	Rename
☐ 📄 EdSoMeWorkshopOct.pdf	64.5KB	2 September 2010, 02:08 PM	Rename
☐ 📄 Lecture_notes_W5Sp.pdf	2.9MB	27 May 2010, 06:46 PM	Rename
☐ 📄 Lecture_notes_W5Sp.ppsx	4.4MB	27 May 2010, 06:46 PM	Rename
☐ 📄 Moodle_CI810W8Sp.pdf	2MB	27 May 2010, 06:46 PM	Rename
☐ 📄 moodle_CI810W8.ppsx	1.5MB	27 May 2010, 06:46 PM	Rename
☐ 📄 moodle_CI810W8_sum10.pdf	2.4MB	10 August 2010, 08:53 PM	Rename
☐ 📄 moodle_CI810W8_sum10.ppsx	3.3MB	10 August 2010, 08:50 PM	Rename
☐ 📄 moodle_CI810W9.ppt	2.2MB	27 May 2010, 06:46 PM	Rename
☐ 📄 moodle_CI810W9Sp.ppsx	5.3MB	27 May 2010, 06:46 PM	Rename
☐ 📄 moodle_CI810W9_sum10.pdf	1.3MB	17 August 2010, 03:17 PM	Rename
☐ 📄 moodle_CI810W9_sum10.ppsx	2.1MB	17 August 2010, 03:22 PM	Rename
☐ 📄 moodle_CI810_W5sum2010.pdf	2.9MB	13 July 2010, 11:39 AM	Rename
☐ 📄 moodle_CI810_W6Sp.pdf	2.8MB	27 May 2010, 06:46 PM	Rename
☐ 📄 moodle_CI810_W6Sp.ppsx	4.2MB	27 May 2010, 06:46 PM	Rename
☐ 📄 moodle_CI810_W6Su2010.pdf	2.8MB	25 July 2010, 05:07 PM	Rename
☐ 📄 moodle_CI810_W6Su2010.ppsx	4.2MB	25 July 2010, 05:10 PM	Rename
☐ 📄 moodle_CI810_week1.pdf	937.9KB	27 May 2010, 06:46 PM	Rename
☐ 📄 moodle_CI810_week1.ppsx	1.4MB	27 May 2010, 06:46 PM	Rename
☐ 📄 moodle_teststudents_coursekey.pdf	330.6KB	17 July 2010, 10:59 PM	Rename
☐ 📄 moodle_teststudents_coursekey.ppsx	525.7KB	17 July 2010, 11:01 PM	Rename
☐ 📄 storyboard_template2.ppt	124.5KB	27 May 2010, 06:46 PM	Rename
☐ 📄 syllabus_studentsample.pdf	62.2KB	22 August 2010, 11:26 AM	Rename
☐ 📄 syllabus_template.doc	38KB	27 May 2010, 06:46 PM	Rename
☐ 📄 wbk1_17a_1.mp3	719.8KB	27 May 2010, 06:46 PM	Rename

With chosen files... ▾

[Make a folder]   [Select all] [Deselect all]   [Upload a file]

Figure 14-2:
The Files
editing
page.

✔ **Make a Folder:** Click the button to create a folder and place files into the folder. You can make this folder available to your learners on the course front page, or you can just use it to organize your files. For a step-by-step explanation on how to create a folder and display it to your learners, see Chapter 5. The process is quite simple.

✔ **Select All and Deselect All:** By clicking one of these two buttons, Moodle enables you to select all the files or deselect them.

You may find these buttons useful if you're deleting or moving many files. Even though you may not want to move or delete all the files, by selecting them all, you can go back and deselect individual files you don't want to move or delete and save a little time. When you click the Delete button and realize that perhaps you didn't want to delete certain files, no worries. Moodle has a safety net: Moodle prompts you to confirm that you want to delete selected files.

✔ **Upload a File:** Click this button to upload any selected file from your computer.

After you've selected the check boxes next to the files you want to manage, select one of these options from the With Chosen Files drop-down list:

✔ **Move to Another Folder:** Moving your files to specific folders you created (such as YouTube tutorials, lecture notes, and so on) takes just a few steps.

1. From the With Chosen Files drop-down list, select Move to Another Folder.

2. Select the folder in which you want to place the files.

   Moodle lists all the folders above the list of files. Empty folders are at the very top. (See Figure 14-3.) In Figure 14-3, above the table of file, notice that Moodle informs you of your actions and instructs you on what to do next: 2 files selected for moving. Now go into the destination folder and press 'Move files to here'.

3. Click the Move Files to Here button at the bottom of the screen.

   Moodle moves your files. (See Figure 14-4.) Notice at the top of the page, in the navigation bar, the new folder where you're moving the files is listed. In this example, it's Example_For_Dummies_Folder.

   Moodle moves the files to the new folder and displays them. Above the new files, you see a folder with an up arrow, called the Parent directory. If you select this folder, Moodle returns you to the list of all folders and files.

Figure 14-3:
On the Files page, Moodle informs you that you selected two files to move.

2 files selected for moving. Now go into the destination folder and press 'Move files to here'

	Name	Size	Modified	Action
☐ 🗀	Example_For_Dummies_Folder	0 bytes	28 December 2010, 11:47 AM	Rename
☐ 🗀	Week_3_notes	3.6MB	27 May 2010, 06:46 PM	Rename
☐ 🗀	backupdata	148.4MB	29 September 2010, 09:27 PM	Rename
	🗀 moddata	1.4MB	15 July 2010, 03:55 PM	
☐ 🗀	week5_notes	3.4MB	27 May 2010, 06:46 PM	Rename
☐ 🗀	week_3	7.3MB	27 May 2010, 06:46 PM	Rename
☐ 🗀	week_6	325.5KB	27 May 2010, 06:46 PM	Rename
☐ 📄	Assignments_grades.pdf	69.3KB	21 June 2010, 06:31 PM	Rename
☐ 📄	Assignments_grades_Spring2010.doc	38.5KB	27 May 2010, 06:46 PM	Rename
☐ 📄	Bb_K12_09_TrendsUpdate.pdf	368.8KB	27 May 2010, 06:46 PM	Rename
☐ 📄	Bb_K12_ParentsReport.pdf	7MB	27 May 2010, 06:46 PM	Rename
☐ 📄	Bb_K12_WP_BlendedLearning.pdf	920.6KB	27 May 2010, 06:46 PM	Rename

Figure 14-4:
Moodle
shows you
files have
been moved
to the
chosen
folder.

	Name	Size	Modified	Action
	🔙 Parent folder			
☐	Assignments_grades.pdf	69.3KB	21 June 2010, 06:31 PM	Rename
☐	Assignments_grades_Spring2010.doc	38.5KB	27 May 2010, 06:46 PM	Rename

With chosen files... ▾

| Make a folder | | Select all | Deselect all | | Upload a file |

In my example, notice that the name of the folder is connected with underscores (_). You don't need to use underscores when you give names to files or folders — Moodle adds them automatically when it saves the folder name. The database doesn't like names that aren't connected.

✔ **Delete Completely:** Selecting this option from the With Chosen Files drop-down list deletes the selected files and folders from your Moodle course and site. Moodle prompts you to make sure you want to delete the selected files.

✔ **Create ZIP Archive:** A Zip file (an archive) consists of a folder that holds any number of files you select, and the Zip utility compresses them in size and creates a Zip file. This utility is very useful for storing files in archives or storing larger files such as audio, images, and video. By using Zip files, you can easily upload or download the files. You can make Zip files available to your learners; however, they need a Zip utility in order to unzip the folders. Most operating systems have a built-in Zip utility, such as WinZip in Windows and MacZip or StuffIt Expander for Macintosh.

To zip a folder of files, follow these steps:

1. From the With Chosen Files drop-down list, select Create Zip Archive.

   Moodle takes you to a new page where you see the files you selected. In the example, I chose a folder with two files, as shown in Figure 14-5. Moodle tells you that you're about to create a Zip file containing the listed files.

2. In the field below Moodle's statement What do you want to call the zip file?, give your Zip folder a name.

   The default name is new.zip.

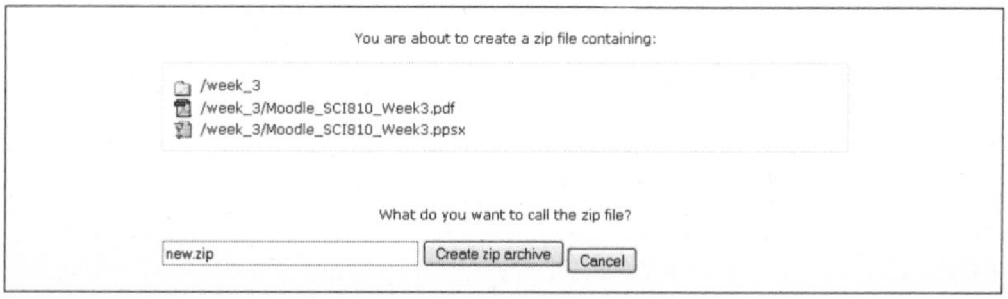

You are about to create a zip file containing:

📁 /week_3
📄 /week_3/Moodle_SCI810_Week3.pdf
📄 /week_3/Moodle_SCI810_Week3.ppsx

What do you want to call the zip file?

| new.zip | | Create zip archive | Cancel |

Figure 14-5:
Creating a
Zip file.

3. Click the Create Zip Archive button.

Moodle returns you to the list of files. You see the Zip folder listed alphabetically in your list of files. Notice three additional links on the right side of the list:

Unzip: This link unzips your archived files and adds them to the files area where the Zip file is stored.

Lists: If you click this link, Moodle displays all the files that are stored in the archive. Note that you can't view the files by click this link. It's there to refresh your memory. Moodle understands that no matter how intuitive and logical your naming structure becomes, you may forget at some point.

Restore: This link is related to the backup tools. After you've backed up your course or specific data within the course and uploaded it to your new course, you use this link to restore the files and content. I cover restoring content in the "Backing Up Your Course and Data" section, later in this chapter.

Organizing Your Data

Creating folders, storing your files in folders, and creating Zip archives of your data are all aspects of organizing your allocated space for your course. Organizing files in folders on your course front page also helps students navigate to and access the content they need. They will be grateful for a clean, clear front page that doesn't contain a long list of resources.

The other important aspect of organizing data is understanding file sizes, how you can optimize your data to keep file sizes smaller, and which file formats are most compatible with Moodle and browsing software. I touch on optimizing file sizes in Chapter 5. Table 14-1 is a brief guide that can help you decide which formats to use to save your data so that it can be viewed by most learners. You most likely are familiar with these formats and have used them at some point.

Table 14-1   File Formats Identification and Recommendations

File Type	Formats Supported by Moodle	Software Required to View	Recommended
Mainly Text Based	RTF, Word, PDF, HTML, PowerPoint (PPT). All widely used for text, though images can be embedded within the text document.	Learners need a PDF reader or PDF Publisher, both of which are free. If docs are saved as RTF, Open Office word-processing software can read them (www. openoffice.org).	PDF
Pictures Images	JPEG, GIF, and PNG. The best formats for browser based applications are JPEG and GIF. You don't need to buy graphic software; you can use Paint, which comes free with Windows, or Paintbrush for Mac.	To view the other formats, learners' computers need compatible viewers.	JPG, GIF
Video	FVL, SWF, MOV, WMV, MPG, AVI, FLV, RAM, RPM, RM, YouTube.	These formats are all supported by Moodle plugins but they need to be enabled. (See Chapter 6.) Some of the formats do not work well with certain browsers.	YouTube, SWF, FLV
Audio	MP3, AAC, WMA, RA, MP4.	They are playable on most computers and any Internet-connected devices your learners will use. Filters need to be enabled. (See Chapter 6.)	MP3

Backing Up Your Course and Data

As you know, backing up your work is important. I believe everyone at some point learned a hard lesson by losing work in some way related to crashes, whether the loss was due to hard drive failure, a virus, sun spots exploding, or satellites falling out of the sky. It's always possible that some problems may occur with the database on the Moodle server. Although Moodle has auto-mated course backups for the whole site your system administrator manages (see Chapter 13), you still want to make sure your work is in safe keeping.

Backing up is the first part of copying and cloning process so you can reuse the course. Get the highlighter out!

To back up your course so you can avoid forget-and-regret scenarios, follow these steps:

1. **In the Administration block on your course front page, click the Backup link.**

   Moodle takes you to the Course Backup page with the course name and number listed, as shown in Figure 14-6.

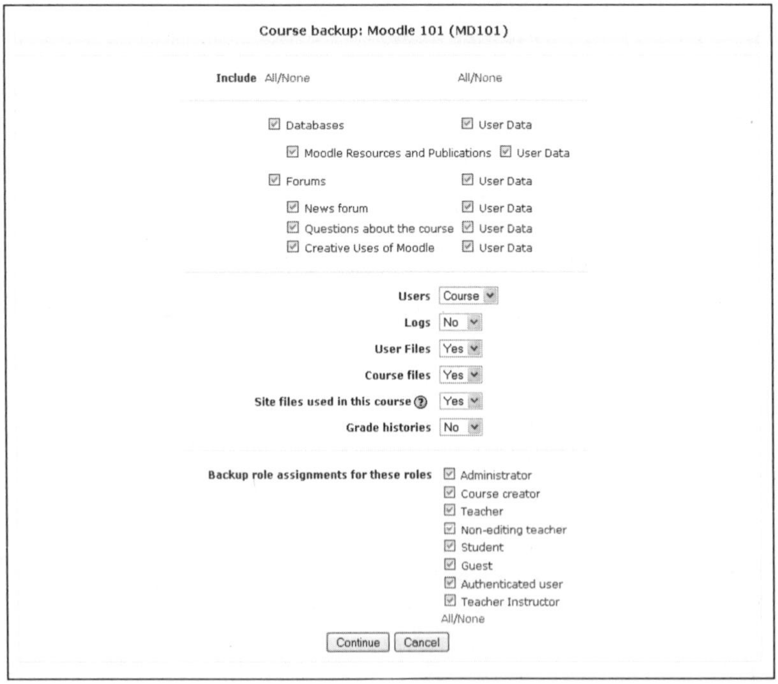

Figure 14-6:
The Course
Backup
page.

2. If you don't want to back up everything, deselect options as desired.

By default, Moodle has everything selected. Backing up everything is recommended for a complete course backup that includes all learners' data.

Notice the left column has Include All/None links, and under those links all your activities are listed. On the right, you have User Data check boxes below All/None links. These check boxes enable you to select which data you want to back up.

For example, you may not want to back up all the data from the Chat activity. If that's the case, deselect the box in front of the User Data for the Chat activity. Be careful not to deselect the activity Chat as you want to back up the whole course.

3. Click the Continue button at the bottom of the page to begin the backup process.

Moodle takes you to the next page in the backup process, which lists the details of the data you've selected for the backup.

4. Change the backup name if you want and then click the Continue button at the bottom of the page.

At the top of the page, the default backup name in the form of *Course_Shortname-Date-Time*.zip. (See Figure 14-7.) You can leave the default name or change it to something more intuitive. (I recommend always including a date in the backup name.)

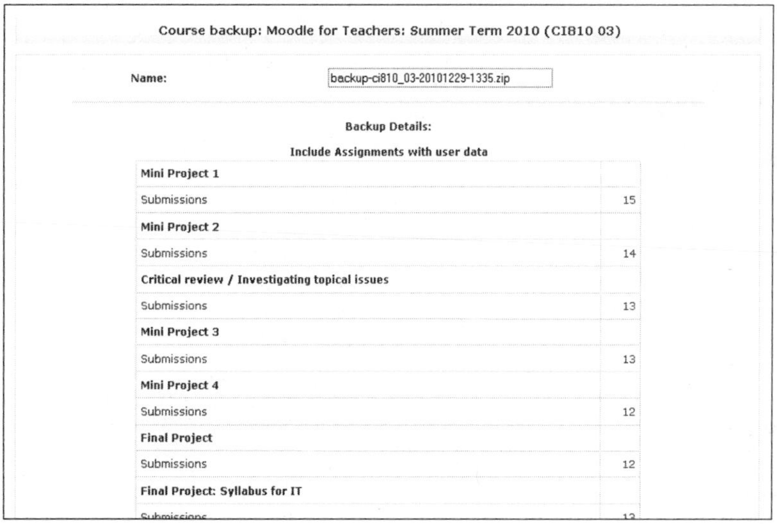

Figure 14-7:
Course
backup
details.

Course backup: Moodle for Teachers: Summer Term 2010 (CI810 03)	
Name:	backup-ci810_03-20101229-1335.zip

Backup Details:

Include Assignments with user data

Mini Project 1	
Submissions	15
Mini Project 2	
Submissions	14
Critical review / Investigating topical issues	
Submissions	13
Mini Project 3	
Submissions	13
Mini Project 4	
Submissions	12
Final Project	
Submissions	12
Final Project: Syllabus for IT	
Submissions	13

Depending on how much data you're backing up, the backup process may take a few seconds. If you aren't convinced you selected correct options or something doesn't look entirely correct, click the Cancel button instead or use the Back button in your browser, and start again.

The next page in this backup process (see Figure 14-8) shows what has been backed up. At the bottom of the page, Moodle gives you a message: Backup completed successfully.

Figure 14-8:
Course
backup
confirmation.

- Wikis
  - Course format data
- Copying user files
- Copying course files
- Copying site files used in course
- Zipping backup
- Copying zip file
- Cleaning temp data

Backup completed successfully

[Continue]

5. **Click the Continue button.**

Moodle takes you to the final page, the backup directory that is accessible anytime from the Files link in the Administration block. In the preceding section, I describe how you can download and organize files in the directory.

Saving Time by Reusing Your Course

After putting in hours of work creating your course, you can sit back and relax because you will never have to create another Moodle course if you offer the same course, or even a similar one, again. The backup and restore processes allow instructors to duplicate — yes, *clone,* as one of my students called it — the entire course so it can be reused. You can also duplicate specific activities from one course for use in another, similar to the import function.

Restoring your entire course

The process for restoring and duplicating a course is straightforward. Unless your system administrator moved the backup, it's stored in the backup data folder located in the course Files folder, accessible from your course Administration block.

To restore your course, follow these steps:

1. **Click the Files link in the course Administration block.**

   Moodle takes you to the list of files and folders.

2. **Click the backupdata folder.**

   Moodle takes you to your backup files directory, as shown in Figure 14-9.

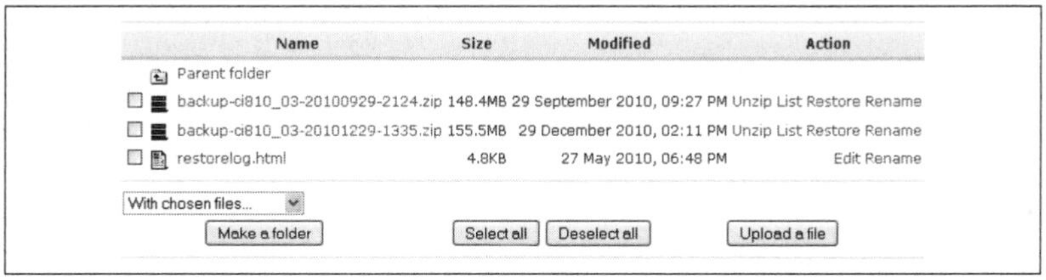

Figure 14-9:
The backup
file
directory.

	Name	Size	Modified	Action
	Parent folder			
☐	backup-ci810_03-20100929-2124.zip	148.4MB	29 September 2010, 09:27 PM	Unzip List Restore Rename
☐	backup-ci810_03-20101229-1335.zip	155.5MB	29 December 2010, 02:11 PM	Unzip List Restore Rename
☐	restorelog.html	4.8KB	27 May 2010, 06:48 PM	Edit Rename

With chosen files...   Make a folder   Select all   Deselect all   Upload a file

3. **Under the Action column, click the Restore link located next to the backup file you want to restore or copy.**

   Moodle takes you to a new page stating `You are about to start the restore process for:`, and then the filename is listed below.

4. **Click the Yes button to answer the question `Do you want to continue?`**

   The restore process begins. Moodle lists all the files on the next page that appears.

5. **Click the Continue button at the bottom of the page.**

   The Course Restore page appears, as shown in Figure 14-10. This page allows you to restore the course. You have an option to add and/or delete data to it first.

6. **Fill in the Category, Short Name, Full Name, and Course Start Date fields.**

   This is where you can *clone* (duplicate) a course by just giving it a new name, such as Physics 101 Winter Term, and new start date.

7. **If needed, deselect the check boxes next to the activities you don't want to include.**

   By default, all check boxes are selected.

8. **At the bottom of the Course Restore page, as shown in Figure 14-11, select the following options:**

   - *Metacourse:* Choose whether this is a meta course.

   - *Users:* Choose Course or None. The default is Course.

   - *Groups:* Choose whether you will use groups.

   - *Logs:* Select No. (You do not want to restore log files.)

   - *Site Files:* Files pertaining to the whole site, meaning available to all courses.

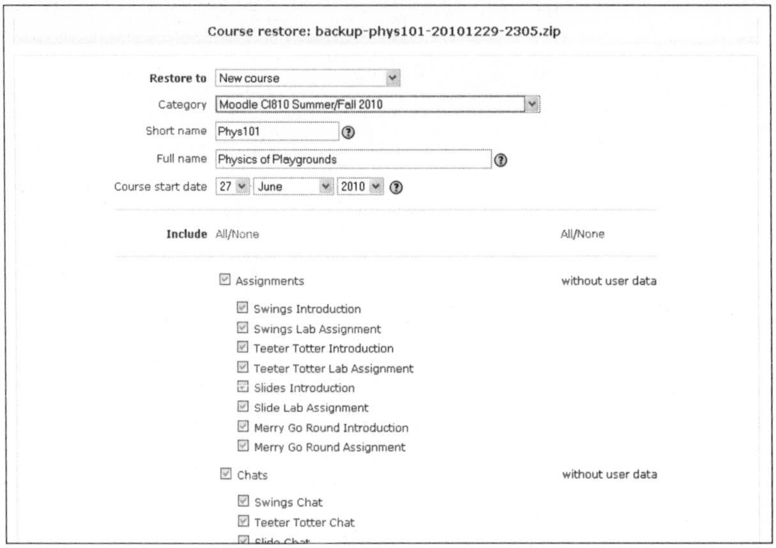

Course restore: backup-phys101-20101229-2305.zip

Restore to   New course

Category   Moodle CI810 Summer/Fall 2010

Short name   Phys101

Full name   Physics of Playgrounds

Course start date   27   June   2010

Include   All/None   All/None

☑ Assignments   without user data
   ☑ Swings Introduction
   ☑ Swings Lab Assignment
   ☑ Teeter Totter Introduction
   ☑ Teeter Totter Lab Assignment
   ☑ Slides Introduction
   ☑ Slide Lab Assignment
   ☑ Merry Go Round Introduction
   ☑ Merry Go Round Assignment
☑ Chats   without user data
   ☑ Swings Chat
   ☑ Teeter Totter Chat
   ☑ Slide Chat

Figure 14-10:
The first half of the options and selections page for restoring a course.

- *Grade Histories:* Grade data related to your course. If you're starting a new course, you don't want to restore the grade histories. Notice in Figure 14-11 that in this example there isn't a drop-down list to make a choice, just the word No, because I deselected restoring grade history.

- *Role Mappings:* Teacher roles, by default, are only given permission to assign roles for Non-Editing Teacher, Student, and Guest.

9. Click the Continue button.

Moodle takes you to the Confirmation page, which is the last page before the restoration begins. This page informs you that certain course data needs to be restored for specific activities and that the process may take a long time.

10. Click the Restore This Course Now! button.

If you include user data for specific activities, this button is available only for users with this capability enabled (moodle/restore: userinfo).

Moodle takes you to a new page informing you about the progress of the restoring procedure. Moodle then tells you whether it was successful.

11. Click the Continue button.

The restoration is complete, and you can see the restored course listed on the site front page and under the courses category you've chosen.

Slide Lab (.pdf)
Physics of Inclined Planes Website
Physics of Inclined Planes YouTube Video
Merry Go Round (text)
Merry Go Round (MS Word)
Merry Go Round (.pdf)
Physics of Merry Go Rounds Website
Physics of Merry Go Rounds YouTube Video

Wikis   without user data
Playground Physics Wiki

Metacourse	No
Users	Course
Groups ⑦	Yes
Logs	No
User Files	Yes
Course files	Yes
Site files	Yes
Grade histories	No

Role mappings

Source role Target role
Teacher (editingteacher) Teacher (editingteacher)
Student (student) Student (student)

[Continue] [Cancel]

Figure 14-11: The second half of the options and selections page for restoring a course.

Importing specific data from your course

You don't need to go through the whole backup and restore process if you want to import data from another course. You can import any number of activities and resources from other courses, including other instructors' courses if you have a Teacher role (or another role with editing rights) in those courses. This importing tool allows you and your colleagues to reuse popular and useful activities and resources, saving everyone time.

The importing tool isn't designed to import student or teacher data from activities (such as forums, chats, and so on). It imports the activity as you have set it up without the discussion threads. The importing tool imports questions from your quizzes, but not students' data if they have taken the quiz.

To import activities or resources from your course, follow these steps:

1. **Go to the course to which you want to import data.**

2. **Click the Import link in the course Administration block.**

   Moodle takes you to the Import Activities from Another Course page, where you choose which course you want to select data from. (See Figure 14-12.)

Figure 14-12:
The Import
Activities
from
Another
Course set-
tings page.

3. **From the Courses I Have Taught drop-down list, select the course you want to import. Then click the Use This Course button immediately below the list.**

   Notice at the bottom of the page you can import your groups.

   Moodle takes you to a new page listing all the activities and resources from the course you want to transfer.

4. **Select the type of activities or resources you want to import. At the bottom of the page, choose whether you want to include course files and site files for the course.**

   By default, everything is selected. The All/None links enable you to deselect everything.

   The site files option imports backups at the site level. For this particular example, the backup would be quiz questions in the question pool. Select the yellow question mark, and Moodle informs you of what's included.

   Moodle displays a reporting page that informs you of what's being imported.

5. **If all looks fine, click the Continue button at the bottom of the page.**

   Be patient. This step can take a little time, so go get yourself a cup of tea and relax.

   Moodle returns another page informing you of what was imported.

6. **Click the Continue button at the bottom of the page.**

You have to wait again, and then another screen appears with an `Import course data` statement and a Continue button.

7. **Click Continue and then, on the next page, click Continue again.**

When everything is completed, Moodle returns you to the front page of the course into which you are importing.

If you imported quizzes or assignments from your course, don't forget to change any dates (that is, starting availability dates and due dates) associated with them; otherwise, the learners will not be able to access the content.

Resetting Your Course to Clear All User Data

The resetting tool enables you to clear your course of all user data, keeping all activities, resources, and settings for the activities. Resetting is useful for activities (such as wikis, glossaries, forums) and for tools (such as groups, grade book, and roles) when you want a new group of students to start on the activities and you need to record their progress.

When you're going through the procedure and selecting items to reset, your user data will be completely deleted, and you'll be unable to recover it. I advise that you back up your course first, including the user data, before you begin experimenting with the resetting tool. (See "Backing Up Your Course and Data," earlier in the chapter.)

To reset your course, follow these steps:

1. **From the course you want to reset, click the Reset link in the course Administration block.**

Moodle takes you to the Reset Course page.

2. **Under the General options, set the new course start date and delete all calendar events, course log reports, and user notes.**

Click the Show Advanced button to display all options in each category.

3. **Under Role options, you can unenroll users with specific roles within your course. You can also remove all overrides and role assignments specific to this course.**

4. **Go through the other sections and make your selections.**

For the Gradebook reset option, note that if you select the option to delete the grade book, individual grades will still be listed in the users' accounts. The Groups reset options enable you to delete all groups, and the Activity reset options enable you to remove data associated specific activities.

5. **After making all your changes, click the Reset Course button.**

   You have three other button: Select Default, Deselect All, and Cancel. Most are self-explanatory. The Select Default button returns all the default selections for the course as when you first set it up.

   Moodle returns you to your course. Go through the course to make sure all is just as you need it.

Viewing Logs, Reports, and Statistics

Moodle can provide teachers and administrators with detailed logs and participation reports of all the activities in a course. These tools are quite useful when you need to track students' activities in a course. You may want to analyze your course reports on a regular basis to monitor, for instance, when your students engage with the material and how long they spend in the course and with certain resources and activities. This analysis is more important if your course is completely online than if your course is a hybrid course or part of blended learning initiative. Logs can inform you about whether students find certain material you give them helpful. For example, if learners don't look at quiz review notes, you may be wasting your time preparing them.

After you retrieve the log files and they're displayed for you, they also provide you with active links to other parts of the course, such as links to user profiles, to specific pages in activities, or to resources.

 If you have administrative privileges, you can access site reports to keep tabs on all the roles for every course in the site, which is handy if you wear an administrative hat and have to prepare reports for your bosses. The site report tool works the same way as the course report tool except that you access it from the Site Administration block on the front page of the Moodle site.

Viewing course logs

The log files for each course show all activity within the course. You can view what resources and activities are being used, when they are being used, and for how long. Course logs show activity within the course. Instructors can use this information to see what resources are being used and when. You can check individual student activity or the whole course.

To access your course log, follow these steps:

1. **Click the Reports link in the Administration block on your course front page.**

   Moodle takes you to a new page with a list of filter options displayed in drop-down lists, as shown in Figure 14-13. Below the drop-down list are links to various reports that are covered in the next section.

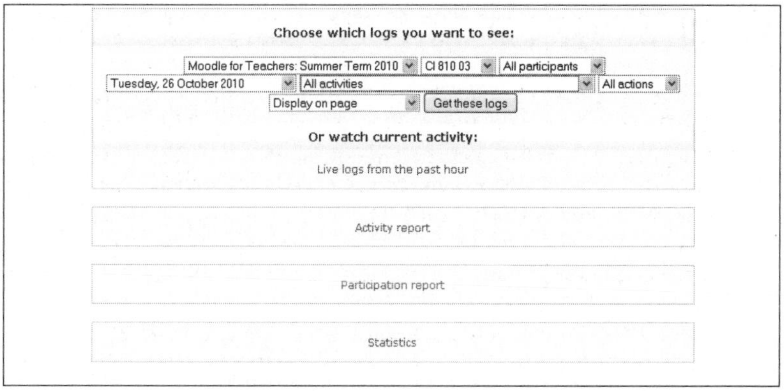

   Choose which logs you want to see:

   Moodle for Teachers: Summer Term 2010 ▾ CI 810 03 ▾ All participants ▾
   Tuesday, 26 October 2010 ▾ All activities ▾ All actions ▾
   Display on page ▾ [Get these logs]

   Or watch current activity:

   Live logs from the past hour

   Activity report

   Participation report

   Statistics

Figure 14-13:
Use the logs
and reports
setup page
to choose
data.

Moodle doesn't give a report on the complete time learners stayed in an activity. That would be quite nice. However, if you need to make sure someone stayed with a task for any particular time, you can work it out by checking the start time and the time he left the activity or logged out. Of course, students are clever, and if they know that you're monitoring time spent, they may just log in, open the activity, and then leave or watch TV.

2. **Select your filter options for the required data.**

   You can use the available filter options to choose the logs required for your reporting needs. Moodle collects a lot of data, so you need to narrow the search by using the filters listed in Table 14-2.

Table 14-2	Log Filters and Their Functionality
Filter	*Description*
Course	Teacher role is required in order for the log filters to appear. This drop-down list includes all courses in which the instructor is a teacher.
Participant	You can choose to see all participants or individual users registered for the selected course.
Day	You can choose any day of the course from the first day the course started.
Activity	All the activities and resources you set up for your course are listed by topics or weeks. You can choose all activities or individual ones.
Action	The default is to view all actions. This filter allows you to select Viewed, Updated, Deleted, or All Changes Made.
Display/ Download	Moodle enables you to display the log files on the page (which is the default) or download them as a text file, in Excel format, or ODS (Open Document Spreadsheet).

3. **Click the Get These Logs button located on the right side of (or below if you're working on a small screen) the Display drop-down list.**

   Moodle retrieves your data. Figure 14-14 displays an individual student's activity for August 9. Notice the student's name links to her profile, and each activity is also a link to that activity page.

   You can return to the logs and reports page by using the navigation bar or the Back button in your browser.

Generating reports

Moodle can generate two different type of reports, one for activities, the other for participants and log files for up-to-date uses. I'm sure that from the various options you will be able to pull out dates to provide you with information you require on how your course is being explored by all your participants.

Live Logs from the Past Hour

Right under the drop-down lists of log filters in Figure 14-13 (shown earlier), Moodle enables you to view live logs from the last hour. Live logs are updated on a regular basis. They display a record of all users and all activities accessed. You don't have a choice of filtering out data. Click the Live Logs from the Past Hour link located in the center of the page.

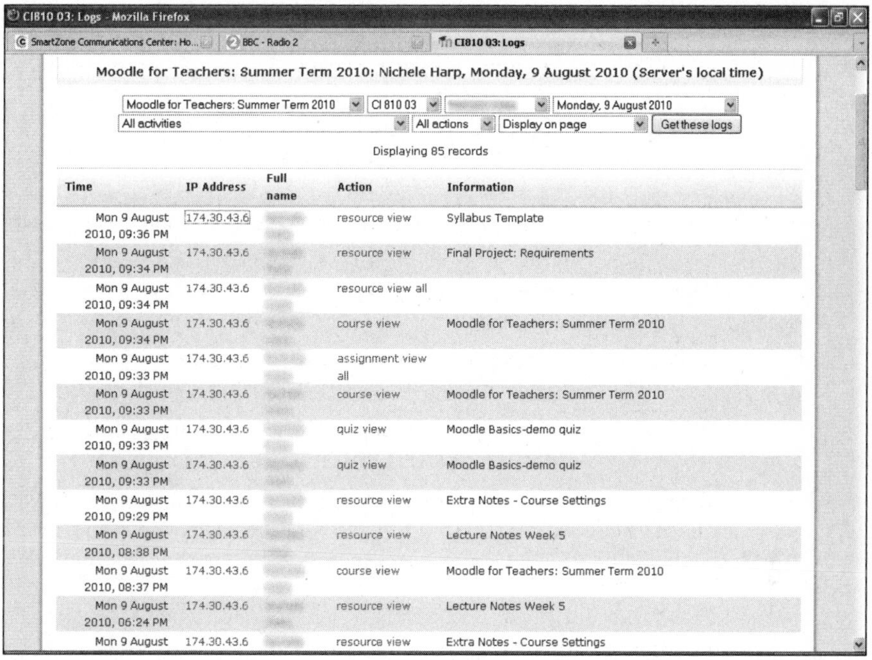

Figure 14-14:
Report for
a particular
student on
a specific
date.

Activity Report

If you need a report a particular activity or all activities in your course, you can use the Activity Report tool, which enables you to filter the exact details you need and generate a report. The activities are displayed by the topic and shown by name. The output of the generated report appears in the following order:

✔ Resource or activity name

✔ Number of times viewed

✔ Date last viewed

✔ Elapsed time since last view

To generate an full activity report, follow these steps:

1. **Click the Reports link in the course Administration block.**

   You arrive at the page shown earlier in Figure 14-13.

2. **Use the filter drop-down lists to narrow your search.**

3. **Click the Activity Report link located under the log files.**

You can also generate an individual user activity report, but you first need to access the learner from the participant's block. This activity report gives you a quick overview of how frequently a particular learner is involved in your course and how much time that person spends with a particular activity. To create an individual leaner report, follow these steps:

1. **On your course front page, go to the People block, located by default at the top-left corner of your front page and click the Participants link.**

   Moodle takes you to a list of all registered users (participants) in your course.

2. **Click the learner's name.**

   Moodle takes to the learner's profile page. You see a number of tabs across the top of the page

3. **Click the Activity Reports tab.**

   Moodle returns an Outline report, as shown in Figure 14-15 with the learner's name at the top of the page. (In this example, it's me.) Notice the other links under the tabs: Complete Report, Today's Logs, All Logs, Statistics, and Grades. You can look at forums or chats and see how involved your learner has been. You can also generate statistics if required for an individual report on the student.

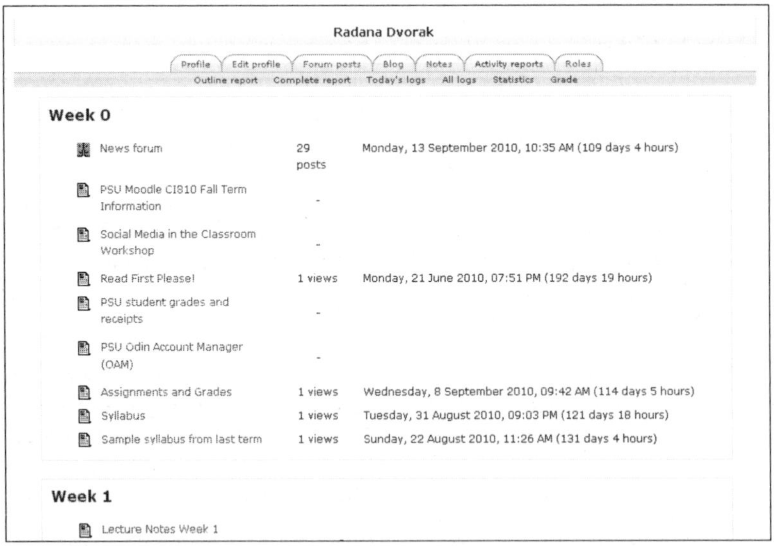

Figure 14-15: The participant Activity Report.

Participation Report

A Participation Report enables you to monitor learners' participation in the course and individual activities. It doesn't give you an individual participant's report as described in the preceding section, but instead it gives reports for the roles assigned in the particular course. Administrator, Teacher, Student, and Guest are the usual default roles. This type of report can be useful, for example, if you created a VIP guest account for guest authors that participated in a forum discussion. You can generate a report on participation between the guests and learners to determine the success of the activity.

To generate a Participation Report, follow these steps:

1. **Click the Reports link in the course Administration block.**

   You arrive at the page shown earlier in Figure 14-16.

2. **Use the filter drop-down lists to narrow your search.**

3. **Click the Participation Report link located under the log files.**

   Moodle presents you with a new page with several drop-down lists.

4. **Select the following options:**

   • Activity module

   • Number of days you want the report to cover the activity

   • Roles

   • Actions (Your choices are All Actions, View, and Post.)

5. **Click the Go button to generate the report.**

Statistics

If you or your administrator enables site statistics, Moodle collects statistics about each course and can produce graphs displaying them, which can be handy for departmental reports or other purposes.

To enable the statistics functionality, you need to have administrative privileges. You can find the statistics options by going to the Site Administration block, clicking the Server link, and then clicking the Statistics link. All options on the page provide you with information on each functionality. (For more on this topic, see Chapter 13.)

Statistics is not enabled because the data can be a heavy burden on the database. If you need statistics for a certain period, make sure that you go back and de-select the functionality after you finish collecting the data.

To view statistics output, follow these steps:

1. **Click the Reports link in the course Administration block.**

   You arrive at the page shown earlier in Figure 14-13.

2. **Use the filter drop-down lists to narrow your search.**

3. Click the Statistics link located under the log files.

Moodle takes you to the statistics page.

4. Choose from the drop-down lists for the following options:

- *Course:* You have choices for all your courses.

- *All Activity:* Select options from the drop-down list.

- *Time Period:* Click the day/time.

5. Click the View button.

Moodle displays the data graphically along with a table, as shown in Figure 14-16. Notice that you have a menu located in the top-right corner that has three options: General Purpose View, Detailed User View, and Back to Report. The Detailed User View report enables you to select a particular learner, guest, or teacher in your course and collect her data; you have an option to download a graphic file of the data if you require it.

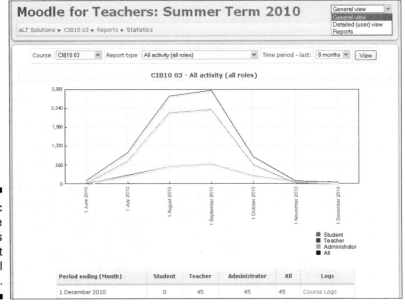

Figure 14-16: The Statistics Output page for All Activities.

Part V
The Part of Tens

The 5th Wave   By Rich Tennant

"It's been like this ever since Hogwarts started offering courses online."

In this part . . .

In true *For Dummies* style, I include The Part of Tens, which is all about the little extras that sometimes just don't go anywhere else in the book. The little extras are important, however, and this part is the perfect place for them. In this part, you find a list of issues to think about before you create online courses and a list of creative ways to keep your students engaged after the novelty of Moodle wears off.

Keep reading, I promise it's worth it!

Chapter 15

Ten Questions to Ask before Building and Launching Your Course

In This Chapter

▶ Nailing the basics before starting

▶ Defining your online teaching model

▶ Supporting learning goals and learning styles

▶ Enhancing the online experience through communication and feedback

*I*t seems so simple to collect your content, prepare your documents, and run through some Moodle demo courses (`http://demo.moodle.net`) or explore your colleagues' courses on your organization's Moodle site. After that, you're ready to leap in and start building your course, right? Wait, hold on. Before you build, take a few minutes to ask yourself these ten questions; they will save you time.

Is the Moodle Site Ready for Use?

If your organization is running a Moodle site, seek out the person who wears the Moodle system administrative hat, tell him what a wonderful job he's doing (getting on your system administrator's good side is worth gold), and ask him to set up your Moodle course for you. Bringing a Coke and Skittles may help.

Also, ask him the following questions:

> ✔ **"Are multimedia filters turned on, including YouTube?"**

> ✔ **"Are pop-up windows blocked? Can you turn them on?"** If your IT asks why they need to be turned on, tell him that you want files and Internet sites to be opened in a new window, which makes navigating the site

easier for your learners and decreases the chances that they will log out of the Moodle course by clicking the red X in the corner.

✔ **"How do my learners access my course?"** Ask for the URL.

✔ **"Do I have a maximum size for my course? What is it?"**

✔ **"Do you run regular backups, and is there a scheduled downtime when you run maintenance on the server? Do you notify everyone, or is this a regularly scheduled occurrence?"**

✔ **"If you need statistics about learners' activities, are statistics turned on?"** If not, ask for them to be turned on and negotiate when you want to collect data. Statistics quickly clog up server space. You may want to collect data on your course activities for a short period to see what and how learners are interacting with your course.

How Do Students Register for My Course?

You need to know whether your learners will be self registering or whether they'll be registered by the system administrator. Alternatively, you may be given permission capabilities on your Teacher account to register them (because that means less work for the administrator). Chapters 4 and 13 cover registration in more detail. Self registration is the easiest — you simply need to give students a URL or point them to a Moodle link on the organization's Web site. If, however, they will be registered by the system admin, let them know they will receive an e-mail with details about how to access your Moodle course.

Who Do I Contact If I Have Problems with the Site?

If you have a Moodle system administrator, make special note of that person's contact information and keep it handy.

If your organization doesn't have a system administrator for the Moodle site, find a knowledgeable Moodle friend. This can be a friend or a colleague in your IT department. Bring her presents, tell her she is the most wonderful person walking this earth. Ego boosting and bribery work very well. You can also try a nice introduction e-mail first, and often that's enough.

If you're on your own, don't forget that the Moodle community is very active — someone will help:

✔ `http://docs.moodle.org`: This is a great place to find documentation about anything and everything to do with Moodle.

✔ `http://moodle.org/community`: The Moodle community is a great place to find information in the forums and post questions. Someone is online helping 24/7. Moodlers span the globe, and they are a friendly bunch. The community has more than 1 million registered users!

I almost forgot: There's me! Contact me at `www.dummies.com/go/moodlefd`.

What Type of Course Am I Offering?

Are you offering a complete online course? Are you creating a hybrid course that's both online and offline? Or do you have a regular class and want to use Moodle to supplement and extend it? If your course includes face-to-face time, your Moodle course organization doesn't not need to make use of the communication tools as much as if you're running a course where you will never see your students. Structure and organize your course around the teaching model you're adapting.

I discuss eLearning models such as blended or hybrid learning in Chapter 2.

What Are My Learning Goals and Objectives?

Learning goals and objectives are important to the way you'll organize your course. Is this a course running for ten weeks or for a semester in an educational organization? Is this a short training course whereby your learners need to be introduced to new policies and then pass an assessment test? Remember that you need to clearly define your learning goals and objectives and then structure and organize your course to support those goals.

When you're organizing your content, also be sure to identify your participants' learning styles and use the capabilities of Moodle to support the variety of learning styles you come across.

If you keep in mind that knowledge is facilitated by the development of effective instructional strategies, and no single medium can support them all, you will be on your way to creating an effective and efficient learning environment. See the companion Web site for more information on learning styles and templates that can help you identify how your instructional methods may support a variety of learning goals.

Did I Brainstorm and Organize My Course Structure?

Take your syllabus, your TOC, and all the resources you want your learners to read and then think how you will organize that content in your Moodle course. Just by picking up this book, I know you've thought about putting your content online and you have some ideas about how you want to extend your conventional course. Don't feel you need to do anything novel and extraordinary; often that isn't the best strategy. Never compromise your teaching methods just because you're using a different form of delivery. After all, Moodle is designed with pedagogy in mind. You can structure your course by weeks, topics, or discussion and build from there.

Thinking and working through exactly how you're going to deliver the teaching are harder than actually doing it, and in my opinion, the delivery is the most critical aspect of any successful course. Your syllabus is a great starting point. Have a look at a few demo courses, plan your course (storyboards are a good tool to help plan), and then begin. The companion Web site offers few planning templates that may help.

How Will I Communicate with My Learners?

As I'm sure you already know, communication and feedback are absolutely vital to a successful outcome of any course. Moodle offers many different ways to communicate with your learners. A whole chapter is dedicated to communication tools, that's how important I feel communicating with your learner is. Start by browsing Chapter 8, and before you start setting up your course, add communicative strategies to your planning stage. Plan how you will communicate with your learners and how your learners can contact each other, work in groups, and have peer time using Moodle. The younger generations live in an online world anyway; they will take to it like fish to water.

Obviously, your communication strategies will differ depending on whether you have a course that's completely online or a course where you have face-to-face interaction with your learners. Even if you do have physical presence, using Moodle for detailed feedback for assignments and quizzes may save you and your learners time — they will come prepared or may even ask questions in chat or e-mail, saving face-to-face time for course work.

How Will I Assess My Learners?

Assessment in Moodle will save you a lot of time. Read Chapter 7 and then have a look at the Assignment and Quiz modules in Chapters 10 and 11, and then add your assessment strategy to your syllabus. You can also grade or give credit for participation in forums, adding to glossaries, wikis . . . actually, most activities can be assessed. The Moodle grades and grade book support most traditional techniques and can take marking burden off of you. Plan and plan and plan and when you decided how to do the assessing, make sure you include ways you will inform your learners about assessment, about how to access online assignments, and about how to upload them and how to use the quizzes (worksheets or tests).

Am I Comfortable Using Moodle?

When you're ready to start developing your course, I recommend you try some of the tools and modules to get a feel for the site and how it works. Either set up a new play course available only to you or start working on the one you will use with your learners. Don't get caught up in thinking that everything has to be perfect; just enjoy it. You can delete anything you don't want, hide resources and activities (the closed eye icon), or reset your course all together.

Getting to know Moodle is essential — you should know at least the core basics before you offer the course. Start slowly and build up. For instance, if you're using Moodle as part of your traditional face-to-face class, start using core basics, like uploading content, setting up a forum, and creating links to resources. Also, be willing to learn with your learners when they get started with your course: They'll take to it quickly and may even offer you advice or give you ideas about how to extend it.

Is My Course Ready to Go Live?

Testing your course is important — even more so if you're offering a complete online course where you'll have minimal interaction with your learners. Recruit a former learner or a colleague to go through it. Watch your helpers and see how they interact with your course. Develop a check list and watch the interactions. Ask your helpers to test all quiz questions. Here are a few suggestions:

✔ Did they find the introduction document/instructions?

✔ Did they read what they were instructed to read first?

✔ Were they confused? Did they click different things before they returned to your instruction? I'm assuming you uploaded a syllabus or instructions. In my courses, I prepare a "Please Read First!" document, upload it to the top section so that learners to see it right away, and also e-mail it to new learners.

✔ Was the syllabus clear?

✔ Identify difficulties.

✔ Interview the testers and ask what they liked, disliked, found useful, confusing, and so on.

The companion Web site (www.dummies.com/go/moodlefd) has a template for a checklist and suggestions about how to run a pilot study or evaluation.

Chapter 16

Ten Creative Ways to Keep Your Learners Involved in Your Course

*E*veryone involved in education and training wants his or her learners to have a good experience. Nothing is more rewarding than seeing learners excelling and enjoying a course. In fact, that's worth all the hours you slaved to put the course together and deliver it. So, what can you do in Moodle to get your learners to be actively involved in the course and have a good experience? As you can imagine, Moodle offers many ways. This chapter features ten suggestions that really work.

Communicate with Your Learners

As an educator or instructor, I don't need to tell you how important communication is; however, people often assume that because a course is online, instructors don't need to be as hands-on. I beg to differ. The most successful online courses are those in which instructors are actively involved and get to know their learners, even though it's only virtually. Here are few suggestions:

✔ **Complete your profile.** Complete your profile with a picture and your skills, likes, dislikes, and a bit about yourself so your learners can get to know you. After all, you tell learners about yourself at the beginning of each face-to-face course or training session. Also, encourage (or make it mandatory) for learners to personalize their profiles.

Make sure your system administrator has not disabled this capability. By default, all Moodle user accounts can personalize their profiles.

✔ **Keep online office hours.** Use the Moodle chat room effectively, followed up with forum discussions.

✔ **Respond to your learners.** Allow learners to e-mail or post messages, and then get back to them quickly. Post the good questions (with answers) to the News forum, which Moodle pushes to e-mail all learners in the course. If appropriate, give the learners credit for brilliance; you may just see more forum activity and participation, and you won't have to answer similar questions again.

✔ **Chat with your learners.** Chats are great for making yourself available to alleviate test panic by holding a session before it. The answers generated can be downloaded and used for future FAQs — a great resource.

✔ **Blog (and encourage your learners to blog, too).** Many people like to blog about themselves or something they're passionate about. Blogs can be individual journals between just you and your learner, or made available to the course or site. They can be used to correct grammar as part of an English course or a foreign language course. Blogs can be topic related and are popular because of the ownership they exhibit.

✔ **Talk.** Sometimes talking accomplishes a lot more if you have a situation that needs attention, in much shorter time. If you think it necessary, don't hesitate to pick up the telephone or use Skype with the learner. (Remember, Skype is free.) Your learners will appreciate your commitment.

Use Forums for Discussions and Other Class-Related Activities

You see a lot more activity if you start the forums and post the first discussion topic. Adding your input to discussions is also valuable because it shows learners that you're engaged and are reading their postings. If learners find replies interesting and useful, they're more likely to get involved in the forum discussion.

You can make forums a required task as part of the course and assign grades, points, or scales. Moodle pushes the marks straight to the grade book, which ensures participation.

Set up a forum leader/monitor, or let learners take turns and share the responsibility. You can set up a *rubric* (a set of rules for assigning grades for scoring) and give learners capabilities to rate or grade postings.

The following list details other ways that you can creatively use forums to keep your learners engaged:

✔ **Debates:** Use forums to set up debates among schools, organizations, courses, or within a course.

✔ **Role-playing:** Set up a forum around characters and use the character to role-play. You can set up courtroom dramas, election scenarios, plays, or major historical decision-making exercises. Learners then have to learn all about the character to be able to take on the persona, answer questions, and debate issues from his or her perspective.

✔ **Storytelling:** Ask learners to take on a character persona and contribute to discussions using the persona of the character.

✔ **FAQs:** Forums can be set up as FAQs or question-and-answer discussions in which everyone can answer.

Give Feedback

At the beginning of the course, inform your learners how they'll be assessed and which activities are part of the assessment. Doing so is standard practice. The next invaluable responsibility is for you to give feedback. You can automate your feedback in the Quiz module by adding feedback for each answer or question, or overall feedback for the quiz based on outcomes. You can also add feedback to assignments that display in the learner's grade book and are automatically e-mailed, with the grade, when you post it.

You can also give feedback for forum contributions and for creating and contributing to resources like wikis, glossaries, chats, and so on. Posting a brief message to a learner to acknowledge and encourage her participation doesn't take up much of your time.

Assign Responsibility to Learners

Let learners monitor forum discussions, glossary entries, database entries, download and mark chat session, decide which great chat topics get posted to forum discussions, or monitor chats. Permissions can be added to individual user accounts, or you can set up a new group leader with enabled capabilities to approve entries, so you can rotate who wears the hat.

Many activities can be set up to require submission approval before something is added, such as a glossary, database, or wiki. Placing learners in charge to approve an entry can create a feel-good factor among your learners and save you valuable time ensuring that what's posted isn't rubbish or malicious.

Set Up Project Learner Groups

You can use many of the activities for projects. You may think that learners who take online courses lack group experience on projects. This thought isn't entirely correct. Projects can be set up for groups, and various communication tools in Moodle help members work together. In a traditional classroom setting, learners don't often meet after class. Instead, they use current social media to communicate, which is what Moodle learners do.

Encourage your learners to use wikis in group projects. Wikis provide a great resource for brainstorming exercises for projects. Their extensibility allows for learners to upload resources to evaluate, link to the Internet, and start organizing the project.

Invite Guests to Participate in the Course

Getting someone to come to your class to talk to your learners about their work or to share adventures, skills, and expertise can be difficult. Well, it is a lot easier to invite guests to participate in similar activities online. If the format isn't in real time (for example, a chat is in real time where the guest is taken from his work and needs to be at a computer at a specific time), the guest is usually happy to answer questions at his convenience. Here are a couple suggestions on how to structure this activity:

✔ **Have students post questions for the guest using a forum:** Enable everyone to rate the questions; then, take the top ten questions and e-mail them to the guest. When the guest e-mails back the answers, you can post the answers to the News forum or on a Web page on the course front page.

✔ **Assign a VIP role to the guest:** Create a VIP role and invite your guest to participate in the forum discussion. I cover roles in Chapter 13.

✔ **Ask the guest to share his work:** Invite a guest, such as an artist, author, or someone with artifacts, to post his work in the Moodle course. Or if that guest has a Web site, you can create a Web page and link to the work.

Reward Your Learners For Contributions

Creating a cool project using Moodle modules that every in the course or site can benefit from or posting individual achievements on blogs or posting suggestions to forums are popular activities for learners to view and be rewarded for. Martin Dougiamas, the original creator of Moodle, states that in a true collaborative environment, people are both teachers and learners.

Why not give your learners a Moodle trophy (or at least acknowledgements and fame) for being a great Moodler and promoting collaborative spirit?

Create Practice Tests

Practice tests are a great tool for learners to check their knowledge before they have to be formally evaluated. The Quiz module can be set up for students to take the test repeatedly until they know the material and feel confident with the subject matter.

The Quiz module can also be used for the end of a reading section or chapter reviews, encouraging learners to keep up with course reading.

Dig In to the Delightful Database

The Database activity module is a resource that all instructors should use in some capacity — if for nothing else than teaching learners how to set up and use a simple database, a skill they'll find useful in their employment, further education, or personal use. Here are just a few ideas for using this module to keep learners engaged:

✔ **Contact information:** The database can be used for learners' personal contact details or portfolio, such as artwork, a photo album, essays for college entrance, resumes, and so on. Learners can create a database that will contain other Moodlers, instructors, business contacts, employment or college information, family, and friends. Having all your contacts organized and accessible makes it easy to set up project work with other Moodlers. You won't have any need to leave to Moodle environment to e-mail, chat, and use other third-party software.

✔ **Project work:** Used to collect information for a group project and then to organize that info into categories to make it easily accessible for future uses. For example:

- *Storage for grant proposals:* A large amount of work goes into collecting data and resources before an actual proposal is submitted. Using a database enables a group to work collaboratively, from different locations, and to store information in an organized repository that's available for future similar projects.

- *Research repository:* Research projects generate an extraordinary amount of data and are often a collaborative exercise, which makes this module ideal for such activity.

✔ **A portfolio:** Learners can create a personal portfolio for potential employers or for admissions offices for art schools, universities, or any other type of training organizations.

Create a Competition

Learners love to compete, especially if there's a reward at the end of it. You can set up competition between learners or create teams. The Groups tool is ideal for such competitions. You and another instructor sharing the same Moodle site can compete between courses. Wikis, databases, glossaries, forums, quizzes, and assignments can all offer fierce challenges. Review the modules in the chapters, put on your referee hat, and see how creative you can get in setting up a competitive activity for your learners.

Index

• *N* •

• *O* •

Notes

Notes